— GEORGE ANNAND —

P9-CCC-188

PENNA. • GETTYSBURG
• PHILADELPHIA
CHAMBERSBUR

OHIO

ANTIETAM

WINCHESTER • *Potomac R.*
CEDAR CREEK • BULL ⊛ WASHINGTON
RUN CENTERVILLE
VALLEY OF THE • MANASSAS
SHENANDOAH

WEST WILDERNESS • SPOTTSYLVANIA
CHANCELLORSVILLE • • FREDERICKSBURG
VIRGINIA *Chickahominy R.* • YORKTOWN
York R.
James R. • COLD HARBOR
Y LYNCHBURG • RICHMOND • MALVERN HILL • FORTRESS MONROE
APPOMATTOX PETERSBURG • • NORFOLK
FIVE FORKS HAMPTON
VIRGINIA ROADS • NEWPORT NEWS

DURHAM STA. • ROANOKE I.

RALEIGH CAROLINA
NOXVILLE SALISBURY • GOLDSBORO HATTERAS
NORTH AVERASBORO • NEWBERN INLET
BENTON-
VILLE FT. MACON

SOUTH
FT. FISHER *Atlantic*
COLUMBIA • *Ocean*
ANTA CAROLINA GEORGETOWN

MACON CHARLESTON
FORT SUMTER

ORGIA SAVANNAH
RSONVILLE

FERNANDINA

JACKSONVILLE

FLORIDA ST. AUGUSTINE

JOHN BROWN'S BODY

JOHN BROWN'S BODY

by Stephen Vincent Benét

Edited and annotated by MABEL A. BESSEY
Late Head of the Department of English
Bay Ridge High School, Brooklyn

With an introductory essay
"The Coming of the American Civil War"
by BERT JAMES LOEWENBERG, Professor of American History,
Sarah Lawrence College

RINEHART & COMPANY, INC.
New York   Toronto

TO MY MOTHER
AND TO THE MEMORY
OF MY FATHER

CONTENTS

LIST OF MAPS

THE AUTHOR

In 1780 Esteban Benét left the Island of Minorca to seek his fortune in the New World and settled in St. Augustine, Florida. From this Spanish ancestry came Stephen Vincent Benét, the grandfather of the poet, Stephen Vincent Benét. The older Stephen was the first appointee from Florida to West Point and became Chief of Ordnance of the United States Army with the rank of Brigadier General. The poet's father, James Walker Benét, Colonel of Ordnance in the United States Regular Army, commanded the only training camp for ordnance officers during the last World War.

Stephen Vincent Benét was born on July 22, 1898, in Bethlehem, Pennsylvania. But it is rarely the lot of army people to remain long in any one place; consequently, Mr. Benét spent most of his young days first in one military post, then in another—six years in California, eight in Georgia. In Augusta, Georgia, he attended the Summerville Academy to prepare for college.

In 1915 Mr. Benét entered Yale and almost immediately became the despair and envy of "other fellows who wanted to make names for themselves in a literary way." At the age of seventeen he had already published one volume of verse, *Five Men and Pompey*. Patterned somewhat on Browning's dramatic monologues, the poems depicted moments in the lives of Sertorius, Lucillus, Crassus, Cicero, Caesar, and Pompey. Since other members of the Benét family have distinguished themselves in the literary world,—his brother William Rose Benét and his sister Laura are both poets and critics—it was not strange that Stephen, too, should reveal a facile pen.

While in Yale, he was winner of the John Masefield poetry prize for his poem entitled "Music," and the Albert Stanburrough Cook prize for "The Drug-Shop, or Endymion in Edmonstown," a sympathetic and intuitive interpretation of John Keats as a young man. He wrote plays and acted in them, was elected to the Editorial Board of the *Yale Record* and, later, to the chairmanship of the *Yale Literary Magazine*. It was of his connection with this magazine that John Farrar remarked that Benét was the despair of all the other fellows who wanted to make the "Lit," for the editorial board could hardly reject its chairman's stuff and "the youngster wrote so much and so well that there was often mighty little room left for any other ambitious verse-maker."

Mr. Benét's first significant volume *Young Adventure* appeared in 1918, a year before his graduation, followed in 1925 by another collection of his poetry, *Tiger Joy*. This last contains "King David," a poem which two years earlier had been awarded a prize by *The Nation*. In the meantime, he had published his first novel, autobiographical in tone, *Beginning of Wisdom*, in 1921, had gone to France, studied at the Sorbonne, and had married Rosemary Carr of the Chicago *Tribune*. In 1926, he published *Spanish Bayonet*, an historical novel of Florida in Revolutionary times dealing with the Minorcan background; and, in 1934, a second novel, *James Shore's Daughter*.

A Guggenheim Memorial Foundation Fellowship granted to Mr. Benét in 1926 made it possible for him to write *John Brown's Body*. The fellowship was established to encourage scholarly and creative work, and in the case of Mr. Benét, permitted the poet time and money to develop his idea of an epic of the Civil War. All of the narrative was written in France, to which he sailed on receiving the award, and where he remained for almost two years.

Mr. Benét, who had felt for some time that America was old enough and rich enough in racial experience to offer epic material, had already been writing ballads and narratives showing his love for the legends and history of his native land. Among these should be especially noted "The Hemp," a legend of the revenge of Sir Henry Gaunt upon the pirate Captain Hawk, "The Ballad of William Sycamore," and "The Mountain Whippoorwill," a Georgian romance of "How Hill-Billy Won the Great Fiddlers' Prize."

John Brown's Body received the Pulitzer Prize in 1929, and in 1933 it was awarded the Roosevelt medal. In 1936 appeared a volume of *Ballads and Poems* followed by *Burning City* and *A Book of Americans*, which Mr. Benét wrote in collaboration with his wife and which was dedicated to their children. His short stories, collected in *Thirteen O'Clock* and *Tales Before Midnight* are varied and interesting. Of them all, "The Devil and Daniel Webster" has achieved the greatest popular acclaim, many critics placing it with "The Legend of Sleepy Hollow," "Rip Van Winkle," and *Huckleberry Finn*. "Death in the Country," in the same collection, is perhaps the most moving.

John Brown's Body is much more than a retelling of the chronicle of the Civil War. For example, the poem is enriched by the poet's complete familiarity with the various sections of his country, its beauty, its origin, its diversity, a familiarity of which the reader becomes aware in the Invocation. The epic itself is rich in action and suspense, with characters expressive of many moods and drawn from various sections and walks of life. The episodes are divided one from another by lyrics and musical interludes planned to prepare the reader's mind for each new scene and contrasting character. The most telling is the "Thirteen sisters beside the sea—" in Book I; the most beautiful and most moving is Mr. Benét's own favorite:

> This is the hidden place that hiders know,
> This is where hiders go.

which introduces the episode of Jack and Melora in Book III.

Two things have been accomplished in the writing of *John Brown's Body*. First, Mr. Benét has taught the average person that poetry can be highly readable, and second, that the finest tales, like the deepest emotions, can be told best in poetry. Henry Seidel Canby, editor of *The Saturday Review of Literature*, points out that the simple verse, sometimes contrasted with prose, which makes the historical backbone of the epic shows that the whole narrative might have been written in prose, but had prose been the medium, there would have been not only a loss in vividness and beauty, in interest and excitement, but a lessening of the possibilities of storytelling as well.

The power in the prose and verse which Stephen Vincent Benét has created suggests to critics that he has not yet produced his masterpiece, that his greatest work is to come.

M. A. B.

New York
November, 1941

xi

CHRONOLOGY OF THE CIVIL WAR

CAMPAIGNS	BATTLES	LEADERS	
		SOUTH	NORTH
Opening Conflict	Fort Sumter, S. C., April 12–14, 1861	Beauregard	Anderson
	First Bull Run, Manassas, Va, July 21, 1861	Beauregard J. E. Johnston	McDowell
Western Campaigns 1862	Fort Henry, Fort Donelson, Tenn., February	Tilghman {Buckner Pillow Floyd}	Grant Flag-Officer Foote
	Shiloh (Pittsburg Landing), Tenn., April 6–7	A. S. Johnston Beauregard	Grant Sherman Buell and Wallace
	Island No. 10 (Mississippi River), surrender, April 7	Polk and Pillow	Pope Flag-Officer Foote
Eastern Campaigns 1862	Siege of Yorktown, Va., April 5–May 4	J. E. Johnston	McClellan

Campaign	Battle	Confederate Commander	Union Commander
Peninsula Campaign	Williamsburg, Va., May 5	J. E. Johnston and Beauregard	McClellan
	Fair Oaks (Seven Pines), Va., May 31–June 1	J. E. Johnston	McClellan
	Seven Days' Battles before Richmond, June 25–July 1	Lee	McClellan
	Second Bull Run, August 29–30	Lee / Jackson	Pope
Jackson's Valley Campaign	Front Royal, Winchester, and other Jackson victories, May	Jackson	Frémont / Banks
First Confederate invasion of the North	Antietam (Sharpsburg), Md., September 17, 1862	Lee	McClellan
	Fredericksburg, Va., December 13, 1862	Lee	Burnside
Naval engagements	Hampton Roads, Va. (*Merrimac* and *Monitor*), March 9, 1862	Jones	Worden
	Surrender of New Orleans, April 29, 1862	Mitchell / Lovell	Farragut / Butler
	Mobile Bay, August 5, 1864	Buchanan	Farragut

CHRONOLOGY OF THE CIVIL WAR

CAMPAIGNS	BATTLES	LEADERS	
		SOUTH	NORTH
Western Campaigns 1863	Murfreesboro (Stone River), Tenn., Dec. 31, 1862–Jan. 2, 1863	Bragg	Rosecrans
	Vicksburg, Miss., Surrender, July 4, 1863	Pemberton	Grant Porter
	Chickamauga, Ga., September 19–20	Bragg	Rosecrans Thomas
	Chattanooga (Lookout Mountain, Missionary Ridge), Tenn., Nov. 23–25	Bragg	Grant Sherman Thomas
Eastern Campaign 1863	Chancellorsville, Va., May 2–4	Lee Jackson	Hooker
	Gettysburg, Pa., July 1–3	Lee	Meade
	Siege of Knoxville, Tenn., Nov. 17–Dec. 4	Longstreet	Burnside

Campaign	Battle	Confederate	Union
Western Campaign 1864-65	Capture of Atlanta, Sept. 2, 1864	Johnston Hood	Sherman
	Sherman's march, Nov. 15-Dec. 10, 1864		Sherman
	Nashville, Tenn., Dec. 15-16, 1864	Hood	Thomas
Eastern Campaigns 1864-65	The Wilderness, Va., May 5-6, 1864	Lee	Grant
	Spottsylvania, Va., May 8-21, 1864	Lee	Grant
	Cold Harbor, Va., June 3, 1864	Lee	Grant
	Petersburg, Va., June 15-18	Beauregard Lee	{ Smith Burnside Warren Hancock
	Siege of Richmond and Petersburg, June 22, 1864-April 2, 1865	Lee	Grant
The Valley Campaign	Cedar Creek, Va., Oct. 19, 1864	Early	Sheridan
	Five Forks, Va., April 1, 1865	Pickett	Sheridan

On April 9, 1865, Lee surrendered to Grant at Appomattox Court House.

THE COMING OF THE AMERICAN CIVIL WAR

All was quiet on the Potomac on the night of the sixteenth of October, 1859. A small band of men moved stealthily in the direction of the federal arsenal at Harper's Ferry on the Virginia side of the river, seized the watchman and forced its way into the armory. But no slaves rose to fight for the freedom that John Brown, leader of the raid, passionately believed to be theirs. Instead a detachment of marines, commanded by Colonel Robert E. Lee, put John Brown and his followers to rout. Brought speedily to trial, convicted of conspiracy against the State of Virginia, of murder and of inciting the slaves to riot, Brown was sentenced to hang until dead.

Precisely a year and seven months after the raid, on the sixteenth of May, 1860, the Republican party, young, aggressive, and eager for victory, assembled in second annual convention at Chicago. To the surprise of the seasoned politicos and the unseasoned public, Abraham Lincoln, Kentucky-born "rail-splitter" from Illinois, was nominated for the Presidency. Lincoln was elected, but even before he was sworn into office South Carolina voted, December 20, 1860, to dissolve "the union between the State of South Carolina and the other States united with her under the compact entitled 'The Constitution of the United States of America.'" Not long thereafter, on April 12, 1861, a gun fired at Fort Sumter splintered the American Union and inaugurated the American Civil War. Yet neither John Brown's raid, the election of Lincoln, nor the secession of South Carolina was a cause of the tragic conflict; they were consequences with origins deep in the American past.

The roots of the Civil War are imbedded in the soil of American experience. The history of American life is a record of controversy as well as co-operation, but the clash between North and South was the first to lead to armed strife. Accordingly few events in American annals are so confused by partisanship and distorted by emotion. Neither constitutional, political, nor economic factors alone account for the struggle. Men do not fight to vindicate articles of a constitutional creed, for belief in the righteousness of a political theory becomes a throbbing faith only when it is the

xvii

cornerstone of a design for living. Nor do mortals accept the ordeal of battle to uphold a moral principle except when that principle is part of the pattern of a vital culture. Southerners did not die for the doctrine of secession, for secession was a method rather than a principle just as states' rights was a means rather than an end. Confederate soldiers did not kill their Yankee kinsmen because of cotton or because of the slaves who planted, harvested, and ginned that all-important crop. Economics divorced from social and intellectual drives will not explain the war between the states any more than politics divorced from the emotional and psychological forces which conditioned it. The American Civil War was a struggle for American nationality and a struggle for Southern independence. It was less a war between states than a war between two nations, two economic sections, and two ways of life.

Long considered pivotal, slavery was a proximate rather than a direct cause. Many Southerners abhorred it no less actively than Northerners and there were as militant supporters of the "peculiar institution" within the Federal Union as in the states which subsequently withdrew. When Lincoln issued the famous Emancipation Proclamation in 1863, only slaves within the fighting Confederacy were freed while the status of those behind the Federal lines remained unchanged. Lincoln never regarded the war as a crusade to abolish slavery, and the "loyal" opposition was as antagonistic to emancipation as those who had earlier objected to interference with it. Nor was slavery sufficiently powerful to keep the states which bordered the Confederacy attached to the South, while the slaves themselves, instead of flocking to the standard of freedom, remained for the most part faithful to their masters.

Abolitionism always remained a minority and William Lloyd Garrison's *Liberator,* founded in 1831, never attained a circulation exceeding three thousand. While a moral revulsion toward slavery had existed since earliest times, abolitionism must be carefully distinguished from opposition to the extension of slavery in the territories ultimately to become states. To exclude slavery from the West, particularly in the territory acquired after the Mexican War (1848), involved not only the morals of slavery, but social, political, and economic considerations as well. Slavery was only a single element in a changing social situation.

The doctrine of states' rights is scarcely more revealing. The United States from this point of view was a compact between sovereignties, not a union of peoples. Accordingly, the federal government was conceived as the agent of the states, not the states as agents of the federal government. It was the states, not the federal government, which represented the people and protected their fundamental liberties. Since the states were originally sovereign, they derived no powers from the government they had created. Such powers as the central government possessed derived from the states by way of the Constitution. What the states had once given, they could later take away. Disagreements between states and the central authority could be resolved only by the states themselves, for if the Constitution was simply the instrument by which the Union came into being the states alone could judge when their rights were impaired. Anything less would limit their sovereignty. Nullification, therefore, was the means of last resort; secession the final step if grievances for which nullification was invoked remained unredressed.

But constitutional doctrines are the reflections of living motivations. They follow rather than precede experience, but whatever the theoretical status of states' rights, secession was certainly not novel in 1861. Thirteen parts of Great Britain seceded from the imperial whole in 1776. As it happened they were thirteen slaveholding parts, although slavery was not the central issue of imperial disagreement. Thomas Jefferson and James Madison in the Virginia and Kentucky Resolutions (1798) invoked the rights of the states since they seemed to offer the best safeguard against federal encroachment upon individual liberties. From 1800 to the end of the second war with England, states' rights was often "the sword wielded by sectionalism." New England, outvoted by Southern planters and Western farmers who cared less for commerce than for crops, raised the specter of secession on several occasions, notably at the Hartford Convention (1814) when "Mr. Madison's War" with England caused ships to rot in North Atlantic ports and goods to pile up on the docks of Boston, Salem, and Marblehead.

Assertion of states' rights with the implication of secession was not confined to New England any more than to the South. John C. Calhoun's beloved South Carolina formally nullified the tariff of 1832, and the Force Bill, President Andrew Jackson's answer, was no less "coercive" than the acts of Lincoln which brought about secession in 1861. Uncompromising abolitionists were willing to scrap the Union rather than remain in federal partnership with those wicked enough to hold other men in bondage. Northern businessmen, even after the secession movement had begun, blamed the abolitionists for their economic plight, while leaders of financial enterprise in New York City expressed themselves in no uncertain terms against the use of force to resist the seceded states. The mayor of New York, Fernando Wood, even suggested that the city declare its independence in order to preserve its trade inviolate. Whenever secession sentiments were voiced before the Civil War, they were voiced in defense of regional rather than state interests. And slavery was never the salient interest. If there was an "irrepressible conflict" in William H. Seward's dramatic and undying phrase, it was initiated neither by slavery nor by states' rights.

Equally unrewarding is the thesis of territorial expansion as the sole cause of division. The westward march of the American people began in colonial days long before the advent of cotton and the slavery system. Movement of population westward was a persistent theme of Western culture of which American expansion was simply a phase. American statesmen, dreamers, and frontiersmen added nothing to the primitive "earth hunger" of the human race and little to the technique of acquisition although they coined a phrase—"manifest destiny"—to justify the urge. Expansionist sentiment was not confined to the South where slavery was entrenched or to the North where nature and a series of historical accidents combined to exclude it. William H. Seward, an ardent adversary of slavery in the territories, was just as ardent a devotee of American destiny to expand within or without the continent. John Quincy Adams, bitter foe of slavery although no abolitionist, was as active an exponent of territorial growth as any citizen in the Republic. Southern leaders, it is true, looked with longing at the former Spanish domain held in feeble Mexican hands, at Cuba, Nicaragua and other points south, but they had an avid interest in the Oregon Territory as well. The westward movement accelerated the impending clash between North and South; it did not create it.

In other words, no simple formula will solve the complicated social equation which yielded disunion. The frontier, conceived as a constantly receding area of free land, continued to be one of the chief molding forces of the American character, yet it was not the prime factor which sundered the Republic. States' rights, still venerated in some quarters, was even then a protective political coloration evolved to conceal special interests. Slavery was a cardinal sin of society corrosive of democracy, but the North was no less guilty than the South. The North not only shared in complicity, but there was only a slight margin of difference between the enslavement of dusky workers on Southern plantations and the enslavement of white workers in Northern shops and mills, a deadly parallel which Southern apologists were quick to perceive. Democracy and slavery of either variety could not co-exist. Slavery and democracy constituted not only a contradiction in terms but a contradiction in ideals, and as long as the social atmosphere was charged with the emotionalism of sectional insecurity pressing problems could not be attacked. And the welfare of the people, the perennial democratic goal, could not be solved within sectional limits.

The Civil War was an epic in the struggle of man and a stage in the drama of American development. Just as its meanings transcend the bloody slaughter of Gettysburg, its origins go far beyond the Kansas-Nebraska Act of 1854. The war lies at the roots of American culture and at the heart of humanity, for it was an interlude in the building of democratic institutions as it was a clash between an old order and an emerging new world. The South strove to anchor society in the past, to stem the irresistible tide of change, and to uphold an aristocratic regionalism against the claims of national unity. While largely unaware of its historic mission, the North, on the other hand, was bound to the future by ties of steam and ties of gold. The Civil War was therefore a contest between two civilizations, one rural, individualistic, static; the other industrial, urban, and dynamic. So conceived, the conflict mirrors the growth of Western society. The antithesis between rural and urban culture represents the most pervasive cleavage of the modern world from the time of the industrial revolutions, roughly coincident with the founding of the American nation, until the present day. The cotton gin, a product of the revolutions in mechanics, prevented the extinction of slavery and more than any other single factor created the cotton kingdom. Ironically it was an invention perfected by Eli Whitney, a Connecticut Yankee, which became the basis of a rural society and delayed economic and social diversification.

No less synoptic of major social trends was the sectional character of national discord. The history of the United States, like the history of the rest of the world, is the record of localisms pitted against nationalisms, of ever larger provincialisms competing against the general welfare on different levels of time and aspiration. Within this framework the controversy appears in sharper focus and permits division into two analytical periods. From the birth of the nation until about 1850 there was rivalry; after 1850 there was conflict. At first the sections were able to accommodate differences, to assuage grievances, and to compromise divergent objectives; during the second stage they were not. In the earlier period the sections were in the process of growth; in the latter they had reached a stage of maturity, but where once there were three sections, there came to be two. East, West, and South existed in a geographical sense, but culturally only the North and the South remained. While there were three sections, political, social, and intellectual lines interpenetrated; when there were two sections, thought and society hardened into a sectional impasse. Security vanished and a blatant aggressiveness took its place. Suspicion and fear created a new inner world in which emotion banished reason and the psychology of human pride succeeded the philosophy of the general welfare.

America is a confederation of sections rather than a union of states. Sectionalism preceded nationalism in the New World as in the Old, but sectionalism was neither peculiar to the South nor to the years during which the South became solid. Just as there have always been sections with different economic, cultural, and political forms, there have always been subsections within them. Thus the South did not always present the unified front which apparently dominated its thought and feeling in 1861. Between the tidewater coastal plain and the back country in the land south of the Potomac, a social and economic disparity obtained almost from the beginning. Tennessee and Kentucky were Western rather than Southern in the late eighteenth and early nineteenth centuries, closer to Ohio, western Pennsylvania, and upstate New York than to Virginia and South Carolina. Georgia was a frontier society on the eve of the Revolution, and Alabama and Mississippi were once less Southern than Western. Louisiana and Texas shared a greater community with the upper Mississippi Valley than with the seaboard South until the economics of cotton and slavery brought them under the cultural sway of Dixie.

Yet three great sections, the East, the West, and the South, have always existed. Although agriculture was the staff of American life in the first hundred years of nationhood, the East was almost immediately distinguished by a diversified economy. While the South and the West were both agricultural, the South was devoted to the production of staples—rice, tobacco, and cotton; the West to a multiple crop system. Western social institutions were reared upon small farms manned by free labor; Southern social institutions upon plantations manned by slave labor.

Sectionalism, however, is relative rather than static. As the industrial process expanded it moved westward from the North Atlantic seaboard into the Northwest and gradually transformed that area into a civilization which resembled New England, commercial, industrial, and urban. As the plantation system expanded it moved westward from the South Atlantic seaboard into the region west of the mountains and west of the Mississippi and transformed a primitive society into a civilization which resembled the older South. And the frontier moved ever farther westward, recapitulating American cultural development from social simplicity to social complexity, until the frontier itself disappeared at the beginning of the twentieth century.

Sectional contests neither began nor ended with slavery. Continuous throughout American life, sectionalism was in part a striving for control of the national government, a struggle for power to protect and further the designs of a region with specific problems, motives, and ends. As long as undeveloped land existed, the West was pivotal, for new states were the inevitable consequence of territorial growth. And in the language of political pressures new states meant additional representatives, apportioned according to population, whose votes affected the political balance.

The objectives of East, West, and South were as diverse as their economic organizations were different. While there were wide differences in detail, the outline of the sectional pattern in the years from 1830 to 1860 is nevertheless clear. Planters and farmers were producers of raw materials and the purchasers of fabricated goods. Whether they grew cotton, corn, or wheat, the welfare of rural America seemed to depend upon markets. They wished to sell in the highest market and to buy in the cheapest. Western farmers and Southern planters agreed on still another important economic item. Both were indebted to the money marts of the East, for capital was required to finance business operations. Farmers who mortgaged their land to pay for agricultural implements, and planters who used their slaves and plantations as collateral to purchase more land and more slaves, tended to favor decentralized banking and fluid credit. Translated into the idiom of economic theory and the vernacular of constitutional law, the values of the rural, debtor, and producing regions made sectional sense. Since agriculturalists sought little direct aid from the government, they were advocates in economics of laissez-faire, in politics of states' rights, and in law of a literal interpretation of the Constitution. While these concepts were not woven into a tight fabric of thought and action, they were nevertheless understood by sectional statesmen.

Almost diametrically opposite was the Eastern economic program. Wedded not to agriculture but to trade, commerce, and industry, Eastern entrepreneurs desired frequent governmental intervention. Tariffs for industry, subsidies for ships and commerce, and federal funds for the construction of harbors, roads, canals, and railways were prime commercial concerns. If the debtor communities were disposed to favor decentralized banking, the creditor communities were active exponents of a United States Bank and of laws to preserve the sanctity of contract. In addition to protection from foreign competition, the East wished to preserve the home market, West and South, and for this reason its spokesmen were as anxious to bargain with the West as with the South. For this reason, too, Eastern business groups found a congenial political haven in the conservative Whig party, which was as hostile to radical Western agrarianism as to radical Northern abolitionism. Control of the federal government was as necessary to attain these ends as to prevent them. The East accordingly evolved a different set of social attitudes. Instead of a literal interpretation of American constitutional law, Easterners advocated a liberal interpretation; instead of noninterference with the so-called law of economics, they wished for active interference; instead of states' rights, they favored more federal powers.

Such fundamental economic drives colored other items on the sectional agenda. The East was hostile to immigration in the early years of the nineteenth century when French émigrés swelled Jeffersonian-Republican ranks, but changed its attitude when mill operators perceived the connection between immigration and the labor supply. With no labor shortage, the South was indifferent to immigration until the relationship of immigrants to the Westward movement and the relationship of Western state making to national power politics was grasped. Nor did the South begin to pride itself upon what its apologists erroneously called racial homogeneity until sectional sensitivity made contrast with the North, obviously peopled by varied stocks, a comfort and a virtue.

Much the same sort of political and social inversion marks opinion on the land question. Cheap and ultimately free land was the goal of the West. The East, however, hardly shared this enthusiasm when the lure of land attracted labor, actually or psychologically, and sent the wage scale for mill and factory workers upwards, but when a growing population and a growing immigration made labor abundant, Eastern manufacturers began to see potential markets in the growing West. Southern sentiments charted a different course. At first Southern leaders were more than willing to trade their votes on land bills in return for Western support on tariff reduction, but after the correlation between Western Congressional votes and the progress of Western statehood was established the bonds of political alliance between the agrarian sections began to wear somewhat thin. Time and again the West introduced favorable land bills into the Congress only to have them blocked by sectional compromise, and when finally a Homestead Law was passed by Congress it was vetoed by James Buchanan, a President sympathetic to the South—not because slavery was endangered, but because the whole economic system of the South was imperilled.

Basic to sectional divergence was not slavery but the tariff. When South Carolina defied the Union in the reign of King Andrew—as Jackson was derisively dubbed by his conservative adversaries—it was protection for Eastern industry rather than aggression against slavery which roused the implacable ire of John C. Calhoun and led to nullification. Compromise brought about the tariff of 1833 which provided for gradual reduction. Displeased though the makers of woolens and hardware were by this economic blow, Western agrarians and Southern planters united to keep the tariff low. Of the 93 House votes cast in opposition to the Tariff of 1846, 63 came from the representatives of New England and the Middle States. As the tariff went still lower in 1857 the restless dissatisfaction in the industrial sectors of American economy is not difficult to comprehend, and it is significant that the party which elected Lincoln in 1860 promised a tariff act satisfactory to Eastern industry and a homestead act satisfactory to Western farmers. Both laws, the tariff in 1861 and homestead in 1862, were enacted as soon as the Southern delegation was out of Congress.

Southern aversion to the tariff was based upon reasoned economic analysis. Convinced that American industry survived only because of tariffs and subsidies, leaders of the staple-producing states concluded that a natural conflict of interests obtained between agriculture and native manufacturing. Eastern manufacturers were the rivals of the European nations which absorbed Southern crops. If the South could exchange its cotton directly for the wares of its customers it would secure an advantage which Eastern selfishness alone prevented. Failing direct trade, a low tariff was the only solution, but even this compromise raised the price of imports and therefore reduced returns from Southern labor and capital investment.

Yet the tariff reveals but a part of the sectional controversy. American agrarians, steeped in Jeffersonian traditions, believed that agriculture outranked industry in the hierarchy of human endeavor. Social rewards should be commensurate with the nobility of occupational calling. And so completely did King Cotton dominate the Southern mind that his subjects felt that the whole national economy rested on the plantation. World prosperity as well as American affluence depended upon it. Bales of cotton crammed the holds of ocean-going ships and its sale provided the exchange, in the alchemy of foreign trade, against which American purchases were made abroad. The real power behind the driving looms of New England no less than the whirring bobbins of France and England was cotton, without which the machinery would come to a sickening halt with calamitous social results. And if prosperity depended upon the white balls of gleaming cotton it depended equally upon the sweating bodies of black Negroes. But when the final accounting was made in plantation ledgers, did the South receive its due share?

Southern leaders answered this persistent query in a wailing negative. They were as certain that the South was the economic appendage of the North as their forebears had been that the South was the economic appendage of Britain, and in both cases they were willing to fight a war for economic liberation. No statistics of the lack of credit facilities, of comparative sectional income, of overproduction of cotton and declining prices suggest Southern resentment more clearly than the comments in 1851 of Professor F. A. P. Barnard of Alabama State University, later president of Columbia University:

At present the North fattens and grows rich upon the South. We depend upon it for our entire supplies. We purchase all our luxuries and necessaries from the North. ... With us every branch and pursuit in life, every trade, profession and occupation is dependent upon the North ... our slaves are clothed with Northern manufactured goods ... work with northern ... implements ... are working for northern more than southern profits.

Another writer remarked four years earlier:

> A contest has been going on between North and South not limited to slavery . . . but a contest for the wealth and commerce of the great Mississippi . . . whether the growing commerce of the great West shall be thrown upon New Orleans or given to the Atlantic cities.

To substitute economic freedom for economic bondage, the South had to capture this coveted prize. Then bustling commercial cities would rise on the Southern seaboard and the Gulf coast; ships from Europe, laden instead of empty, would dock at Southern wharves bringing the manufactured articles from Europe and returning with cargoes of cotton. Relieved of middlemen's charges, increased costs due to tariffs and high freight rates, the profit of the planters and the wealth of the South would be assured and the depressing pall of insecurity would finally be lifted.

The virtual monopoly of cotton had first to be broken if this ambition was to be realized. Perspicacious leaders sought to establish manufacturing in the South and to develop direct trade with Europe. No less important was the effort to link South and West by rail, as much to divert domestic commerce from the North Atlantic seaboard as to strengthen the political bonds between the two sections. But local capital, largely invested in land and slaves, was unavailable for speculative ventures, while the pressures to produce cotton were too great to resist. With the price of cotton fixed in a world market over which planters exerted little control, the margin of profit tended to shrink while planters were constantly impelled to plant more cotton and buy more slaves to meet the downward trend.

Escape from the thralldom of cotton was difficult. Cotton was not merely king; cotton was Southern culture. The plantation and its social code was more than a material goal; it was a social aspiration and a cultural ideal. Professionals in the towns whose existence revolved about cotton—lawyers, doctors, ministers, merchants, and teachers—dreamed of manorial halls in the black belt, for the plantation was the index of achievement and the measure of success. Poor whites whose very position in Southern society depended upon Negro servitude sweetened their bitter lives with endless reveries in which cotton and slaves played the principal roles. To them white domination was even more compelling than to the master of slaves. The South had long been an economic unit; it had become a social unit. Political unity, based upon both, was only a matter of time.

Efforts to diversify Southern economic life proved unavailing. The city of New York exercised financial dominion over Dixie as the city of London had done in the age of the American Revolution. Yankee notions poured into the Southland and cotton continued to feed the mills of New England. While economic dependence was a gloomy prospect, gloom was intensified as the South realized it was also to be a sectional minority. Dependence added to minority status created a new psychology which, combined with vicious attacks on slavery, forged Southern nationalism. As long as the South had an ally in the agrarian West the South could retain its composure, but when that ally was lost the South came to feel victimized. Thereafter, the South was ripe for secession.

Slavery was indeed a peculiar institution but cotton was scarcely less so. Climate and soil severely limited its expansion and, as cotton was practically a one-crop system, climate and soil exercised almost dictatorial powers. In the struggle for economic gain, inextricably related to the struggle for sectional power, the non-slaveholding states had an insuperable advantage. Unlike cotton capitalism, Northern economy was less rigorously restricted by physical factors. Western prairies could be sown with wheat and corn, Western plains awaited the cattleman, factories and cities were growing on the shores of Western rivers, and gold and iron were already being extracted from Western mines. Southern fears were verified during the critical period from 1850 to 1860. The value of Southern staples increased only 25 per cent; the output of Northern mines, mills, shops, and fisheries nearly doubled. The future of cotton seemed bounded by the stubborn material facts of land, soil, and climate, but none could set limits to the machine, to the endless variety of goods it could produce, or to the staggering series of digits necessary to compute potential Northern profits.

While statesmen of the old South were distraught by unmistakable portents of future inequality, the Northeast girded itself for a mighty industrial effort. The ten years from the Compromise of 1850 to the election of Lincoln were crucial, for a vast transformation, beside which the political reverberations of the sectional combat pale by comparison, had already begun. Machines changed the contours of society and initiated the process which was ultimately to change American civilization. In 1834 Cyrus H.

McCormick invented the reaper and sixteen years later over 4000 had been manufactured and sold. By contracting the time of operation and reducing the amount of labor, the reaper speeded agricultural expansion. If wheat did not dethrone cotton as agricultural king, it was auxiliary to a greater rival. The new contender for dominion over America was the machine, symbolized by the reaper which presaged an agricultural revolution and the railroad which heralded another series of epoch-making social changes. Likewise, Samuel F. B. Morse in 1844 contributed to the development of the electrical telegraph, and two years thereafter Elias Howe patented the sewing machine. Applied to shoes, boots, and textiles, the sewing machine generated a revolution in industry second in magnitude only to the revolution in communication wrought by the telegraph which united society as well as business. By 1857 Chicago became the transportation hub of the Western economic universe with thousands of miles of track leading to and from its sprawling freight yards. To all who appraised these magical changes it was apparent that—except within the narrow confines of cotton, land, and slaves—the society of the machine was dynamic and the society of the plantation static.

As a consequence of steam locomotives, of electric telegraphs and machine technology, the industrial salient pushed farther westward. Villages on the banks of the Ohio, the Wabash, the Illinois, and the Mississippi grew into diminutive cities with mills and factories of their own. Pioneer economy followed pioneer society into the memory of the past. Linked by finance as well as by trade the politics of the older West took on an Eastern cast. Protected markets, stable currency, and contractual sanctity were as much the ideals of farmers who moved into nascent industrial towns and invested their capital in hardware plants, sawmills, and local banks as they had earlier been to textile magnates of Massachusetts and ironmongers of Pennsylvania. And as the wheels of industry turned in response to the power of accumulating capital, minds attuned to the needs of business were more keenly aware of a "slave power" which menaced the industrial trinity of tariffs, land, and banking.

While the North became confident, the South became defensive. Even after the election of Lincoln, allegedly the direct cause of secession, the South still retained administrative control of the federal government, but the census returns faithfully indexed the continuing triumphs of American capital, the growth of the West, and the increase of industrial urban population. No clairvoyance was required to foresee mutations in political balance; no prevision to chart the relative decline of the South. Senator Jefferson Davis of Mississippi uttered more than a half truth when he rose to attack the Free Soil party on the eve of secession. "Do you propose," he challenged them, "to better the condition of the slave? It is that you may have an opportunity of cheating us that you want to limit slave territory. . . . It is that you may have a majority in the Congress . . . and convert the Government into an engine of northern aggrandizement. It is that your section may grow in power. . . . Because you want, by an unjust system of legislation, to promote the industry of the New England states. . . ."

Northern industry, apprehensive of Southern agrarian domination, was determined to break it. The South, fearful of the future and alarmed by repeated assaults upon slavery, was determined to prevent it. Adolescent, blatant, self-confident, the North refused to permit the South to expand if expansion meant the stultification of Northern industrial desires. Sensitive, protective, self-conscious, the South refused to play the sectional game according to rules not of its own making, especially if the new rules demoted the South to a minor role and a subordinate position. As Southerners became more frustrated, they became more belligerent; as they became more aggressive, they became more emotional. Emotion generated emotion just as irrational conduct called forth irrational responses.

The irrepressible conflict was a conflict between two civilizations, two opposing capitalisms, two ways of life. Whether the clash was inevitable depends upon a larger question. Can issues between peoples be solved by reason and reason alone? Sensitive men of high intellectual endowments rationalized slavery as a moral virtue sanctioned by the laws of man and the laws of God. They scorned the North as a nation of shopkeepers, as a polyglot civilization, while they regarded the South as the lost Athenian paradise finally regained. Great and good men in the North, on the other hand, spirited slaves across the international border in defiance of law and loathed slaveholders as the agents of Satan.

Economic and cultural sectionalism combined with humanitarian impulses and religious fervor in a crusade against slavery. Irreconcilable with the elemental precepts of democracy, slavery was looked upon as the besetting sin of society by those still moved by the American spirit. Immigrants to the New World, not uninfluenced by economics, were yet sustained by the American dream to which opportunity to live and work on Western farms gave measurable reality. They were as quick to respond to appeals for liberty as their Eastern fellows who with native workers shared the conviction that rights for white men in Northern shops and rights for colored men on Southern plantations were parts of the same mighty battle. Devout men who walked with God were sorely troubled when human beings fled through Northern streets hunted by other humans whose duty it was to send them back into servitude. As the multiplication of books, periodicals, and newspapers goaded the American conscience into action, politicians, however unwillingly, were forced to take a stand. Nor were businessmen, also anxious to bar the question of slavery from the forum of politics, any less active in widening the breach, for their economics was as inimical to Southern welfare as were the ethics of humanitarian reformers.

Sectionalism, territorial expansion, and the antislavery impulse coincided to bring about the American Civil War. Cotton was coupled with the westward movement and the westward movement with political power. When expansion, sectional power, and slavery fused, the South had become a conscious minority. The impact of Northern industrial development simultaneously sharpened the ethical problem posed by slavery and intensified Southern nationalism. Of this tangled story John Brown and the raid he led were simply incidents, yet John Brown is a symbol; a symbol of tragic futility, of unleashed human emotion, of misguided fervor. But John Brown is also a living part of the folklore of the American people. In a larger and perhaps a truer sense John Brown is an American symbol, of social aspiration, of a fighting faith in freedom, and of the unquenchable human spirit.

BERT JAMES LOEWENBERG

Sarah Lawrence College
Bronxville, New York

FOREWORD

John Brown's Body is a long poem dealing with some of the things that happened in our Civil War and how they affected various kinds of Americans, North and South, East and West. A good many of the people described in it are real people who played their part in history—Lincoln, Lee, Judah P. Benjamin, John Brown. A good many others—Jack Ellyat, Clay Wingate, Melora Vilas—are imaginary people, fictional characters. All I can claim is that nothing happens to any one of the fictional characters that did not happen or could not have happened to real people who lived in that time. It was a remarkable time—one of the great and crucial periods of our history—and it summoned forth great men and small, strong figures and weak ones. It decided how we were going to live as a nation—whether we were going to live as two nations or as one—and all the America we know today is built upon that decision. If we had decided to live as two nations instead of as one, our own daily lives would be very different. Moreover, the Civil War produced, on both sides, men and deeds of the heroic kind. And such things are worth writing about so that they can be remembered.

Nevertheless, I do not think of the poem as being primarily a poem about war itself. What I was trying to do was to show certain realities, legends, ideas, landscapes, ways of living, faces of men that were ours, that did not belong to any other country. Our history is not just a list of names and dates, declarations and proclamations. It is made up of the lives of millions upon millions of ordinary men and women who lived through war and peace, strove, struggled, succeeded, failed, built something together. It is made of the look of mountains and the flow of rivers, heat and cold, wind and rain, the stones in the old burying-grounds and the casual ballads of the people. It is not tucked away in the past, to be learned by rote and forgotten. Those who came before us in this country were living people, they faced problems very like our own, they made decisions that affect us still. Because I felt this, and feel it, I tried to write a poem that could deal with all sorts of Americans, from Jack Ellyat, the Connecticut Yankee, to Luke Breckinridge, the Southern mountaineer.

The scheme of the poem is a fairly simple one. It begins shortly before John Brown's raid upon Harper's Ferry—it ends just after the close of the war and Lincoln's assassination. There are two main fictional characters, Jack Ellyat, the Northerner, and Clay Wingate, the Southerner, and the poem follows their various adventures, shifting from side to side. The Border States and the growing West are represented by Melora Vilas and her father, John Vilas. Other fictional characters, a runaway slave, a Pennsylvania farmer, a Southern belle, appear and disappear during the course of the narrative, and we hear something of their various stories and different points of view. To Clay Wingate the war means one thing, to Luke Breckinridge another, to Bailey, the sergeant in Sherman's army, a third. Not all were particularly heroic, not every thread is wound up. But there were people like each of them, though not with those names.

The poem is written in a variety of meters and that is deliberate. When I planned it first, I had rather an elaborate scheme for it—historical characters were always to be dressed in blank verse, and so forth. Such a scheme proved too complicated to follow rigidly. But, as it stands, three meters do most of the work: blank verse itself, as in the soliloquies of Benjamin and Lincoln; the light, swift meter, suggesting dancing and riding, which is used for most of the Wingate episodes; and the longer and rougher line, "They reached the Maryland Bridge of Harper's Ferry," which is particularly evident in Book Three. You can think of them, if you want, as musical themes, particularly the Wingate meter which, to me, suggests something of the courtesy and dash of the prewar South. The long rough line is used for a purpose. I wanted a meter in which I could talk about a lot of different American things, such as johnnycake and Harper's Ferry, and still have it sound as if I were talking, not orating. Also, it gives a change from the rhythm of blank verse.

In closing this brief foreword, I should like to say one thing more. Poetry is meant to be read, it is meant to be heard. It is meant for everybody, not only for the scholars. It is not a highly complicated puzzle box which you can open only with a special set of keys. It tells its story in a different way from prose—it uses rhyme and meter and the words go to a beat. You cannot read it precisely as you read prose, any more than you can sing the words of a song without knowing the tune. With poetry, the tune is in the words themselves—and once you begin to hear it, it will stay with you. Nor is it so difficult to hear. Most of the basic rhythms of poetry are very old ones—rhythms hammered but by men who wanted to tell a story or convey an idea more intensely, more swiftly and memorably than they could in prose. Sometimes they succeeded in this, sometimes they did not. You will be able to judge for yourself whether an individual poem succeeds in making you see more clearly or feel more deeply—whether it enters your stock of memories and remains there. But poetry itself is not restricted to any special class, to any special section of life. It is open to any reader who likes the sound and the swing of rhythm, the color and fire of words.

STEPHEN VINCENT BENÉT

New York
November, 1941

INTRODUCTION TO THE POEM

Although he uses the historical background in *John Brown's Body*, Stephen Vincent Benét does not treat the Civil War merely as a "military adventure" or as a crusade for a principle or as a defense of a certain type of society. Instead, he presents two types of civilization engaged in a gigantic struggle, and he reveals not only dramatic action on the field of battle but conflict in the minds and emotions of the antagonists.

Mr. Benét himself says that *John Brown's Body* is not primarily a war poem but another experiment, among many, attempting to express the essence of American life. In his Invocation he shows his knowledge and delight in the ever-changing aspects of his native land. He seems to love the very name of its localities, and responds to the feel of winds, the curve of mountains, the sweep of plains. He is aware of both America's spiritual shortcomings and her lofty ideals.

To him, America is epic material in setting and in historical event; just as, long ago, Greece and Rome provided Homer and Virgil epic setting and epic episode for *The Iliad* and *The Aeneid*. Mr. Benét chooses for his theme the effect of four years of civil strife, and for his symbol, John Brown, the fierce, liberty-loving abolitionist with the Old Testament eyes. His opening situation looks back two centuries to the slave ships that used to round the Horn bearing their human cargo to New England's shores.

In form, the poem is as near, perhaps, the epic as any modern poet has yet achieved. It differs from the traditional epic in that it glorifies no national hero. And it is more than a pageant, although it employs swiftly shifting episodes to intensify dramatic effect, for the poet portrays the sweeping devastation of war upon a nation.

He peoples his canvas with a mingling of characters, historical and fictitious, selecting them from all walks of life and from various localities. With unusual fidelity to chronology and events, he creates for us memorable pictures of the men who controlled the situation. In addition, he presents a host of individuals in whose hopes and fears, moments of greatness and private suffering, cowardice and bravery, we are permitted to share. Unforgettable are the word portraits of John Brown, Lincoln, Lee, and Stonewall Jackson.

Of the story people, we shall not soon forget Sally Dupré, whose moods reflect the conflict of her inheritance; Clay Wingate, who must graduate from his shining boots and saber, his conventional bringing-up as a "Southern gentleman" before he can become a man; Jack Ellyat with his inchoate thoughts, who spent so much of the war years in and out of prisons; Melora, heroine of that sylvan interlude among the hiders, possessing the loveliness of all womanhood in strange surroundings; Cudjo, the most loyal of slaves. Nor shall we soon forget Mr. Benét's pictures of plantation life, vivid descriptions of the beauty in each locality as the seasons change, the thrilling battle scenes, interspersed with lyric bits of philosophy.

The main plan swings into view the whole course of the Civil War, the poet indulging in the episodic technique of the motion-picture, interspersed with swift dramatic glimpses and flash backs. His meter changes with the mood; and although the narrative is carried in blank verse, to suit the mood, the poet feels free to change to rhyme, or to prose.

In this day of mechanized warfare, the story of the Civil War seems very remote—the last war to be fought in the "grand manner." Perhaps the greatest tribute to *John Brown's Body* is the feeling, as we close the book, that the tremendous panorama on which we have looked happened only yesterday.

CHARACTERS IN THE POEM

The Prelude

> Captain of the slave ship—a strange mixture of ruthlessness and Puritan religion
>
> The Mate—too young to be hardened to the sights and sounds of the slave ship
>
> Tarbarrel—one of the slaves, who claimed he was once a king

Books I–VIII

> Fictional characters necessary to the plot

> *Jack Ellyat*—Connecticut born
>
> *Clay Wingate*—Georgian heir to Wingate Hall
>
> *Cudjo*—major-domo of Wingate Hall
>
> *Fat Aunt Bess*—devoted slave of Wingate Hall
>
> *Huger Shepley*
> *Wainscott Bristol*
> *The Cazenove boys* } friends and neighbors of Clay Wingate
> *The Cotter brothers*
>
> *Sally Dupré* of Appleton—daughter of "French" Dupré the dancingmaster
>
> *Marse Billy*—father of Clay Wingate
>
> "*Ole Mistis*,"—Mary Lou Wingate—mother of Clay
>
> *Jake Diefer*—the "barrel-chested Pennsylvanian"
>
> *Luke Breckinridge*—mountain man
>
> *Jim*—Luke's cousin
>
> *Henry Fairfield*—Nothern officer
>
> *Curley Hatton*—Southern soldier
>
> *Shippy*—a Northern spy
>
> *Charley Bailey*—companion of Jack Ellyat
>
> *Melora Vilas*
> *John Vilas*, Melora's father
> *Harriet Vilas*, Melora's mother } the "hiders"
> *Bent Vilas*, the young brother
>
> *Lucy Weatherby*—a Virginia cousin of the Shepleys
>
> *Spade*—a runaway slave
>
> *Sophy*—a chambermaid at Pollet's Hotel

Historical characters

Abraham Lincoln and his Cabinet
Jefferson Davis and his Cabinet
John Brown, "bearded patriarch with the Old Testament eyes"
General Robert E. Lee
General Ulysses S. Grant
General "Stonewall" Jackson
General George McClellan

Leaders of the various campaigns
    For the North: McDowell, Pope, Burnside, Rosecrans, Thomas, Hooker, Meade, Sheridan, Sherman, Farragut
    For the South: Beauregard, A. Johnston, J. E. Johnston, Bragg, Longstreet, Hood, Early, Pickett, Buchanan

Other prominent people of the time, referred to in the course of the narrative, are identified in the notes.

INVOCATION

As in olden times when poets called upon the muse for inspiration, so in his Invocation, Stephen Vincent Benét dedicates his poem to the Spirit of America, the American Muse. Although he is fully aware of the difficulty of his task, he hopes that his epic will truthfully interpret the American way of life. He fears that America is too vast and too diversified to be successfully portrayed; yet he, like many other poets, cannot resist the temptation to undertake the impossible.

The poet pictures the various aspects of the American scene and the growth of America through exploration and settlement from earliest times to our own day.

John Brown's Body

INVOCATION = Calling in muse

AMERICAN muse, whose strong and diverse heart
So many men have tried to understand
But only made it smaller with their art,
Because you are as various as your land,

As mountainous-deep, as flowered with blue rivers,
Thirsty with deserts, buried under snows,
As native as the shape of Navajo quivers,
And native, too, as the sea-voyaged rose.

Swift runner, never captured or subdued,
Seven-branched elk beside the mountain stream,   10
That half a hundred hunters have pursued
But never matched their bullets with the dream,

Where the great huntsmen failed, I set my sorry
And mortal snare for your immortal quarry.

You are the buffalo-ghost, the broncho-ghost
With dollar-silver in your saddle-horn,
The cowboys riding in from Painted Post,
The Indian arrow in the Indian corn,

And you are the clipped velvet of the lawns
Where Shropshire grows from Massachusetts sods,   20
The grey Maine rocks—and the war-painted dawns
That break above the Garden of the Gods.

The prairie-schooners crawling toward the ore
And the cheap car, parked by the station-door.

3

Where the skyscrapers lift their foggy plumes
Of stranded smoke out of a stony mouth
You are that high stone and its arrogant fumes,
And you are ruined gardens in the South

And bleak New England farms, so winter-white
Even their roofs look lonely, and the deep
The middle grainland where the wind of night
Is like all blind earth sighing in her sleep.

A friend, an enemy, a sacred hag
With two tied oceans in her medicine-bag.   10

They tried to fit you with an English song
And clip your speech into the English tale.
But, even from the first, the words went wrong,
The catbird pecked away the nightingale.

The homesick men begot high-cheekboned things
Whose wit was whittled with a different sound
And Thames and all the rivers of the kings
Ran into Mississippi and were drowned.

They planted England with a stubborn trust.
But the cleft dust was never English dust.   20

Stepchild of every exile from content
And all the disavouched, hard-bitten pack
Shipped overseas to steal a continent
With neither shirts nor honor to their back.

Pimping grandee and rump-faced regicide,
Apple-cheeked younkers from a windmill-square,
Puritans stubborn as the nails of Pride,
Rakes from Versailles and thieves from County Clare,

The black-robed priests who broke their hearts in vain
To make you God and France or God and Spain.   30

These were your lovers in your buckskin-youth.
And each one married with a dream so proud
He never knew it could not be the truth
And that he coupled with a girl of cloud.

4

And now to see you is more difficult yet
Except as an immensity of wheel
Made up of wheels, oiled with inhuman sweat
And glittering with the heat of ladled steel.

All these you are, and each is partly you,
And none is false, and none is wholly true.

So how to see you as you really are,
So how to suck the pure, distillate, stored
Essence of essence from the hidden star
And make it pierce like a riposting sword. 10

For, as we hunt you down, you must escape
And we pursue a shadow of our own
That can be caught in a magician's cape
But has the flatness of a painted stone.

Never the running stag, the gull at wing,
The pure elixir, the American thing.

And yet, at moments when the mind was hot
With something fierier than joy or grief,
When each known spot was an eternal spot
And every leaf was an immortal leaf, 20

I think that I have seen you, not as one,
But clad in diverse semblances and powers,
Always the same, as light falls from the sun,
And always different, as the differing hours.

Yet, through each altered garment that you wore
The naked body, shaking the heart's core.

All day the snow fell on that Eastern town
With its soft, pelting, little, endless sigh
Of infinite flakes that brought the tall sky down
Till I could put my hands in the white sky 30

And taste cold scraps of heaven on my tongue
And walk in such a changed and luminous light
As gods inhabit when the gods are young.
All day it fell. And when the gathered night

5

Was a blue shadow cast by a pale glow
I saw you then, snow-image, bird of the snow.

And I have seen and heard you in the dry
Close-huddled furnace of the city street
When the parched moon was planted in the sky
And the limp air hung dead against the heat.

I saw you rise, red as that rusty plant,
Dizzied with lights, half-mad with senseless sound,
Enormous metal, shaking to the chant
Of a triphammer striking iron ground.   10

Enormous power, ugly to the fool,
And beautiful as a well-handled tool.

These, and the memory of that windy day
On the bare hills, beyond the last barbed wire,
When all the orange poppies bloomed one way
As if a breath would blow them into fire,

I keep forever, like the sea-lion's tusk
The broken sailor brings away to land,
But when he touches it, he smells the musk,
And the whole sea lies hollow in his hand.   20

So, from a hundred visions, I make one,
And out of darkness build my mocking sun.

And should that task seem fruitless in the eyes
Of those a different magic sets apart
To see through the ice-crystal of the wise
No nation but the nation that is Art,

Their words are just. But when the birchbark-call
Is shaken with the sound that hunters make
The moose comes plunging through the forest-wall
Although the rifle waits beside the lake.   30

Art has no nations—but the mortal sky
Lingers like gold in immortality.

This flesh was seeded from no foreign grain
But Pennsylvania and Kentucky wheat,
And it has soaked in California rain
And five years tempered in New England sleet

To strive at last, against an alien proof
And by the changes of an alien moon,
To build again that blue, American roof
Over a half-forgotten battle-tune

And call unsurely, from a haunted ground,
Armies of shadows and the shadow-sound.   10

In your Long House there is an attic-place
Full of dead epics and machines that rust,
And there, occasionally, with casual face,
You come awhile to stir the sleepy dust;

Neither in pride nor mercy, but in vast
Indifference at so many gifts unsought,
The yellowed satins, smelling of the past,
And all the loot the lucky pirates brought.

I only bring a cup of silver air,
Yet, in your casualness, receive it there.   20

Receive the dream too haughty for the breast,
Receive the words that should have walked as bold
As the storm walks along the mountain-crest
And are like beggars whining in the cold.

The maimed presumption, the unskilful skill,
The patchwork colors, fading from the first,
And all the fire that fretted at the will
With such a barren ecstasy of thirst.

Receive them all—and should you choose to touch them
With one slant ray of quick, American light,   30
Even the dust will have no power to smutch them,
Even the worst will glitter in the night.

If not—the dry bones littered by the way
May still point giants toward their golden prey.

7

~~~~~~

PRELUDE:
The Slaver

~~~~~~

The poet pictures one of the slave ships of the early seventeenth century on its return trip from Africa to New England. The conditions described are supported by historical fact, for the barbaric Africans were packed uncomfortably close together in the hot, stuffy holds of the slave ships, and were frequently chained. Once a day, perhaps, the slave deck was washed down, sometimes less often. Consequently we can understand the mate's aversion to going below.

Some of the trips lasted as long as three months, and many of the slaves, because of privation, undernourishment, homesickness, and terror, died on the voyage.

We note that this trip is shorter, for the mate looks forward to reaching port in six weeks, and at the opening of the episode, the ship has been on its way barely a week.

PRELUDE—THE SLAVER

He closed the Bible carefully, putting it down
As if his fingers loved it.
                              Then he turned.
"Mr. Mate."
           "Yes, sir."
                     The captain's eyes held a shadow.
"I think, while this weather lasts," he said, after a pause,
"We'd better get them on deck as much as we can.
They keep better that way. Besides," he added, unsmiling,
"She's begun to stink already. You've noticed it?"   10

The mate nodded, a boyish nod of half-apology,
"And only a week out, too, sir."
                                "Yes," said the skipper.
His eyes looked into themselves. "Well. The trade," he said,
"The trade's no damn perfume-shop." He drummed with his
     fingers.
"Seem to be quiet tonight," he murmured, at last.
"Oh yes sir, quiet enough." The mate flushed. "Not
What you'd call quiet at home but—quiet enough."

"Um," said the skipper. "What about the big fellow?"   20

"Tarbarrel, sir? The man who says he's a king?
He was praying to something—it made the others restless.
Mr. Olsen stopped it."
                      "I don't like that," said the skipper.

"It was only an idol, sir."
                          "Oh."
                               "A stone or something."
"Oh."
     "But he's a bad one, sir—a regular sullen one—
He—eyes in the dark—like a cat's—enough to give you—"   30
The mate was young. He shivered. "The creeps," he said.

"We've had that kind," said the skipper. His mouth was hard
Then it relaxed. "Damn cheating Arabs!" he said,
"I told them I'd take no more of their pennyweight kings,
Worth pounds to look at, and then when you get them aboard

11

Go crazy so they have to be knocked on the head
Or else just eat up their hearts and die in a week
Taking up room for nothing."

The mate hardly heard him, thinking of something else.
"I'm afraid we'll lose some more of the women," he said.
"Well, they're a scratch lot," said the skipper, "Any sickness?"

"Just the usual, sir."
                              "But nothing like plague or—"
                                                      "No sir."
"The Lord is merciful," said the skipper.   10
His voice was wholly sincere—an old ship's bell
Hung in the steeple of a meeting-house
With all New England and the sea's noise in it.
"Well, you'd better take another look-see, Mr. Mate."
The mate felt his lips go dry. "Aye aye, sir," he said,
Wetting his lips with his tongue. As he left the cabin
He heard the Bible being opened again.

Lantern in hand, he went down to the hold.
Each time he went he had a trick of trying
To shut the pores of his body against the stench   20
By force of will, by thinking of salt and flowers,
But it was always useless.
                              He kept thinking:
When I get home, when I get a bath and clean food,
When I've gone swimming out beyond the Point
In that cold green, so cold it must be pure
Beyond the purity of a dissolved star,
When I get my shore-clothes on, and one of those shirts
Out of the linen-closet that smells of lavender,
Will my skin smell black even then, will my skin smell black?   30

The lantern shook in his hand.
                              This was black, here,
This was black to see and feel and smell and taste,
The blackness of black, with one weak lamp to light it
As ineffectually as a firefly in Hell,
And, being so, should be silent.
                              But the hold
Was never silent.

There was always that breathing.
Always that thick breathing, always those shivering cries.

A few of the slaves
Knew English—at least the English for water and Jesus.
"I'm dying." "Sick." "My name Caesar."
                              Those who knew
These things, said these things now when they saw the lantern
Mechanically, as tamed beasts answer the whipcrack.
Their voices beat at the light like heavy moths.
But most made merely liquid or guttural sounds   10
Meaningless to the mate, but horribly like
The sounds of palateless men or animals trying
To talk through a human throat.
                              The mate was used
To the confusion of limbs and bodies by now.
At first it had made him think of the perturbed
Blind coil of blacksnakes thawing on a rock
In the bleak sun of Spring, or Judgment Day
Just after the first sounding of the trump
When all earth seethes and crumbles with the slow   20
Vast, mouldy resurrection of the dead.
But he had passed such fancies.
                              He must see
As much as he could. He couldn't see very much.
They were too tightly packed but—no plague yet,
And all the chains were fast. Then he saw something.
The woman was asleep but her baby was dead.
He wondered whether to take it from her now.
No, it would only rouse the others. Tomorrow.
He turned away with a shiver.   30
                              His glance fell
On the man who said he had been a king, the man
Called Tarbarrel, the image of black stone
Whose eyes were savage gods.
                              The huge suave muscles
Rippled like stretching cats as he changed posture,
Magnificence in chains that yet was ease.
The smolder in those eyes. The steady hate.

The mate made himself stare till the eyes dropped.
Then he turned back to the companionway.   40

13

His forehead was hot and sweaty. He wiped it off,
But then the rough cloth of his sleeve smelt black.

The captain shut the Bible as he came in.
"Well, Mister Mate?"
                        "All quiet, sir."
                                    The captain
Looked at him sharply. "Sit down," he said in a bark.
The mate's knees gave as he sat. "It's—hot down there,"
He said, a little weakly, wanting to wipe
His face again, but knowing he'd smell that blackness   10
Again, if he did.
                "Takes you that way, sometimes,"
Said the captain, not unkindly, "I remember
Back in the twenties."
                        Something hot and strong
Bit the mate's throat. He coughed.
                            "There," said the captain,
Putting the cup down. "You'll feel better now.
You're young for this trade, Mister, and that's a fact."

The mate coughed and didn't answer, much too glad   20
To see the captain change back to himself
From something made of steam, to want to talk.
But, after a while, he heard the captain talking,
Half to himself.
                "It's a fact, that," he was saying,
"They've even made a song of me—ever heard it?"
The mate shook his head, quickly, "Oh yes you have.
You know how it goes." He cleared his throat and hummed:

    "Captain Ball was a Yankee slaver,
    Blow, blow, blow the man down!   30
    He traded in niggers and loved his Saviour,
    Give me some time to blow the man down."

The droning chanty filled the narrow cabin
An instant with grey Massachusetts sea,
Wave of the North, wave of the melted ice,
The hard salt-sparkles on the harder rock.
The stony islands.
                Then it died away.

14

"Well," said the captain, "if that's how it strikes them—
They mean it bad but I don't take it bad.
I get my sailing-orders from the Lord."
He touched the Bible. "And it's down there, Mister,
Down there in black and white—the sons of Ham—
Bondservants—sweat of their brows." His voice trailed off
Into texts. "I tell you, Mister," he said fiercely,
"The pay's good pay, but it's the Lord's work, too.
We're spreading the Lord's seed—spreading his seed—"

His hand made the outflung motion of a sower   10
And the mate, staring, seemed to hear the slight
Patter of fallen seeds on fertile ground,
Black, shining seeds, robbed from a black king's storehouse,
Falling and falling on American earth
With light, inexorable patter and fall,
To strike, lie silent, quicken.
                          Till the Spring
Came with its weeping rains, and the ground bore
A blade, a shadow-sapling, a tree of shadow,
A black-leaved tree whose trunk and roots were shadow,   20
A tree shaped like a yoke, growing and growing
Until it blotted all the seamen's stars.

Horses of anger trampling, horses of anger,
Trampling behind the sky in ominous cadence,
Beat of the heavy hooves like metal on metal,
Trampling something down. . . .
                          Was it they, was it they?
Or was it cold wind in the leaves of the shadow-tree
That made such grievous music?

                    Oh Lordy Je-sus   30
                    Won't you come and find me?
                    They put me in jail, Lord,
                    Way down in the jail.
                    Won't you send me a pro-phet
                    Just one of your prophets
                    Like Moses and Aaron
                    To get me some bail?

15

I'm feeling poorly
Yes, mighty poorly,
I ain't got no strength, Lord,
I'm all trampled down.
So send me an angel
Just any old angel
To give me a robe, Lord,
And give me a crown.

Oh Lordy Je-sus
It's a long time comin'   10
It's a long time co-o-min'
That Jubilee time.
We'll wait and we'll pray, Lord,
We'll wait and we'll pray, Lord,
But it's a long time, Lord,
Yes, it's a long time.

The dark sobbing ebbed away.
The captain was still talking. "Yes," he said,
"And yet we treat 'em well enough. There's no one
From Salem to the Guinea Coast can say   20
They lose as few as I do." He stopped.
                              "Well, Mister?"

The mate arose. "Good night sir and—"
                              "Good night."

The mate went up on deck. The breeze was fresh.
There were the stars, steady. He shook himself
Like a dog coming out of water and felt better.
Six weeks, with luck, and they'd be back in port
And he could draw his pay and see his girl.
Meanwhile, it wasn't his watch, so he could sleep.   30
The captain still below, reading that Bible. . . .
Forget it—and the noises, still half-heard—
He'd have to go below to sleep, this time,
But after, if the weather held like this,
He'd have them sling a hammock up on deck.
You couldn't smell the black so much on deck
And so you didn't dream it when you slept.

BOOK ONE:

The Singing Bones

October, 1859, sees Jack Ellyat and his dog on a day's hunt through the Connecticut woods. Ellyat is happy. He is glad to be Connecticut-born and young enough to enjoy each season as it comes. Yet, as he returns home through the dusk, his thoughts become grave. His mind shivers with the wind of premonition. He finds himself thinking of the rumors he hears of dissension on the slavery question between the North and the South; of catch-word phrases; of conventional pictures of the South in the books he has read; of remarks made by bitter abolitionists in Massachusetts.

That same autumn day sees Clay Wingate of Georgia whose home, Wingate Hall, is one of the great plantations of the South and whose family can be traced back to the Stuart kings of England. He, too, riding home after a day's hunting, feels the chill wind of premonition.

Meanwhile, at Harper's Ferry, John Brown, the famous abolitionist of Kansas, with twenty-two followers, takes possession of the Maryland bridge. Colonel Robert E. Lee and Lieut. J. E. B. Stuart, later General Stuart, one of the most dashing figures of the Civil War, are ordered to join the marines and surround the arsenal held by Brown and his followers.

John Brown is vanquished; he is brought to trial; sentenced to be hanged; is hanged. And with that hanging is kindled a great conflagration between the North and the South.

John Brown's body cannot rest. His story renews the old legend of the bones of one who, feeling himself unjustly killed, tells the tale until he is avenged. John Brown's body may be moldering in the grave, but the cause of freedom for which he sacrificed his life becomes a common cause.

I. *Jack Ellyat feels the chill wind of premonition*

Jack Ellyat had been out all day alone,
Except for his new gun and Ned, the setter,
The old wise dog with Autumn in his eyes,
Who stepped the fallen leaves so delicately
They barely rustled. Ellyat trampled them down
Crackling, like cast-off skins of fairy snakes.
He'd meant to hunt, but he had let the gun
Rest on his shoulder.
                    It was enough to feel
The cool air of the last of Indian summer   10
Blowing continually across his cheek
And watch the light distill its water of gold
As the sun dropped.
                    Here was October, here
Was ruddy October, the old harvester,
Wrapped like a beggared sachem in a coat
Of tattered tanager and partridge feathers,
Scattering jack-o-lanterns everywhere
To give the field-mice pumpkin-colored moons.
His red clay pipe had trailed across the land   20
Staining the trees with colors of the sumach:
East, West, South, North, the ceremonial fume
Blue and enchanted as the soul of air
Drifted its incense.
                    Incense of the wild,
Incense of earth fulfilled, ready to sleep
The stupefied dark slumber of the bear
All winter, underneath a frozen star.

Jack Ellyat felt that turning of the year
Stir in his blood like drowsy fiddle-music   30
And knew he was glad to be Connecticut-born
And young enough to find Connecticut winter
Was a black pond to cut with silver skates
And not a scalping-knife against the throat.
He thought the thoughts of youth, idle and proud.

            Since I was begotten
            My father's grown wise

19

But he has forgotten
The wind in the skies.
I shall not grow wise.

Since I have been growing
My uncle's got rich.
He spends his time sowing
A bottomless ditch.
I will not grow rich.

For money is sullen
And wisdom is sly,   10
But youth is the pollen
That blows through the sky
And does not ask why.

O wisdom and money
How can you requite
The honey of honey
That flies in that flight?
The useless delight?

So, with his back against a tree, he stared
At the pure, golden feathers in the West   20
Until the sunset flowed into his heart
Like a slow wave of honey-dropping dew
Murmuring from the other side of Sleep.
There was a fairy hush
Everywhere. Even the setter at his feet
Lay there as if the twilight had bewitched
His russet paws into two russet leaves,
A dog of russet leaves who did not stir a hair.

Then something broke the peace.
Like wind it was, the flutter of rising wind,   30
But then it grew until it was the rushing
Of winged stallions, distant and terrible,
Trampling beyond the sky.
                          The hissing charge
Of lightless armies of angelic horse
Galloping down the stars.
                          There were no words

In that implacable and feathery thunder,
And yet there must have been, or Ellyat's mind
Caught them like broken arrows out of the air.

Thirteen sisters beside the sea,
(Have a care, my son.)
Builded a house called Liberty
And locked the doors with a stately key.
None should enter it but the free.
(Have a care, my son.)

The walls are solid as Plymouth Rock.   10
(Rock can crumble, my son.)
The door of seasoned New England stock.
Before it a Yankee fighting-cock
Pecks redcoat kings away from the lock.
(Fighters can die, my son.)

The hearth is a corner where sages sit.
(Sages pass, my son.)
Washington's heart lies under it.
And the long roof-beams are chiseled and split
From hickory tough as Jackson's wit.   20
(Bones in the dust, my son.)

The trees in the garden are fair and fine.
(Trees blow down, my son.)
Connecticut elm and Georgia pine.
The warehouse groans with cotton and swine.
The cellar is full of scuppernong-wine.
(Wine turns sour, my son.)

Surely a house so strong and bold,
(The wind is rising, my son,)
Will last till Time is a pinch of mould!   30
There is a ghost, when the night is old.
There is a ghost who walks in the cold.
(The trees are shaking, my son.)

The sisters sleep on Liberty's breast,
(The thunder thunders, my son,)
Like thirteen swans in a single nest.

But the ghost is naked and will not rest
Until the sun rise out of the West.
(The lightning lightens, my son.)

All night long like a moving stain,
(The trees are breaking, my son,)
The black ghost wanders his house of pain.
There is blood where his hand has lain.
It is wrong he should wear a chain.
(The sky is falling, my son.)

The warning beat at his mind like a bird and passed.   10
Ellyat roused. He thought: they are going South.
He stared at the sky, confused. It was empty and bleak.
But still he felt the shock of the hooves on his heart.
—The riderless horses never bridled or tamed—
He heard them screaming like eagles loosed from a cloud
As they drove South to trample the indolent sun,
And darkness sat in his mind like a shadow enthroned.
He could not read the riddle their flight had set
But he felt wretched, and glad for the dog's cold nose
That now came nuzzling his hand.   20
                         Who has set you free?
Who has driven you out in the sky with an iron whip
Like blind, old thunders stubbornly marching abreast
To carry a portent high on shoulders of stone
The length and breadth of the Union?
The North and South are at peace and the East and West,
The tomahawk is buried in prairie-sod.
The great frontier rolls westward with the sun,
And the new States are crowding at the door,
The buckskin-States, the buffalo-horned, the wild   30
Mustangs with coats the color of crude gold.
Their bodies, naked as the hunter's moon,
Smell of new grass and the sweet milk of the corn.
Defiant virgins, fiercely unpossessed
As the bird-stars that walk the night untrodden.
They drag their skies and sunsets after them
Like calico ponies on a rawhide rope,
And who would ride them must have iron thighs
And a lean heart, bright as a bowie-knife.

Were they not foaled with treasure in their eyes
Between the rattlesnake and the painted rock?
Are they not matches for vaquero gods?
Are they not occupation for the strength
Of a whole ruffian world of pioneers?
And must they wait like spayed mares in the rain,
While Carolina and Connecticut
Fight an old quarrel out before a ghost?

So Ellyat talked to his young indignation,
Walking back home with the October moon.   10
But, even as he mused, he tried to picture
The South, that languorous land where Uncle Toms
Groaned Biblically underneath the lash,
And grinning Topsies mopped and mowed behind
Each honeysuckle vine.
                          They called them niggers
And cut their ears off when they ran away,
But then they loved their mammies—there was that—
Although they sometimes sold them down the river—
And when the niggers were not getting licked   20
Or quoting Scripture, they sang funny songs,
By the Swanee river, on the old plantation.

The girls were always beautiful. The men
Wore varnished boots, raced horses and played cards
And drank mint-juleps till the time came round
For fighting duels with their second cousins
Or tar-and-feathering some God-damn Yankee. . . .
The South . . . the honeysuckle . . . the hot sun . . .
The taste of ripe persimmons and sugar-cane . . .
The cloyed and waxy sweetness of magnolias . . .   30
White cotton, blowing like a fallen cloud,
And foxhounds belling the Virginia hills . . .

And then the fugitive slave he'd seen in Boston,
The black man with the eyes of a tortured horse. . . .

He whistled Ned. What do you think of it, Ned?
We're abolitionists, I suppose, and Father
Talks about Wendell Phillips and John Brown
But, even so, that doesn't have to mean

We'll break the Union up for abolition,
And they can't want to break it up for slavery—
It won't come to real fighting, will it, Ned?
But Ned was busy with a rabbit-track.
There was the town—the yellow window of home.

Meanwhile, in Concord, Emerson and Thoreau
Talked of an ideal state, so purely framed
It never could exist.
                                    Meanwhile, in Boston
Minister Higginson and Dr. Howe   10
Waited for news about a certain project
That had to do with pikes and Harper's Ferry.

Meanwhile, in Georgia, Clay Wingate dreamed.

II. *The proud Georgian family of Wingate Hall*

Settled more than a hundred year
By the river and county of St. Savier,
The Wingates held their ancestry
As high as Taliaferro or Huger,
Maryland Carroll, Virginia Lee.
They had ill-spelt letters of Albemarle's
And their first grant ran from the second Charles,   20
Clerkly inscribed upon parchmentries
"To our well-beloved John Wingate, these,"
Though envy hinted the royal mood
Held more of humor than gratitude
And the well-beloved had less applied
To honest John than his tall young bride,
At least their eldest to John's surprise,
Was very like Monmouth about the eyes,
Till his father wondered if every loyalty
Was always so richly repaid by royalty,   30
But, having long found that the principal question
In a happy life is a good digestion
And the worst stomachic of all is jealousy
He gave up the riddle, and settled zealously
To farming his acres, begetting daughters,
And making a study of cordial waters

24

Till he died at ninety of pure senility
And was greatly mourned by the local gentility.

John the Second was different cloth.
He had wings—but the wings of the moth.
Courtly, unlucky, clever and wise,
There was a Stuart in his eyes,
A gambler that played against loaded dice.
He could harrow the water and plough the sand,
But he could not do the thing at hand.
A fencing-foil too supple for use,   10
A racing colt that must run at loose.
And the Wingate acres had slipped away
If it had not been for Elspeth Mackay.
She was his wife, and her heart was bold
As a broad, bright guinea of Border gold.
Her wit was a tartan of colored weather.
Her walk was gallant as Highland heather.
And whatever she had, she held together.

It was she who established on Georgia soil
Wingate honor and Wingate toil   20
When John and his father's neighbors stood
At swords' points over a county feud
And only ill-fortune and he were friends.
—They prophesied her a dozen ends,
Seeking new ground for a broken man
Where only the deer and the rabbit ran
And the Indian arrow harried both,
But she held her word and she kept her troth,
Cleared the forest and tamed the wild
And gave the breast to the new-born child   30
While the painted Death went whooping by
—To die at last as she wished to die
In the fief built out of her blood and bone
With her heart for the Hall's foundation-stone.

Deep in her sons, and the Wingate blood,
She stamped her sigil of fortitude.
Thrift and love for the house and the chief
And a scone on the hob for the son of grief.
But a knife in the ribs for the pleasant thief.

And deep in her sons, when she was gone,
Her words took root, and her ghost lived on.
The slow voice haunting the ocean-shell
To counsel the sons of her sons as well.
And it was well for the Wingate line
To have that stiffening set in its spine.
For once in each breeding of Wingate kin
There came a child with an olive skin
And the mouth of Charles, the merry and sad,
And the bright, spoilt charm that Monmouth had.   10
Luckily seldom the oldest born
To sow the nettle in Wingate corn
And let the cotton blight on its stalk
While he wasted his time in witty talk,
Or worse, in love with no minister handy,
Or feeding a spaniel on nuts and brandy
And taking a melancholy pride
In never choosing the winning side.

Clay Wingate was the last to feel
The prick of that spur of tarnished steel,   20
Gilt, but crossed with the dubious bar
Of arms won under the bastard's star,
Rowel his mind, at that time or this,
With thoughts and visions that were not his.
A sorrow of laughter, a mournful glamor
And the ghostly stroke of an airy hammer
Shaking his heart with pity and pride
That had nothing to do with the things he eyed.
He was happy and young, he was strong and stout,
His body was hard to weary out.   30
When he thought of life, he thought of a shout.
But—there was a sword in a blackened sheath,
There was a shape with a mourning wreath:
And a place in his mind was a wrestling-ring
Where the crownless form of an outlawed king
Fought with a shadow too like his own,
And, late or early, was overthrown.

It is not lucky to dream such stuff—
Dreaming men are haunted men.
Though Wingate's face looked lucky enough   40

26

To any eye that had seen him then,
Riding back through the Georgia Fall
To the white-pillared porch of Wingate Hall.
Fall of the possum, fall of the 'coon,
And the lop-eared hound-dog baying the moon.
Fall that is neither bitter nor swift
But a brown girl bearing an idle gift,
A brown seed-kernel that splits apart
And shows the Summer yet in its heart,
A smokiness so vague in the air   10
You feel it rather than see it there,
A brief, white rime on the red clay road
And slow mules creaking a lazy load
Through endless acres of afternoon,
A pine-cone fire and a banjo-tune,
And a julep mixed with a silver spoon.

Your noons are hot, your nights deep-starred,
There is honeysuckle still in the yard,
Fall of the quail and the firefly-glows
And the pot-pourri of the rambler-rose,   20
Fall that brings no promise of snows . . .

Wingate checked on his horse's rein
With a hand as light as a butterfly
And drank content in body and brain
As he gazed for a moment at the sky.
This was his Georgia, this his share
Of pine and river and sleepy air,
Of summer thunder and winter rain
That spills bright tears on the window-pane
With the slight, fierce passion of young men's grief,   30
Of the mockingbird and the mulberry-leaf.
For, wherever the winds of Georgia run,
It smells of peaches long in the sun,
And the white wolf-winter, hungry and frore,
Can prowl the North by a frozen door
But here we have fed him on bacon-fat
And he sleeps by the stove like a lazy cat.
Here Christmas stops at everyone's house
With a jug of molasses and green, young boughs,
And the little New Year, the weakling one,   40

Can lie outdoors in the noonday sun,
Blowing the fluff from a turkey-wing
At skies already haunted with Spring—

Oh, Georgia . . . Georgia . . . the careless yield!
The watermelons ripe in the field!
The mist in the bottoms that tastes of fever
And the yellow river rolling forever. . . !

So Wingate saw it, vision or truth,
Through the colored window of his own youth,
Building an image out of his mind
To live or die for, as Fate inclined.

He drank his fill of the air, and then,
Was just about to ride on again
When—what was that noise beyond the sky,
That harry of unseen cavalry
Riding the wind?
                                    His own horse stirred,
Neighing. He listened. There was a word.
He could not hear it—and yet he heard.
It was an arrow from ambush flung,
It was a bell with a leaden tongue
Striking an hour.
                                    He was young
No longer. He and his horse were old,
And both were bound with an iron band.
He slipped from the saddle and tried to stand.
He struck one hand with the other hand.
But both were cold.

The horses, burning-hooved, drove on toward the sea,
But, where they had passed, the air was troubled and sick
Like earth that the shoulder of earthquake heavily stirs.
There was a whisper moving that air all night,
A whisper that cried and whimpered about the house
Where John Brown prayed to his God, by his narrow bed.

JOHN BROWN'S PRAYER

Omnipotent and steadfast God,
Who, in Thy mercy, hath

Upheaved in me Jehovah's rod
And his chastising wrath,

For fifty-nine unsparing years
Thy Grace hath worked apart
To mould a man of iron tears
With a bullet for a heart.

Yet, since this body may be weak
With all it has to bear,
Once more, before Thy thunders speak,
Almighty, hear my prayer.   10

I saw Thee when Thou did display
The black man and his lord
To bid me free the one, and slay
The other with the sword.

I heard Thee when Thou bade me spurn
Destruction from my hand
And, though all Kansas bleed and burn,
It was at Thy command.

I hear the rolling of the wheels,
The chariots of war!   20
I hear the breaking of the seals
And the opening of the door!

The glorious beasts with many eyes
Exult before the Crowned.
The buried saints arise, arise
Like incense from the ground!

Before them march the martyr-kings,
In bloody sunsets drest,
O, Kansas, bleeding Kansas,
You will not let me rest!   30

I hear your sighing corn again,
I smell your prairie-sky,
And I remember five dead men
By Pottawattomie.

Lord God it was a work of Thine,
And how might I refrain?

But Kansas, bleeding Kansas,
I hear her in her pain.

Her corn is rustling in the ground,
An arrow in my flesh.
And all night long I staunch a wound
That ever bleeds afresh.

Get up, get up, my hardy sons,
From this time forth we are
No longer men, but pikes and guns
In God's advancing war.   10

And if we live, we free the slave,
And if we die, we die.
But God has digged His saints a grave
Beyond the western sky.

Oh, fairer than the bugle-call
Its walls of jasper shine!
And Joshua's sword is on the wall
With space beside for mine.

And should the Philistine defend
His strength against our blows,   20
The God who doth not spare His friend,
Will not forget His foes.

III.   The tale of Harper's Ferry

They reached the Maryland bridge of Harper's Ferry
That Sunday night. There were twenty-two in all,
Nineteen were under thirty, three not twenty-one,
Kagi, the self-taught scholar, quiet and cool,
Stevens, the cashiered soldier, Puritan-fathered,
A singing giant, gunpowder-tempered and rash.
Dauphin Thompson, the pippin-cheeked country-boy,
More like a girl than a warrior; Oliver Brown,   30
Married last year when he was barely nineteen;
Dangerfield Newby, colored and born a slave,
Freeman now, but married to one not free
Who, with their seven children, waited him South,
The youngest baby just beginning to crawl;

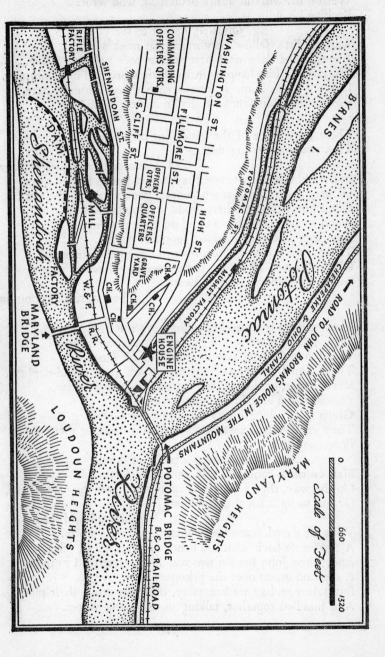

The Raid at Harper's Ferry

Watson Brown, the steady lieutenant, who wrote
Back to his wife,
                    "Oh, Bell, I want to see you
And the little fellow very much but must wait.
There was a slave near here whose wife was sold South.
They found him hanging in Kennedy's orchard next morning.
I cannot come home as long as such things are done here.
I sometimes think that we shall not meet again."

These were some of the band. For better or worse
They were all strong men.   10
                                The bearded faces look strange
In the old daguerreotypes: they should be the faces
Of prosperous, small-town people, good sons and fathers,
Good horse-shoe pitchers, good at plowing a field,
Good at swapping stories and good at praying,
American wheat, firm-rooted, good in the ear.
There is only one whose air seems out of the common,
Oliver Brown. That face has a masculine beauty
Somewhat like the face of Keats.
                                They were all strong men. 20

They tied up the watchmen and took the rifleworks.
Then John Brown sent a raiding party away
To fetch in Colonel Washington from his farm.
The Colonel was George Washington's great-grand-nephew,
Slave-owner, gentleman-farmer, but, more than these,
Possessor of a certain fabulous sword
Given to Washington by Frederick the Great.
They captured him and his sword and brought them along
Processionally.
                                The act has a touch of drama,   30
Half costume-romance, half unmerited farce.
On the way, they told the Washington slaves they were free,
Or free to fight for their freedom.
                                The slaves heard the news
With the dazed, scared eyes of cattle before a storm.
A few came back with the band and were given pikes,
And, when John Brown was watching, pretended to mount
A slipshod guard over the prisoners.
But, when he had walked away, they put down their pikes
And huddled together, talking in mourning voices.   40

32

It didn't seem right to play at guarding the Colonel
But they were afraid of the bearded patriarch
With the Old Testament eyes.
                                    A little later
It was Patrick Higgins' turn. He was the night-watchman
Of the Maryland bridge, a tough little Irishman
With a canny, humorous face, and a twist in his speech.
He came humming his way to his job.
                                    "Halt!" ordered a voice.
He stopped a minute, perplexed. As he told men later,   10
"Now I didn't know what 'Halt!' mint, any more
Than a hog knows about a holiday."
                                    There was a scuffle.
He got away with a bullet-crease in his scalp
And warned the incoming train. It was half-past-one.
A moment later, a man named Shepherd Heyward,
Free negro, baggage-master of the small station,
Well-known in the town, hardworking, thrifty and fated,
Came looking for Higgins.
                                    "Halt!" called the voice again,   20
But he kept on, not hearing or understanding,
Whichever it may have been.
                                    A rifle cracked.
He fell by the station-platform, gripping his belly,
And lay for twelve hours of torment, asking for water
Until he was able to die.
                                    There is no stone,
No image of bronze or marble green with the rain
To Shepherd Heyward, free negro of Harper's Ferry,
And even the books, the careful, ponderous histories,   30
That turn live men into dummies with smiles of wax
Thoughtfully posed against a photographer's background
In the act of signing a treaty or drawing a sword,
Tell little of what he was.
                                    And yet his face
Grey with pain and puzzled at sudden death
Stares out at us through the bookworm-dust of the years
With an uncomprehending wonder, a blind surprise.
"I was getting along," it says, "I was doing well.
I had six thousand dollars saved in the bank.   40
It was a good town, a nice town, I liked the folks
And they liked me. I had a good job there, too.

On Sundays I used to dress myself up slick enough
To pass the plate in church, but I wasn't proud
Not even when trashy niggers called me Mister,
Though I could hear the old grannies over their snuff
Mumbling along, 'Look, chile, there goes Shepherd Heyward.
Ain't him fine in he Sunday clo'es—ain't him sassy and fine?
You grow up decent and don't play ball in the street,
And maybe you'll get like him, with a gold watch and chain.'
And then, suddenly—and what was it all about?
Why should anyone want to kill me? Why was it done?"   10

So the grey lips. And so the hurt in the eyes.
A hurt like a child's, at punishment unexplained
That makes the whole child-universe fall to pieces.
At the time of death, most men turn back toward the child.

Brown did not know at first that the first man dead
By the sword he thought of so often as Gideon's sword
Was one of the race he had drawn that sword to free.
It had been dark on the bridge. A man had come
And had not halted when ordered. Then the shot
And the scrape of the hurt man dragging himself away.   20
That was all. The next man ordered to halt would halt.
His mind was too full of the burning judgments of God
To wonder who it had been. He was cool and at peace.
He dreamt of a lamb, lying down by a rushing stream.

So the night wore away, indecisive and strange.
The raiders stuck by the arsenal, waiting perhaps
For a great bell of jubilation to toll in the sky,
And the slaves to rush from the hills with pikes in their hands,
A host redeemed, black rescue-armies of God.
It did not happen.   30
                    Meanwhile, there was casual firing.
A townsman named Boerley was killed. Meanwhile, the train
Passed over the bridge to carry its wild news
Of abolition-devils sprung from the ground
A hundred and fifty, three hundred, a thousand strong
To pillage Harper's Ferry, with fire and sword.
Meanwhile the whole countryside was springing to arms.
The alarm-bell in Charlestown clanged "Nat Turner has come.
Nat Turner has come again, all smoky from Hell,

Setting the slave to murder and massacre!"
The Jefferson Guards fell in. There were boys and men.
They had no uniforms but they had weapons.
Old squirrel-rifles, taken down from the wall,
Shot guns loaded with spikes and scraps of iron.
A boy dragged a blunderbuss as big as himself.
They started for the Ferry.
                              In a dozen
A score of other sleepy, neighboring towns
The same bell clanged, the same militia assembled.   10

The Ferry itself was roused and stirring with dawn.
And the firing began again.
                              A queer, harsh sound
In the ordinary streets of that clean, small town,
A desultory, vapid, meaningless sound.

God knows why John Brown lingered! Kagi, the scholar,
Who, with two others, held the rifle-works,
All morning sent him messages urging retreat.
They had the inexorable weight of common sense
Behind them, but John Brown neither replied   20
Nor heeded, brooding in the patriarch-calm
Of a lean, solitary pine that hangs
On the cliff's edge, and sees the world below
A tiny pattern of toy fields and trees,
And only feels its roots gripping the rock
And the almighty wind that shakes its boughs,
Blowing from eagle-heaven to eagle-heaven.

Of course they were cut off. The whole attempt
Was fated from the first.
                              Just about noon   30
The Jefferson Guards took the Potomac Bridge
And drove away the men Brown posted there.

There were three doors of possible escape
Open to Brown. With this the first slammed shut.
The second followed it a little later
With the recapture of the other bridge
That cut Brown off from Kagi and the arsenal
And penned the larger body of the raiders
In the armory.

Again the firing rolled,
And now the first of the raiders fell and died,
Dangerfield Newby, the freed Scotch-mulatto
Whose wife and seven children, slaves in Virginia,
Waited for him to bring them incredible freedom.
They were sold South instead, after the raid.
His body lay where the townspeople could reach it.
They cut off his ears for trophies.

                  If there are souls,
As many think that there are or wish that there might be,   10
Crystalline things that rise on light wings exulting
Out of the spoilt and broken cocoon of the body,
Knowing no sorrow or pain but only deliverance,
And yet with the flame of speech, the patterns of memory,
One wonders what the soul of Dangerfield Newby
Said, in what terms, to the soul of Shepherd Heyward,
Both born slave, both freed, both dead the same day.
What do the souls that bleed from the corpse of battle
Say to the tattered night?
                 Perhaps it is better   20
We have no power to visage what they might say.

The firing now was constant, like the heavy
And drumming rains of summer. Twice Brown sent
Asking a truce. The second time there went
Stevens and Watson Brown with a white flag.
But things had gone beyond the symbol of flags.
Stevens, shot from a window, fell in the gutter
Horribly wounded. Watson Brown crawled back
To the engine house that was the final fort
Of Brown's last stand, torn through and through with slugs.   30

A Mr. Brua, one of Brown's prisoners,
Strolled out from the unguarded prison-room
Into the bullets, lifted Stevens up,
Carried him over to the old hotel
They called the Wager House, got a doctor for him,
And then strolled back to take his prisoner's place
With Colonel Washington and the scared rest.
I know no more than this of Mr. Brua
But he seems curiously American,
And I imagine him a tall, stooped man   40

A little yellow with the Southern sun,
With slow, brown eyes and a slow way of talking.
Shifting the quid of tobacco in his cheek
Mechanically, as he lifted up
The dirty, bloody body of the man
Who stood for everything he most detested
And slowly carrying him through casual wasps
Of death to the flyspecked but sunny room
In the old hotel, wiping the blood and grime
Mechanically from his Sunday coat,   10
Settling his black string-tie with big, tanned hands,
And, then, incredibly, going back to jail.
He did not think much about what he'd done
But sat himself as comfortably as might be
On the cold bricks of that dejected guard-room
And slowly started cutting another quid
With a worn knife that had a brown bone-handle.

He lived all through the war and died long after,
This Mr. Brua I see. His last advice
To numerous nephews was "Keep out of trouble,   20
But if you're in it, chew and don't be hasty,
Just do whatever's likeliest at hand."

I like your way of talking, Mr. Brua,
And if there still are people interested
In cutting literary clothes for heroes
They might do worse than mention your string-tie.

There were other killings that day. On the one side, this,
Leeman, a boy of eighteen and the youngest raider,
Trying to flee from the death-trap of the engine-house
And caught and killed on an islet in the Potomac.   30
The body lay on a tiny shelf of rock
For hours, a sack of clothes still stung by bullets.

On the other side—Fontaine Beckham, mayor of the town,
Went to look at Heyward's body with Patrick Higgins.
The slow tears crept to his eyes. He was getting old.
He had thought a lot of Heyward. He had no gun
But he had been mayor of the town for a dozen years,
A peaceful, orderly place full of decent people,
And now they were killing people, here in his town,

37

He had to do something to stop it, somehow or other.
He wandered out on the railroad, half-distraught
And peeped from behind a water-tank at the raiders.
"Squire, don't go any farther," said Higgins, "It ain't safe."
He hardly heard him, he had to look out again.
Who were these devils with horns who were shooting his people?
They didn't look like devils. One was a boy
Smooth-cheeked, with a bright half-dreamy face, a little
Like Sally's eldest.
                              Suddenly, the air struck him   10
A stiff, breath-taking blow. "Oh," he said, astonished.
Took a step and fell on his face, shot through the heart.
Higgins watched him for twenty minutes, wanting to lift him
But not quite daring. Then he turned away
And went back to the town.
                              The bars had been open all day,
Never to better business.
When the news of Beckham's death spread from bar to bar,
It was like putting loco-weed in the whiskey,
The mob came together at once, the American mob,   20
They mightn't be able to take Brown's last little fort
But there were two prisoners penned in the Wager House.
One was hurt already, Stevens, no fun killing him.
But the other was William Thompson, whole and unwounded,
Caught when Brown tried to send his first flag of truce.

They stormed the hotel and dragged him out to the bridge,
Where two men shot him, unarmed, then threw the body
Over the trestle. It splashed in the shallow water,
But the slayers kept on firing at the dead face.
The carcass was there for days, a riven target,   30
Barbarously misused.
                              Meanwhile the armory yard
Was taken by a new band of Beckham's avengers,
The most of Brown's prisoners freed and his last escape cut off.

What need to tell of the killing of Kagi the scholar,
The wounding of Oliver Brown and the other deaths?
Only this remains to be told. When the drunken day
Reeled into night, there were left in the engine-house
Five men, alive and unwounded, of all the raiders.
Watson and Oliver Brown   40

38

Both of them hurt to the death, were stretched on the floor
Beside the corpse of Taylor, the young Canadian.
There was no light, there. It was bitterly cold.
A cold chain of lightless hours that slowly fell
In leaden beads between two fingers of stone.
Outside, the fools and the drunkards yelled in the streets,
And, now and then, there were shots. The prisoners talked
And tried to sleep.
                        John Brown did not try to sleep,
The live coals of his eyes severed the darkness;   10
Now and then he heard his young son Oliver calling
In the thirsty agony of his wounds, "Oh, kill me!
Kill me and put me out of this suffering!"
John Brown's jaw tightened. "If you must die," he said,
"Die like a man." Toward morning the crying ceased.
John Brown called out to the boy but he did not answer.
"I guess he's dead," said John Brown.
                              If his soul wept
They were the incredible tears of the squeezed stone.
He had not slept for two days, but he would not sleep.   20
The night was a chained, black leopard that he stared down,
Erect, on his feet. One wonders what sights he saw
In the cloudy mirror of his most cloudy heart,
Perhaps God clothed in a glory, perhaps himself
The little boy who had stolen three brass pins
And been well whipped for it.
                              When he was six years old
An Indian boy had given him a great wonder,
A yellow marble, the first he had ever seen.
He treasured it for months but lost it at last,   30
Boylike. The hurt of the loss took years to heal.
He never quite forgot.
                        He could see it now,
Smooth, hard and lovely, a yellow, glistening ball,
But it kept rolling away through cracks of darkness
Whenever he tried to catch it and hold it fast.
If he could only touch it, he would be safe,
But it trickled away and away, just out of reach,
There by the wall . . .
                        Outside the blackened East   40
Began to tarnish with a faint, grey stain
That caught on the fixed bayonets of the marines.

39

Lee of Virginia, Light Horse Harry's son,
Observed it broaden, thinking of many things,
But chiefly wanting to get his business done,
A curious, wry, distasteful piece of work
For regular soldiers.
                    Therefore to be finished
As swiftly and summarily as possible
Before this yelling mob of drunk civilians
And green militia once got out of hand.
His mouth set. Once already he had offered   10
The honor of the attack to the militia,
Such honor as it was.
                    Their Colonel had
Declined with a bright nervousness of haste.
"Your men are paid for doing this kind of work.
Mine have their wives and children." Lee smiled briefly,
Remembering that. The smile had a sharp edge.
Well, it was time.
                    The whooping crowd fell silent
And scattered, as a single man walked out   20
Toward the engine-house, a letter in his hand.
Lee watched him musingly. A good man, Stuart.
Now he was by the door and calling out.
The door opened a crack.
                    Brown's eyes were there
Over the cold muzzle of a cocked carbine.
The parleying began, went on and on,
While the crowd shivered and Lee watched it all
With the strict commonsense of a Greek sword
And with the same sure readiness.   30
                    Unperceived,
The dawn ran down the valleys of the wind,
Coral-footed dove, tracking the sky with coral . . .
Then, sudden as powder flashing in a pan,
The parleying was done.
                    The door slammed shut.
The little figure of Stuart jumped aside
Waving its cap.
            And the marines came on.

Brown watched them come. One hand was on his carbine.   40
The other felt the pulse of his dying son.

"Sell your lives dear," he said. The rifle-shots
Rattled within the bricked-in engine-room
Like firecrackers set off in a stone jug,
And there was a harsh stink of sweat and powder.
There was a moment when the door held firm.
Then it was cracked with sun.
                          Brown fired and missed.
A shadow with a sword leaped through the sun.
"That's Ossawattomie," said the tired voice
Of Colonel Washington.   10
                    The shadow lunged
And Brown fell to his knees.
                          The sword bent double,
A light sword, better for parades than fighting,
The shadow had to take it in both hands
And fairly rain his blows with it on Brown
Before he sank.
              Now two marines were down,
The rest rushed in over their comrades' bodies,
Pinning one man of Brown's against the wall   20
With bayonets, another to the floor.

Lee, on his rise of ground, shut up his watch.
It had been just a quarter of an hour
Since Stuart gave the signal for the storm,
And now it was over.
                    All but the long dying.

IV. Sally Dupré and Clay Wingate dance and dream

Cudjo, the negro, watched from the pantry
The smooth glissades of the dancing gentry,
His splay-feet tapping in time to the tune
While his broad face beamed like a drunken moon   30
At candles weeping in crystal sconces,
Waxed floors glowing like polished bronzes,
Sparkles glinting on Royal Worcester
And all the stir and color and luster
Where Miss Louisa and Miss Amanda,
Proud dolls scissored from silver paper,
With hoopskirts wide as the front veranda
And the gypsy eyes of a caged frivolity,

Pointed their toes in a satin caper
To the nonchalant glory of the Quality.

And there were the gentlemen, one and all,
Friends and neighbors of Wingate Hall—
Old Judge Brooke from Little Vermilion
With the rusty voice of a cracked horse-pistol
And manners as stiff as a French cotillion.
Huger Shepley and Wainscott Bristol,
Hawky arrogant sons of anger
Who rode like devils and fought like cocks   10
And watched, with an ineffable languor
Their spoilt youth tarnish a dicing-box.
The Cazenove boys and the Cotter brothers,
Pepperalls from Pepperall Ride.
Cummings and Crowls and a dozen others,
Every one with a name and a pride.
Sallow young dandies in shirts with ruffles,
Each could dance like a blowing feather,
And each had the voice that Georgia muffles
In the lazy honey of her May weather.   20

Cudjo watched and measured and knew them,
Seeing behind and around and through them
With the shrewd, dispassionate, smiling eye
Of the old-time servant in days gone by.
He couldn't read and he couldn't write,
But he knew Quality, black or white,
And even his master could not find
The secret place in the back of his mind
Where witch-bones talked to a scarlet rag
And a child's voice spoke from a conjur-bag.   30
For he belonged to the hidden nation,
The mute, enormous confederation
Of the planted earth and the burden borne
And the horse that is ridden and given corn.
The wind from the brier-patch brought him news
That never went walking in white men's shoes
And the grapevine whispered its message faster
Than a horse could gallop across a grave,
Till, long ere the letter could tell the master,
The doomsday rabbits had told the slave.   40

He was faithful as bread or salt,
A flawless servant without a fault,
Major-domo of Wingate Hall,
Proud of his white folks, proud of it all.
They might scold him, they might let him scold them,
And he might know things that he never told them,
But there was a bond, and the bond would hold,
On either side until both were cold.

So he didn't judge, though he knew, he knew,
How the yellow babies down by the Slough,   10
Had a fourth of their blood from old Judge Brooke,
And where Sue Crowl got her Wingate look,
And the whole, mad business of Shepley's Wager,
And why Miss Harriet married the Major.
And he could trace with unerring ease
A hundred devious pedigrees
Of man and horse, from the Squire's Rapscallion
Back to the stock of the Arab stallion,
And the Bristol line through its baffling dozens
Of doubly-removed half-second-cousins,   20
And found a creed and a whole theology
On the accidents of human geology.

He looked for Clay in the dancing whirl,
There he was, coming down the line,
Hand in hand with a dark, slim girl
Whose dress was the color of light in wine
Sally Dupré from Appleton
Where the blackshawled ladies rock in the sun
And young things labor and old things rule,
A proud girl, taught in a humbling school   30
That the only daughters of misalliance
Must harden their hearts against defiance
Of all the uncles and all the aunts
Who succour such offspring of mischance
And wash them clean from each sinful intention
With the kindliest sort of incomprehension.

She had the Appleton mouth, it seemed,
And the Appleton way of riding,
But when she sorrowed and if she dreamed,

Something came out from hiding.
She could sew all day on an Appleton hem
And look like a saint in plaster,
But when the fiddles began to play
And her feet beat fast but her heart beat faster
An alien grace inhabited them
And she looked like her father, the dancing-master,
The scapegrace elegant, "French" Dupré,
Come to the South on a luckless day,
With bright paste buckles sewn on his pumps.   10
A habit of holding the ace of trumps,
And a manner of kissing a lady's hand
Which the county failed to understand.
He stole Sue Appleton's heart away
With eyes that were neither black nor grey,
And broke the heart of the Brookes' best mare
To marry her safely with time to spare
While the horsewhip uncles toiled behind—
He knew his need and she knew her mind.
And the love they had was as bright and brief   20
As the dance of the gilded maple-leaf,
Till she died in Charleston of childbed fever
Before her looks or his heart could leave her.
It took the flavor out of his drinking
And left him thoughts he didn't like thinking,
So he wrapped his child in the dead girl's shawl
And sent her politely to Uncle Paul
With a black-edged note full of grief and scruples
And half the money he owed his pupils,
Saw that Sue had the finest hearse   30
That I. O. U.'s could possibly drape her
And elegized her in vile French verse
While his hot tears spotted the borrowed paper.

He still had manners, he tried to recover,
But something went when he buried his lover.
No women with eyes could ever scold him
But he would make places too hot to hold him,
He shrugged his shoulders and kept descending—
Life was a farce, but it needed ending.
The tag-line found him too tired to dread it   40
And he died as he lived, with an air, on credit,

44

In his host's best shirt and a Richmond garret,
Talking to shadows and drinking claret.
He passed when Sally was barely four
And the Appleton kindred breathed once more
And, with some fervor, began to try
To bury the bone of his memory
And strictly expunge from his daughter's semblance
All possible traces of a resemblance.
Which system succeeded, to outward view,
As well as most of such systems do   10
And resulted in mixing a martyr's potions
For "French" Dupré in his daughter's notions.

And slander is sinful and gossip wrong,
But country memories are long,
The Appleton clan is a worthy clan
But we remember the dancing-man.
The girl is pretty, the girl seems wise,
The girl was born with her father's eyes.
She will play with our daughters and know our sons,
We cannot offend the Appletons.   20
Bristols and Wingates, Shepleys and Crowls,
We wouldn't hurt her to save our souls.
But after all—and nevertheless—
For one has to think—and one must confess—
And one should admit—but one never knows—
So it has gone, and so it goes,
Through the sun and the wind and the rainy weather
Whenever ladies are gathered together,
Till, little by little and stitch by stitch,
The girl is put in her proper niche   30
With all the virtues that we can draw
For someone else's daughter-in-law,
A girl to be kind to, a girl we're lucky in,
A girl to marry some nice Kentuckian,
Some Alabaman, some Carolinian—
In fact, if you ask me for my opinion,
There are lots of boys in the Northern sections
And some of them have quite good connections—
She looks charming this evening, doesn't she?
If she danced just a little less *dashingly!*   40

45

Cudjo watched her as she went by,
"She's got a light foot," thought Cudjo, "Hi!
A light, swif' foot and a talkin' eye!
But you'll need more'n dat, Miss Sally Dupré
Before you proposals with young Marse Clay.
And as soon as de fiddles finish slewin'
Dey's sixteen things I ought to be doin'.
The Major's sure to be wantin' his dram,
We'll have to be cuttin' a second ham,
And dat trashy high-yaller, Parker's Guinea,   10
Was sayin' some Yankee name Old John Brown
Has raised de Debil back in Virginny
And freed de niggers all over town,
He's friends with de ha'nts and steel won't touch him
But the paterollers is sure to cotch him.
How come he want to kick up such a dizziness!
Nigger-business ain't white-folks' business."

There was no real moon in all the soft, clouded night,
The rats of night had eaten the silver cheese,
Though here and there a forgotten crumb of old brightness   20
Gleamed and was blotted.
                          But there was no real moon,
No bowl of nacre, dripping an old delusive
Stain on the changed, strange grass, making faces strange;
There was only a taste of warm rain not yet fallen,
A wine-colored dress, turned black because of no moon,
—It would have been spangled in moon—and a broadcloth coat,
And two voices talking together, quite softly, quite calmly.
The dance. Such a lovely dance. But you dance so lightly.
Amanda dances so well. But you dance so lightly.   3
Louisa looks so pretty in pink, don't you think?
Are you fond of Scott? Yes, I'm very fond of Scott.
Elegant extracts from gilt-edged volumes called Keepsakes
And Godey's Lady's Book words.

                         (If I were a girl,
A girl in a Godey's Lady's Book steel-engraving,
I would have no body or legs, no aches or delusions.
I would know what to do. I would marry a man called Mister.
We would live in a steel-engraving, in various costumes

46

Designed in the more respectable Paris modes,
With two little boys in little plush hats like muffins,
And two little girls with pantalettes to their chins.
I must do that, I think.
                But now my light feet know
That they will be tired and burning with all my dancing
Before I cool them in the exquisite coolness
Of water or the cool virginal sheets of virgins,
And a face comes swimming toward me out of black broadcloth
And my heart knocks.   10
                 Who are you, why are you here?
Why should you trouble my eyes?)

                     No, Mr. Wingate,
I cannot agree with you on the beauties of Byron.

(But why should something melt in the stuff of my hand,
And my voice sound thin in my ears?
                      This face is a face
Like any other face. Did my mother once
Hear thin blood sing in her ears at a voice called Mister?
And wish for—and not wish for—and when the strange thing   20
Was consummate, then, and she lay in a coil of darkness,
Did she feel so much changed? What is it to be
A woman?
          No, I must live in a steel-engraving.)

His voice said. But there was other than his voice.
Something that heard warm rain on unopened flowers
And spoke or tried to speak across swimming blackness
To the slight profile and the wine-colored dress.
Her hair was black. Her eyes might be black or grey.
He could not remember, it irked him not to remember.   30
But she was just Sally Dupré from Appleton
Only she was not. Only she was a shadow
And a white face—a terrible, white shut face
That looked through windows of inflexible glass
Disdainfully upon the beauties of Byron
And every puppy that ever howled for the moon
To brush warm raindrops across the unopened flower
And so quiet the heart with—what?
                     But you speak to her aunts.

You are Wingate of Wingate Hall. You are not caught
Like a bee drunk with the smell of honey, the smell of sleep,
In a slight flower of glass whose every petal
Shows eyes one cannot remember as black or grey.
You converse easily on elegant subjects
Suitable for young ladies.

      You do not feel
The inexorable stairs of the flesh ascended
By an armed enemy with a naked torch.
This has been felt before, this has been quenched   10
With fitting casualness in flesh that has
A secret stain of the sun.

       It is not a subject
Suitable for the converse of young ladies.

"My God, My God, why will she not answer the aching?
My God, My God, to lie at her side through the darkness!"
(And yet—is it real—do I really—)

         The wine-colored dress
Rose. Broadcloth rose and took her back to the dance.

V. *Jack Ellyat visions the result of the hanging of John Brown*

  The nickeled lamp threw a wide yellow disk   20
  On the red tablecloth with the tasseled fringes.
  Jack Ellyat put his book down with a slight
  Impatient gesture.
      There was mother, knitting
  The same grey end of scarf while Father read
  The same unaltered paper through the same
  Old-fashioned spectacles with the worn bows.

  Jane with one apple-cheek and one enshadowed,
  Soundlessly conjugated Latin verbs,
  "Amo, amas, amat," through sober lips,   30
  "Amamus, amatis, amant," and still no sound.
  He glanced at the clock. On top of it was Phaëton
  Driving bronze, snarling horses down the sharp,
  Quicksilver, void, careening gulfs of air.
  Until they smashed upon a black-marble sea.

48

The round spiked trophy of the brazen sun
Weighed down his chariot with its heavy load
Of ponderous fire.
                    To be like Phaëton
And drive the trophy-sun!
                              But he and his horses
Were frozen in their attitude of snarling,
Frozen forever to the tick of a clock.
Not all the broomstick witches of New England
Could break that congealed motion and cast down   10
The huge sun thundering on the black marble
Of the mantelpiece, streaked with white veins of foam.
If once such things could happen, all could happen,
The snug, safe world crack up like broken candy
And the young rivers, roaring, rush to the sea;
White bulls that caught the morning on their horns
And shook the secure earth until they found
Some better recompense for life than life,
The untamed ghost, the undiminished star.

But it would not happen. Nothing would ever happen.   20
He had been here, like this, ten thousand times,
He would be here, like this, ten thousand more,
Until at last the little ticks of the clock
Had cooled what had been hot, and changed the thin,
Blue, forking veins across the back of his hand
Into the big, soft veins on Father's hand.
And the world would be snug.
                              And he would sit
Reading the same newspaper, after dinner,
Through spectacles whose bows were getting worn   30
While a wife knitted on an endless scarf
And a child slowly formed with quiet lips
"Amo, amas, amat," and still no sound.
And it would be over. Over without having been.

His father turned a creaking page of paper
And cleared his throat. "The *Tribune* calls," he said,
"Brown's raid the work of a madman. Well, they're right,
But—"
            Mrs. Ellyat put her knitting down.

"Are they going to hang him, Will?"
                              "It looks that way."
"But, Father, when—"
                    "They have the right, my son,
He broke the law."
                    "But, Will! You don't believe—"
A little spark lit Mr. Ellyat's eyes.
"I didn't say I thought that he was wrong.
I said they had the right to hang the man,
But they'll hang slavery with him."   16
                              A quick pulse
Beat in Jack Ellyat's wrist. Behind his eyes
A bearded puppet creaked upon a rope
And the sky darkened because he was there.
Now it was Mother talking in a strange
Iron-bound voice he'd never heard before.
"I prayed for him in church last Sunday, Will.
I pray for him at home here every night.
I don't know—I don't care—what laws he broke.
I know that he was right. I pray to God   20
To show the world somehow that he was right
And break these Southern people into knowing!
And I know this—in every house and church,
All through the North—women are praying for him,
Praying for him. And God will hear those prayers."

"He will, my dear," said Mr. Ellyat gently,
"But what will be His answer?"
                              He took her hand,
Smoothing it for a moment. Then she sighed
And turned back to the interminable scarf.   30
Jack Ellyat's pulse beat faster.
                    Women praying,
Praying at night, in every house in the North,
Praying for old John Brown until their knees
Ached with stiff cold.
                    Innumerable prayers
Inexorably rising, till the dark
Vault of the midnight was so thronged and packed
The wild geese could not arrow through the storm
Of terrible, ascendant, women's prayers. . . .   40

The clock struck nine, and Phaëton still stood
Frozenly urging on his frozen horses,
But, for a moment, to Jack Ellyat's eyes,
The congealed hoofs had seemed to paw the air
And the bronze car roll forward.

VI.   *The poet remembers a Courthouse in a Square and tells of
the trial of John Brown*

On Saturday, in Southern market towns,
When I was a boy with twenty cents to spend,
The carts began to drift in with the morning,
And, by the afternoon, the slipshod Square
And all broad Center Street were lined with them;   10
Moth-eaten mules that whickered at each other
Between the mended shafts of rattletrap wagons,
Mud-spattered buggies, mouldy phaetons,
And, here and there, an ox-cart from the hills
Whose solemn team had shoulders of rough, white rock,
Innocent noses, black and wet as snailshells,
And that inordinate patience in their eyes.

There always was a Courthouse in the Square,
A cupolaed Courthouse, drowsing Time away
Behind the grey-white pillars of its porch   20
Like an old sleepy judge in a spotted gown;
And, down the Square, always a languid jail
Of worn, uneven brick with moss in the cracks
Or stone weathered the grey of weathered pine.
The plump jail-master wore a linen duster
In summer, and you used to see him sit
Tilted against the wall in a pine-chair,
Spitting reflectively in the warm dust
While endless afternoons slowly dissolved
Into the longer shadow, the dust-blue twilight.   30
Higgledy-piggledy days—days that are gone—
The trotters are dead, all the yellow-painted sulkies
Broken for firewood—the old Courthouse grins
Through new false-teeth of Alabama limestone—
The haircloth lap-robe weeps on a Ford radiator—

But I have seen the old Courthouse. I have seen
The flyspecked windows and the faded flag
Over the judge's chair, touched the scuffed walls,
Spat in the monumental brass spittoons
And smelt the smell that never could be aired,
Although one opened windows for a year,
The unforgettable, intangible
Mixture of cheap cigars, worm-eaten books,
Sweat, poverty, negro hair-oil, grief and law.
I have seen the long room packed with quiet men,   10
Fit to turn mob, if need were, in a flash—
Cocked-pistol men, so lazily attentive
Their easy languor knocked against your ribs
As, hour by hour, the lawyers droned along,
And minute on creeping minute, your cold necknape
Waited the bursting of the firecracker,
The flare of fury.
           And yet, that composed fury
Burnt itself out, unflaring—was held down
By a dry, droning voice, a faded flag.   20
The kettle never boiled, the pistol stayed
At cock but the snake-head hammer never fell. . . .
The little boys climbed down beyond the windows. . . .

So, in the cupolaed Courthouse there in Charlestown,
When the jail-guards had carried in the cot
Where Brown lay like a hawk with a broken back,
I hear the rustle of the moving crowd,
The buzz outside, taste the dull, heavy air,
Smell the stale smell and see the country carts
Hitched in the streets.   30
           For a long, dragging week
Of market-Saturdays the trial went on.
The droning voices rise and fall and rise.
Stevens lies quiet on his mattress, breathing
The harsh and difficult breath of a dying man,
Although not dying then.
           Beyond the Square
The trees are dry, but all the dry leaves not fallen—
Yellow leaves falling through a grey-blue dusk,
The first winds of November whirl and scatter them. . . .   40

52

Read as you will in any of the books,
The details of the thing, the questions and answers,
How sometimes Brown would walk, sometimes was carried,
At first would hardly plead, half-refused counsel,
Accepted later, made up witness-lists,
Grew fitfully absorbed in his defense,
Only to flare in temper at his first lawyers
And drive them from the case.
                              Questions and answers,
Wheels creaking in a void.   10
                    Sometimes he lay
Quiet upon his cot, the hawk-eyes staring.
Sometimes his fingers moved mechanically
As if at their old task of sorting wool,
Fingertips that could tell him in the dark
Whether the wool they touched was from Ohio
Or from Vermont. They had the shepherd's gift.
It was his one sure talent.
                    Questions creaking
Uselessly back and forth.   20
                    No one can say
That the trial was not fair. The trial was fair,
Painfully fair by every rule of law,
And that it was made not the slightest difference.
The law's our yardstick, and it measures well
Or well enough when there are yards to measure.
Measure a wave with it, measure a fire,
Cut sorrow up in inches, weigh content.
You can weigh John Brown's body well enough,
But how and in what balance weigh John Brown?   30

He had the shepherd's gift, but that was all.
He had no other single gift for life.
Some men are pasture Death turns back to pasture,
Some are fire-opals on that iron wrist,
Some the deep roots of wisdoms not yet born.
John Brown was none of these,
He was a stone,
A stone eroded to a cutting edge
By obstinacy, failure and cold prayers.
Discredited farmer, dubiously involved   40
In lawsuit after lawsuit, Shubel Morgan

53

Fantastic bandit of the Kansas border,
Red-handed murderer at Pottawattomie,
Cloudy apostle, whooped along to death
By those who do no violence themselves
But only buy the guns to have it done,
Sincere of course, as all fanatics are,
And with a certain minor-prophet air,
That fooled the world to thinking him half-great
When all he did consistently was fail.
So far one advocate.   10
                    But there is this.

Sometimes there comes a crack in Time itself.
Sometimes the earth is torn by something blind.
Sometimes an image that has stood so long
It seems implanted as the polar star
Is moved against an unfathomed force
That suddenly will not have it any more.
Call it the *mores*, call it God or Fate,
Call it Mansoul or economic law,
That force exists and moves.   20
                            And when it moves
It will employ a hard and actual stone
To batter into bits an actual wall
And change the actual scheme of things.
                                            John Brown
Was such a stone—unreasoning as the stone,
Destructive as the stone, and, if you like,
Heroic and devoted as such a stone.
He had no gift for life, no gift to bring
Life but his body and a cutting edge,   30
But he knew how to die.
                        And yardstick law
Gave him six weeks to burn that hoarded knowledge
In one swift fire whose sparks fell like live coals
On every State in the Union.
                            Listen now,
Listen, the bearded lips are speaking now,
There are no more guerilla-raids to plan,
There are no more hard questions to be solved
Of right and wrong, no need to beg for peace,   40
Here is the peace unbegged, here is the end,

54

Here is the insolence of the sun cast off,
Here is the voice already fixed with night.

I have, may it please the Court, a few words to say.

In the first place I deny everything but what I have all along admitted: of a design on my part to free slaves. . . .

Had I interfered in the matter which I admit, and which I admit has been fairly proved . . . had I so interfered in behalf of the rich, the powerful, the intelligent, or the so-called great . . . and suffered and sacrificed, what I have in this interference, it would have been all right. Every man in this Court 10 would have deemed it an act worthy of reward rather than punishment.

I see a book kissed which I suppose to be the Bible, or at least the New Testament, which teaches me that all things whatsoever I would that men should do unto me, I should do even so to them. It teaches me further to remember them that are in bonds as bound with them. I endeavored to act up to that instruction. I say I am yet too young to understand that God is any respecter of persons. I believe that to have interfered as I have done, as I have always freely admitted I have done in behalf of 20 His despised poor, I did no wrong, but right. Now, if it is deemed necessary that I should forfeit my life for the furtherance of the ends of justice and mingle my blood further with the blood of my children and with the blood of millions in this slave country whose rights are disregarded by wicked, cruel and unjust enactments, I say, let it be done.

Let me say one word further. I feel entirely satisfied with the treatment I have received on my trial. Considering all the circumstances, it has been more generous than I expected. But I feel no consciousness of guilt. I have stated from the first what 30 was my intention and what was not. I never had any design against the liberty of any person, nor any disposition to commit treason or incite slaves to rebel or make any general insurrection. I never encouraged any man to do so but always discouraged any idea of that kind.

Let me say also, in regard to the statements made by some of those connected with me, I hear it has been stated by some of them that I have induced them to join with me. But the contrary is true. I do not say this to injure them, but as regretting their weakness. Not one but joined me of his own accord, and 40 the greater part at their own expense. A number of them I

never saw, and never had a word of conversation with, till the day they came to me, and that was for the purpose I have stated.
   Now I have done.

The voice ceased. There was a deep, brief pause.
The judge pronounced the formal words of death.
One man, a stranger, tried to clap his hands.
The foolish sound was stopped.
There was nothing but silence then.
                       No cries in the court,
No roar, no slightest murmur from the thronged street,   10
As Brown went back to jail between his guards.
The heavy door shut behind them.
There was a noise of chairs scraped back in the court-room,
And that huge sigh of a crowd turning back into men.

A month between the sentence and the hanging.
A month of endless visitors, endless letters.
A Mrs. Russell came to clean his coat.
A sculptor sketched him.
               In the anxious North,
The anxious Dr. Howe most anxiously   20
Denied all godly connection with the raid,
And Gerrit Smith conveniently went mad
For long enough to sponge his mind of all
Memory of such an unsuccessful deed.
Only the tough, swart-minded Higginson
Kept a grim decency, would not deny.
Pity the portly men, pity the pious,
Pity the fool who lights the powder-mine,
They need your counterfeit penny, they will live long.

In Charlestown meanwhile, there were whispers of rescue.   30
Brown told them,
"I am worth now infinitely more to die than to live."
And lived his month so, busily.
A month of trifles building up a legend
And letters in a pinched, firm handwriting
Courageous, scriptural, misspelt and terse,
Sowing a fable everywhere they fell
While the town filled with troops.
               The Governor came,

Enemies, friends, militia-cavaliers,
Old Border Foes.
                    The month ebbed into days,
The wife and husband met for the last time,
The last letter was written:

"To be inscribed on the old ramily Monument at North Elba,
Oliver Brown born 1839 was killed at Harpers Ferry, Va. Nov.
    17th 1859
Watson Brown born 1835 was wounded at Harpers Ferry Nov.
    17th and died Nov. 19th 1859   10
(My Wife can) supply *blank* dates to above
John Brown born May 9th 1800 was executed at Charlestown
    Va. December 2nd 1859."

At last the clear warm day, so slow to come.

The North that had already now begun
To mold his body into crucified Christ's,
Hung fables about those hours—saw him move
Symbolically, kiss a negro child,
Do this and that, say things he never said,
To swell the sparse, hard outlines of the event   20
With sentimental omen.
                    It was not so.
He stood on the jail-porch in carpet-slippers,
Clad in a loose ill-fitting suit of black,
Tired farmer waiting for his team to come.
He left one last written message:

    "I, John Brown, am now quite *certain* that the crimes of this
guilty land: will never be purged *away:* but with Blood. I had
as I now think: vainly flattered myself that without *very much*
bloodshed; it might be done."   30

They did not hang him in the jail or the Square.
The two white horses dragged the rattling cart
Out of the town. Brown sat upon his coffin.
Beyond the soldiers lay the open fields
Earth-colored, sleepy with unfallen frost.
The farmer's eye took in the bountiful land.
"This *is* a beautiful country," said John Brown.

The gallows-stairs were climbed, the death-cap fitted.
Behind the gallows,
Before a line of red-and-grey cadets,
A certain odd Professor T. J. Jackson
Watched disapprovingly the ragged militia
Deploy for twelve long minutes ere they reached
Their destined places.
The Presbyterian sabre of his soul
Was moved by a fey breath.

                      He saw John Brown,   10
A tiny blackened scrap of paper-soul
Fluttering above the Pit that Calvin barred
With bolts of iron on the unelect;
He heard the just, implacable Voice speak out
"Depart ye wicked to eternal fire."
And sternly prayed that God might yet be moved
To save the predestined cinder from the flame.

Brown did not hear the prayer. The rough black cloth
Of the death-cap hid his eyes now. He had seen
The Blue Ridge Mountains couched in their blue haze.   20
Perhaps he saw them still, behind his eyes—
Perhaps just cloth, perhaps nothing any more.
"I shall look unto the hills from whence cometh my help."

The hatchet cut the cord. The greased trap fell.

Colonel Preston:

    "So perish all such enemies of Virginia,
        All such enemies of the Union,
        All such foes of the human race."

John Brown's body lies a-mouldering in the grave.
He will not come again with foolish pikes   30
And a pack of desperate boys to shadow the sun.
He has gone back North. The slaves have forgotten his eyes.
John Brown's body lies a-mouldering in the grave.
John Brown's body lies a-mouldering in the grave.
Already the corpse is changed, under the stone,
The strong flesh rotten, the bones dropping away.
Cotton will grow next year, in spite of the skull.

Slaves will be slaves next year, in spite of the bones.
Nothing is changed, John Brown, nothing is changed.

"There is a song in my bones. There is a song
In my white bones."

I hear no song. I hear
Only the blunt seeds growing secretly
In the dark entrails of the preparate earth,
The rustle of the cricket under the leaf,
The creaking of the cold wheel of the stars.

"Bind my white bones together—hollow them   10
To skeleton pipes of music. When the wind
Blows from the budded Spring, the song will blow."

I hear no song. I only hear the roar
Of the Spring freshets, and the gushing voice
Of mountain-brooks that overflow their banks,
Swollen with melting ice and crumbled earth.

"That is my song.
It is made of water and wind. It marches on."

No, John Brown's body lies a-mouldering,
A-mouldering.   20

"My bones have been washed clean
And God blows through them with a hollow sound,
And God has shut his wildfire in my dead heart."

I hear it now,
Faint, faint as the first droning flies of March,
Faint as the multitudinous, tiny sigh
Of grasses underneath a windy scythe.

"It will grow stronger."

It has grown stronger. It is marching on.
It is a throbbing pulse, a pouring surf,   30
It is the rainy gong of the Spring sky
Echoing,
John Brown's body.

John Brown's body.
But still it is not fierce. I find it still
More sorrowful than fierce.

*"You have not heard it yet. You have not heard
The ghosts that walk in it, the shaking sound."*

Strong medicine,
Bitter medicine of the dead,
I drink you now. I hear the unloosed thing,
The anger of the ripe wheat—the ripened earth
Sullenly quaking like a beaten drum
From Kansas to Vermont. I hear the stamp
Of the ghost-feet. I hear the ascending sea.

10

     "Glory, Glory, Hallelujah,
     Glory, Glory, Hallelujah,
     Glory, Glory, Hallelujah!"

What is this agony of the marching dust?
What are these years ground into hatchet blades?

*"Ask the tide why it rises with the moon,
My bones and I have risen like that tide
And an immortal anguish plucks us up
And will not hide us till our song is done."*

20

The phantom drum diminishes—the year
Rolls back. It is only winter still, not spring,
The snow still flings its white on the new grave,
Nothing is changed, John Brown, nothing is changed
John . . . Brown . . .

BOOK TWO:

The Stone in the Pool

On April 12, 1861, the Confederate forces began the bombardment of Fort Sumter in Charleston harbor. This action the poet calls "the stone that falls in the pool." The ripples spread to the home of Sally Dupré. The ripples scatter the news to Stroudsburg Siding.

They establish Jefferson Davis, with his Cabinet, as President of the Confederacy at Richmond. The ripples spread to Washington where Lincoln and his Cabinet send out the call for seventy-five thousand volunteers. The ripples spread from Georgia to Maine as the young men answer the call.

Wingate perceives the ripples; the slaves in the cabins, half-fearful, half-wishful for freedom, sense them.

Jake Diefer from Pennsylvania, Luke Breckinridge from the mountains of Tennessee respond, neither quite sure what the ripples tell.

Jack Ellyat follows the slogan "On to Richmond." Curly Hatton marches drearily with the Virginia recruits. Both are confident that in three months the war will be over.

July comes and with it the first battle at Manassas or Bull Run, a Confederate victory, but ending in complete confusion of both Union and Confederate soldiers. The battle brings into prominence names that are to become great in the history of the war: Johnston, McDowell, Beauregard, Jackson and his brigade standing on the Henry House plateau; Burnside, Bell, and Bartow.

The results of Bull Run bring tumult to Washington, bitterness and scorn toward Lincoln; to that same Lincoln renewed determination to protect the Union; rumors of a mighty man in the South, Robert E. Lee.

I. The stubborn guns of Fort Sumter

A smoke-stained Stars-and-Stripes droops from a broken tooth-
pick and ninety tired men march out of fallen Sumter to their
ships, drums rattling and colors flying.

Their faces are worn and angry, their bellies empty and cold,
but the stubborn salute of a gun, fifty times repeated, keeps their
backs straight as they march out, and answers something stubborn
and mute in their flesh.

Beauregard, *beau sabreur*, hussar-sword with the gilded hilt,
the gilded metal of the guard twisted into lovelocks and roses,
vain as Murat, dashing as Murat, Pierre Gustave Toutant Beau- 10
regard is a pose of conquering courtesy under a palmetto-banner.
The lugubrious little march goes grimly by his courtesy, he
watches it unsmiling, a light half-real, half that of invisible foot-
lights on his French, dark, handsome face.

II. The soul begins to march

The stone falls in the pool, the ripples spread.
The colt in the Long Meadow kicked up his heels.
"That was a fly," he thought, "It's early for flies."
But being alive, in April, was too fine
For flies or anything else to bother a colt.
He kicked up his heels again, this time in pure joy,   20
And started to run a race with the wind and his shadow.
After the stable stuffiness, the sun.
After the straw-littered boards, the squelch of the turf.
His little hoofs felt lighter than dancing-shoes,
He scared himself with a blue-jay, his heart was a leaf.
He was pure joy in action, he was the unvexed
Delight of all moving lightness and swift-footed pace,
The pride of the flesh, the young Spring neighing and rearing.
Sally Dupré called to him from the fence.
He came like a charge in a spatter of clean-cut clods,   30
Ears back, eyes wide and wild with folly and youth.
He drew up snorting.
        She laughed and brushed at her skirt
Where the mud had splashed it.
        "There, Star—there, silly boy!

Why won't you ever learn sense?"
                              But her eyes were hot,
Her hands were shaking as she offered the sugar
—Long-fingered, appleblossom-shadow hands—
Star blew at the sugar once, then mumbled it up.
She patted the pink nose. "There, silly Star!
That's for Fort Sumter, Star!" How hot her eyes were!
"Star, do you know you're a Confederate horse?
Do you know I'm going to call you Beauregard?"

Star whinnied, and asked for more sugar. She put her hand   10
On his neck for a moment that matched the new green leaves
And sticky buds of April.
                              You would have said
They were grace in quietness, seen so, woman and horse. . . .

The widened ripple breaks against a stone
The heavy noon walks over Chancellorsville
On brazen shoes, but where the squadron rode
Into the ambush, the blue flies are coming
To blow on the dead meat.

Carter, the telegraph-operator, sighed   20
And propped his eyes awake again.
                              He was tired.
Dog-tired, stone-tired, body and mind burnt up
With too much poker last night and too little sleep.
He hated the Sunday trick. It was Riley's turn
To take it, but Riley's wife was having a child.
He cursed the child and the wife and Sunday and Riley.
Nothing ever happened at Stroudsburg Siding
And yet he had to be here and keep awake
With the flat, stale taste of too little sleep in his mouth   30
And wait for nothing to happen.
                              His bulky body
Lusted for sleep with every muscle and nerve.
                              The sounder chattered
And his head snapped back with a sharp, neck-breaking jerk.
By God, he'd nearly— *chat—chitter-chatter-chat-chat—*
For a moment he took it in without understanding
And then the vein in his forehead began to swell

And his eyes bulged wide awake.

"By Jesus!" he said,

And stared at the sounder as if it had turned to a snake.
"By Jesus!" he said, "By Jesus, they've done it!" he said.

The cruelty of cold trumpets wounds the air.
The ponderous princes draw their gauntlets on.
The captains fit their coal-black armor on.

Judah P. Benjamin, the dapper Jew,
Seal-sleek, black-eyed, lawyer and epicure,
Able, well-hated, face alive with life,
Looked round the council-chamber with the slight
Perpetual smile he held before himself
Continually like a silk-ribbed fan.
Behind the fan, his quick, shrewd, fluid mind
Weighed Gentiles in an old balance.

There they were.

Toombs, the tall, laughing, restless Georgian,
As fine to look at as a yearling bull,
As hard to manage.

Stephens, sickly and pale,

Sweet-voiced, weak-bodied, ailingly austere,
The mind's thin steel wearing the body out,
The racked intelligence, the crippled charm.
Mallory—Reagan—Walker—at the head
Davis.

The mind behind the silk-ribbed fan
Was a dark prince, clothed in an Eastern stuff,
Whose brown hands cupped about a crystal egg
That filmed with colored cloud. The eyes stared, searching.

"I am the Jew. What am I doing here?
The Jew is in my blood and in my hands,
The lonely, bitter and quicksilver drop,
The stain of myrrh that dyes no Gentile mind
With tinctures out of the East and the sad blare
Of the curled ramshorn on Atonement Day.
A river runs between these men and me,
A river of blood and time and liquid gold,
—Oh white rivers of Canaan, running the night!—
And we are colleagues. And we speak to each other

Across the roar of that river, but no more.
I hide myself behind a smiling fan.
They hide themselves behind a Gentile mask
And, if they fall, they will be lifted up,
Being the people, but if I once fall
I fall forever, like the rejected stone.
That is the Jew of it, my Gentile friends,
To see too far ahead and yet go on
And I can smile at it behind my fan
With a drowned mirth that you would find uncouth. 10
For here we are, the makeshift Cabinet
Of a new nation, gravely setting down
Rules, precedents and cautions, never once
Admitting aloud the cold, plain Franklin sense
That if we do not hang together now
We shall undoubtedly hang separately.
It is the Jew, to see too far ahead—

I wonder what they're doing in the North,
And how their Cabinet shapes, and how they take
Their railsplitter, and if they waste their time 20
As we waste ours and Mr. Davis's.

Jefferson Davis, pride of Mississippi,
First President of the Confederate States,
What are you thinking now?
                              Your eyes look tired.
Your face looks more and more like John Calhoun.
And that is just, because you are his son
In everything but blood, the austere child
Of his ideas, the flower of states-rights.
I will not gird against you, Jefferson Davis. 30
I sent you a challenge once, but that's forgotten,
And though your blood runs differently from mine,
The Jew salutes you from behind his fan,
Because you are the South he fell in love with
When that young black-haired girl with the Gentile-eyes,
Proud, and a Catholic, and with honey-lips,
First dinted her French heels upon his heart. . . .
We have changed since, but the remembered Spring
Can change no more, even in the Autumn smokes.
We cannot help that havoc of the heart 40

66

But my changed mind remembers half the spring
And shall till winter falls.
                    No, Jefferson Davis,
You are not she—you are not the warm night
On the bayou, or the New Orleans lamps,
The white-wine bubbles in the crystal cup,
The almond blossoms, sleepy with the sun:
But, nevertheless, you are the South in word,
Deed, thought and temper, the cut cameo
Brittle but durable, refined but fine,   10
The hands well-shaped, not subtle, but not weak,
The mind set in tradition but not unjust,
The generous slaveholder, the gentleman
Who neither forces his gentility
Nor lets it be held lightly—
                    and yet, and yet
I think you look too much like John Calhoun,
I think your temper is too brittly-poised,
I think your hands too scholar-sensitive,
And though they say you mingle in your voice   20
The trumpet and the harp, I think it lacks
That gift of warming men which coarser voices
Draw from the common dirt you tread upon
But do not take in your hands. I think you are
All things except success, all honesty
Except the ultimate honesty of the earth,
All talents but the genius of the sun.
And yet I would not have you otherwise,
Although I see too clearly what you are.

Except—except—oh honeydropping Spring,   30
Oh black-haired woman with the Gentile eyes!
Tell me, you Gentiles, when your Gentile wives
Pray in the church for you and for the South,
How do they pray?—not in that lulling voice
Where some drowned bell of France makes undertones
To the warm river washing the levee.
You do not have so good a prayer as mine.
You cannot have so good a prayer as mine."

67

Lincoln, six feet one in his stocking feet,
The lank man, knotty and tough as a hickory rail,
Whose hands were always too big for white-kid gloves,
Whose wit was a coonskin sack of dry, tall tales,
Whose weathered face was homely as a plowed field—
Abraham Lincoln, who padded up and down
The sacred White House in nightshirt and carpet-slippers,
And yet could strike young hero-worshipping Hay
As dignified past any neat, balanced, fine
Plutarchan sentences carved in a Latin bronze;   10
The low clown out of the prairies, the ape-buffoon,
The small-town lawyer, the crude small-time politician,
State-character but comparative failure at forty
In spite of ambition enough for twenty Caesars,
Honesty rare as a man without self-pity,
Kindness as large and plain as a prairie wind,
And a self-confidence like an iron bar:
This Lincoln, President now by the grace of luck,
Disunion, politics, Douglas and a few speeches
Which make the monumental booming of Webster   20
Sound empty as the belly of a burst drum,
Lincoln shambled in to the Cabinet meeting
And sat, ungainly and awkward. Seated so
He did not seem so tall nor quite so strange
Though he was strange enough. His new broadcloth suit
Felt tight and formal across his big shoulders still
And his new shiny top-hat was not yet battered
To the bulging shape of the old familiar hat
He'd worn at Springfield, stuffed with its hoard of papers.
He was pretty tired. All week the office-seekers   30
Had plagued him as the flies in fly-time plague
A gaunt-headed, patient horse. The children weren't well
And Mollie was worried about them so sharp with her tongue.
But he knew Mollie and tried to let it go by.
Men tracked dirt in the house and women liked carpets.
Each had a piece of the right, that was all most people could stand

Look at his Cabinet here. There were Seward and Chase,
Both of them good men, couldn't afford to lose them,
But Chase hates Seward like poison and Seward hates Chase

And both of 'em think they ought to be President
Instead of me. When Seward wrote me that letter
The other day, he practically told me so.
I suppose a man who was touchy about his pride
Would send them both to the dickens when he found out,
But I can't do that as long as they do their work.
The Union's too big a horse to keep changing the saddle
Each time it pinches you. As long as you're sure
The saddle fits, you're bound to put up with the pinches
And not keep fussing the horse.   10
                              When I was a boy
I remember figuring out when I went to town
That if I had just one pumpkin to bump in a sack
It was hard to carry, but once you could get two pumpkins,
One in each end of the sack, it balanced things up.
Seward and Chase'll do for my pair of pumpkins.
And as for me—if anyone else comes by
Who shows me that he can manage this job of mine
Better than I can—well, he can have the job.
It's harder sweating than driving six cross mules,   20
But I haven't run into that other fellow yet
And till or supposing I meet him, the job's my job
And nobody else's.
                    Seward and Chase don't know that.
They'll learn it, in time.
                          Wonder how Jefferson Davis
Feels, down there in Montgomery, about Sumter.
He must be thinking pretty hard and fast,
For he's an able man, no doubt of that.
We were born less than forty miles apart,   30
Less than a year apart—he got the start
Of me in age, and raising too, I guess,
In fact, from all you hear about the man,
If you set out to pick one of us two
For President, by birth and folks and schooling,
General raising, training up in office,
I guess you'd pick him, nine times out of ten
And yet, somehow, I've got to last him out.

These thoughts passed through the mind in a moment's flash.
Then that mind turned to business.
                              It was the calling
Of seventy-five thousand volunteers.

IV.   Lincoln calls his volunteers

Shake out the long line of verse like a lanyard of woven steel
And let us praise while we can what things no praise can deface,
The corn that hurried so fast to be ground in an iron wheel
The obdurate, bloody dream that slept before it grew base.

Not the silk flag and the shouts, the catchword patrioteers,
The screaming noise of the press, the preachers who howled for 10
    blood,
But a certain and stubborn pith in the hearts of the cannoneers
Who hardly knew their guns before they died in the mud.

They came like a run of salmon where the ice-fed Kennebec flings
Its death at the arrow-silver of the packed and mounting host,
They came like the young deer trooping to the ford by Eutaw
    Springs,
Their new horns fuzzy with velvet, their coats still rough with
    the frost.

North and South they assembled, one cry and the other cry,   20
And both are ghosts to us now, old drums hung up on a wall,
But they were the first hot wave of youth too-ready to die,
And they went to war with an air, as if they went to a ball.

Dress-uniform boys who rubbed their buttons brighter than gold,
And gave them to girls for flowers and raspberry-lemonade,
Unused to the sick fatigue, the route-march made in the cold,
The stink of the fever camps, the tarnish rotting the blade.

We in our time have seen that impulse going to war
And how that impulse is dealt with. We have seen the circle
    complete.   30
The ripe wheat wasted like trash between the fool and the whore.
We cannot praise again that anger of the ripe wheat.

This we have seen as well, distorted and half-forgotten
In what came before and after, where the blind went leading the
    blind,
The first swift rising of youth before the symbols were rotten,
The price too much to pay, the payment haughty in kind.

So with these men and then. They were much like the men you
    know,
Under the beards and the strangeness of clothes with a different
    fit.
They wrote mush-notes to their girls and wondered how it would 10
    go,
Half-scared, half-fierce at the thought, but none yet ready to
    quit.

Georgia, New York, Virginia, Rhode Island, Florida, Maine,
Piney-woods squirrel-hunter and clerk with the brand-new gun,
Thus they were marshalled and drilled, while Spring turned
    Summer again,
Until they could stumble toward death at gartersnake-crooked
    Bull Run.

    V. *Wingate takes his stand for Dixie*

Wingate sat in his room at night
Between the moon and the candle-light,   20
Reading his Byron with knitted brows,
While his mind drank in the peace of his house,
It was long past twelve, and the night was deep
With moonlight and silence and wind and sleep,
And the small, dim noises, thousand-fold,
That all old houses and forests hold.
The boards that creak for nothing at all,
The leaf that rustles, the bough that sighs,
The nibble of mice in the wainscot-wall,
And the slow clock ticking the time that dies   30
All distilled in a single sound
Like a giant breathing underground,
A sound more sleepy than sleep itself.
Wingate put his book on the shelf

71

And went to the window. It was good
To walk in the ghost through a silver wood
And set one's mettle against the far
Bayonet-point of the fixed North Star.
He stood there a moment, wondering.
North Star, wasp with the silver sting
Blue-nosed star on the Yankee banners,
We are coming against you to teach you manners!
With crumbs of thunder and wreaths of myrtle
And cannon that dance to a Dixie chorus,   10
With a song that bites like a snapping-turtle
And the tiger-lily of Summer before us,
To pull you down like a torn bandanna,
And drown you deeper than the Savannah!

And still, while his arrogance made its cry,
He shivered a little, wondering why.

There was his uniform, grey as ash,
The boots that shone like a well-rubbed table,
The tassels of silk on the colored sash
And sleek Black Whistle down in the stable,   20
The housewife, stitched from a beauty's fan,
The pocket-Bible with Mother's writing,
The sabre never yet fleshed in man,
And all the crisp new toys of fighting.
He gloated at them with a boyish pride,
But still he wondered, Monmouth-eyed.
The Black Horse Troop was a cavalier
And gallant name for a lady's ear.
He liked the sound and the ringing brag
And the girls who stitched on the county flag,   30
The smell of horses and saddle-leather
And the feel of the squadron riding together,
From the loose-reined canter of colts at large,
To the crammed, tense second before the charge:
He liked it all with the young, keen zest
Of a hound unleashed and a hawk unjessed.

And yet—what happened to men in war?
Why were they all going out to war?

He brooded a moment. It wasn't slavery,
That stale red-herring of Yankee knavery
Nor even states-rights, at least not solely,
But something so dim that it must be holy.
A voice, a fragrance, a taste of wine,
A face half-seen in old candleshine,
A yellow river, a blowing dust,
Something beyond you that you must trust,
Something so shrouded it must be great,
The dead men building the living State   10
From 'simmon-seed on a sandy bottom,
The woman South in her rivers laving
That body whiter than new-blown cotton
And savage and sweet as wild-orange-blossom,
The dark hair streams on the barbarous bosom,
If there ever has been a land worth saving—
In Dixie land, I'll take my stand,
And live and die for Dixie! . . .

And yet—and yet—in some cold Northern room,
Does anyone else stare out the obdurate moon   20
With doubtful passion, seeing his toys of fighting
Scribbled all over with such silver writing
From such a heart of peace, they seem the stale
Cast properties of a dead and childish tale?
And does he see, too soon,
Over the horse, over the horse and rider,
The grey, soft swathing shadowness of the spider,
Spinning his quiet loom?
No—no other man is cursed
With such doubleness of eye,   30
They can hunger, they can thirst,
But they know for what and why.

I can drink the midnight out,
And rise empty, having dined.
For my courage and my doubt
Are a double strand of mind,
And too subtly intertwined.
They are my flesh, they are my bone,
My shame and my foundation-stone.
I was born alone, to live alone.   40

73

Sally Dupré, Sally Dupré,
Eyes that are neither black nor grey,
Why do you haunt me, night and day?

Sea-changing eyes, with the deep, drowned glimmer
Of bar-gold crumbling from sunken ships,
Where the sea-dwarfs creep through the streaked, green shimmer
To press the gold to their glass-cold lips.
They sculpture the gold for a precious ring,
In the caverns under the under-skies,
They would marry the sea to a sailor-king!   10
You have taken my heart from me, sea-born eyes.
You have taken it, yes, but I do not know.
There are too many roads where I must go.
There are too many beds where I have slept
For a night unweeping, to quit unwept,
And it needs a king to marry the sea.

Why have you taken my heart from me?
I am not justice nor loyalty.
I am the shape of the weathercock,
That all winds come to and all winds mock.   20
You are the image of sea-carved stone,
The silent thing that can suffer alone,
The little women are easier,
The easy women make lighter love,
I will not take your face to the war,
I will not carry your cast-off glove.

Sally Dupré, Sally Dupré,
Heart and body like sea-blown spray,
I cannot forget you, night or day.

So Wingate pondered in Wingate Hall,   30
And hated and loved in a single breath,
As he tried to unriddle the doubtful scrawl
Of war and courage and love and death,
And then was suddenly nothing but sleep—
And tomorrow they marched—to a two-months chasing
Of Yankees running away like sheep
And peace in time for the Macon racing.

74

He got in his bed. Where the moonlight poured,
It lay like frost on a sleeping sword.

VI. *Wingate's slaves wonder about freedom*

It was stuffy at night in the cabins, stuffy but warm.
And smells are a matter of habit. So, if the air
Was thick as black butter with the commingled smells
Of greens and fried fat and field-sweat and heavy sleep,
The walls were well-chinked, the low roof kept out the rain.
Not like the tumble-down cabins at Zachary's place
Where the field-hands lived all year on hominy-grits
And a piece of spoiled pork at Christmas.   10
                         But Zachary
Was a mean man out of the Bottoms, no quality to him.
Wingate was quality. Wingate cared for its own.
A Wingate cabin was better than most such cabins,
You might have called it a sty, had they set you there;
A Middle Age serf might have envied the well-chinked walls.
While as for its tenants then, being folk unversed
In any law but the law of the Wingate name,
They were glad to have it, glad for fire on the hearth,
A roof from the dark-veined wind.   20

"What you so wakeful for, black boy?"
                          "Thinkin', woman."
"You got no call to be thinkin', little black boy,
Thinkin's a trouble, a h'ant lookin' over de shoulder,
Set yo' head on my breas' and forget about thinkin'."

"I got my head on yo' breas', and it's sof' dere, woman,
Sof' and sweet as a mournin' out of de Scriptures,
Sof' as two Solomon doves. But I can't help thinkin'."

"Ain't I good enough for you no more, black boy?
Don' you love me no more dat you mus' keep thinkin'?"   30

"You's better'n good to me and I loves you, woman,
Till I feels like Meshuck down in de fiery furnace,
Till I feels like God's own chile. But I keeps on thinkin',
Wonderin' what I'd feel like if I was free."

"Hush, black boy, hush for de Lord's sake!"
                              "But listen, woman——"

"Hush yo'self, black boy, lean yo'self on my breas',
Talk like that and paterollers'll git you,
Swinge you all to bits with a blacksnake whip,
Squinch-owl carry yo' talk to de paterollers,
It ain't safe to talk like that."
                              "I got to, woman,
I got a feelin' in my heart."
                              "Den you sot on dat feelin'!   10
Never heard you talk so in all my born days!
Ain't we got a good cabin here?"
                              "Sho', we got a good cabin."
"Ain't we got good vittles, ain't old Mistis kind to us?"

"Sho' we got good vittles, and ole Mistis she's kind.
I'se mighty fond of ole Mistis."
                              "Den what you talkin',
You brash fool-nigger?"
                              "I just got a feelin', woman.
Ole Marse Billy, he's goin' away tomorrow,   20
Marse Clay, he's goin' with him to fight de Yankees,
All of 'em goin', yes suh."
                              "And what if dey is?"

"Well, sposin' de Yankees beats?"
                              "Ain't you got *no* sense,
   nigger?
Like to see any ole Yankees lick ole Marse Billy
And young Marse Clay!"
                              "Hi, woman, ain't dat de trufe!"
"Well, den——"   30
                   "But I sees 'em all, jus' goin' and goin',
Goin' to war like Joshua, goin' like David,
And it makes me want to be free. Ain't you never thought
At all about bein' free?"
                              "Sho', co'se I thought of it.
I always reckoned when ole Marse Billy died,
Old Mistis mebbe gwine to set some of us free,
Mebbe she will."
                              "But we-uns gwine to be old den,

76

We won't be young and have the use of our hands,
We won't see our young 'uns growin' up free around us,
We won't have the strength to hoe our own co'n ourselves,
I want to be free, like me, while I got my strength."

"You might be a lot worse off and not be free,
What'd you do if ole man Zachary owned us?"

"Kill him, I reckon."
                    "Hush, black boy, for God's sake hush!"

"I can't help it, woman. Dey ain't so many like him
But what dey is is too pizen-mean to live.   10
Can't you hear dat feelin' I got, woman? I ain't scared
Of talk and de paterollers, and I ain't mean.
I'se mighty fond of ole Mistis and ole Marse Billy,
I'se mighty fond of 'em all at de Big House,
I wouldn't be nobody else's nigger for nothin'.
But I hears 'em goin' away, all goin' away,
With horses and guns and things, all stompin' and wavin',
And I hears de chariot-wheels and de Jordan River,
Rollin' and rollin' and rollin' thu' my sleep,
And I wants to be free. I wants to see my chillun   20
Growin' up free, and all bust out of Egypt!
I wants to be free like an eagle in de air,
Like an eagle in de air."

VII. *The armies gather*

Iron-filings scattered over a dusty
Map of crook-cornered States in yellow and blue.
Little, grouped male and female iron-filings,
Scattered over a patchwork-quilt whose patches
Are the red-earth stuff of Georgia, the pine-bough green of Ver-
      mont.
Here you are clustered as thick as a clump of bees   30
In swarming time. The clumps make cities and towns.
Here you are strewn at random, like single seeds
Lost out of the wind's pocket.
                    But now, but now,

77

The thunderstone has fallen on your map
And all the iron-filings shiver and move
Under the grippings of that blinded force,
The cold pull of the ash-and-cinder star.

The map is vexed with the long battle-worms
Of filings, clustered and moving.
                              If it is
An enemy of the sun who has so stolen
Power from a burnt star to do this work,
Let the bleak essence of the utter cold   10
Beyond the last gleam of the most outpost light
Freeze in his veins forever.
                              But if it is
A fault in the very metal of the heart,
We and our children must acquit that fault
With the old bloody wastage, or give up
Playing the father to it.
                              O vexed and strange,
Salt-bitter, apple-sweet, strong-handed life!
Your million lovers cast themselves like sea   20
Against your mountainy breast, with a clashing noise
And a proud clamor—and like sea recoil,
Sucked down beneath the forefoot of the new
Advancing surf. They feed the battle-worms,
Not only War's, but in the second's pause
Between the assaulting and the broken wave,
The voices of the lovers can be heard,
The sea-gull cry.

VIII. *Jake Diefer leaves his native Pennsylvania*

Jake Diefer, the barrel-chested Pennsylvanian,
Hand like a ham and arms that could wrestle a bull,   30
A roast of a man, all solid meat and good fat,
A slow-thought-chewing Clydesdale horse of a man,
Roused out of his wife's arms. The dawn outside
Was ruddy as his big cheeks. He yawned and stretched
Gigantically, hawking and clearing his throat.
His wife, hair tousled around her like tousled corn,

78

Stared at him with sleep-blind eyes.

"Jake, it ain't come morning,
Already yet?"

He nodded and started to dress.
She burrowed deeper into the bed for a minute
And then threw off the covers.

They didn't say much
Then, or at breakfast. Eating was something serious.
But he looked around the big kitchen once or twice
In a puzzled way, as if trying hard to remember it.   10
She too, when she was busy with the first batch
Of pancakes, burnt one or two, because she was staring
At the "SALT" on the salt-box, for no particular reason.
The boy ate with them and didn't say a word,
Being too sleepy.

Afterwards, when the team
Was hitched up and waiting, with the boy on the seat,
Holding the reins till Jake was ready to take them,
Jake didn't take them at once.

The sun was up now,   20
The spilt-milk-mist of first morning lay on the farm,
Jake looked at it all with those same mildly-puzzled eyes,
The red barn, the fat rich fields just done with the winter,
Just beginning the work of another year.
The boy would have to do the rest of the planting.

He blew on his hands and stared at his wife dumbly.
He cleared his throat.

"Well, good-by, Minnie," he said,
"Don't you hire any feller for harvest without you write me,
And if any more of those lightning-rodders come around,   30
We don't want no more dum lightning-rods."

He tried
To think if there was anything else, but there wasn't.
She suddenly threw her big, red arms around his neck,
He kissed her with clumsy force.

Then he got on the wagon
And clucked to the horses as she started to cry.

IX. *The mountain men*

Up in the mountains where the hogs are thin
And razorbacked, wild Indians of hogs,
The laurel's green in April—and if the nights
Are cold as the cold cloud of watersmoke
Above a mountain-spring, the midday sun
Has heat enough in it to make you sweat.

They are a curious and most native stock,
The lanky men, the lost, forgotten seeds
Spilled from the first great wave-march toward the West
And set to sprout by chance in the deep cracks   10
Of that hill-billy world of laurel-hells.
They keep the beechwood-fiddle and the salt
Old-fashioned ballad-English of our first
Rowdy, corn-liquor-drinking, ignorant youth;
Also the rifle and the frying-pan,
The old feud-temper and the old feud-way
Of thinking strangers better shot on sight
But treating strangers that one leaves unshot
With border-hospitality.
              The girls   20
Have the brief-blooming, rhododendron-youth
Of pioneer women, and the black-toothed age.
And if you yearn to meet your pioneers,
You'll find them there, the same men, inbred sons
Of inbred sires perhaps, but still the same;
A pioneer-island in a world that has
No use for pioneers—the unsplit rock
Of Fundamentalism, calomel,
Clan-virtues, clannish vices, fiddle-tunes
And a hard God.   30
              They are our last frontier.
They shot the railway-train when it first came,
And when the Fords first came, they shot the Fords.
It could not save them. They are dying now
Or being educated, which is the same.
One need not weep romantic tears for them,
But when the last moonshiner buys his radio,
And the last, lost, wild-rabbit of a girl
Is civilized with a mail-order dress,

Something will pass that was American
And all the movies will not bring it back.

They are misfit and strange in our new day,
In Sixty-One they were not quite so strange,
Before the Fords, before the day of the Fords . . .

Luke Breckinridge, his rifle on his shoulder,
Slipped through green forest alleys toward the town,
A gawky boy with smoldering eyes, whose feet
Whispered the crooked paths like moccasins.
He wasn't looking for trouble, going down,   10
But he was on guard, as always. When he stopped
To scoop some water in the palm of his hand
From a sweet trickle between moss-grown rocks,
You might have thought him careless for a minute,
But when the snapped stick cracked six feet behind him
He was all sudden rifle and hard eyes.
The pause endured a long death-quiet instant,
Then he knew who it was.
                          "Hi, Jim," he said,
Lowering his rifle. The green laurel-screen   20
Hardly had moved, but Jim was there beside him.
The cousins looked at each other. Their rifles seemed
To look as well, with much the same taut silentness.

"Goin' to town, Luke?"
                        "Uh-huh, goin' to town,
You goin'?"
            "Looks as if I was goin'."
                                        "Looks
As if you was after squirrels."
                                "I might be.
You goin' after squirrels?" "I might be, too."   30
"Not so many squirrels near town."
                                    "No, reckon there's not."

Jim hesitated. His gaunt hands caressed
The smooth guard of his rifle. His eyes were sharp.
"Might go along a piece together," he said.
Luke didn't move. Their eyes clashed for a moment,
Then Luke spoke, casually.
                            "I hear the Kelceys

81

Air goin' to fight in this here war," he said.
Jim nodded slowly, "Yuh, I heerd that too."
He watched Luke's trigger-hand.
                                "I might be goin'
Myself sometime," he said reflectively
Sliding his own hand down. Luke saw the movement.
"We-uns don't like the Kelceys much," he said
With his eyes down to pinpoints.
                                Then Jim smiled.
"We-uns neither," he said.   10
                                His hand slid back.

They went along together after that
But neither of them spoke for half-a-mile,
Then finally, Jim said, half-diffidently,
"You know who we air goin' to fight outside?
I heard it was the British. Air that so?"
"Hell, no," said Luke, with scorn. He puckered his brows.
"Dunno's I rightly know just who they air."
He admitted finally, "But 'tain't the British.
It's some trash-lot of furriners, that's shore.   20
They call 'em Yankees near as I kin make it,
But they ain't Injuns neither."
                                "Well," said Jim
Soothingly, "Reckon it don't rightly matter
Long as the Kelceys take the other side."

X. *On to Richmond*

It was noon when the company marched to the railroad-station.
The town was ready for them. The streets were packed.
There were flags and streamers and pictures of Lincoln and
    Hamlin.
The bad little boys climbed up on the trees and yelled,   30
The good little boys had clean paper-collars on,
And swung big-eyed on white-painted wicket-gates,
Wanting to yell, and feeling like Fourth of July.
Somebody fastened a tin can full of firecrackers
To a yellow dog's tail and sent him howling and racketing
The length of the street.
                                "There goes Jeff Davis!" said somebody,

82

And everybody laughed, and the little boys
Punched each other and squealed between fits of laughing
"There goes Jeff Davis—lookit ole yellow Jeff Davis!"
And then the laugh died and rose again in a strange
Half-shrill, half-strangled unexpected shout
As they heard the Hillsboro' Silver Cornet Band
Swinging "John Brown's Body" ahead of the soldiers.
I have heard that soul of crowd go out in the queer
Groan between laughter and tears that baffles the wise.
I have heard that whanging band.   10

"We'll hang Jeff Davis on a sour-apple tree."
Double-roll on the snare-drums, double squeal of the fife,
"We'll hang Jeff Davis on a sour-apple tree!"
Clash of the cymbals zinging, throaty blare of cornets,
"We'll hang Jeff Davis on a sour-apple tree!"
"On to Richmond! On to Richmond! On to Richmond!"
"Yeah! There they come! *Yeah! Yeah!"*
And they came, the bearskin drum-major leading the band,
Twirling his silver-balled baton with turkey-cock pomp,
The cornet-blowers, the ranks. The drum-major was fine,   20
But the little boys thought the captain was even finer,
He looked just like a captain out of a book
With his sword and his shoulder-straps and his discipline-face.
He wasn't just Henry Fairfield, he was a captain,
—Henry Fairfield worried about his sword,
Hoping to God that he wouldn't drop his sword,
And wondering hotly whether his discipline-face
Really looked disciplined or only peevish—
"Yeah! There they come! There's Jack! There's Charlie! Yeah!
    Yeah!"
The color-guard with the stiff, new flapping flag,   30
And the ranks and the ranks and the ranks, the amateur
Blue, wavering ranks, in their ill-fitting tight coats,
Shoulders galled already by their new guns,
—They were three-months' men, they had drilled in civilian
    clothes
Till a week ago—"There's Charlie! There's Hank, yeah, yeah!"
"On to Richmond, boys! Three cheers for Abe Lincoln!
Three cheers for the boys! Three groans for old Jeff Davis
And the dirty Rebs!"   40
"We'll hang Jeff Davis on a sour-apple tree!"

83

Jack Ellyat, marching, saw between blue shoulders
A blur of faces. They all were faces he knew,
Old Mrs. Cobb with her wart and her Paisley shawl,
Little·George Freeman, the slim Tucker girls,
All of them cheering and shouting—and all of them strange
Suddenly, different, faces he'd never seen.
Faces somehow turned into one crowd-face.
His legs went marching along all right but they felt
Like somebody else's legs, his mind was sucked dry.
It was real, they were going away, the town was cheering them. 10
Henry Fairfield was marching ahead with his sword.
Just as he'd thought about it a thousand times,
These months—but it wasn't the way that he'd thought about it.
"On to Richmond! On to Richmond! On to Richmond!"
There were Mother and Father and Jane and the house.
Jane was waving a flag. He laughed and called to them.
But his voice was stiff in his throat, not like his real voice.
This, everything, it was too quick, too crowded, not Phaëton
Charging his snarling horses at a black sea,
But a numb, hurried minute with legs that marched   20
Mechanically, feeling nothing at all.
The white crowd-face—the sweat on the red seamed neck
Of the man ahead—"On to Richmond!"—blue shoulders bobbing—
Flags—cheering—somebody kissed him—Ellen Baker—
She was crying—wet mouth of tears—didn't want her to kiss him—
Why did she want to—the station—*halt*—Mother and Jane.
The engineer wore a flag in his coat-lapel.
The engine had "On to Richmond!" chalked all over it.
Nothing to say now—Mother looks tired to death—
I wish I weren't going—no, I'm glad that I am—   30
The damn band's playing "John Brown's Body" again,
I wish they'd stop it!—I wish to God we could start—
There—*close up, men!*—oh my God, they've let Ned out!
I told them for God's sake to lock him up in the cellar,
But they've let him out—maybe he got out by himself—
He's got too much sense—"No, down, Ned! Down, good dog!
Down, I tell you!—"
                    *"Good-by, boys! Good-by! We'll hang Jeff
                    Davis!"*

The engine squealed, the packed train started to move.   40

84

Ned wanted to come, but they wouldn't let him come.
They had to kick him away, he couldn't see why.

XI. *A Virginia column*

In another column, footsore Curly Hatton
Groaned at the thought of marching any more.
His legs weren't built for marching and they knew it,
Butterball-legs under a butterball-body.
The plump good-tempered face with its round eyes
Blue and astonished as a china-doll's,
Stared at the road ahead and hated it
Because there was so much of it ahead   10
And all of it so dry.
                        He didn't mind
The rest so much. He didn't even mind
Being the one sure necessary joke
Of the whole regiment. He'd always been
A necessary joke—fat people were.
Fat babies always were supposed to laugh.
Fat little boys had fingers poked at them.
And, even with the road, and being fat,
You had a good time in this funny war,   20
Considering everything, and one thing most.

His mind slipped back two months. He saw himself
In the cool room at Weatherby's Retreat
Where all the girls were sewing the new star
In the new flag for the first volunteers.
He hadn't thought of fighting much before,
He was too easy-going. If Virginia
Wanted secession, that was her affair.
It seemed too bad to break the Union up
After some seventy years of housekeeping.   30
But he could understand the way you'd feel
If you were thin and angry at the Yanks.
He knew a lot of Yankees that he liked,
But then he liked most people, on the whole
Although most girls and women made him shy.
He loved the look of them and the way they walked,

He loved their voices and their little sweet mouths,
But something always seemed to hold him back,
When he was near them.
                        He was too fat, too friendly,
Too comfortable for dreams, too easy-shy.
The porcelain dolls stood on the mantelpiece,
Waiting such slim and arrant cavaliers
As porcelain dolls must have to make them proud,
They had no mercy for fat Cupidons,
Not even Lucy, all the years before,   10
And Lucy was the porcelain belle of the world!
And so when she said.
                        And he couldn't believe
At first.
        But she was silver and fire and steel
That day of the new stars and the new flag,
Fire and bright steel for the invading horde
And silver for the men who drove them off,
And so she sewed him in her flag and heart:
Though even now, he couldn't believe she **had**   20
In spite of all the letters and the socks
And kissing him before he went away.
But it was so—the necessary joke
Made into a man at last, a man in love
And loved by the most porcelain belle of the world.
And he was ready to march to the world's end
And fight ten million Yanks to keep it so.

"Oh God, after we're married—the cool night
Over the garden—and Lucy sitting there
In her blue dress while the big stars come out."   30
His face was funny with love and footsore pride,
The man beside him saw it, gave a laugh,
"Curly's thinking it's time for a julep, boys!
Hot work for fat men, Curly!"

XII. Before Bull Run

The crows fly over the Henry House, through the red sky of
    evening, cawing,
Judith Henry, bedridden, watches them through the clouded
    glass of old sight.

(July is hot in Virginia—a parched, sun-leathered farmer sawing
Dry sticks with a cicada-saw that creaks all the lukewarm night.)

But Judith Henry's hands are cool in spite of all midsummer's
    burning,
Cool, muted and frail with age like the smoothness of old yellow
    linen, the cool touch of old, dulled rings.
Her years go past her in bed like falling waters and the waters
    of a millwheel turning,
And she is not ill content to lie there, dozing and calm, remem-
    bering youth, to the gushing of those watersprings.   10

She has known Time like the cock of red dawn and Time like a
    tired clock slowing;
She has seen so many faces and bodies, young and then old, so
    much life, so many patterns of death and birth.
She knows that she must leave them soon. She is not afraid to
    flow with that river's flowing.
But the wrinkled earth still hangs at her sufficed breast like a
    weary child, she is unwilling to go while she still has milk for
    the earth.

She will go in her sleep, most likely, she has the sunk death-sleep 20
    of the old already,

(War-bugles by the Potomac, you cannot reach her ears with
    your brass lyric, piercing the crowded dark.)

It does not matter, the farm will go on, the farm and the children
    bury her in her best dress, the plow cut its furrow, steady,

(War-horses of the Shenandoah, why should you hurry so fast
    to tramp the last ashy fire from so feeble and retired a spark?)

There is nothing here but a creek and a house called the Henry
    House, a farm and a bedridden woman and people with coun-
    try faces.
                                                     30
There is nothing for you here. And La Haye Sainte was a quiet
    farm and the mile by it a quiet mile.
And Lexington was a place to work in like any one of a dozen
    dull, little places.
And they raised good crops at Blenheim till the soldiers came
    and spoiled the crops for a while.

The red evening fades into twilight, the crows have gone to
     their trees, the slow, hot stars are emerging.
It is cooler now on the hill—and in the camps it is cooler, where
     the untried soldiers find their bivouac hard.
Where, from North and South, the blind wrestlers of armies
     converge on the forgotten house like the double pincers of an
     iron claw converging.
And Johnston hurries his tired brigades from the Valley, to
     bring them up in time before McDowell can fall on Beauregard.

The congressmen came out to see Bull Run,   10
The congressmen who like free shows and spectacles.
They brought their wives and carriages along,
They brought their speeches and their picnic-lunch,
Their black constituent-hats and their devotion:
Some even brought a little whiskey, too,
(A little whiskey is a comforting thing
For congressmen in the sun, in the heat of the sun.)
The bearded congressmen with orator's mouths,
The fine, clean-shaved, Websterian congressmen,
Come out to see the gladiator's show   20
Like Iliad gods, wrapped in the sacred cloud
Of Florida-water, wisdom and bay-rum,
Of free cigars, democracy and votes,
That lends such portliness to congressmen.
(The gates fly wide, the bronze troop marches out
Into the stripped and deadly circus-ring,
"*Ave, Caesar!*" the cry goes up, and shakes
The purple awning over Caesar's seat.)
"*Ave, Caesar! Ave,* O congressmen,
We who are about to die,   30
Salute you, congressmen!"
Eleven States,
New York, Rhode Island, Maine,
Connecticut, Michigan and the gathered West,
Salute you, congressmen!
The red-fezzed Fire-Zouaves, flamingo-bright,
Salute you, congressmen!
The raw boys still in their civilian clothes,
Salute you, congressmen!
The second Wisconsin in its homespun grey,
Salutes you, congressmen!

The Garibaldi Guards in cocksfeather hats,
Salute you, congressmen!
The Second Ohio with their Bedouin-caps,
Salutes you, congressmen!
Sherman's brigade, grey-headed Heintzelman,
Ricketts' and Griffin's doomed and valiant guns,
The tough, hard-bitten regulars of Sykes
Who covered the retreat with the Marines,
Burnside and Porter, Willcox and McDowell,
All the vast, unprepared, militia-mass   10
Of boys in red and yellow Zouave pants,
Who carried peach-preserves inside their kits
And dreamt of being generals overnight;
The straggling companies where every man
Was a sovereign and a voter—the slack regiments
Where every company marched a different step;
The clumsy and unwieldy-new brigades
Not yet distempered into battle-worms;
The whole, huge, innocent army, ready to fight
But only half-taught in the tricks of fighting,
Ready to die like picture-postcard boys   20
While fighting still had banners and a sword
And just as ready to run in blind mob-panic,
Salutes you with a vast and thunderous cry,
Ave, Caesar, ave, O congressmen,
Ave, O Iliad gods who forced the fight!
You bring your carriages and your picnic-lunch
To cheer us in our need.
                              You come with speeches,
Your togas smell of heroism and bay-rum.   30
You are the people and the voice of the people
And, when the fight is done, your carriages
Will bear you safely, through the streaming rout
Of broken troops, throwing their guns away.
You come to see the gladiator's show,
But from a high place, as befits the wise:
You will not see the long windrows of men
Strewn like dead pears before the Henry House
Or the stone-wall of Jackson breathe its parched
Devouring breath upon the failing charge,   40
Ave, Caesar, ave, O congressmen,
Cigar-smoke wraps you in a godlike cloud,

And if you are not to depart from us
As easily and divinely as you came,
It hardly matters.
                              Fighting Joe Hooker once
Said with that tart, unbridled tongue of his
That made so many needless enemies,
"Who ever saw a dead cavalryman?"
                              The phrase
Stings with a needle sharpness, just or not,
But even he was never heard to say,   10
"Who ever saw a dead congressman?"
And yet, he was a man with a sharp tongue.

XIII.   *The first day*

The day broke, hot and calm. In the little farm-houses
That are scattered here and there in that rolling country
Of oak and rail-fence, crooked creeks and second-growth pine,
The early-risers stand looking out of the door
At the long dawn-shadows for a minute or two
—Shadows are always cool—but the blue-glass sky
Is fusing with heat even now, heat that prickles the hairs
On the back of your hand.   20
                              They sigh and turn back to the house.
"Looks like a scorcher today, boys!"
                              They think already
Of the cool jug of vinegar-water down by the hedge.

Judith Henry wakened with the first light,
She had the short sleep of age, and the long patience.
She waited for breakfast in vague, half-drowsy wonderment
At various things. Yesterday some men had gone by
And stopped for a drink of water. She'd heard they were soldiers.
She couldn't be sure. It had seemed to worry the folks   30
But it took more than soldiers and such to worry her now.
Young people always worried a lot too much.
No soldiers that had any sense would fight around here.
She'd had a good night. Today would be a good day.

A mile and a half away, before the Stone Bridge,
A Union gun opened fire.

Six miles away, McDowell had planned his battle
And planned it well, as far as such things can be planned—
A feint at one point, a flanking march at another
To circle Beauregard's left and crumple it up.
There were Johnston's eight thousand men to be reckoned with
But Patterson should be holding them, miles away,
And even if they slipped loose from Patterson's fingers
The thing might still be done.
                              If you take a flat map
And move wooden blocks upon it strategically,   10
The thing looks well, the blocks behave as they should.
The science of war is moving live men like blocks.
And getting the blocks into place at a fixed moment.
But it takes time to mold your men into blocks
And flat maps turn into country where creeks and gullies
Hamper your wooden squares. They stick in the brush,
They are tired and rest, they straggle after ripe blackberries,
And you cannot lift them up in your hand and move them.
—A string of blocks curling smoothly around the left
Of another string of blocks and crunching it up—   20
It is all so clear in the maps, so clear in the mind,
But the orders are slow, the men in the blocks are slow
To move, when they start they take too long on the way—
The General loses his stars and the block-men die
In unstrategic defiance of martial law
Because still used to just being men, not block-parts.
McDowell was neither a fool nor a fighting fool;
He knew his dice, he knew both armies unready,
But congressmen and nation wanted a battle
And he felt their hands on his shoulders, forcing his play.   30
He knew well enough when he played that he played for his head
As Beauregard and Johnston were playing for theirs,
So he played with the skill he had—and does not lie
Under a cupolaed gloom on Riverside Drive.
Put Grant in his place that day and with those same dice,
Grant might have done little better.
                                    Wherefore, now,
Irvin McDowell, half-forgotten general,
Who tried the game and found no luck in the game
And never got the chance to try it again   40
But did not backbite the gamblers who found more luck in it
Then or later in double-edged reminiscences;

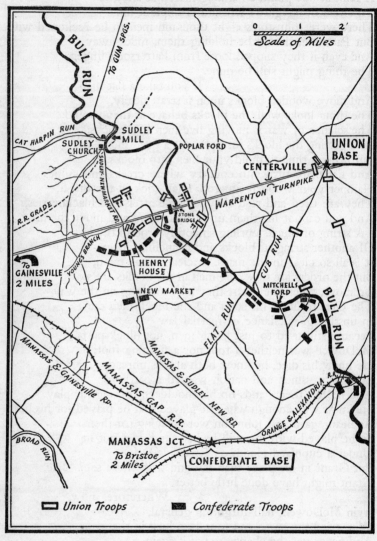

The First Battle of Bull Run (*Manassas*)

If any laurel can grow in the sad-colored fields
Between Bull Run and Cub Run and Cat Hairpin Bend
You should have a share of it for your hardworking ghost
Because you played as you could with your cold, forced dice
And neither wasted your men like the fighting fools
Nor posed as an injured Napoleon twenty years later.
Meanwhile, McDowell watched his long flanking column
File by, on the Warrentown pike, in the first dawn-freshness.
"Gentlemen, that's a big force," he said to his staff.

    A full rifled battery begins to talk spitefully to Evans' Caro- 10
linians. The grey skirmish-line, thrown forward on the other
side of Bull Run, ducks its head involuntarily as a locomotive
noise goes by in the air above it, and waits for a flicker of blue
in the scrub-oaks ahead.

XIV. *Vignettes of battle*

Beauregard, eager *sabreur*, whose heart was a French
Print of a sabretasche-War with "La Gloire" written under it,
Lovable, fiery. bizarre, picturesque as his name,
Galloped toward Mitchell's Ford with bald, quiet Joe Johnston,
The little precise Scotch-dominie of a general,
Stubborn as flint, in advance not always so lucky,   20
In retreat more dangerous than a running wolf—
Slant shadow, sniffing the traps and the poisoned meat,
And going on to pause and slash at the first
Unwary dogs before the hunters came up.
Grant said of him once,
"I was always anxious with Joe Johnston in front of me,
I was never half so anxious in front of Lee."
He kissed his friends in the Nelson-way we've forgotten,
He could make men cheer him after six-weeks retreating.
Another man said of him, after the war was done,   30
Still with that puzzled comparison we find
When Lee, the reticent sword, comes into the question,
"Yes, Lee was a great general, a good man;
But I never wanted to put my arms round his neck
As I used to want to with Johnston."
                        The two sayings

Make a good epitaph for so Scotch a ghost,
Or would if they were all.
                                    They are not quite all,
He had to write his reminiscences, too,
And tell what he would have done if it had not been
For Davis and chance and a dozen turns of the wheel.
That was the thistle in him—the other strain—
But he was older then.
                                    I'd like to have seen him
That day as he galloped along beside Beauregard,   10
Sabreur and dominie planning the battle-lines.
They'd ordered Jackson up to the threatened left
But Beauregard was sure that the main assault
Would come on the right. He'd planned it so—a good plan—
But once the blocks start moving, they keep on moving.

The hands of the scuffed brown clock in the kitchen of the
    Henry House point to nine-forty-five.
Judith Henry does not hear the clock, she hears in the sky a
    vast dim roar like piles of heavy lumber crashingly falling.
They are carrying her in her bed to a ravine below the Sudley   20
    Road, maybe she will be safe there, maybe the battle will go
    by and leave her alive.
The crows have been scared from their nests by the strange
    crashing, they circle in the sky like a flight of blackened leaves,
    wheeling and calling.

Back at Centerville, there are three-months' men,
A Pennsylvania regiment, a New York Battery.
They hear the spent wave of the roar of the opening guns,
But they are three-months' men, their time is up today.
They would have fought yesterday or a week ago,   30
But then they were still enlisted—today they are not—
Their time is up, and there can't be much use or sense
In fighting longer than you've promised to fight.
They pack up their things and decide they'd better go home,
And quietly march away from that gathering roar.

Luke Breckinridge, crouched by the Warrentown pike,
Saw stuffed dolls in blue coats and baggy trousers
Go down like squirrels under the rifle-cracks.
His eyes glowed as a bullet ripped his sleeve
And he felt well. Armies weren't such a much,
Too damn many orders, too damn much saluting,
Too many damn officers you weren't allowed
To shoot when they talked mean to you because
They were your officers, which didn't make sense.
But this was something he could understand,   10
Except for those dirty stinkers of big guns,
It wasn't right to shoot you with big guns
But it was a good scrap except for that—
Carried a little high, then . . . change it . . . good . . .
Though men were hard to miss when you were used
To squirrels. His eyes were narrow. He hardly heard
The officer's voice. The woods in front of him
Were full of Kelceys he was going to kill,
Blue-coated Kelcey dolls in baggy trousers.
It was a beautiful and sufficing sight.   20

    The first blue wave of Burnside is beaten back from the pike to
stumble a little way and rally against Porter's fresh brigade.
    Bee and Bartow move down from the Henry House plateau—
grey and butternut lines trampling the bullet-cut oak-leaves,
splashing across Young's Branch.
    Tall, black-bearded Bee rides by on his strong horse, his long
black hair fluttering.
    Imboden's red-shirted gunners unlimber by the Henry House
to answer the Parrotts and howitzers of Ricketts and Griffin.
The air is a sheet of iron, continually and dully shaken.   30

Shippy, the little man with the sharp rat-eyes,
Saw someone run in front of them waving a sword;
Then they were going along toward a whining sound
That ran like cold spring-water along his spine.
(God, he was in for it now!) His sharp rat-eyes
Flickered around and about him hopelessly.

95

If a fellow could only drop out, if a fellow could only
Pretend he was hurt a little and then drop out
Behind a big, safe oak-tree—no use—no use—
He was in for it, now. He couldn't get away.
*"Come on, boys—come on, men—clean them out with the
bayonet!"*
He saw a rail-fence ahead, a quiet rail-fence,
But men were back of it—grey lumps—a million bees
Stinging the air—
He couldn't shoot, even—he was too scared to shoot—   10
His legs took him on—he couldn't stop his legs.

Curly Hatton, toiling along the slow
Crest of the Henry Hill, over slippery ground,
Glanced at the still-blue sky that lay so deep
Above the little pines, so pooled, so calm.
He thought, with the slow drowsiness of fatigue,
Of Lucy feeding the white, greedy swans
On the blue pool by Weatherby's Retreat.
They stretched their necks, and clattered with their wings.
There was a fragrance sleeping in her hair.   20
"Close up, folks—don't straggle—we're going into action!"
His butterball-legs moved faster—Lucy—Lucy—

Bee and Bartow's brigades are broken in their turn—it is fight
and run away—fight and run away, all day—the day will go to
whichever of the untried wrestlers can bear the pain of the grips
an instant longer than the other.

Beauregard and Johnston hurry toward the firing—McDowell
has already gone—

The chessplayers have gone back to little pieces on the shaken
board—little pieces that cannot see the board as a whole.   30

The block-plan is lost—there is no plan any more—only the
bloodstained, fighting blocks, the bloodstained and blackened
men.

Jack Ellyat heard the guns with a knock at his heart
When he first heard them. They were going to be in it, soon.
He wondered how it would feel. They would win, of course,

But how would it feel? He'd never killed anything much.
Ducks and rabbits, but ducks and rabbits weren't men.
He'd never even seen a man killed, a man die,
Except Uncle Amos, and Uncle Amos was old.
He saw a red sop spreading across the close
Feathers of a duck's breast—it had been all right,
But now it made him feel sick for a while, somehow.
Then they were down on the ground, and they were firing,
And that was all right—just fire as you fired at drill.
Was anyone firing at them? He couldn't tell.   10
There was a stone bridge. Were there rebels beyond the bridge?
The shot he was firing now might go and kill rebels
But it didn't feel like it.
                         A man down the line
Fell and rolled flat, with a minor coughing sound
And then was quiet. Ellyat felt the cough
In the pit of his stomach a minute.
But, after that, it was just like a man falling down.
It was all so calm except for their guns and the distant
Shake in the air of cannon. No more men were hit,   20
And, after a while, they all got up and marched on.
If Rebels had been by the bridge, the rebels were gone,
And they were going on somewhere, you couldn't say where,
Just marching along the way that they always did.
The only funny thing was, leaving the man
Who had made that cough, back there in the trampled grass
With the red stain sopping through the blue of his coat
Like the stain on a duck's breast. He hardly knew the man
But it felt funny to leave him just lying there.

   The wreckage of Bee, Bartow and Evans' commands streams 30
back into a shallow ravine below a little wood—broken blocks
hammered into splinters by war—two thousand confused men
reeling past their staggering flags and the hoarse curses and
rallying cries of their officers, like sheep in a narrow run.
   Bee tries to halt them furiously—he stands up in his stirrups,
tree-tall, while the blue flood of the North trickles over the
stream and pours on and on.
   He waves his sword—the toyish glitter sparkles—he points to
a grey dyke at the top of the ravine—a grey dyke of musket-
holding Virginians, silent and ready.   40

"Look, men, there's Jackson's brigade! It stands there like a stone wall. Rally behind the Virginians!"

They rally behind them—Johnston and Beauregard are there —the Scotch dominie plucks a flag and carries it forward to rally the Fourth Alabama—the French hussar-sword rallies them with bursting rockets of oratory—his horse is shot under him, but he mounts again.

And the grey stone wall holds like a stiff dyke while the tired men get their breath behind it—and the odd, lemon-sucking, ex-professor of tactics who saw John Brown hung in his carpet-slippers and prayed a Presbyterian prayer for his damned soul, has a new name that will last as long as the face they cut for him on Stone Mountain, and has the same clang of rock against the chisel-blade.

Judith Henry, Judith Henry, they have moved you back at
      last, in doubt and confusion, to the little house where
      you know every knothole by heart.
It is not safe, but now there is no place safe, you are between the
      artillery and the artillery, and the incessant noise comes
      to your dim ears like the sea-roar within a shell where
      you are lying.
The walls of the house are riddled, the brown clock in the kitchen
      gouged by a bullet, a jar leaks red preserves on the cup-
      board shelf where the shell-splinter came and tore the
      cupboard apart.
The casual guns do not look for you, Judith Henry, they find
      you in passing merely and touch you only a little, but the
      touch is enough to give your helpless body five sudden
      wounds and leave you helplessly dying.

Wingate gentled Black Whistle's pawing
With hand and wisdom and horseman's play
And listened anew to the bulldogs gnawing
Their bone of iron, a mile away.
There was a wood that a bonfire crowned
With thick dark smoke without flame for neighbor,
And the dull, monotonous, heavy sound

Of a hill or a woman in too-long labor,
But that was all for the Black Horse Troop
And had been all since the day's beginning,
That stray boy beating his metal hoop
And the tight-lipped wonder if they were winning.
Wainscott Bristol, behind his eyes,
Was getting in bed with a sweet-toothed wench,
Huger Shepley felt for his dice
And Stuart Cazenove swore in French
"*Mille diables* and Yankee blood!   10
How long are we going to stick in the mud?"
While a Cotter hummed with a mocking sigh,
" 'If you want a good time, jine the cavalry!' "
"Stuart's in it, Wade Hampton's in it."
"The Yanks'll quit in another minute!"
"General Beau's just lost us!"
                                 "Steady!"
"And he won't find us until he's ready!"
"It must be two—we've been here since six."
"It's Virginia up to her old-time tricks!   20
They never did trust a Georgia man,
But Georgia'll fight while Virginia can!"

An aide rode up on a sweating mare
And they glowered at him with hostile stare.
He had been in it and they had not.
He had smelt the powder and heard the shot,
And they hated his soul and his martial noise
With the envious hate of little boys.
Then "Yaaih! Yaaih!"
                       —and Wingate felt   30
The whole troop lift like a lifted dart
And loosened the sabre at his belt,
And felt his chest too small for his heart.

Curly Hatton was nothing any more
But a dry throat and a pair of burnt black hands
That held a hot gun he was always firing
Though he no longer remembered why he fired.
They ran up a cluttered hill and took hacked ground

99

And held it for a while and fired for a while,
And then the blue men came and they ran away,
To go back, after a while, when the blue men ran.
There was a riddled house and a crow in a tree,
There was uneven ground. It was hard to run.
The gun was heavy and hot. There once had been
A person named Lucy and a flag and a star
And a cane chair beside wistarias
Where a nigger brought you a drink. These had ceased to exist.
There was only very hot sun and being thirsty.   10
Yells—crashings—screams from black lips—a dead, tattered crow
In a tattered tree. There had once been a person named Lucy
Who had had an importance. There was none of her now.

Up the hill again. Damn tired of running up hill.
And then he found he couldn't run any more,
He had to fall down and be sick. Even that was hard,
Because somebody near kept making a squealing noise—
The dolefully nasty noise of a badly-hurt dog.
It got on his nerves and he tried to say something to it,
But it was he who made it, so he couldn't stop it.   20

Jack Ellyat, going toward the battle again,
Saw the other side of the hill where Curly was lying,
Saw, for a little while, the two battered houses,
The stuffed dead stretched in numb, disorderly postures,
And heard for a while again that whining sound
That made you want to duck, and feel queer if you did.

To him it was noise and smoke and the powder-taste
And, once and again, through the smoke, for a moment seen,
Small, monstrous pictures, gone through the brain like light,
And yet forever bitten into the brain;   30
A marsh, a monstrous arras of live and dead
Still shaking under the thrust of the weaver's hand,
The crowd of a deadly fair.
                            Then, orders again.
And they were going away from the smoke once more.

The books say "Keyes' brigade made a late and weak
Demonstration in front of the Robinson house

And then withdrew to the left, by flank, down Young's Branch,
Taking no further part in the day."

To Jack Ellyat

It was a deadly fair in a burning field
Where strange crowds rushed to and fro and strange drunkards
　lay
Sprawled in a stupor deeper than wine or sleep,
A whining noise you shrank from and wanted to duck at,
And one dead cough left behind them in the tall grass
With the slow blood sopping its clothes like the blood on a shot 10
　duck's breast.

　Imboden is wounded, Jackson is shot through the hand, the
guns of Ricketts and Griffin, on the Henry House plateau, are
taken and retaken; the gunners shot down at their guns while
they hold their fire, thinking the advancing Thirty-Third Virginia is one of their own regiments, in the dimness of the battle-
cloud.
　It is nearly three o'clock—the South gathers for a final charge
—on the left, Elzey's brigade, new-come from the Shenandoah,
defiles through the oaks near the Sudley Road to reinforce the 20
grey wrestler—the blue wrestler staggers and goes back, on
unsteady heels.
　The charge sweeps the plateau—Bartow is killed, black-haired
Bee mortally wounded, but the charge goes on.
　For a moment, the Union line is a solid crescent again—a
crescent with porcupine-pricks of steel—and then a crescent of
sand—and then spilt sand, streaming away.
　There is no panic at first. There is merely a moment when
men have borne enough and begin to go home. The panic comes
later, when they start to jostle each other.　　　　　　　30
　Jefferson Davis, riding from Manassas, reaches the back-wash
of the battle. A calm grey-bearded stranger tells him calmly
that the battle is lost and the South defeated. But he keeps on,
his weak eyes stung with the dust, a picture, perhaps, of a Plutarch
death on a shield in his schooled mind—and is in time to see the
last blue troops disappear beyond Bull Run, and hear the last
sour grumble of their guns.

Judith Henry, Judith Henry, your body has born its ghost at
　last, there are no more pictures of peace or terror left in the

broken machine of the brain that was such a cunning pic-
    ture-maker:

Terrified ghost, so rudely dishoused by such casual violence, be
    at rest; there are others dishoused in this falling night, the
    falling night is a sack of darkness, indifferent as Saturn to
    wars or generals, indifferent to shame or victory.

War is a while but peace is a while and soon enough the earth-
    colored hands of the earth-workers will scoop the last buried
    shells and the last clotted bullet-slag from the racked em-
    bittered acre,   10

And the rustling visitors drive out fair Sundays to look at the
    monument near the rebuilt house, buy picture postcards and
    wonder dimly what you were like when you lived and what
    you thought when you knew you were going to die.

Wingate felt a frog in his throat
As he patted Black Whistle's reeking coat
And reined him in for a minute's breath.
He was hot as the devil and tired to death,
And both were glad for the sun in the West
And a panting second of utter rest,   20
While Wingate's mind went patching together
Like a cobbler piecing out scraps of leather
The broken glimmers of what they'd done
Since the sun in the West was a rising sun,
The long, bored hours of shiftless waiting
And that single instant of pure, fierce hating
When the charge came down like a cataract
On a long blue beach of broken sand
And Thought was nothing but all was Act
And the sabre seemed to master the hand.   30
Wainscott Bristol, a raging terrier
Killing the Yankee that shot Phil Ferrier
With a cut that spattered the bloody brains
Over his saddle and bridle-reins,
One Cotter cursing, the other praying,
And both of them slashing like scythes of slaying,
Stuart Cazenove singing "Lord Randall"
And Howard Brooke as white as a candle,
While Father fought like a fiend in satin,
And killed as he quoted tag-ends of Latin,   40

The prisoners with their sick, dazed wonder
And the mouths of children caught in a blunder
And over it all, the guns, the thunder,
The pace, the being willing to die,
The stinging color of victory.

He remembered it all like a harsh, tense dream.
It had a color. It had a gleam.
But he had outridden and lost the rest
And he was alone with the bloody West
And a trampled road, and a black hill-crest.   10

The road and the bushes all about
Were cluttered with relics of Yankee rout,
Haversacks spilling their shirts and socks,
A burst canteen and a cartridge-box.
Rifles and cups trampled underfoot,
A woman's locket, a slashed black boot
Stained and oozing along the slash
And a ripe pear crushed to a yellow mash.
Who had carried the locket and munched the pear,
And why was a dead cat lying there,   20
Stark and grinning, a furry sack,
With a red flannel tongue and a broken back?
You didn't fight wars with a tabby-cat. . . .
He found he was telling the Yankees that,
They couldn't hear him of course, but still . . .
He shut his eyes for a minute until
He felt less dizzy. There, that was better,
And the evening wind was chilly and keen—
—He'd have to write Mother some sort of letter—
—He'd promised Amanda a Yank canteen,   30
But he didn't feel like getting it here,
Where that dead cat snickered from ear to ear—

Back in the pinewoods, clear and far,
A bugle sang like a falling star.
He shivered, turned Black Whistle around
And galloped hastily toward the sound.

Curly Hatton opened his eyes again.

A minute ago he had been marching, marching,
Forever up and down enormous hills
While his throat scratched with thirst and something howled—
But then there was a clear minute—and he was lying
In a long, crowded, strangely-churchly gloom
Where lanterns bobbed like marshlights in a swamp
And there was a perpetual rustling noise
Of dry leaves stirred by a complaining wind.
No, they were only voices of wounded men.
"Water. Water. Water. Water. Water."   10
He heard the rain on the roof and sucked his lips.
"Water. Water. Water. Water. Water."

(Oh, heavy sluices of dark, sweet, Summer rain,
Pour down on me and wash me free again,
Cleanse me of battles, make my flesh smell sweet,
I am so sick of thirst, so tired of pain,
So stale with wounds and the heat!)

Somebody went by, a doctor with red sleeves;
He stared at the red sleeves and tried to speak
But when he spoke, he whispered. This was a church.   20
He could see a dim altar now and a shadow-pulpit.
He was wounded. They had put the wounded men in a church.
Lucy's face came to him a minute and then dissolved,
A drowned face, ebbing away with a smile on its mouth.
He had meant to marry that face in another church.
But he was dying instead. It was strange to die.

All night from the hour of three, the dead man's hour, the rain
    falls in heavy gusts, in black irresistible streams as if the whole
    sky were falling in one wet huddle.
All night, living and dead sleep under it, without moving, on   30
    the field; the surgeons work in the church; the wounded moan;
    the dissevered fragments of companies and regiments look
    for each other, trying to come together.
In the morning, when the burial-parties go out, the rain is still
    falling, damping the powder of the three rounds fired over the
    grave; before the grave is well-dug, the bottom of the grave
    is a puddle.

All day long the Southern armies bury their dead to the sodden
   drums of the rain; all day the bugle calls a hoarse-throated
      "Taps"; the bugler lets the water run from his bugle-
         mouth and wipes it clean again and curses the rainy
            weather.

XV. *The Union retreat*

All night the Union army fled in retreat
Like horses scared by a shadow—a stumbling flood
Of panicky men who had been brave for a while
And might be brave again on another day
But now were merely children chased by the night   10
And each man tainting his neighbor with the same
Blind fear.
               When men or horses begin to run
Like that, they keep on running till they tire out
Unless a strong hand masters a bridle-rein.
Here there was no hand to master, no rein to clutch,
Where the riderless horses kicked their way through the crowd
And the congressmen's carriages choked Cat Hairpin Bend.
Sykes and the regulars covered the retreat,
And a few brigades were kept in some sort of order,   20
But the rest—They tried to stop them at Centerville.
McDowell and his tired staff held a haggard conference.
But before the officers could order retreat
The men were walking away.
                           They had fought and lost.
They were going to Washington, they were going back
To their tents and their cooking-fires and their letters from Susie.
They were going back home to Maine or Vermont or Ohio,
And they didn't care who knew it, and that was that.

Meanwhile, on the battlefield, Johnston and Beauregard,   30
Now joined by the dusty Davis, found themselves
As dazed by their victory as their foes by defeat.
They had beaten one armed mob with another armed mob
And Washington was theirs for the simple act
Of stretching a hand to the apple up on the bough,
If they had known. But they could not know it then.
They too saw spectres—unbroken Union reserves

Moving to cut their supply-line near Manassas.
They called back the pursuit, such scattered pursuit as it was.
Their men were tired and disordered. The chance went by
While only the stiff-necked Jackson saw it clear
As a fighting-psalm or a phrase in Napoleon's tactics.
He said to the surgeon who was binding his wound,
With a taciturn snap, "Give me ten thousand fresh troops
And I will be in Washington by tomorrow."
But they could not give him the troops while there yet was time.
He had three days' rations cooked for the Stonewall Brigade   10
And dourly awaited the order that never came.
He had always been at God's orders, and God had used him
As an instrument in winning a certain fight.
Now, if God saw fit to give him the men and guns,
He would take Washington for the glory of God.
If He didn't, it was God's will and not to be questioned.

Meanwhile he could while the hours of waiting away
By seeing the Stonewall Brigade was properly fed,
Endeavoring, with that rigid kindness of his
To show Imboden his error in using profanity   20
—In the heat of battle many things might be excused,
But nothing excused profanity, even then—
And writing his Pastor at Lexington a letter
Enclosing that check for the colored Sunday-school
Which he'd promised, and, being busy, had failed to send.
There is not one word of Bull Run in all that letter
Except the mention of "a fatiguing day's service."
It would not have occurred to Jackson there might have been.

Walt Whitman, unofficial observer to the cosmos, reads of the
defeat in a Brooklyn room. The scene rises before him, more real   30
than the paper he stares upon. He sees the defeated army pouring
along Pennsylvania Avenue in the drizzling rain, a few regiments
in good order, marching in silence, with lowering faces—the rest a
drenched, hungry mob that plods along on blistered feet and falls
asleep on the stoops of houses, in vacant lots, in basement-areas
huddled, too tired to remember battle or be ashamed of flight.
     Nothing said—no cries or cheers from the windows, no jeers
from the secessionists in the watching crowd—half the crowd is
secessionist at heart, even now, more than ever now.

Two old women, white-haired, stand all day in the rain, giving coffee and soup and bread to the passing men. The tears stream down their faces as they cut the bread and pour out the coffee.

Whitman sees it all in his mind's eye—the tears of the two women—the strange look on the men's faces, awake or asleep—the dripping, smoke-colored rain. Perplexed and deep in his heart, something stirs and moves—he is each one of them in turn—the beaten men, the tired women, the boy who sleeps there quietly with his musket still clutched tightly to him. The long lines of a poem begin to lash themselves against his mind, with the lashing 10 surge and long thunder of Montauk surf.

Horace Greeley has written Lincoln an hysterical letter—he has not slept for seven nights—in New York, "on every brow sits sullen, scorching, black despair."

He was trumpeting "On to Richmond!" two weeks ago. But then the war was a thing for an editorial—a triumphal parade of Unionists over rebels. Now there has been a battle and a defeat. He pleads for an armistice—a national convention—anything on almost any terms to end this war.

Many think as he does; many fine words ring hollow as the 20 skull of an orator, the skull of a maker of war. They have raised the Devil with slogans and editorials, but where is the charm that will lay him? Who will bind the Devil aroused?

Only Lincoln, awkwardly enduring, confused by a thousand counsels, is neither overwhelmed nor touched to folly by the madness that runs along the streets like a dog in August scared of itself, scaring everyone who crosses its path.

Defeat is a fact and victory can be a fact. If the idea is good, it will survive defeat, it may even survive the victory.

His huge, patient, laborious hands start kneading the stuff of 30 the Union together again; he gathers up the scraps and puts them together; he sweeps the corners and the cracks and patches together the lost courage and the rags of belief.

The dough didn't rise that time—maybe it will next time. God must have tried and discarded a lot of experiment-worlds before he got one even good enough to whirl for a minute—it is the same with a belief, with a cause.

It is wrong to talk of Lincoln and a star together—that old rubbed image is a scrap of tinsel, a scrap of dead poetry—it dries up and blows away when it touches a man. And yet Lincoln had a star, if you will have it so—and was haunted by a prairie-star.

Down in the South another man, most unlike him but as steadfast, is haunted by another star that has little to do with tinsel, and the man they call "Evacuation" Lee begins to grow taller and to cast a longer shadow.

BOOK THREE:

The Wilderness Stone

April of the next year, 1862, finds Jack Ellyat in camp above Pittsburg Landing in Grant's Army of the Tennessee. He has re-enlisted after the Battle of Bull Run, but he is homesick for his old company and not at all popular with Western strangers.

The nine months since Bull Run have brought new people into prominence: rough-bearded Tecumseh Sherman; neat, handsome McClellan; Grant of Galena, hero, in February of this same year, of Fort Henry and Fort Donelson, now Major-General Grant.

The time is ripe for Shiloh in which Grant, Sherman, and Buell are to oppose Johnston and Beauregard. Johnston catches Grant off guard, but in the end Shiloh is counted a Union victory.

Of the battle itself we see but little, for "this is Ellyat's tune, this is no tune but his"—and Ellyat with his tent-companion Bailey are taken prisoner soon after the surprise attack. But, as the prison column is marched in the direction opposite to the fighting, Ellyat and Bailey find opportunity to escape. Bailey is recaptured at once, but Ellyat loses himself in the trackless woods.

Exhausted and starving, he is cared for by a family of draft-evaders—hiders. Strangely attracted to the young girl of the family, Melora Vilas, he remains content to stay hidden in the woods. The young lovers, Melora and Jack, take no thought of consequences or of the future until one day Ellyat is surprised by a Confederate scout and again taken prisoner.

1. *Tennessee wilderness*

By Pittsburg Landing, the turbid Tennessee
Sucks against black, soaked spiles with soil-colored waters.
That country is huge and disorderly, even now.
—This is Ellyat's tune, this is no tune but his—
Country of muddy rivers, sombre and swollen,
Country of bronze wild turkeys and catfish-fries
And brushpile landings going back to the brush.
A province of mush and milk, a half-cleared forest,
A speckled guinea-cock that never was cooped
But ran away to grow his spurs by himself.   10
Neither North nor South, but crunching a root of its own
Between strong teeth—perhaps a wild-onion-root,
Perhaps a white stalk of arbutus, hardier there,
Than any phantom-arbutus of Eastern Springs.
A mudsill man with the river-wash in his ears,
Munching the coarse, good meal of a johnny-cake
Hot from the hob—even now it tastes of the brush,
The wilderness, the big lost star in the pines,
The brown river-dirt, the perpetual river-sound,
In spite of the sidewalks, in spite of the trolley-cars.   20
No trolley-car-bell can drown that river-sound,
Or take the loneliness out of the lost moon,
The night too big for a man, too lonesome and wide.
The vastness has been netted in railroad tracks
But it is still vast, uneasy.
                                And when the brief
Screech of the railway-whistle stabs at the trees
That grow so thick, so unplanned, so untidily strong
On either side of the two planned ribs of steel,
Ghost-steamboats answer it from the sucking brown water.   30
In Sixty-two, it was shaggy with wilderness still
For stretches and stretches of close-packed undergrowth,
Wild as a muskrat, ignorant of the axe;
Stretches and stretches where roughly-chinked log-cabins,
Two shouts and a holler away from the nearest neighbors,
Stood in a wisp of open. All night long
The cabin-people heard the chant of the trees,
The forest, hewn away from the painful clearing
For a day or a year, with sweat and back-breaking toil,
But waiting to come back, to crush the crude house   40

III

And the planted space with vines and trailers of green,
To quench the fire on the hearth with running green saps,
With a chant of green, with tiny green tendrils curling,
—This is Ellyat's tune, this is no tune but his—
The railway-train goes by with a shrill, proud scream
And the woman comes to the door in a butternut dress
Hair tousled up in a knot on the back of her head,
A barefoot child at her skirt.
                              The train goes by.
They watch it with a slow wonder that is not pathos   10
Nor heroism but merely a slow wonder.

II. *Thoughts of Jack Ellyat*

Jack Ellyat, in camp above Pittsburg Landing,
Speck in Grant's Army of the Tennessee,
Thought of old fences in Connecticut
With a homesick mind.
                        This country was too new,
Too stragglingly-unplanned, too muddy with great,
Uncomfortable floods, too roughly cut
With a broad hatchet out of a hard tree.

It had seemed fine when he was mustered out   20
After Bull Run, to wear a veteran air,
And tell pink Ellen Baker about war
And how, as soon as he could re-enlist
He'd do it where he got a chance to fight—
Wet mouth of tears—he hadn't wanted to kiss her
At first, but it was easier later on.
Why had he ever gone out to Chicago?
Why had he ever heard that shallow band
Whanging its brass along a Western street
And run to sign the muster-roll again?   30
Why had he ever talked about Bull Run
To these green, husky boys from Illinois
And Iowa, whose slang was different slang,
Who called suspenders galluses and swore
In the sharp pops of a mule-driver's whip?
Bull Run—it had impressed them for a week
But then they started to call him "Bull Run Jack." . . .

Henry Fairfield marching along with his sword,
All the old company marching after him
Back in McClellan's army, back by the known
Potomac, back in the safe and friendly East;
All the papers telling how brave they were
And how, as soon as the roads dried up in the spring,
"The little Napoleon" would hammer the South to bits
With a blue thunderbolt.

                         And here he was
A lost pea, spilt at random in a lost war;   10
A Tennessee war that had no *Tribunes* or polish
Where he was the only Easterner in the whole
Strange-swearing regiment of Illinois farmers,
Alien as Rebels, and rough as all outdoors.

He wanted to get transferred, he wanted to be
Back with the company, back with the Eastern voices,
Back where nobody called him "Bull Run Jack"
And snickered at him for shaving every two days.
He'd written about it and Father knew a congressman
But nothing would happen—he'd never get away,   20
He'd stay being Bull Run Jack till the end of the war
And march through acres of hostile Tennessee mud
Till his legs dropped off, and never get to be Corporal.
He was sick of the war and the mud and the Western faces.
He hated the sight of his Illinois uniform.
He was sorry for himself. He felt with a vague
Soft blur of self-pity that he was really quite brave,
And if people only knew, they'd do something about it.

This is Ellyat's tune, this is no tune but his.
Nine months have passed since McDowell reddened Bull Run,
Nine strong-hoofed months, but they have meant little to Ellyat.   30
What means the noise of the wind to the dust in the wind?
But the wind calls strange things out, calls strange men out,
A dozen pictures flash in front of the eyes
And are gone in a flash—
                         rough-bearded Tecumseh Sherman,
Who had tried most things, but being cursed with a taste
For honesty, had found small luck in his stars;
Ex-soldier, banker, lawyer, each in its turn,

Ex-head of a Southern military-school,
Untidy ex-president of a little horse-railroad;
Talkative, nervous, salty, Scotch-Irish fighter,
High-strung, quick-tempered, essentially modern-minded,
Stamping the length of the dusty corridors
Of a Western hotel with a dead cigar in his teeth,
Talking the war to himself, till the word goes round
The new general is crazy—

                    neat, handsome McClellan,
Ex-railroad president too, but a better railroad;   10
The fortunate youth, the highly-modern boy-wonder,
The snapping-eyed, brisk banner-salesman of war
With all the salesman's gifts and the salesman's ego;
Great organizer, with that magnetic spark
That pulls the heart from the crowd—and all of it spoiled
By the Napoleon-complex that haunts such men.
There never has been a young banner-salesman yet
That did not dream of a certain little cocked-hat
And feel it fit. McClellan felt that it fitted.
—After a year and a day, the auditors come,   20
Dry auditors, going over the books of the company,
Sad auditors, with groups of red and black figures
That are not moved by a dream of precious cocked hats.
And after the auditors go, the board of directors
Decides, with a sigh, to do without banner-salesmen—
It is safer to dream of a rusty Lincoln stovepipe.
That dream has more patience in it.

                      And yet, years later,
Meeting the banner-salesman in some cheap street
With the faded clippings of old success in his pocket,   30
One cannot help feeling sorry for the cocked hat
So briefly worn in a dream of luck and the ego.
One cannot help feeling sorry for George McClellan,
He should have been a hero by every rule.
He looked the part—he could have acted the part
Word perfectly. He looked like an empire-maker.
But so few empire-makers have looked the part.

Fate has a way of picking unlikely material.
Her stiff hands were busy now with an odd piece of wood,
Sometime Westpointer, by accident more than choice,   40
Sometime brevet-captain in the old Fourth Infantry,

Mentioned in Mexican orders for gallant service
And, six years later, forced to resign from the Army
Without enough money to pay for a stateroom home.
Turned farmer on Hardscrabble Farm, turned bill-collector,
Turned clerk in the country-store that his brothers ran,
The eldest-born of the lot, but the family-failure,
Unloading frozen hides from a farmer's sleigh
With stoop-shouldered strength, whittling beside the stove,
And now and then turning to whiskey to take the sting
From winter and certain memories.   10
                              It didn't take much.
A glass or two would thicken the dogged tongue
And flush the fair skin beneath the ragged brown beard.
Poor and shabby—old "Cap" Grant of Galena,
Who should have amounted to something but hadn't so far
Though he worked hard and was honest.
                              A middle-aged clerk,
A stumpy, mute man in a faded army overcoat,
Who wrote the War Department after Fort Sumter,
Offering them such service as he could give   20
And saying he thought that he was fit to command
As much as a regiment, but getting no answer.
So many letters come to a War Department,
One can hardly bother the clerks to answer them all—
Then a Volunteer colonel, drilling recruits with a stick,
A red bandanna instead of an officer's sash;
A brigadier-general, one of thirty-seven,
Snubbed by Halleck and slighted by fussy Frémont;
And then the frozen February gale
Over Fort Henry and Fort Donelson,   30
The gunboats on the cold river—the brief siege—
"Unconditional surrender"—and the newspapers.

Major-General Grant, with his new twin-stars,
Who, oddly, cared so little for reading newspapers,
Though Jesse Grant wrote dozens of letters to them
Pointing out all the wonders his son had done
And wringing one dogged letter from that same son
That should have squelched anybody but Jesse Grant.
It did not squelch him. He was a business man,
And now Ulysses had astonished Galena   40
By turning out to be somebody after all;

115

Ulysses' old father was going to see him respected
And, incidentally, try to wangle a contract
For army-harness and boom the family tannery.
It was a great surprise when Ulysses refused,
The boy was so stubborn about it.

                            And everywhere
Were business-people, picking up contraband cotton,
Picking up army-contracts, picking up shoddy,
Picking up shoes and blankets, picking up wagons,
Businesslike robins, picking up juicy earthworms,
Picking up gold all over Tom-Tiddler's Ground,
And Ulysses wouldn't see it.

                            Few people have been
More purely Yankee, in essence, than Jesse Grant.

More pictures—Jefferson Davis, in dripping Spring rain,
Reading a chilly inauguration-address
To an unstirred crowd. He is really President now.
His eyes are more tired, his temper beginning to fray.
A British steamer in the Bahama Channel
Stopped by a Captain Wilkes and a Union cruiser.
They take two men, and let the steamer puff on
—And light a long hissing fuse that for a month
Nearly brings war with England. Lincoln and Seward
Stamp out the fuse, and let the Confederates go—
Wooden frigates at anchor in Hampton Roads
Burning and sinking with tattered banners apeak
Under the strange new, armadillo-bite
Of something plated with iron that yet can float,
The *Merrimac*—and all Washington and the North
In a twenty-four-hours' panic—then, next day—
As Lincoln stares from the window of the White House
For the sooty sign in the sky that means defeat—
The armadillo, smoking back in her pride
To crunch up another meal of weak wooden ships,
Is beaten off by another leaky prodigy
A tin-can cylinder on a floating shingle,
The *Monitor*—the first fight of iron-clads,
The sinking of all the world's old sea-bitten names,
Temeraire, *Victory*, and *Constellation*,
Serapis, *Bon Homme Richard*, *Golden Hind*,
Galleys of Antony, galleys of Carthage,

Galleons with gilded Virgins, galleasses,
Viking long-serpents, siren-haunted galliots,
Argos and argosies and the Achæan pride,
Moving to sea in one long wooden wall
Behind the huge ghost-flagship of the Ark
In such a swelling cloud of phantom sail
They whitened Ocean—going down by the head,
Green water seeping through the battened ports,
Spreading along the scrubbed and famous decks,
Going down—going down—going down—to mermaid-pools,   10
To Fiddler's Green—to the dim barnacle-thrones,
Where Davy Jones drinks everlasting rum
With the sea-horses of his sunken dreams.

But this is Ellyat's tune—and if the new
Army of the Potomac stands astrain
To end Secession with its "little Napoleon."
If Lee is just about to find his hour;
If, among many mirrors and gilt chairs,
Under the flare of the gas-chandeliers
A sallow-faced and puffy Emperor   20
With waxed mustachios and a slick goatee
Gave various Southern accents, talking French,
Evasive answers and no definite help,
Ready enough to recognize the South
If he were sure of profit in the scheme
But not yet finding such a profit sure;
If in the foggy streets of Westminster,
The salty streets of Liverpool and Hull,
The same mole-struggle in the dark went on
Between Confederate and Unionist—   30
The *Times* raved at the North—Mr. Gladstone thought
England might recognize the South next year,
While Palmerston played such a tangled game
It is illegible yet—and Henry Adams
Added one more doubt to his education
By writing propaganda for the North,
It is all mist to Ellyat.
               And when he sleeps,
He does not dream of Grant or Lee or Lincoln.
He only dreams that he is back at home
With a heroic wound that does not hurt.   40

117

A uniform that never stings with lice,
And a sword like Henry Fairfield's to show Ellen Baker.

III. Battle of Shiloh

As far as the maps and the blocks on the maps have meaning
The situation is this.
                                    A wide Western river,
A little lost landing, with a steamboat-store,
A post office where the roads from the landings meet,
A plank church three miles inland called Shiloh Chapel,
An undulating and broken table-land
Roughed into a triangle by bordering creeks.   10
Each side of the triangle runs about four miles long
And, scattered in camps from the tip of the triangle
To the base at the landing, are thirty-three thousand men,
Some fairly seasoned in war, but many green sticks,
Grant's Army of the Tennessee.
                                    Down the river
Don Carlos Buell has twenty-five thousand more
In the Army of the Ohio.
                                    Opposing these
Are Albert Sidney Johnston and Beauregard   20
With something like forty thousand butternut fighters,
Including a martial bishop.
                                    Johnston plans
To smash Grant's army to bits, before Buell can join it,
And water his wagon-trains in the Tennessee.
He has sneaked his army along through wilderness roads
Till now they are only a mile and a half away
Tonight from the Union lines.
                                    He is tall and active.
Light brown hair streaked with grey feathers, blue claymore eyes 30
That get steel shadows in battle, a face like Hamilton's,
Old Westpointer, old cavalry-colonel, well-schooled in war.
Lincoln offered to make him a major-general
And rumor says that he could have had the command
Of the Union armies, once.
                                    But he resigned
And later, went with his State. It is hard to say

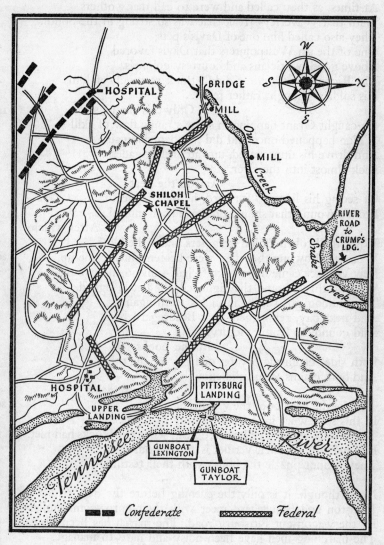

West compass rose: W, S, N, E

HOSPITAL

BRIDGE

MILL

MILL

SHILOH CHAPEL

Owl Creek

RIVER ROAD to CRUMP'S LDG.

Snake Creek

HOSPITAL

UPPER LANDING

PITTSBURG LANDING

Tennessee River

GUNBOAT LEXINGTON

GUNBOAT TAYLOR

▬ ▬ *Confederate*   ✕✕✕✕ *Federal*

The Battle of Shiloh

What he might have been.
                                They called him the "*preux chevalier*"
At times, as they called and were to call many others
With that Waverley-streak that was so strong in the South.
They also called him one of Davis's pets,
One of the tin Westpointers that Davis favored
Above good politicians and courtesy colonels.
The Richmond *Enquirer* didn't think so much of him,
His soldiers thought rather more.
                                Only this can be said.   10
He caught Grant napping in some strange flaw of skill
Which happened once and did not happen again.
And drove his unprepared, unwatchful brigades
Back almost into the river.
                                And in the heat
Of seeing his lines go forward, he bled to death
From a wound that should not have been mortal.
                                After which,
While the broken Union stragglers under the bluff
Were still howling that they were beaten, Buell came up,   20
Lew Wallace came up, the knife half-sunk in the wound
Was not thrust home, the night fell, the battle lagged.
The bulldog got the bone in his teeth again
And next day, reinforced, beat Beauregard back
And counted a Union victory.
                                In the books
Both sides claim victory on one day or the other
And both claims seem valid enough.
                                It only remains
To take the verdict of the various dead   30
In this somewhat indecisive meeting of blocks.
There were thirty-five hundred dead when the blocks had met.
But, being dead, their verdict is out of court.
They cannot puzzle the books with their testimony.

Now, though, it is only the evening before the day.
Johnston and Beauregard meet with their corps-commanders
By the wagon-cut Pittsburg road. The march has been slow.
The marching men have been noisy and hard to manage.
By every rule of war, Grant must have been warned
Long before now, and is planning an ambush for them.   40
They are being marched into an open Union trap.

So Beauregard thinks and says—and is perfectly right
According to rules. There is only one difficulty.
There is no ambush.

                    Sherman has just reported
The presence of enemy troops in front of his lines
But says he expects nothing more than some picket-firing
And Grant that evening telegraphs General Halleck,
"I have scarcely the faintest idea of an attack."

So much for the generals. Beauregard makes his point
And is overruled.   10
                    The April night comes down.
The butternut men try to get some sleep while they can.
They are to be up and fighting by five in the morning.

IV. *Ellyat gives the alarm*

Jack Ellyat, least of any, expected attack.
He woke about five with a dazzle struck in his eyes
Where a long dawn-ray slid through a crack in the tent.
He cursed at the ray and tried to go back to sleep
But he couldn't do it, although he was tired enough,
Something ate at his mind as soon as he wakened
And kept on eating.   20
                    This morning was Sunday morning.
The bells would be jangling for church back home, pretty soon,
The girls would be going to church in white Sunday dresses,
No, it was too early for that—they'd be muffled up
In coats and galoshes. Their cheeks would be pink as apples.
O frosty churchbells jangling across the thin
Crust of packed frost, under Connecticut sky,
Put snow on my tongue, and the grey, cool flower of rain—
He had to get up. He couldn't lie here and listen
To Bailey and the rest of them, snoring away.   30
His throat was dry. He needed a drink of water
But not from a muddy river—put rain on my tongue!
Souse me with chilly, sweet flaws of Puritan rain—
He started to put on his boots, looking over at Bailey.
Bailey was bearded, Bailey was thirty-two,
Bailey had been a teamster and was a corporal.
The waking Bailey looked like a stupid horse,

The sleeping Bailey looked like a dirty sack,
Bailey called him "Colonel" and didn't mean it,
Bailey had had him tossed in a blanket once,
Somehow he hated Bailey worse than the rest.
He managed to leave the tent without waking Bailey.
It was very early still. The sun was just up.
A fair sky, a very fair day. The air still held
That bloom which is not the bloom on apple or peach
But the bloom on a fruit made up of pure water and light,
The freshness of dawn, still trembling, being new-born.
He sucked at it gratefully.
                              The camp was asleep.
All that length of tents still asleep. He could see through the tents.
He could see all those sleeping, rough, lousy, detested men
Laden with sleep as with soft leaden burdens laden,
Movelessly lying between the brown fawns of sleep
Like infants nuzzled against the flanks of a doe,
In quietness slumbering, in a warm quietness,
While sleep looked at them with her fawn's agate eyes
And would not wake them yet.
                                      And he was alone,
And for a moment, could see this, and see them so
And, being free, stand alone, and so being free
To love or hate, do neither, but merely stand
Above them like sleep and see them with untouched eyes.
In a while they would wake, and he would hate them again.
But now he was sleep. He was the sun on the coat
Of the halted fawn at the green edge of the wood
Staring at morning.
                              He could not hate them yet.

Somebody near by, in the woods, took a heap of dry sticks,
And began to break them quickly, first one by one,
Then a dozen together, then hard-cracking axe-helves breaking.
Ellyat was running. His mouth felt stiff with loud words
Though he heard no sound from his mouth. He could see the
    white
Fine pine-splinters flying from those invisible axe-helves. . . .

For a minute all of them were tangled together
In the bucking tent like fish in a canvas scoop,
Then they were out of it somehow—falling in line—

122

Bailey's hair looked angry and sleepy. The officers
Were yelling the usual things that officers yelled.
It was a surprise. They were going to be licked again.
It did not matter yet. It would matter soon.
Bailey had lost his blouse and his pants weren't buttoned.
He meant to tell Bailey about it. There wasn't time.
His eyes felt bald as glass but that was because
He kept looking for flying pine-splinters in the air.
Now they were setting off firecrackers under a boiler
And a man ran past with one hand dripping red paint,   10
Holding the hand with his other hand and talking
As if the hurt hand were a doll.

                      An officer hit him
With the flat of a sword. It spanked some dust from his coat
And the man's face changed from a badly-fitting mask
Of terror, cut into ridges of sallow wax,
To something pink and annoyed, but he kept on running.
All this happened at once as they were moving.
The dawn had been hit to pieces with a hard mallet.
There were no fawns. There was an increasing noise   20
Through which he heard the lugubrious voice of Bailey
Singing off-key, like a hymn,
      "When I was a weaver, I lived by myself,
        And I worked at the weaver's tra-a-de—"

The officers were barking like foxes now.

As the last tent dropped behind them, Ellyat saw
A red, puzzled face, looking out from under a tent-flap,
Like a bear from a cave. The face had been drunk last night,
And it stared at the end of the column with a huge and stupid
    wisdom.   30

V. Capture

"When I was a weaver, I lived by myself,
And I worked at the weaver's trade—"

Jack Ellyat found himself back behind somebody's tent
After a while. He had been out in the woods.
He remembered scrouging against a too-porous tree

For a day or a number of minutes while he jerked
A rattling ramrod up and down in a gun.
But they couldn't stay in the woods—they had to come back.
They had called him "Bull Run Jack" but they had to come back,
Bailey and all the rest. He had come back with them,
But that was different—that was all right for him.
This red-colored clang of haste was different for him.
Bailey and all the rest could run where they liked.
He was an old soldier. He would stay here and fight.
Running, he tripped on a rope, and began to fall,   10
Bailey picked him back on his feet. "Did they get you, Bud?"
"No, they didn't get me."
                              Ellyat's voice was a snarl.
What business had Bailey steadying him like that?
He hadn't been running.
                           Suddenly he saw
Grey shouting strangers bursting into the tents
And his heart shrank up in a pea.
                                    "Oh hell," he said,
Hopelessly ramming a cartridge. He was an old soldier.   20
He wasn't going to run. He was going to act
Vast fictive heroisms in front of Bailey,
If they only gave him time, just a little time.

A huge horse rose above the wall of the tent
And hung there a second like a bad prodigy,
A frozen scream full of hoofs.
                                He struck at its head
And tried to get out from under as it lunged down
But he wasn't quite quick enough.
                                    As he slipped and fell   30
He saw the laughter pasted on Bailey's face
But before he could hear the laugh, the horse had fallen,
Jarring the world.
                    After blunt, sickly time
A fat young man with a little pink moustache
Was bawling "Hey, Yank, surrender!" into his ear
And nervously waving a pistol in front of his eyes.
He nodded weakly. "Hey, boys," called the fat young man,
"I got two Yanks!" His mouth was childish with pleasure.
He was going to tell everybody he had two Yanks.   40
"Here, Yank, come and pull the horse off the other Yank."

The prisoner's column straggled along the road
All afternoon. Jack Ellyat marched in it numbly.
He was stiff and sore. They were going away from the battle
But they could still hear it, quaking,
The giant stones rolled over the grumbling bridge.

Some of the prisoners tried to joke with the guards,
Some walked in silence, some spoke out now and then,
As if to explain to the world why they were there.
One man said, "I got a sore heel." Another said,
"All the same the Tenth Missouri's a damn good regiment."   10
Another said, "Listen, boys, don't it beat all hell?
I left my tobacco behind me, back in the tent,
Don't it beat all hell to lose your tobacco like that?"

Bailey kept humming the "Weaver," but now and then
He broke it off, to say, with a queer satisfaction,
"Well, we surely did skedaddle—we surely did."
Jack Ellyat had said nothing for a long time.
This was war, this was Phaëton, this was the bronze chariot
Rolling the sky. If he had a soul any more
It felt scrawny and thin as a sick turkey-poult.   20
It was not worth the trouble to fatten. He tried to fatten it
With various thoughts, now and then, but the thoughts were
   spoilt
Corn. They had damn well skedaddled. They damn well had.
That was all. The rest of the army could win or lose
They had surely skedaddled. They had been whipped again.
He had been whipped again.
                     He was no longer
The old soldier—no longer even "Bull Run Jack."
He had lost a piece of himself. It had ragged edges   30
That piece. He could see it left behind in the tents
Under a dirty coat and a slab of tobacco.

After a while he knocked against Bailey's arm.
"Where are we going?" he said, in a shy voice.
Bailey laughed, not badly, "Well, Colonel, Corinth I guess,
Corinth first—and then some damn prison-camp."
He spat in the road. "It won't be good grub," he said.
"Bacon and hominy-grits. They don't eat right.

They don't eat nothing but bacon and hominy-grits.
God, I'm goin' to get tired of bacon and hominy-grits!"

Ellyat looked. There was something different about him.
He stated a fact. "You've buttoned your pants," he said.
"I remember you didn't have 'em buttoned this morning."

"That's so," said Bailey, impressed, "Now when did I button
    'em?"
They chewed at the question, trying to puzzle it out.
It seemed very important to both for quite a long time.

VI. Escape

It was night now. The column still marched. But Bailey and 10
    Ellyat
Had dropped to the rear of the column, planning escape.
There were few guards and the guards were as tired as they.
Two men could fall in a ditch by the side of the road
And get away, perhaps, if they picked a good time.
They talked it over in stupid whispers of weariness.
The next bend—no, the guard was coming along.
The next bend after—no, there was light for a moment
From a brief star, then clouded—the top of the hill—
The bottom of the hill—and they still were marching.   20
Rain began to fall, a drizzle at first, then faster.
Ellyat's eyes were thick. He walked in a dream,
A heavy dream, cut from leaden foil with blunt shears.
Then Bailey touched him—he felt the tired bones of his skull
Click with a sudden spark—his feet stopped walking—
He held his breath for an instant,
And then wearily slumped in the ditch with enormous noise,
Hunching his shoulders against a phantom bayonet.

But when he could raise his head, the column had gone.
He felt fantastic. They couldn't escape like this.   30
You had to escape like a drawing in *Harper's Weekly*
With stiff little men on horses like sickle-pears
Firing round frozen cream-puffs into your back.
But they had escaped.
                    Life came back to him in a huge

Wave of burnt stars. He wanted to sing and yell.
He crackled out of the ditch and stood beside Bailey.
Had he ever hated Bailey? It could not have been.
He loved Bailey better than anything else in the world.

They moved slyly toward the woods, they were foxes escaped.
Wise foxes sliding away to a hidden earth
To a sandy floor, to the warm fawn-flanks of sweet sleep. . . .
And then an awful molasses-taffy voice
Behind them yelled "Halt!" and "Halt!" and—sudden explosion
Of desultory popcorn in iron poppers—   10
Wild running at random—a crash among broken boughs—
A fighting sound—Bailey's voice, half-strangled but clear,
"Run like hell, Jack, they'll never catch you!"

                                  He ran like hell.

Time passed like the rain. Time passed and was one with the
    rain.

VII. Sylvan interlude

Ellyat woke from a nightmare and put out his hand
To touch the wall by his bed, but there was no wall.
Then he listened for Bailey's snoring.
                            And he heard   20
The gorged, sweet pouring of water through infinite boughs,
The hiss of the big spilt drop on the beaten leaf,
The bird-voiced and innumerable rain,
A wet quail piping, a thousand soaked black flutes
Building a lonely castle of sliding tears,
Strange and half-cruel as a dryad's bright grief.

Ellyat huddled closer under the tree,
Remembering what he could. He had run for years,
He had slept for years—and yet it was still not dawn.
It seemed cruel to him that it should never be dawn.   30
It seemed cruel that Bailey was lost. He had meant to show
Some fictive heroisms in front of Bailey.
He had not. Bailey had saved his skin instead,
And Bailey was lost. And in him something was lost,
Something worse than defeat or this rain—some piece of himself.
Some piece of courage.

                    Now the slant rain began
To creep through his sodden heart. He thought, with wild awe,
"This is Nibelung Hall. I am lying in Nibelung Hall.
I am long dead. I fell there out of the sky
In a wreck of horses, spilling the ball of the sun,
And they shut my eyes with stone runes and put me to sleep
On a bier where the living stream perpetually flows
Past Ygdrasil and waters the roots of the world.
I can hear the ravens scream from the cloudy roof.
I can hear the bubbles rising in the clear stream.
I can hear the old gods shout in the heathen sky
As the hawk-Valkyrie carry the stiffened lumps
Of corpse-faced heroes shriekingly to Valhalla.
This is Nibelung Hall. I must break the runes from my eyes.
I must escape it or die."
                              He slept. The rain fell.

Melora Vilas, rising by candlelight,
Looked at herself in the bottom of the tin basin
And wished that she had a mirror.
                                        Now Spring was here,
She could kneel above the well of a forest pool
And see the shadow hidden under the water,
The intent brown eyes, the small face cut like a heart.
She looked at the eyes and the eyes looked back at her,
But just when it seemed they could start to talk to each other—
"What are you like? Who are you?"—
                                        a ripple flawed
The deep glass and the shadow trembled away.

If she only had a mirror, maybe she'd know
Something, she didn't know what, but something important,
Something like knowing your skin and you were alive
On a good day, something as drenched as sleep,
As wise as sleep, as piercing as the bee's dagger.
But she'd never know it unless she could get a mirror
And they'd never get a mirror while they were hiders.
They were bound to be hiders as long as the war kept on.
Pop was that way. She remembered roads and places.
She was seventeen. She had seen a lot of places,

A lot of roads. Pop was always moving along.
Everybody she'd ever known was moving along.
—Dusty wagons full of chickens and children,
Full of tools and quilts, Rising Sun and Roses of Sharon,
Mahogany dressers out of Grandmother's house,
Tin plates, cracked china, a couple of silver spoons,
Moving from State to State behind tired, scuffed horses
Because the land was always better elsewhere.

Next time they'd quit. Next stop they'd settle right down.
Next year they'd have time to rub up the mahogany dresser.   10
Next place, Mom could raise the flowers she wanted to raise.
But it never began. They were always moving along.

She liked Kansas best. She wished they'd go back to Kansas.
She liked the smell of the wind there.
But Pop hadn't wanted to join with the Free-Soilers
And then the slavery men had shot up the town
And killed the best horse they had. That had settled Pop.
He said something about a plague on both of your houses
And moved along. So now they were hiders here
And whenever you wanted to ask Pop about the war   20
All he said was that same old thing about the plague.
She mustn't call him Pop—that was movers'-talk.
She must call him Father, the way Mom, Mother wanted.
But it was hard to remember. Mom talked a lot
About old times back in the East and Grandmother's house.
She couldn't remember an East. The East wasn't real.
There was only the dusty road and moving along.
Although she knew that Mom had worn a silk dress
And gone to a ball, once. There was a picture of Pop
And Mom, looking Eastern, in queer old Eastern clothes.   30
They weren't white trash. She knew how to read and figure.
She'd read *Macbeth* and *Beulah* and *Oliver Twist*.
She liked *Beulah* best but *Macbeth* would have suited Pop.
Sometimes she wondered what had happened to them,
When Mother used to live in Grandmother's house
And wear silk dresses, and Father used to read Latin—
When had they started to go just moving along,
And how would it feel to live in Grandmother's house?

But it was so long ago, so hard to work out
And she liked it this way—she even liked being hiders.   40

It was exciting, especially when the guns
Coughed in the sky as they had all yesterday,
When Bent hid out in the woods to keep from recruiters,
And you knew there were armies stumbling all around you,
Big, blundering cows of armies, snuffling and tramping
The whole scuffed world with their muddy, lumbering hoofs,
Except the little lost brushpile where you were safe.
There were guns in the sky again today. Big armies.
An army must be fine to look at.
                                        But Pop   10
Would never let her do it or understand.
An army or a mirror. She didn't know
Which she'd rather find, but whenever she thought of it
The mirror generally won. You could keep a mirror yourself.

She had to call the hogs that afternoon.
You had to call them once or twice a month
And give them food or else they ran too wild
And never came for butchering in the Fall,
Though they lived well enough without your calling,
Fat in the forest, feeding on beech mast,   20
Wild muscadines and forest provender
That made their flesh taste sweet as hazelnuts.

She liked the hogs, they weren't tame, sleepy hogs
Grunting in a black wallow, they were proud
Rapid and harsh and savage as Macbeth.
There was a young boar that she called Macbeth,
She'd seen him fight grey-bristled, drowsy Duncan
And drive him from the trough.
                                        Fagin was there,
Bill Sikes was there and Beulah the black sow,   30
And Lady Macduff whose grunt was half a whine.
You could learn lots about a book from hogs.
She poured the swill and cupped her hands to call.
Sometimes they'd help her with it, Pop or Bent,
But Pop was off with Bent this afternoon
And Mom was always busy.
                                        Slim and straight
She stood before the snake-rail pen that kept
Macbeths on their own proper side of the fence.
"Piggy," she called, "Here, piggy, piggy, piggy!"   40

It wasn't the proper call, but the hogs knew
That sweet clear loudness with its sleepy silver
Trembling against a chanter of white ash.
"Here, piggy, piggy, piggy, piggy, piggy!
Here, piggy, piggy!" There was a scrambling noise
At the edge of the woods. "Here, piggy!"

                                              It was Banquo.
Greedy, but hesitant.
                      The Artful Dodger
Slim, black and wicked, had two feet in the trough   10
Before that obese indecision moved.
"Here, piggy! Here, piggy, piggy!"
                           The gleaming call
Floated the air like a bright glassy bubble,
Far, far, with its clean silver and white ash.
And Ellyat, lost and desperate in the wood,
Heard it, desirous as the elvish blast
Wound on a tiny horn of magic grass
To witch steel riders into a green hill.
He stumbled toward its music.   20
                        "Piggy, piggy,
Here, piggy, piggy!"
                    The swine grunted and jostled.
Melora watched them, trying to count them up
With grave eyes, brown as nuts in rainwater.
They were all there, she thought—she must be sure.
She called again. No, something moved in the woods.
She stared past the clearing, puzzled. So Ellyat saw her
Beyond the swine, head lifted like a dark foal
That listens softly for strangeness.
                         And she saw   30
An incoherent scarecrow in blue clothes
Stagger on wooden feet from the deep wood.
She called to him to keep away from the hogs,
Half-frightenedly.
                    He did not hear or obey.
He was out of Nibelung Hall.
                        She put one hand
On the rail of the fence to steady herself and waited.
"You can't come in here," she said, fiercely. "The hogs'll kill 40
    you."
But he was past the fed hogs and over the fence.

She saw a queer look on his face. "You're hungry," she said.
He grinned, made a noise in his throat, and fell, trying to touch
  her.

SONG OF ELLYAT'S HEART

Now that I am clean again,
Now I've slept and fed,
How shall I remember when
I was someone dead?

Now the balm has worked its art
And the gashes dry,
And the lizard at my heart   10
Has a sleepy eye,

How shall I remember yet
Freezing underground,
With the wakened lizard set
To the living wound?

Do not ponder the offence
Nor reject the sore,
Do not tear the cerements
Flesh may need once more.

Cold comes back and pain comes back   20
And the lizard, too.
And the burden in the sack
May be meant for you.

Do not play the risen dunce
With unrisen men.
Lazarus was risen once
But earth gaped again.

So Ellyat swam back to life, swam back to warmth
And the smell of cooking food. It was night. He heard
Impenetrable rain shake a low roof   36
And hiss stray, scattering drops on an open fire.
But he was safe. That rain was caged in the sky.

It could not fall on him.
                    He lay in a lax
Idleness, warm and hungry, not wanting to move.
A grub in a close cocoon neither bold nor wise, but content.

A tall woman was cooking mush in an iron pot.
The smell of the mush was beautiful, the shape of the pot
More beautiful than an urn by sea-nymphs carved
From sunken marbles stained with the cold sea-rose.
The woman was a great Norn, in her pot she cooked a new world,
Made of pure vapors and the juices of unspoilt light,   10
A new globe of sulliless amber and grains of white corn,
An orbed perfection. All life was beautiful now.

A girl came into the room upon light, quick feet.
He stared at her, solemnly. She was young and thin.
The small, just head was set on the slender neck
With a clean sureness. The heavy hair was a helm
Of bronze cooled under a ripple, marked by that flowing.
It was not slight but it could not weight her down.
Her hands and feet were well made and her body had
That effortless ease, that blood that flies with the bird.   20
She saw his open eyes and came over to him,
Not shyly but not concernedly.
                              Their eyes met.
The older woman kept stirring her melted world.
"Well," said the girl, "You look better." He nodded, "Yes."
Their eyes said, "I have seen a new thing. In the deep cells
Below the paltry clockwork of the ticked heart,
I have seen something neither light nor night,
A new thing, a new picture. It may mean
The lifting of a shut latch. It may mean nothing."   30

She made an escaping gesture with her right hand.
"You didn't say who you were," she said. "You just fell.
You better tell who you are, Pop'll want to know."
A shadow crossed her. "Pop won't want to keep you," she said.
"But I reckon we'll have to keep you here for a piece,
You're not fit to travel yet and that's a fact.
You look a little bit like Young Seward," she said
Reflectively, "But sometimes you look more like Oliver.
I dunno. What's your name?"
                              Ellyat put forth his hand   40

133

Toward being alive again, slowly, hauling it down.
He remembered. He was Jack Ellyat. He had been lost.
He had lain with hel-shoes on in Nibelung Hall
For twenty years. This was the girl with the swine
Whose loud sweet calling had come to him in the wood
And lifted him back to warmth and a cooking world.
He had lost a piece of himself, a piece of life,
He must find it, but now—

"What's your name?" he said in a whisper.

SONG OF THE HIDERS

This is the hidden place that hiders know.   10
This is where hiders go.
Step softly, the snow that falls here is different snow,
The rain has a different sting.
Step softly, step like a cloud, step softly as the least
Whisper of air against the beating wing,
And let your eyes be sealed
With two blue muscadines
Stolen from secret vines,
Or you will never find in the lost field
The table spread, the signs of the hidden feast.   20

This is where hiders live.
This is the tentative
And outcast corner where hiders steal away
To bake their hedgehogs in a lump of clay,
To raise their crops and children wild and shy,
And let the world go by
In accidental marches of armed wrath
That stumble blindly past the buried path.
Step softly, step like a whisper, but do not speak
Or you will never see   30
The furriness curled within the hollow tree,
The shadow-dance upon the wilderness-creek.

This is the hiders' house.
This is the ark of pine-and-willow-boughs.
This is the quiet place.
You may call now, but let your call be sweet
As clover-honey strained through silver sieves

And delicate as the dust upon the moth
Or you will never find your fugitives.
Call once, and call again,
Then, if the lifted strain
Has the true color and substance of the wild,
You may perceive, if you have lucky eyes,
Something that ran away from being wise
And changed silk ribbons for a greener cloth,
Some budding-horned and deer-milk-suckled child
Some lightness, moving toward you on light feet,   10
Some girl with indolent passion in her face.

Jack Ellyat wondered about things, six days later.
The world had come back to its shape. He was well and strong.
He had seen the old man with the burnt dreams in his eyes,
Who had fallen from something years ago in his youth
Or risen from something with an effort too stark;
The runaway who had broken the pasture-bars
To test the figments of life on a wild stone.
You could see the ultimate hardness of that strange stone
Cut in his face—but then, there was something else,   20
That came at moments and went, and answered no questions.
Had the feel of the stone been worth it, after all?
It puzzled Ellyat.
                    He couldn't figure it out.
Going West to get fat acres was common enough,
But, once you got the acres, you settled down,
You sent your children to school. You put up a fence.
When a war came along, you fought on your proper side;
You didn't blast both sides with Mercutio's curse
And hide in a wilderness.
                         The man was all wrong,   30
And yet the man was not weak. It was very strange.
If the man had been weak, you could understand him all right.

The woman was more easy to understand.
He liked the woman—he liked the rough shaggy boy
Who had lived so much in the woods to keep from the armies
That his ears were sharp as a squirrel's, and all his movements
Had something untamed about them, something leafy and strange.
Of course he ought to be fighting for the North,
He was really a skulk—but things were different here.   40

135

You couldn't reason about the difference in words
But you felt it inside your skin.
                                    Things were different here.
Like Nibelung Hall in the rain of his fever-dream,
But with no terror, with an indolent peace.

He'd have to get back to the regiment pretty soon.
He couldn't stay here. They none of them wanted him here.
He'd have to get back. But he didn't know where to go.
They could tell him how to get back to Pittsburg Landing
But how did he know if the army was there or not?   10
He didn't even know who'd won in the battle,
And, if the Rebs had won, he'd be captured again
As soon as he got on a road.
                                    Well, he'd have to chance it.
He couldn't stay here and fall in love with Melora.
Melora came walking down the crooked path
With a long shadow before her. It was the hour
When the heat is out of the gold of afternoon
And the cooled gold has not yet turned into grey,
The hour of the paused tide, neither flow nor ebb,   20
The flower beginning to close but not yet closed.

He saw her carry her fairy head aloft
Against that descending gold,
He saw the long shadow that her slight body made.

When she came near enough to him, she heard him humming
A tune he had thought forgotten, the weaver's tune.
"And the only harm that I've ever done,
Was to love a pretty maid."

She halted, trying to listen. He stopped the tune.   30
"What's that you were singing?" she said.
                                    "Oh, just trash," he said.
"I liked it. Sing it some more."
                                    But he would not sing it.

They regarded each other a foot or so apart.
Their shadows blotted together into one shadow.

She put her hand to both cheeks, and touched them lightly,

As if to cool them from something.
                              A soft, smooth shock
Inexplicable as the birth of a star
And terrible as the last cry of the flesh
Ran through his cords and struck.
                              He stared at the shadows.
Then she took her shadow into the house with her
But he still stood looking where the shadows had touched.

John Vilas watched them go off through the wood
To get the water from the other spring,   10
The big pail clanking between them.
                              His hard mouth
Was wry with an old nursery-rhyme, but his eyes
Looked somewhere beyond hardness.
                              Let them go.
Harriet said and Harriet always said
And Harriet was right, but let them go.
Men who go looking for the wilderness-stone
And find it, should not marry or beget,
But, having done so, they must take the odds   20
As the odds are.
                              Faustus and I are old.
We creep about among the hollow trees
Where the bright devils of our youth have gone
Like a dissolving magic, back to earth.
But in our tarnished and our antique wands
And in the rusty metal of our spells
There still remain such stubbornness and pith
As may express elixirs from a rock
Or pick a further quarrel with the gods   30
Should we find cause enough.
                              I know this girl,
This boy, this youth, this honey in the blood,
This kingly danger, this immediate fire.
I know what comes of it and how it lies
And how, long afterwards, at the split core
Of the prodigious and self-eaten lie,
A little grain of truth lies undissolved
By all the acids of philosophy.
Therefore, I will not seek a remedy   40
Against a sword but in the sword itself

137

Nor medicine life with anything but life.
I am too old to try the peddler's tricks,
Too wise, too foolish, too long strayed in the wood,
The custom of the world is not my custom,
Nor its employments mine.
                                        I know this girl
As well as if I never lay with her mother.
I know her heart touched with that wilderness-stone
That turns good money into heaps of leaves
And builds an outcast house of apple-twigs
Beside a stream that never had a name.
She will forget what I cannot forget,
And she may learn what I shall never learn,
But, while the wilderness-stone is strong in her,
I'd have her use it for a touchstone yet
And see the double face called good and bad
With her own eyes. So, if she stares it down,
She is released, and if it conquers her,
She was not weighted with a borrowed shield.

We are no chafferers, my daughter and I.
We give what pleases us and when we choose,
And, having given, we do not take back.
But once we shut our fists upon a star
It will take portents to unloose that grip
And even then the stuff will keep the print.
It is a habit of living.
                                        For the boy
I do not know but will not stand between.
He has more toughness in him than he thinks.
—I took my wife out of a pretty house.
—I took my wife out of a pleasant place.
—I stripped my wife of comfortable things.
—I drove my wife to wander with the wind.
—And we are old now, Faustus.
                                        Let it be so.
There was one man who might have understood,
Because he was half-oriole and half-fox,
Not Emerson, but the man by Walden Pond.
But he was given to the birds in youth
And never had a woman or a daughter.

The filled pail stood on a stone by the lip of the spring,
But they had forgotten the pail.
                              The spring was a cool
Wavering mirror that showed them their white, blurred faces
And made them wonder to see the faces so like
And yet so silent and distant.
                              Melora turned.
"We ought to go back," she said in a commonplace voice.
"Not yet, Melora."
                              Something, as from the spring   10
Rising, in silver smoke, in arras of silvers,
Drifting around them, pushed by a light, slow wind.
"Not yet Melora."
                              They sat on a log above.
Melora's eyes were still looking down at the spring.
Her knees were hunched in her arms.
                              "You'll be going," she said,
Staring at the dimmed glass. "You'll be going soon."
The silver came closer, soaking into his body,
Soaking his flesh with bright, impalpable dust.   20
He could smell her hair. It smelt of leaves and the wind.
He could smell the untaken whiteness of her clean flesh,
The deep, implacable fragrance, fiercer than sleep,
Sweeter than long sleep in the sun.
                              He touched her shoulder.
She let the hand stay but still she gazed at the spring.
Then, after a while, she turned.
                              The mirrored mouths
Fused in one mouth that trembled with the slow waters.

Melora, in the room she had to herself   30
Because they weren't white-trash and used to be Eastern,
Let the rain of her hair fall down,
In a stream, in a flood, on the white birch of her body.
She was changed, then. She was not a girl any more.
She was the white heart of the birch,
Half hidden by a fleece that a South wind spun
Out of bronze air and light, on a wheel of light.
Her sharp clear breasts
Were two young victories in the hollow darkness
And when she stretched her hands above her head   40

139

And let the spun fleece ripple to her loins,
Her body glowed like deep springs under the sun.

She had no song to sing herself asleep
Tonight, but she would need no song to sing.
A thousand thoughts ran past her in a brief
Unhurrying minute, on small, quiet feet
But did not change her. Nothing could change her now.
—Black winter night against the windowpane
And she, a child, singing her fear to sleep
With nursery-rhymes and broken scraps of tunes.   10
How well she could remember those old songs.
But this night she would sleep without a song
Except the song the earth knows in the night
After the huge embrace of the bright day,
And that was better.
                      She thought to herself.
"I don't know. I can't think. I ought to be scared.
I ought to have lots of maybes. I can't find them.
It's funny. It's different. It's a big pair of hands
Pushing you somewhere—but you've got to go.   20
Maybe you're crazy but you've got to go.
That's why Mom went. I know about Mom now.
I know how she used to be. It's pretty sweet.
It's rhymes, it's hurting, it's feeling a bird's heart
Beat in your hand, it's children growing up,
It's being cut to death with bits of light,
It's wanting silver bullets in your heart,
It's not so happy, but it's pretty sweet,
I've got to go."
                      She passed her narrow hands   30
Over her body once, half-wonderingly.

"Divide this transitory and temporal flesh
Into twelve ears of red and yellow corn
And plant each ear beside a different stream.
Yet, in the summer, when the harvesters
Come with their carts, the grain shall change again
And turn into a woman's body again
And walk across a heap of sickle-blades
To find the naked body of its love."

She slipped her dress back on and stole downstairs.
The bare feet, whispering, made little sound.
A sleeper breathed, a child turned in its sleep.
She heard the tiny breathings. She shut the door.

The moon rode a high heaven streaked with cloud.
She watched it for a moment. Then she drank
That moon from its high heaven with her mouth
And felt the immaculate burning of that frost
Run from her fingers in such corporal silver
Her whole slight body was a corposant   10
Of hollow light and the cold sap of the moon.

She knew the dark grass cool beneath her feet.
She knew the opening of the stable door.
It shut behind her. She was in darkness now.

Jack Ellyat, lying in a warm nest of hay,
Stared at the sweet-smelling darkness with troubled eyes.
He was going tomorrow. He couldn't skulk any more.
—Oh, reasonless thirst in the night, what can slake your thirst,
Reasonless heart, why will you not let me rest?
I have seen a woman wrapped in the grace of leaves,   20
I have kissed her mouth with my mouth, but I must go—
He was going back to find a piece of himself
That he had lost in a tent, in a red loud noise,
Under a sack of tobacco. Until he found it
He could never be whole again
                              —but the hunger creeps
Like a vine about me, crushing my narrow wisdom,
Crushing my thoughts—
                    He couldn't stay with Melora.
He couldn't take her back home. If he were Bailey   30
He would know what to do. He would follow the weaver's tune.
He would keep Melora a night from the foggy dew
And then go off with the sunrise to tell the tale
Sometime for a campfire yarn. But he wasn't Bailey.
He saw himself dead without ever having Melora
And he didn't like it.
                    Maybe, after the war.
Maybe he could come back to the hider's place,

Maybe—it is a long time till after the war
And this is now—you took a girl when you found her—

He heard something move and rustle in the close darkness
"What's that?" he said. He got no answering voice
But he knew what it was. He saw a light-footed shadow
Come toward the nest where he lay. For a moment then
He felt weak, half-sickened almost.
                                        Then his heart began
To pound to a marching rhythm that was not harsh
Nor sweet, but enormous cadence.   10
                              "Melora," he said.
His hand went out and touched the cup of her breast.

SONG OF ELLYAT'S HEART

What things shall be said of you,
Terrible beauty in armor?
What things shall be said of you,
Horses riding the sky?
The fleetness, the molten speed,
The rhythm rising like beaten
Drums of barbaric gold
Until fire mixes with fire?   20

The night is a sparkling pit
Where Time no longer has power
But only vast cadence surging
Toward an instant of tiny death.
Then, with the slow withdrawal
Of seas from a rock of moonlight,
The clasping bodies unlock
And the lovers have little words.

What is this spear, this burnished
Arrow in the deep waters   30
That is not quenched by them
Until it has found its mark?
What is this beating of wings
In the formless heart of the tempest?
This wakening of a sun
That was not wakened before?

They have dragged you down from the sky
And broken you with an ocean
Because you carried the day,
Phaëton, charioteer.
But still you loose from the cloud
The matched desires of your horses
And sow on the ripened earth
The quickened, the piercing flame.

What things shall be said of you,
Terrible beauty in armor?   10
Dance that is not a dance,
Brief instant of welded swords.
For a moment we strike the black
Door with a fist of brightness.
And then it is over and spent,
And we sink back into life.

Back to the known, the sure,
The river of sleep and waking,
The dreams floating the river,
The nearness, the conquered peace.   20
You have come and smitten and passed,
Poniard, poniard of sharpness.
The child sleeps in the planet.
The blood sleeps again.

He wasn't going away when he went to the wood.
He told himself that. They had broken the dime together.
They had cut the heart on the tree.
                              The jack-knife cut
Two pinched half-circles of white on the green bark.
The tree-gum bled from the cuts in sticky, clear drops,   30
And there you were.
                    And shortly the bark would dry
Dead on the living wood and leave the white heart
All through the winter, all through the rain and snow,
A phantom-blaze to guide a tall phantom-hunter
Who came in lightness along a leaf-buried path.
All through the snowing winter it would be white.
It would take many springs to cover that white again.

What have I done in idleness, in sweet idleness,
What have I done to the forest?
                                    I have marked
A tree to be my own with a jack-knife blade
In idleness, in sweet idleness. I have loosed
A dryad out of the tree to chain me with wild
Grapevines and forest trailers forever and ever
To the hider's place, to the outcast house of the lost,
And now, when I would be free, I am free no more.
He thought of practical matters. There ought to be   10
A preacher and a gold ring and a wedding-dress,
Only how could there be?

If he only could go away without going away
And have everything turn out just as it ought to be
Without rings or hiding!
                                    He told himself "I'm all right.
I'm not like Bailey. I wouldn't sleep with a girl
Who never slept with anybody before
And then just go off and leave her."
                                    But it was Melora.   20
It wasn't seducing a girl. It was all mixed up.
All real where it ought to be something told in a sermon,
And all unreal when you had to do something about it,
His thoughts went round and round like rats in a cage,
But all he knew was—
                    he was sick for a room
And a red tablecloth with tasselled fringes,
Where a wife knitted on an end of a scarf,
A father read his paper through the same
Unchanging spectacles with the worn bows   30
And a young girl beneath a nickeled lamp
Soundlessly conjugated Latin verbs,
"Amo, amas, amat," and still no sound—

Slight dryad, trailing the green, curled vines of the Spring,
I hate you for this moment, I hate your white breast
And idleness, sweet, hidden idleness—
He started awake. He had been walking through dreams.
How far had he come? He studied the sun and the trees.
Was he lost? No, there was the way.
                                    He turned back slowly,   40

144

To the dryad, the idleness—to the cheesecloth veil,
The incredible preacher, the falling out of life.
He'd ask her this evening where you could find such preachers.
The old man mustn't know till the thing was done
Or he would turn to a father out of a cheap
Play, a cheap shotgun father with a wool beard
Roaring gilt rhetoric—and loading a musket.
He got the dry grins.
                    If the property-father shot him
Would they carve his name on the soldiers' monument   10
After the war?
                There should be a special tablet.
"Here lies John Ellyat Junior, shot and killed
By an angry father for the great cause of Union.
'How sleep the brave.'"
                 He stumbled and looked around him.
"Well, I might go on as far as the road," he said.

A little while later he burst through the screen of brush.
And saw the highroad below him.
                    He wiped his face.   20
The road dipped down a hill to a little bridge.
He was safe enough now.
                What was it Melora had said?
The highroad was six miles away from the farm,
Due west, and he could tell the west by the sun.
He must have covered a dozen, finding the road,
But getting back would be easy.
                The sun was high.
He ought to be starting soon. But he lay down
And stared for a while at the road. It was good to see   30
A road in the open again, a dust-bitten road
Where people and horses went along to a town.
—Dryad, deep in the woods, your trails are small,
Winding and faint—they run between grass and flowers—
But it is good once more to come on a road
That is not drowsy with your idleness—
He looked down toward the bridge. There were moving blobs
   of dust
Crossing it—men on horses. His heart gave a strange
Throb of desire. What were they? They looked like soldiers.   40

Blue coats or grey? He could not tell for the dust.
He'd have to get back in the woods before they passed,
He was a hider now. But he kept on staring
A long two minutes, trying to make them out,
Till his eyes stung. One man had a yellow beard
And carried his rifle slung the Missouri way
But there were Missouri troops on either side.
In a minute he could tell—and wriggle away—

A round stick jabbed in his back.
                              A slow voice said   10
"Reach for the sky, Yank, or I'll nachully drill yuh."
His hands flew up.
                    "Yuh're the hell of a scout," said the voice
With drawling scorn. "Yuh h'ain't even got a gun.
I could have picked yuh off ten minutes ago,
Yuh made more noise than a bear, bustin thru' that bresh.
What'd yuh ust to work at—wrappin' up corsets?
Yeah—yuh kin turn around."
                              Jack Ellyat turned
Incredulously.   20
              "Well, I'll be damned," said the boy
In butternut clothes with the wrinkled face of a leaf.
"Yuh're a young 'un all right—aw, well, don't take it so hard.
Our boys get captured, too. Hey, Billy!" he called,
"Got a Yankee scout."
                      The horse-hoofs stopped in the road.
"Well, bring him along," said a voice.
                                      Jack Ellyat slid
Down a little bank and stood in front of the horses.
He was dazed. This was not happening. But the horses   30
Were there, the butternut men on the horses were there.

A gaunt old man with a sour, dry mouth was talking,
"He's no scout," he said, "He's one of their lousy spies.
Don't he look like a spy? Let's string him up to a tree."
His eye roved, looking for a suitable branch,
His mouth seemed pleased.
                          Ellyat saw two little scooped dishes,
Hung on a balance, wavering in the air.
One was bright tin and carried his life and breath,

146

The other was black. They were balanced with dreadful even-
ness.
But now the black dish trembled, starting to fall.

"Hell, no," said the boy with the face like a wrinkled leaf.
"He's a scout all right. What makes yuh so savage, Ben?
Yuh're always hankerin' after a necktie-party.
Who captured the bugger anyhow?"
                                        "Oh, well,"
Said the other man. "Oh, well." He spat in the dust.
"Anyhow," he said, with a hungry look at Ellyat,   10
"He's got good boots."
                        The boy with the wrinkled face
Remarked that, as for the boots, no Arkansaw catfish
Was going to take them away from their lawful captor.

The rest sat their horses loosely and looked at him
With mild curiosity, ruminating tobacco.
Ellyat tried to think. He could not think.
                                        He was free,
These stuffless men on stuffless horses had freed him
From dryads and fathers, from cheesecloth veils and Melora.   20
He began to talk fast. He didn't hear what he said.
"But I've got to get back," he said. Then he stopped. They
    laughed.
"Oh, yuh'll get over it, Bub," said the wrinkled boy,
"It ain't so bad. You won't have to fight no more.
Maybe yuh'll git exchanged. Git up on that horse.
No, take off them boots first, thanks."
                                        He slung the boots
Around his neck. "Now I got some good boots," he said.
And grinned at the gaunt man with the sour mouth.   30
"Now, Bub, I'll just tie yuh a little with this yere rope
And then you won't be bustin' loose from the gang.
Grab the pommel as well as yuh kin."
                                        The gaunt man coughed.
"I tell you," he said, in a disappointed voice,
"If we just strung him up it'd make things a hull lot easier.
He's a spy for sure, and everyone strings up spies.
We got a long piece to go yet and he's a nuisance."

"Aw, shut yore face," said Jim Breckinridge in a drawl,
"Yuh kin hang any Yanks yuh ketch on a piece uh dishrag,   40

147

Yuh ain't caught no armies yit."
                              The gaunt man was silent.
Ellyat saw the little tin dish that carried the life
Slowly sink down, to safety, the black dish rise.
"Come on," said Billy. The horses started to move,
Stirring a dust that rose for a little while
In a faint cloud. But after the horses had gone,
The cloud settled, the road went to sleep again.

BOOK FOUR:

The Last of Wingate Glory

The war takes its toll of the gentle living of the South. Wingate Hall is feeling the pinch of poverty, but the three stout pillars that have held up its tradition, the two royal slaves, Aunt Bess and Cudjo, and the mistress, Mary Lou, will not let fear of what the future may bring lessen their preparedness for Clay Wingate's brief return home.

Sally Dupré finds herself no match for Lucy Weatherby's coquettish smile. Clay wavers between the two girls until once again the Black Horse Troop starts back and Sally is left to feed her heart to the hawk while Lucy dreams of new conquests.

Now the scene expands and the campaigns of the East and of the West are seen. We learn that McClellan is slow to take Richmond, that Washington remains guarded, that generals come and go. We look into the future and discover what the Army of the Potomac and the Army of Northern Virginia must yet undergo.

The people we have known live on their lives, in action, at home, in prison.

It is three years since John Brown was buried. His song goes on, but the slave is still a slave.

I. Cudjo mourns the days of plenty

Strike up, strike up for Wingate's tune,
Strike up for Sally Dupré!
Strike up, strike up for the April moon,
And the rain on the lilac spray!
For Wingate Hall in its pride once more,
For the branch of myrtle over the door,
Because the men are back from the war;
For the clean bed waiting the dusty rider
And the punchbowl cooling for thirsty throttles,
For the hot cooks boiling the hams in cider   10
And Cudjo grinning at cobwebbed bottles—
The last of the wine, the last of the wine,
The last of the '12 and the '29!
Three times voyaged around the Cape
Till old Judge Brooke, with an oath oracular,
Pronounced it the living soul of the grape,
And the veriest dregs to be supernacular!

Old Judge Brooke with his double chins
Sighing over his hoarded claret
And sending the last of his cherished bins   20
To the hospital-doctors with "I can spare it
But if you give it to some damned layman
Who doesn't know brandy from licorice-water
And sports a white ribbon, by fire and slaughter,
I'll hang the lot of you higher than Haman!"

The Wingate cellars are nearly bare
But Miss Louisa is doing her hair
In the latest style of Napoleon's court.
(A blockade-runner brought the report,
A blockade-runner carried the silk,   30
Heavy as bullion and white as milk,
That makes Amanda a gleaming moth.
For the coasts are staked with a Union net
But the dark fish slip through the meshes yet,
Shadows sliding without a light,
Through the dark of the moon, in the dead of night,
Carrying powder, carrying cloth,
Hoops for the belle and guns for the fighter,

151

Guncotton, opium, bombs and tea.
Fashionplates, quinine and history.
For Charleston's corked with a Northern fleet
And the Bayou City lies at the feet
Of a damn-the-torpedoes commodore;
The net draws tighter and ever tighter,
But the fish dart past till the end of the war,
From Wilmington to the Rio Grande,
And the sandy Bahamas are Dixie Land
Where the crammed, black shadows start for the trip   10
That, once clean-run, will pay for the ship.
They are caught, they are sunk with all aboard.
They scrape through safely and praise the Lord,
Ready to start with the next jammed hold
To pull Death's whiskers out in the cold,
The unrecorded skippers and mates
Whom even their legend expurgates,
The tough daredevils from twenty ports
Who thumbed their noses at floating forts
And gnawed through the bars of a giant's cage   20
For a cause or a laugh or a living-wage,
Who five long years on a sea of night,
Pumped new blood to the vein bled white
—And, incidentally, made the money
For the strangely rich of the after years—
For the flies will come to the open honey,
And, should war and hell have the same dimensions,
Both have been paved with the best intentions
And both are as full of profiteers.)

The slaves in the quarters are buzzing and talking.   30
—All through the winter the ha'nts went walking,
Ha'nts the size of a horse or bigger,
Ghost-patrollers, scaring a nigger,
But now the winter's over and broken,
And the sun shines out like a lovin' token,
There's goin' to be mixin's and mighty doin's,
Chicken-fixin's and barbecuin's,
Old Marse Billy's a-comin' home!
He's slewn a brigade with a ha'nts's jaw-bone,
He's slewn an army with one long sabre,   40
He's scared old Linkum 'most to death,

152

Now he's comin' home to rest from he labor,
Play on he fiddle and catch he breath!

The little black children with velvet eyes
Tell each other tremendous lies.
They play at Manassas with guns of peeled
Willow-stalks from the River Field,
Chasing the Yanks into Kingdom Come
While one of them beats on a catskin drum.
They are happy because they don't know why.
They scare themselves pretending to die,   10
But all through the scare, and before and after,
Their voices are rich with the ancient laughter,
The negro laughter, the blue-black rose,
The laughter that doesn't end with the lips
But shakes the belly and curls the toes
And prickles the end of the fingertips.

Up through the garden, in through the door,
That undercurrent of laughter floats,
It mounts like a sea from floor to floor,
A dark sea, covering painted boats,   20
A warm sea, smelling of earth and grass,
It seeps through the back of the cheval-glass
Where Amanda stares at her stately self
Till her eyes are bright with a different spark,
It sifts like a dye, where Louise's peering
In a shagreen-case for a garnet ear-ring
Till the little jewels shine in the dark,
It spills like a wave in the crowded kitchen
Where the last good sugar of Wingate Hall
Is frosting a cake like a Polar Highland   30
And fat Aunt Bess in her ice-wool shawl
Spends the hoarded knowledge her heart is rich in
On oceans of trifle and floating-island.

Fat Aunt Bess is older than Time
But her eyes still shine like a bright, new dime,
Though two generations have gone to rest
On the sleepy mountain of her breast.
Wingate children in Wingate Hall,
From the first weak cry in the bearing-bed

She has petted and punished them, one and all,
She has closed their eyes when they lay dead.
She raised Marse Billy when he was puny,
She cared for the Squire when he got loony,
Fed him and washed him and combed his head,
Nobody else would do instead.
The matriarch of the weak and the young,
The lazy crooning, comforting tongue.
She has had children of her own,
But the white-skinned ones are bone of her bone.   10
They may not be hers, but she is theirs,
And if the shares were unequal shares,
She does not know it, now she is old.
They will keep her out of the rain and cold.
And some were naughty, and some were good,
But she will be warm while they have wood,
Rule them and spoil them and play physician
With the vast, insensate force of tradition,
Half a nuisance and half a mother
And legally neither one nor the other,   20
Till at last they follow her to her grave,
The family-despot, and the slave.

—Curious blossom from bitter ground,
Master of masters who left you bound,
Who shall unravel the mingled strands
Or read the anomaly of your hands?
They have made you a shrine and a humorous fable,
But they kept you a slave while they were able,
And yet, there was something between the two
That you shared with them and they shared with you,   30
Brittle and dim, but a streak of gold,
A genuine kindness, unbought, unsold,
Graciousness founded on hopeless wrong
But queerly living and queerly strong. . . .

There were three stout pillars that held up all
The weight and tradition of Wingate Hall.
One was Cudjo and one was you
And the third was the mistress, Mary Lou.
Mary Lou Wingate, as slightly made
And as hard to break as a rapier-blade.   40

154

Bristol's daughter and Wingate's bride,
Never well since the last child died
But staring at pain with courteous eyes.
When the pain outwits it, the body dies,
Meanwhile the body bears the pain.
She loved her hands and they made her vain,
The tiny hands of her generation
That gathered the reins of the whole plantation;
The velvet sheathing the steel demurely
In the trained, light grip that holds so surely. 10

She was at work by candlelight,
She was at work in the dead of night,
Smoothing out troubles and healing schisms
And doctoring phthisics and rheumatisms,
Guiding the cooking and watching the baking,
The sewing, the soap-and-candle-making,
The brewing, the darning, the lady-daughters,
The births and deaths in the negro-quarters,
Seeing that Suke had some new, strong shoes
And Joe got a week in the calaboose, 20
While Dicey's Jacob escaped a whipping
And the jellybag dripped with its proper dripping,
And the shirts and estrangements were neatly mended,
And all of the tasks that never ended.

Her manner was gracious but hardly fervent
And she seldom raised her voice to a servant.
She was often mistaken, not often blind,
And she knew the whole duty of womankind,
To take the burden and have the power
And seem like the well-protected flower, 30
To manage a dozen industries
With a casual gesture in scraps of ease,
To hate the sin and to love the sinner
And to see that the gentlemen got their dinner
Ready and plenty and piping-hot
Whether you wanted to eat or not.
And always, always, to have the charm
That makes the gentlemen take your arm
But never the bright, unseemly spell
That makes strange gentlemen love too well, 40

155

Once you were married and settled down
With a suitable gentleman of your own.

And when that happened, and you had bred
The requisite children, living and dead,
To pity the fool and comfort the weak
And always let the gentlemen speak
To succor your love from deep-struck roots
When gentlemen went to bed in their boots,
And manage a gentleman's whole plantation
In the manner befitting your female station.   10

This was the creed that her mother taught her
And the creed that she taught to every daughter.
She knew her Bible—and how to flirt
With a swansdown fan and a brocade skirt.
For she trusted in God but she liked formalities
And the world and Heaven were both realities.
—In Heaven, of course, we should all be equal,
But, until we came to that golden sequel,
Gentility must keep to gentility
Where God and breeding had made things stable,   20
While the rest of the cosmos deserved civility
But dined in its boots at the second-table.
This view may be reckoned a trifle narrow,
But it had the driving force of an arrow,
And it helped Mary Lou to stand up straight,
For she was gentle, but she could hate
And she hated the North with the hate of Jael
When the dry hot hands went seeking the nail,
The terrible hate of women's ire,
The smoky, the long-consuming fire.   30
The Yankees were devils, and she could pray,
For devils, no doubt, upon Judgment Day,
But now in the world, she would hate them still
And send the gentlemen out to kill.

The gentlemen killed and the gentlemen died,
But she was the South's incarnate pride
That mended the broken gentlemen
And sent them out to the war again,
That kept the house with the men away

And baked the bricks where there was no clay,
Made courage from terror and bread from bran
And propped the South on a swansdown fan
Through four long years of ruin and stress,
The pride—and the deadly bitterness.

Let us look at her now, let us see her plain,
She will never be quite like this again.
Her house is rocking under the blast
And she hears it tremble, and still stands fast,
But this is the last, this is the last.   10
The last of the wine and the white corn meal,
The last high fiddle singing the reel,
The last of the silk with the Paris label,
The last blood-thoroughbred safe in the stable
—Yellow corn meal and a jackass colt,
A door that swings on a broken bolt,
Brittle old letters spotted with tears
And a wound that rankles for fifty years—
This is the last of Wingate Hall,
The last bright August before the Fall,   20
Death has been near, and Death has passed,
But this is the last, this is the last.
There will be hope, and a scratching pen,
There will be cooking for tired men,
The waiting for news with shut, hard fists,
And the blurred, strange names in the battle-lists,
The April sun and the April rain.
But never this day come back again.

But she is lucky, she does not see
The axe-blade sinking into the tree   30
Day after day, with a slow, sure stroke
Till it chops the mettle from Wingate oak.
The house is busy, the cups are filling
To welcome the gentlemen back from killing,
The hams are boiled and the chickens basting,
Fat Aunt Bess is smiling and tasting,
Cudjo's napkin is superfine,
He knows how the gentlemen like their wine,
Amanda is ready, Louisa near her,
Glistering girls from a silver mirror,   40

Everyone talking, everyone scurrying,
Upstairs and downstairs, laughing and hurrying,
Everyone giving and none denying,
There is only living, there is no dying.
War is a place but it is not here,
The peace and the victory are too near.
One more battle, and Washington taken,
The Yankees mastered, the South unshaken,
Fiddlers again, and the pairing season,
The old-time rhyme and the old-time reason,   10
The grandchildren, and the growing older
Till at last you need a gentleman's shoulder,
And the pain can stop, for the frayed threads sever,
But the house and the courtesy last forever.

So Wingate found it, riding at ease,
The cloud-edge lifting over the trees,
A white-sail glimmer beyond the rise,
A sugar-castle that strained the eyes,
Then mounting, mounting, the shining spectre
Risen at last from the drop of nectar,   20
The cloud expanding, the topsails swelling,
The doll's house grown to a giant's dwelling,
Porches and gardens and ells and wings
Linking together like puzzle-rings,
Till the parts dissolved in a steadfast whole,
And Wingate saw it, body and soul.

Saw it completely, and saw it gleam,
The full-rigged vessel, the sailing dream,
The brick and stone that were somehow quick
With a ghost not native to stone and brick,   30
The name held high and the gift passed on
From Wingate father to Wingate son,
No longer a house but a conjur-stone
That could hate and sorrow and hold its own
As long as the seed of Elspeth Mackay
Could mix its passion with Wingate clay
And the wind and the river had memories. . . .

Wingate saw it all—but with altered eyes.
He was not yet broken on any wheel,

He had no wound of the flesh to heal,
He had seen one battle, but he was still
The corn unground by the watermill,
He had ridden the rainy winter through
And he and Black Whistle were good as new,
The Black Horse Troop still carried its pride
And rode as the Yankees could not ride,
But, when he remembered a year-old dawn,
Something had come and something gone,
And even now, when he smelt the Spring,   10
And his heart was hot with his homecoming,
There was a whisper in his ear
That said what he did not wish to hear,

(This is the last, this is the last,
Hurry, hurry, this is the last,
Drink the wine before yours is spilled,
Kiss the sweetheart before you're killed,
She will be loving, and she will grieve,
And wear your heart on her golden sleeve
And marry your friend when he gets his leave.   20
It does not matter that you are still
The corn unground by the watermill,
The stones grind till they get their will.
Pluck the flower that hands can pluck,
Touch the walls of your house for luck,
Eat of the fat and drink the sweet,
There is little savor in dead men's meat.
It does not matter that you once knew
Future and past and a different you,
That went by when the wind first blew.   30
There is no future, there is no past,
There is only this hour and it goes fast,
Hurry, hurry, this is the last,
This is the last,
This is the last.)

He heard it and faced it and let it talk.
The tired horses dropped to a walk.
And then Black Whistle lunged at the bit
And whinnied because he was alive,
And he saw the porch where the evenings sit   40

And the tall magnolias shading the drive,
He heard the bell of his father's mirth,
"Tallyho, Yanks—we've gone to earth!
Home, boy, home to Wingate Hall,
Home in spite of them, damn them all!"
He was stabbed by the rays of the setting sun,
He felt Black Whistle break to a run,
And then he was really there again,
Before he had time to think or check,
And a boy was holding his bridle-rein,   10
And Mary Lou's arms were around his neck.

II. *Sally Dupré and Wingate talk with the music*

Sally Dupré and Wingate talk with the music. . . .

The dance. Such a lovely dance. But you dance so lightly.
Amanda dances so well. But you dance so lightly.

(Do you remember the other dance?)

Phil Ferrier was here, remember, last year.

(He danced with me. He could dance rather well. He is dead.)

We were all so sorry when we heard about Phil.

(How long will you live and be able to dance with me?)

Yes. Phil was a fine fellow. We all liked Phil.   20

(Do not talk of the dead.
At first we talk of the dead, we write of the dead,
We send their things to their people when we can find them,
We write letters to you about them, we say we liked him,
He fought well, he died bravely, here is his sword,
Here is his pistol, his letters, his photograph case;
You will like to have these things, they will do instead.
But the war goes on too long.
After a while you still want to talk of the dead.
But we are too tired. We will send you the pistol still,   30

160

The photograph-case, the knickknacks, if we can find them,
But the war has gone on too long.
We cannot talk to you still, as we used to, about the dead.)

Nancy Huguenot's here tonight. Have you danced with her yet?
She didn't want to come. She was brave to come.

(Phil Ferrier was Nancy's lover.
She sent him off. She cut her hair for a keepsake.
They were going to be married as soon as he came back.
For a long time she dressed in black.
Then one morning she rose, and looked at the sun on the wall,   10
She put on a dress with red sleeves and a red, striped shawl,
She said "Phil was my beau. He wouldn't have liked me in black."
She used to cry quite a lot but she hasn't cried much since then.
I think she'll get well and marry somebody else.
I think she's right. If I had to wear grief for a lover,
I wouldn't wear black.
I would wear my best green silk and my Empire sacque
And walk in the garden at home and feel the wind
Blow through my rags of honor forever and ever.
And after that, when I married some other beau,   20
I would make a good wife and raise my children on sweet
Milk, not on poison, though it might have been so.
And my husband would never know
When he turned to me, when I kissed him, when we were kind,
When I cleaned his coat, when we talked about dresses and
    weather,
He had married something that belonged to the wind
And felt the blind
And always stream of that wind on her too-light bones,
Neither fast nor slow, but never checked or resigned,   30
Blowing through rags of honor forever and ever.)

They are calling for partners again. Shall we dance again?

(Why do we hate each other so well, when we
Are tied together by something that will not free us?
If I see you across a room, I will go to you,
If you see me across a room, you will come to me,
And yet we hate each other.)

Not yet, for a minute. I want to watch for a minute.

(I do not hate you. I love you. But you must take me.
I will not take your leavings nor you my pity.
I must break you first for a while and you must break me.
We are too strong to love the surrendered city.
So we hate each other.)

That's a pretty girl over there. Beautiful hair.

(She is the porcelain you play at being.)

Yes, isn't she. Her name is Lucy Weatherby.

(I hate her hair. I hate her porcelain air.)   10

She can't be from the county or I'd remember her.

(I know that kind of mouth. Your mouth is not that.
Your mouth is generous and bitter and sweet.
If I kissed your mouth, I would have to be yours forever.
Her mouth is pretty. You could kiss it awhile.)

No, they're kin to the Shepleys. Lucy comes from Virginia.

(I know that kind of mouth. I know that hair.
I know the dolls you like to take in your hands,
The dolls that all men like to take in their hands,
I will not fight with a doll for you or any one.)   20

We'd better dance now.

(Lucy Weatherby.
When this dance is done, I will leave you and dance with her.
I know that shallow but sufficient mouth.)

As you please.

(Lucy Weatherby.
I will make an image of you, a doll in wax.
I will pierce the little wax palms with silver bodkins.
No, I will not.)

162

That's good music. It beats in your head.

(It beats in the head, it beats in the head,
It ties the heart with a scarlet thread,
This is the last,
This is the last,
Hurry, hurry, this is the last.
We dance on a floor of polished sleet,
But the little cracks are beginning to meet,
Under the play of our dancing feet.
I do not care. I am Wingate still.   10
The corn unground by the watermill.
And I am yours while the fiddles spill,
But my will has a knife to cut your will,
My birds will never come to your hill.

You are my foe and my only friend,
You are the steel I cannot bend,
You are the water at the world's end.

But Wingate Hall must tumble down,
Tumble down, tumble down,
A dream dissolving, a ruined thing,
Before we can melt from the shattered crown   20
Gold enough for a wedding-ring.
And Wingate Hall must lie in the dust,
And the wood rot and the iron rust
And the vines grow over the broken bust,
Before we meet without hate or pride,
Before we talk as lover and bride,
Before the daggers of our offence
Have the color of innocence,
And nothing is said and all is said,   30
And we go looking for secret bread,
And lie together in the same bed.)

Yes, it's good music, hear it lift.

(It is too mellow, it is too swift,
I am dancing alone in my naked shift,
I am dancing alone in the snowdrift.
You are my lover and you my life,

My peace and my unending strife
And the edge of the knife against my knife.
I will not make you a porcelain wife.

We are linked together for good and all,
For the still pool and the waterfall,
But you are married to Wingate Hall.
And Wingate Hall must tumble down,
Tumble down, tumble down,
Wingate Hall must tumble down,
An idol broken apart,   10
Before I sew on a wedding gown
And stitch my name in your heart.
And Wingate Hall must lie in the grass,
And the silk stain and the rabbits pass
And the sparrows wash in the gilded glass,
Before the fire of our anger smothers,
And our sorrows can laugh at their lucky brothers,
Before the knives of our enmity
Are buried under the same green tree
And nothing is vowed and all is vowed   20
And we have forgotten how to be proud,
And we sleep like cherubs in the same cloud.)

III.   The Dixie Angel

Lucy Weatherby, cuddled up in her bed,
Drifted along toward sleep with a smile on her mouth,
"I was pretty tonight," she thought, "I was pretty tonight.
Blue's my color—blue that matches my eyes.
I always ought to wear blue. I'm sorry for girls
Who can't wear that sort of blue. Her name is Sally
But she's too dark to wear the colors I can,
I'd like to give her my blue dress and see her wear it,   30
She'd look too gawky, poor thing.
                                        He danced with her
For a while at first but I hadn't danced with him then,
He danced with me after that. He's rather a dear.
I wonder how long he'll be here. I think I like him.
I think I'm going to be pretty while I am here.

Lucy Weatherby—Lucy Shepley—Lucy Wingate—
Huger's so jealous, nearly as jealous as Curly,
Poor Curly—I ought to answer his mother's letter
But it's so hard answering letters."

                              She cried a little,
Thinking of Curly. The tears were fluent and warm,
They did not sting in her eyes. They made her feel brave.
She could hardly remember Curly any more
But it was right to cry for him, now and then,
Slight tears at night and a long, warm, dreamless sleep   10
That left you looking pretty.
                              She dried the tears
And thought to herself with a pleasant little awe,
"You really are mighty brave, dear. You really are.
Nobody would think your beau was killed at Manassas."
—She could hardly remember Curly any more—
She tried to make Curly's face come out of the darkness
But it was too hard—the other faces kept coming—
Huger Shepley and all the Virginia boys
And now this new boy's face with the dark, keen eyes.   20

Boys who were privates, boys who were majors and captains,
Nice old Generals who patted your shoulder,
Darling convalescents who called you an angel—
A whole, great lucky-bag of nice, thrilling boys,
Fighting for you—and the South and the Cause, of course.
You were a flame for the Cause. You sang songs about it.
You sent white feathers to boys who didn't enlist
And bunches of flowers to boys who were suitably wounded.
You wouldn't dream of making peace with the North
While a single boy was left to fight for the Cause   30
And they called you the Dixie Angel.
                             They fought for the Cause
But you couldn't help feeling, too, that they fought for you,
And when they died for you—and the Cause and the flag—
Your heart was tender enough. You were willing to say
You had been engaged to them, even when you hadn't
And answer their mothers' letters in a sweet way,
Though answering letters was hard.
                           She cuddled closer,
"Pillow, tell me I'm pretty, tell me I'm lovely,   40
Tell me I'm nicer than anybody you know,

Tell me that nice new boy is thinking about me,
Tell me that Sally girl couldn't wear my blue,
Tell me the war won't end till we've whipped the Yankees,
Tell me I'll never get wrinkles and always have beaus."

IV. *The runaway slave*

The slave got away from Zachary's place that night.
He was a big fellow named Spade with one cropped ear.
He had splay feet and sometimes walked with a limp.
His back was scarred. He was black as a pine at night.
He'd tried to run away a couple of times
—That was how he got some of the marks you could tell him   10
    by—
But he'd been pretty quiet now for a year or so
And they thought he had settled down.
                                    When he got away
He meant to kill Zachary first but the signs weren't right.
He talked to the knife but the knife didn't sweat or heat,
So he just got away instead.
                        When he reached the woods
And was all alone, he was pretty scared for a while,
But he kept on going all night by the big soft stars,   20
Loping as fast as he could on his long splay feet
And when morning broke, he knew he was safe for a time.

He came out on a cleared place, then. He saw the red
Sun spill over the trees.
                        He threw his pack
Down on the ground and started to laugh and laugh,
"Spade, boy, Spade, you's lucky to git dis far.
You never managed to git dis far before,
De Lawd's sho'ly with you, Spade."
                                He ate and drank.   30
He drew a circle for Zachary's face in the ground
And spat in the circle. Then he thought of his woman.
"She's sho'ly a grievin' woman dis mawnin', Spade."
The thought made him sad at first, but he soon cheered up.
"She'll do all right as soon as she's thu with grievin'.
Grievin' yaller gals always does all right.
Next time I'se gwine to git me a coal-black gal.

166

I'se tired of persimmon-skins.
                              I'se gwine to break loose.
De signs is right dis time. I'se gwine to be free,
Free in de Norf."
                        He saw himself in the North.
He had a stovepipe hat and a coal-black gal.
He had a white-folks' house and a regular mule.
He worked for money and nobody ever owned him.
He got religion and dollars and lucky dice
And everybody he passed in the white folks' street   1C
Said "Good mawnin', Mr. Spade—Mr. Spade, good mawnin'."
He chuckled aloud. "Good mawnin', Mistuh Spade,
Gwine to be free, Mistuh Spade—yes, suh, Mistuh Spade!"
For a lazy moment, he was already there—
Then he stiffened, nostrils flaring, at a slight sound.
It couldn't be dogs already.
                              "Jesus," he whispered,
"Sweet, lovin' Jesus, don't let 'em git me again,
Burn me up, but don't let 'em git me again,
Dey's gwine to cut me apart."   20
                              The rabbit ran past.
He stared at it for a moment with wild, round eyes,
Started a yell of laughter—and choked it off.
"Dat ain't no nachul rabbit dere, Spade, boy.
Dat's a sign. Yes, suh. You better start makin' tracks.
Take your foot in your hand, Mistuh Spade."
                              He swung the bundle
Up on his shoulders and slid along through the trees.
The bundle was light. He was going to be hungry soon
And the big splay feet would soon be bleeding and sore,   30
But, as he went, he shook with uncanny chuckles.
"Good mawnin', Mr. Spade—glad to see you dis mawnin'
How's Mrs. Spade, Mr. Spade?"

V. The Black Horse Troop returns to war

Sally Dupré, from the high porch of her house
Stared at the road.
                        They would be here soon enough.
She had waved a flag the last time they went away.

167

This time she would wave her hand or her handkerchief.
That was what women did. The column passed by
And the women waved, and it came back and they waved,
And, in between, if you loved, you lived by a dull
Clock of long minutes that passed like sunbonneted women
Each with the same dry face and the same set hands.

(I have read; they have told me that love is a pretty god
With light wings stuck to his shoulders.
                                        They did not tell me
That love is nursing a hawk with yellow eyes,   10
That love is feeding your heart to the beak of the hawk
Because an old woman, gossiping, uttered a name.)

They were coming now.
She remembered the first time.
They were different now. They rode with a different rein.
They rode all together. They knew where they were going.
They were famous now, but she wondered about the fame.
And yet, as she wondered, she felt the tears in her blood
Because they could ride so easily.
                                        He was there.   20
She fed her heart to the hawk and watched him ride.

She thought, "But they like this, too. They are like small boys
Going off to cook potatoes over a fire
Deep in the woods, where no women can ever come
To say how blackened and burnt the potatoes are
And how you could cook them better back in a house.
Oh, they like to come home. When they're sick they like to come
    home,
They dream about home—they write you they want to come
    back,   30
And they come back and live in the house for a while
And raise their sons to hear the same whistle-tune
Under the window, the whistle calling the boys
Out to the burnt potatoes.
                        O whistler Death,
What have we done to you in a barren month,
In a sterile hour, that our lovers should die before us?"
Then she thought. "No, no, I can't bear it. It cannot be borne."
And knowing this, bore it.

He saw her. He turned his horse.
"If he comes here, I can't keep it back, I can't keep it back,
I can't stand it, don't let him come." He was coming now.
He rides well, she thought, while her hands made each other cold.
I will have to remember how. And his face is sharper.
The moustache quite changes his face. The face that I saw
While he was away was clean-shaven and darker-eyed.
I must change that, now. I will have to remember that.
It is very important.

          He swung from Black Whistle's back.   10
His spurs made a noise on the porch. She twisted her hands.
"If I shut my eyes, I can make him kiss me. I will not."

They were saying good-by, now. She heard polite voices say-
    ing it.
Then the voices ended. "No, no, it is not to be borne,
It is the last twist of the vise."
                    Her will snapped then.
When she looked at him, she knew that the knives were edgeless.
In an instant life would begin, life would be forever.

His eyes wavered. There was a thin noise in her ears,   20
A noise from the road.
            The instant fell and lay dead
Between them like something broken.

She turned to see what had killed it.

Lucy Weatherby, reining a bright bay mare,
Played with the braided lash of a riding-whip
And talked to Wingate's father with smiling eyes,
While Huger Shepley tried to put in a word
And the whole troop clustered about her.
                 Her habit was black   30
But she had a knot of bright ribbons pinned at her breast,
Red and blue—the Confederate colors.
                They had cheered her.
They had cheered her, riding along with her colored ribbons.
It was that which had killed the instant.
              Sally looked
At the face with the new moustache she had to remember.
"Good-by," she said. The face bent over her hand

And kissed it acceptably.
                          Then the face had gone.
He was back with the others now. She watched for a minute.
Lucy was unpinning her knot of ribbons.
She saw a dozen hands go up for the knot
And Lucy laugh her sweet laugh and shake her bright head,
Glance once at Huger Shepley and once at Clay,
And then toss the colored knot to the guidon-bearer
Who grinned and tied the ribbons around the staff
While some of them cheered again.   10
                          Then the horses moved.
They went by Lucy. Lucy was waving her hand.
She had tears in her eyes and was saying brave words to the
     soldiers.
Sally watched a back and a horse go out of sight.
She was tired, then.
When the troop had quite disappeared
Lucy rode up to the house.
                          The two women kissed
And talked for a while about riding-habits and war.   20
"I just naturally love every boy in the Black Horse Troop,
Don't you, Sally darling? They're all so nice and polite,
Quite like our Virginia boys, and the Major's a dear,
And that nice little one with the guidon is perfectly sweet.
You ought to have heard what he said when I gave him the knot.
Though, of course, I can tell why you didn't come down to the
     road,
War's terrible, isn't it? All those nice boys going off—
I feel just the way you do, darling—we just have to show them
Whenever we can that we know they are fighting for us,   30
Fighting for God and the South and the cause of the right—
'Law, Chile, don't you fret about whether you's pretty or plain,
You just do what you kin, and the good Lawd'll brighten your
     tracks.'
That's what my old mammy would tell me when I was knee-high
And I always remember and just try to do what I can
For the boys and the wounded and—well, that's it, isn't it, dear?
We've all got to do what we can in this horrible war."
Sally agreed that we had, and drank from a cup.
She thought. "Lucy Weatherby. Yes. I must look for a doll.   40
I must make a doll with your face, an image of wax.
I must call that doll by your name."

VI. *The scene expands*

Now the scene expands, we must look at the scene as a whole.
How are the gameboards chalked and the pieces set? *chess*
There is an Eastern game and a Western game.
In the West, blue armies try to strangle the long
Snake of the Mississippi with iron claws;
Buell and Grant against Bragg and Beauregard.
They have hold of the head of the snake where it touches the
  Gulf,
New Orleans is taken, the fangs of the forts drawn out,
The ambiguous Butler wins ambiguous fame   10
By issuing orders stating that any lady
Who insults a Union soldier in uniform
Shall be treated as a streetwalker plying her trade.
The orders are read and hated. The insults stop
But the ladies remember Butler for fifty years
And make a fabulous devil with pasteboard horns
—"Beast" Butler, the fiend who pilfered the silver spoons—
From a slightly-tarnished, crude-minded, vain politician
Who loved his wife and ached to be a great man.
You were not wise with the ladies, Benjamin Butler,   20
It has been disproved that you stole New Orleans spoons
But the story will chime at the ribs of your name and stain it,
Ghost-silver, clinking against the ribs of a ghost,
As long as the ladies have tongues.
                          Napoleon was wiser
But he could not silence one ugly, clever De Staël. *—learned lady of napoleon*
Make war on the men—the ladies have too-long memories.

The head of the snake is captured—the tail gripped fast—
But the body in between still writhes and resists,
Vicksburg is still unfallen—Grant not yet master—   30
Sheridan, Sherman, Thomas still in the shadow.
The eyes of the captains are fixed on the Eastern game,
The presidents—and the watchers oversea— *England & France*
For there are the two defended kings of the board,
Muddy Washington, with its still-unfinished Capitol,
Sprawling, badly-paved, beset with sharp hogs
That come to the very doorsteps and grunt for crumbs,
Full of soldiers and clerks, full of all the baggage of war,
"Bombproof" officers, veterans back on leave,

Recruits, spies, spies on the spies, politicians, contractors,
Reporters, slackers, ambassadors, bands and harlots,
Negro-boys who organize butting-matches
To please the recruits, tattooers and fortune-tellers,
Rich man, poor man, soldier, beggarman, thief,
And one most lonely man in a drafty White House *Lincoln*
Whose everlasting melancholy runs
Like a deep stream under the funny stories,
The parable-maker, humble in many things
But seldom humble with his fortitude,   10
The sorrowful man who cracked the sure-fire jokes,
Roared over Artemus Ward and Orpheus C. Kerr *Humorous writers*
And drove his six cross mules with a stubborn hand. *of the time*
He has lost a son, but he has no time to grieve for him.
He studies tactics now till late in the night
With the same painful, hewing industry
He put on studying law.
                              McClellan comes, *Book 3*
McClellan goes, McClellan bustles and argues, *Napolean complex*
McClellan is too busy to see the President,   20
McClellan complains of this, complains of that,
The Government is not supporting him,
The Government cannot understand grand strategy,
The Government—
                   McClellan feels abused. *about 35*
McClellan is quite sincere and sometimes right.
They come to the lonely man about McClellan
With various tales.
                   McClellan lacks respect, *1826*
McClellan dreams about a dictatorship,
McClellan does that and this.   30
                   The lonely man
Listens to all the stories and remarks,
"If McClellan wins, I will gladly hold his horse."

A hundred miles away in an arrow-line *Straight South*
Lies the other defended king of the giant chess,
Broad-streeted Richmond.
                        All the baggage of war
Is here as well, the politicians, the troops,
The editors who scream at the government,   40
The slackers, the good and the bad, but the flavor is different:

172

There is something older here, and smaller and courtlier,
The trees in the streets are old trees used to living with people,
Family-trees that remember your grandfather's name.
It is still a clan-city, a family-city, a city
That thinks of the war, on the whole, as a family-matter,
A woman city, devoted and fiercely jealous
As any of the swan-women who ruled it then—
Ready to give their lives and hearts for the South,
But already a little galled by Jefferson Davis
And finding him rather too much of a doctrinaire
With a certain comparative touch of the parvenu.
He is not from Virginia, we never knew his grandfather.

The South is its husband, the South is not quite its master.
It has a soul while Washington is a symbol,
Beautiful, witty, feminine, narrow and valiant,
Unwisely-chosen, perhaps, for a king of the game,
But playing the part with a definite air of royalty
Until, in the end, it stands for the South completely
And when it falls, the sword of the South snaps short.

At present, the war has not yet touched it home.   20
McClellan has landed, on the Peninsula,
But his guns are still far away.
                              The ladies go
To Mrs. Davis's parties in last year's dresses.
Soon they are to cut the green and white chintz curtains
That shade their long drawing-rooms from the lazy sun
To bandage the stricken wounded of Seven Pines.

The lonely man with the chin like John Calhoun's
Works hard and is ill at ease in his Richmond White House.
His health was never too strong—it is tiring now   30
Under a mass of detail, under the strain
Of needless quarrels with secretaries and chiefs
And a Congress already beginning to criticize him.
He puts his trust in God with a charmed devotion
And his faith, too often, in men who can feed his vanity.
They mock him for it. He cannot understand mocking.
There is something in him that prickles the pride of men
Whom Lincoln could have used, and makes them his foes.
Joe Johnston and he have been at odds from the first,

173

Beauregard and he are at odds and will be at odds,
One could go through a list—
                          He is quite as stubborn as Lincoln
In supporting the people he trusts through thick and thin,
But—except for Lee—the people he trusts so far
Seldom do the work that alone can repay the trust.
They fail in the end and his shoulders carry the failure,
And leave him, in spite of his wife, in spite of his God,
Lonely, beginning and end, with that other's loneliness.
The other man could have understood him and used him.   10
He could never have used or comprehended the other.
It is their measure.
                    And yet, a deep loneliness,
A deep devotion, a deep self-sacrifice,
Binds the strange two together.
                              He, too, is to lose
A child in his White House, ere his term is accomplished.
He, too, is to be the scapegoat for all defeat.
And he is to know the ultimate bitterness,
The cause lost after every expense of mind,   20
And bear himself with decent fortitude
In the prison where the other would not have kept him.
One cannot balance tragedy in the scales
Unless one weighs it with the tragic heart.
The other man's tragedy was the greater one
Since the blind fury tore the huger heart,
But this man's tragedy is the more pitiful.
Thus the Eastern board and the two defended kings.
But why is the game so ordered, what crowns the kings?
They are cities of streets and houses like other cities.   30
Baltimore might be taken, and war go on,
Atlanta will be taken and war go on,
Why should these two near cities be otherwise?
We do not fight for the real but for shadows we make.
A flag is a piece of cloth and a word is a sound,
But we make them something neither cloth nor a sound,
Totems of love and hate, black sorcery-stones,
So with these cities.
                    And so the third game is played,
The intricate game of the watchers oversea,   40
The shadow that falls like the shadow of a hawk's wing
Over the double-chessboard until the end—

174

The shadow of Europe, the shadows of England and France,
The war of the cotton against the iron and wheat.
The shadows ponder and mutter, biding their time;
If the knights and bishops that play for the cotton-king
Can take the capital-city of wheat and iron,
The shadow-hands will turn into hands of steel
And intervene for the cotton that feeds the mills.
But if the fable throned on a cotton-bale
Is checkmated by the pawns of iron and wheat,
The shadows will pause, and cleave to iron and wheat,   10
They will go their ways and lift their eyes from the game,
For iron and wheat are not to be lightly held.
So the watchers, searching the board.
                              And so the game.
The blockade grips, the blockade-runners break through,
There are duels and valors, the Western game goes on
And the snake of the Mississippi is tamed at last,
But the fight in the East is the fight between the two kings.
If Richmond is threatened, we threaten Washington,
You check our king with McClellan or Hooker or Grant,   20
We will check your king with Jackson or Early or Lee
And you must draw back strong pieces to shield your king,
For we hold the chord of the circle and you the arc
And we can shift our pieces better than you.

So it runs for years until Jubal Early, riding,
A long twelve months after Gettysburg's high tide,
Sees the steeples of Washington prick the blue June sky
And the Northern king is threatened for the last time.
But, by then, the end is too near, the cotton is withered.
Now the game still hangs in the balance—the cotton in bloom— 30
The shadows of the watchers long on the board.
McClellan has moved his men from their camps at last
In a great sally.
                       There are many gates he can try.
The Valley gate and the old Manassas way,
But he has chosen to ferry his men by sea,
To the ragged half-island between the York and the James
And thrust up a long, slant arm from Fortress Monroe
Northwest toward Richmond.
                                   The roads are sticky and soft,   40
There are forts at Yorktown and unmapped rivers to cross.

175

He has many more men than Johnston or John Magruder
But the country hinders him, and he hinders himself
By always thinking the odds on the other side
And that witches of ruin haunt each move he makes.
But even so—he has boarded that jutting deck
That is the Peninsula, and his forces creep
Slowly toward Richmond, slowly up to the high
Defended captain's cabin of the great ship.
—There was another force that came from its ships
To take a city set on a deck of land,   10
The cause unlike, but the fighting no more stark,
The doom no fiercer, the fame no harder to win.
There are no gods to come with a golden smoke
Here in the mud between the York and the James
And wrap some high-chinned hero away from death.
There are only Bibles and buckles and cartridge belts
That sometimes stop a bullet before it kills
But oftener let it pass.
                         And when Sarpedon
Falls and the heavy darkness stiffens his limbs   20
They will let him lie where he fell, they will not wash him
In the running streams of Scamander, the half-divine,
They will bury him in a shallow and cumbered pit.
But, if you would sing of fighters, sing of these men,
Sing of Fair Oaks and the battered Seven Days,
Not of the raging of Ajax, the cry of Hector,
These men were not gods nor shielded by any gods,
They were men of our shape: they fought as such men may fight
With a mortal skill: when they died it was as men die.

VII. The Army of the Potomac

Army of the Potomac, advancing army,   30
Alloy of a dozen disparate, alien States,
City-boy, farm-hand, bounty-man, first volunteer,
Old regular, drafted recruit, paid substitute,
Men who fought through the war from First Bull Run,
And other men, nowise different in look or purpose,
Whom the first men greeted at first with a ribald cry
"Here they come! Two hundred dollars and a ka-ow!"
Rocks from New England and hickory-chunks from the West,

Bowery boy and clogging Irish adventurer,
Germans who learnt their English under the shells
Or didn't have time to learn it before they died.
Confused, huge weapon, forged from such different metals,
Misused by unlucky swordsmen till you were blunt
And then reforged with anguish and bloody sweat
To be blunted again by one more unlucky captain
Against the millstone of Lee.
                        Good stallion,
Ridden and ridden against a hurdle of thorns   10
By uncertain rider after uncertain rider.
The rider fails and you shiver and catch your breath,
They plaster your wounds and patch up your broken knees,
And then, just as you know the grip of your rider's hands
And begin to feel at home with his horseman's tricks,
Another rider comes with a different seat,
And lunges you at the bitter hurdle again,
And it beats you again—and it all begins from the first,
The patching of wounds, the freezing in winter camps,
The vain mud-marches, the diarrhea, the wastage,   20
The grand reviews, the talk in the newspapers,
The sour knowledge that you were wasted again,
Not as Napoleons waste for a victory
But blindly, unluckily—
                        until at last
After long years, at fish-hook Gettysburg,
The blade and the millstone meet and the blade holds fast.
And, after that, the chunky man from the West,
Stranger to you, not one of the men you loved
As you loved McClellan, a rider with a hard bit,   30
Takes you and uses you as you could be used,
Wasting you grimly but breaking the hurdle down.
You are never to worship him as you did McClellan,
But at the last you can trust him. He slaughters you
But he sees that you are fed. After sullen Cold Harbor
They call him a butcher and want him out of the saddle,
But you have had other butchers who did not win
And this man wins in the end.
                        You see him standing,
Reading a map, unperturbed, under heavy fire.   40
You do not cheer him as the recruits might cheer
But you say "Ulysses doesn't scare worth a darn.

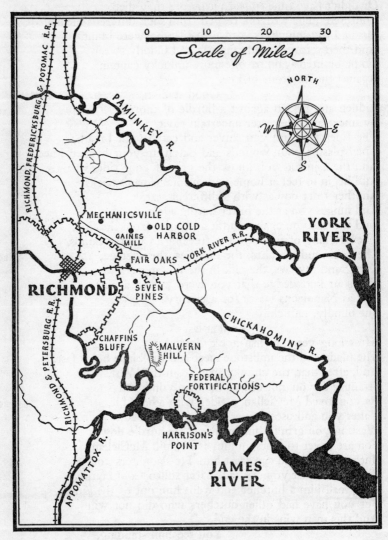

The Peninsula Campaign (Seven Days' Battles)

Ulysses is all right. He can finish the job."
And at last your long lines go past in the Grand Review
And your legend and his begin and are mixed forever.

Now, though, he is still just one of the Western leaders,
And Little Mac is your darling.
                                        You are unshaken
By the ruin of Fredericksburg, the wounds of Antietam,
Chancellorsville is a name in the Wilderness,
Your pickets, posted in front of the Chickahominy,
Hear the churchbells of Richmond, ringing;   10
Listen well to those bells, they are very near tonight,
But you will not hear them again for three harsh years.

Black months of war, hard-featured, defeated months
Between Fair Oaks and Gettysburg,
What is your tale for this army?
What do the men,
So differently gathered for your word to devour,
Say to your ears, deaf with cannon? What do they bring
In powder-pocked hands to the heart of the burst shell?
Let us read old letters awhile,   20
Let us try to hear
The thin, forgotten voices of men forgotten
Crying out of torn scraps of paper, notes scribbled and smudged
On aces, on envelope-backs, on gilt-edged cards stolen out of a
    dead man's haversack.

—Two brothers lay on the field of Fredericksburg
After the assault had failed.
They were unwounded but they could not move,
The sharpshooters covered that patch of ground too well.
They had a breastwork to hide them from the bullets,   30
A shelter of two dead men. One had lost his back,
Scooped out from waist to neck with a solid shot.
The other's legs were gone. They made a good breastwork.
The brothers lay behind them, flat in the mud,
All Sunday till night came down and they could creep off.
They did not dare move their hands for fourteen hours.
—A middle-aged person named Fletcher from Winchester
Enlisted in the Massachusetts Sharpshooters.
He was a crack-duckshooter, skilful and patient.

They gave him the wrong sort of rifle and twenty rounds
And told him to join his company.
It took him days to find it. He had no rations,
He begged bread and green corn and peaches and shot a hog;
So got there at last. He joined just before Antietam.
He'd never been drilled but he knew how to shoot,
Though at first his hands kept shaking.
"It was different kind of gunning from what I was used to,
I was mad with myself that I acted so like a coward."
But as soon as they let him lie down and fight on his own,   10
He felt all right. He had nineteen cartridges now.
The first five each killed a man—he was a good shot—
Then the rifle fouled. He began to get up and fix it,
Mechanically. A bullet went through his lung.
He lay on the field all day. At the end of the day
He was captured, sent to prison, paroled after weeks,
Died later, because of the wound.
That was his war—
Other voices, rising out of the scraps of paper,
Till they mix in a single voice that says over and over   20
"It is cold. It is wet. We marched till we couldn't stand up.
It is muddy here. I wish you could see us here.
I wish everybody at home could see us here.
They would know what war is like. We are still patriotic.
We are going to fight. We hope this general's good.
We hope he can make us win. We'll do all we can.
But I wish we could show everybody who stays at home
What this is like."
Voices of tired men,
Sick, convalescent, afraid of being sick.   30

(Nurses and doctors, savagely, tenderly working,
Trying to beat off death without enough knowledge,
Trying and failing.
Clara Barton, Old Mother Bickerdyke,
Overworked evangels of common sense,
Nursing, tending, clearing a ruthless path
Through the cant and red tape, through the petty jealousies
To the bitter front, bringing up the precious supplies
In spite of hell and high water and pompous fools,
To the deadly place where the surgeons' hands grew stiff   40
Under the load of anguish they had to deal,

Where they bound men's wounds and swabbed them with green
    corn leaves,
There being no other lint.
Whitman, with his sack of tobacco and comfits,
Passing along the terrible, crowded wards,
Listening, writing letters, trying to breathe
Strong life into lead-colored lips.
He does what he can. The doctors do what they can.
The nurses save a life here and another there,
But the sick men die like flies in the hospitals.)   10

Voices of boys and men,
Homesick, stubborn, talking of little things,
"We get better food. I'm getting to be a good cook.
The food's bad. The whole company yelled 'Hard Bread!' today.
There are only three professed Christians in my whole regiment,
I feel sad about that.
I wish you could see the way we have to live here,
I wish everybody at home could see what it's like.
It's muddy. It's cold. My shoes gave out on the march.
We lost the battle. The general was drunk.   20
This is the roughest life that you ever saw.
If I ever get back home—"
And, over and over, in stiff, patriotic phrases,
"I am resigned to die for the Union, mother.
If we die in this battle, we will have died for the right,
We will have died bravely—you can trust us for that.
It is only right to die for our noble Union.
We will save it or die for it. There's just one thing.
I hope I die quick. I hope I don't have to die
In the hospital.   30
There is one thought that to me is worse than death.
(This, they say over and over) it is the thought
Of being buried as they bury us here
After a battle. Sometimes they barely cover us.
I feel sick when I think of getting buried like that,
Though if nothing except our death will rescue our Union,
You can trust us to die for it."
And, through it all, the deep diapason swelling,
"It is cold. We are hungry. We marched all day in the mud.
We could barely stand when we got back into camp.   40
Don't believe a thing the newspapers say about us.
It's all damn lies.

                We are willing to die for our Union,
But I wish you could all of you see what this is like,
Nobody at home can imagine what it is like.
We are ready to fight. We know we can fight and win.
But why will they waste us in fights that cannot be won?
When will we get a man that can really lead us?"
These are the articulate that write the letters.
The inarticulate merely undergo.
There are times of good food and times of campfire jokes,
Times of good weather, times of partial success   10
In those two years.
                "The mail came. Thanks for the papers.
We had a good feed at Mrs. Wilson's place.
I feel fine today. We put on a show last night.
You ought to have seen Jim Wheeler in 'Box and Cox.'
Our little band of Christians meets often now
And the spirit moves in us strongly, praise be to God.
The President reviewed us two days ago.
You should have seen it, father, it was majestic.
I have never seen a more magnificent sight.   20
It makes me proud to be part of such an army.
We got the tobacco. The socks came. I'm feeling fine."
All that—but still the deep diapason throbs
Under the rest.
                The cold. The mud. The bleak wonder.
The weakening sickness—the weevils tainting the bread—
We were beaten again in spite of all we could do.
We don't know what went wrong but something went wrong.
When will we find a man who can really lead us?
When will we not be wasted without success?   30

Army of the Potomac, army of brave men,
Beaten again and again but never quite broken,
You are to have the victory in the end
But these bleak months are your anguish.
                        Your voice dies out.
Let us hear the voice of your steadfast enemy

            VIII. The Army of Northern Virginia

Army of Northern Virginia, fabulous army,
Strange army of ragged individualists,

The hunters, the riders, the walkers, the savage pastorals,
The unmachined, the men come out of the ground,
Still for the most part, living close to the ground
As the roots of the cow-pea, the roots of the jessamine,
The lazy scorners, the rebels against the wheels,
The rebels against the steel combustion-chamber
Of the half-born new age of engines and metal hands.
The fighters who fought for themselves in the old clan-fashion.
Army of planters' sons and rusty poor-whites,
Where one man came to war with a haircloth trunk   10
Full of fine shirts and a body-servant to mend them,
And another came with a rifle used at King's Mountain
And nothing else but his pants and his sun-cracked hands,
Aristo-democracy armed with a forlorn hope,
Where a scholar turned the leaves of an Arabic grammar
By the campfire-glow, and a drawling mountaineer
Told dirty stories old as the bawdy world,
Where one of Lee's sons worked a gun with the Rockbridge
   Battery
And two were cavalry generals.   20
                    Praying army,
Full of revivals, as full of salty jests,
Who debated on God and Darwin and Victor Hugo,
Decided that evolution might do for Yankees
But that Lee never came from anything with a tail,
And called yourselves "Lee's miserables faintin' "
When the book came out that tickled your sense of romance,
Army of improvisators of peanut-coffee
Who baked your bread on a ramrod stuck through the dough,
Swore and laughed and despaired and sang "Lorena,"   30
Suffered, died, deserted, fought to the end.
Sentimental army, touched by "Lorena,"
Touched by all lace-paper-valentines of sentiment,
Who wept for the mocking-bird on Hallie's grave
When you had better cause to weep for more private griefs,
Touched by women and your tradition-idea of them,
The old, book-fed, half-queen, half-servant idea,
False and true and expiring.
                    Starving army,
Who, after your best was spent and your Spring lay dead,   40
Yet held the intolerable lines of Petersburg
With deadly courage.

You too are a legend now
And the legend has made your fame and has dimmed that fame,
—The victor strikes and the beaten man goes down
But the years pass and the legend covers them both,
The beaten cause turns into the magic cause,
The victor has his victory for his pains—
So with you—and the legend has made a stainless host
Out of the dusty columns of footsore men
Who found life sweet and didn't want to be killed,
Grumbled at officers, grumbled at Governments.   10
That stainless host you were not. You had your cowards,
Your bullies, your fakers, your sneaks, your savages.
You got tired of marching. You cursed the cold and the rain.
You cursed the war and the food—and went on till the end.
And yet, there was something in you that matched your fable.
What was it? What do your dim, faint voices say?
"Will we ever get home? Will we ever lick them for good?
We've got to go on and fight till we lick them for good.
They've got the guns and the money and lots more men
But we've got to lick them now.   20
We're not fighting for slaves.
Most of us never owned slaves and never expect to,
It takes money to buy a slave and we're most of us poor,
But we won't lie down and let the North walk over us
About slaves or anything else.
                              We don't know how it started
But they've invaded us now and we're bound to fight
Till every last damn Yankee goes home and quits.
We used to think we could lick them in one hand's turn.
We don't think that any more.   30
                              They keep coming and coming.
We haven't got guns that shoot as well as their guns,
We can't get clothes that wear as well as their clothes,
But we've got to keep on till they're licked and we're independent,
It's the only thing we can do.
                              Though some of us wonder—
Some of us try and puzzle the whole thing through,
Some of us hear about Richmond profiteers,
The bombproofs who get exempted and eat good dinners,
And the rest of it, and say, with a bitter tongue,   40
'This is the rich man's war and the poor man's fight.'
And more of us, maybe, say that, after a while,

184

But most of us just keep on till we're plumb worn out,
We just keep on.
                    We've got the right men to lead us,
It doesn't matter how many the Yankees are,
Marse Robert and Old Jack will take care of that,
We'll have to march like Moses and fight like hell
But we're bound to win unless the two of them die
And God wouldn't be so mean as to take them both,
So we just keep on—and keep on—"
                                    To the Wilderness,   10
To Appomattox, to the end of the dream.
Army of Northern Virginia, army of legend,
Who were your captains that you could trust them so surely?
Who were your battle-flags?
                            Call the shapes from the mist,
Call the dead men out of the mist and watch them ride.
Tall the first rider, tall with a laughing mouth,
His long black beard is combed like a beauty's hair,
His slouch hat plumed with a curled black ostrich-feather,
He wears gold spurs and sits his horse with the seat   20
Of a horseman born.
                    It is Stuart of Laurel Hill,
"Beauty" Stuart, the genius of cavalry,
Reckless, merry, religious, theatrical,
Lover of gesture, lover of panache,
With all the actor's grace and the quick, light charm
That makes the women adore him—a wild cavalier
Who worships as sober a God as Stonewall Jackson,
A Rupert who seldom drinks, very often prays,
Loves his children, singing, fighting, spurs, and his wife.   30
Sweeney his banjo-player follows him.
And after them troop the young Virginia counties,
Horses and men, Botetort, Halifax,
Dinwiddie, Prince Edward, Cumberland, Nottoway,
Mecklenburg, Berkeley, Augusta, the Marylanders,
The horsemen never matched till Sheridan came.
Now the phantom guns creak by. They are Pelham's guns.
That quiet boy with the veteran mouth is Pelham.
He is twenty-two. He is to fight sixty battles
And never lose a gun.   40
                    The cannon roll past,
The endless lines of the infantry begin.

185

A. P. Hill leads the van. He is small and spare,
His short, clipped beard is red as his battleshirt,
Jackson and Lee are to call him in their death-hours.
Dutch Longstreet follows, slow, pugnacious and stubborn,
Hard to beat and just as hard to convince,
Fine corps commander, good bulldog for holding on,
But dangerous when he tries to think for himself,
He thinks for himself too much at Gettysburg,
But before and after he grips with tenacious jaws.
There is D. H. Hill—there is Early and Fitzhugh Lee— 10
Yellow-haired Hood with his wounds and his empty sleeve,
Leading his Texans, a Viking shape of a man,
With the thrust and lack of craft of a berserk sword,
All lion, none of the fox.
                          When he supersedes
Joe Johnston, he is lost, and his army with him,
But he could lead forlorn hopes with the ghost of Ney.
His bigboned Texans follow him into the mist.
Who follows them?
                          These are the Virginia faces, 20
The Virginia speech. It is Jackson's foot-cavalry,
The Army of the Valley,
It is the Stonewall Brigade, it is the streams
Of the Shenandoah, marching.
                          Ewell goes by,
The little woodpecker, bald and quaint of speech,
With his wooden leg stuck stiffly out from his saddle,
He is muttering, "Sir, I'm a nervous Major-General,
And whenever an aide rides up from General Jackson
I fully expect an order to storm the North Pole." 30
He chuckles and passes, full of crotchets and courage,
Living on frumenty for imagined dyspepsia,
And ready to storm the North Pole at a Jackson phrase.
Then the staff—then little Sorrel—and the plain
Presbyterian figure in the flat cap,
Throwing his left hand out in the awkward gesture
That caught the bullet out of the air at Bull Run,
Awkward, rugged and dour, the belated Ironside
With the curious, brilliant streak of the cavalier
That made him quote Mercutio in staff instructions, 40
Love lancet windows, the color of passion-flowers,
Mexican sun and all fierce, taut-looking fine creatures;

Stonewall Jackson, wrapped in his beard and his silence,
Cromwell-eyed and ready with Cromwell's short
Bleak remedy for doubters and fools and enemies,
Hard on his followers, harder on his foes,
An iron sabre vowed to an iron Lord,
And yet the only man of those men who pass
With a strange, secretive grain of harsh poetry
Hidden so deep in the stony sides of his heart
That it shines by flashes only and then is gone.
It glitters in his last words.   10
                                        He is deeply ambitious,
The skilled man, utterly sure of his own skill
And taking no nonsense about it from the unskilled,
But God is the giver of victory and defeat,
And Lee, on earth, vicegerent under the Lord.
Sometimes he differs about the mortal plans
But once the order is given, it is obeyed.
We know what he thought about God. One would like to know
What he thought of the two together, if he so mingled them.
He said two things about Lee it is well to recall.   20
When he first beheld the man that he served so well,
"I have never seen such a fine-looking human creature."
Then, afterwards, at the height of his own fame,
The skilled man talking of skill, and something more.
"General Lee is a phenomenon,
He is the only man I would follow blindfold."
Think of those two remarks and the man who made them
When you picture Lee as the rigid image in marble.
No man ever knew his own skill better than Jackson
Or was more ready to shatter an empty fame.   30
He passes now in his dusty uniform.
The Bible jostles a book of Napoleon's Maxims
And a magic lemon deep in his saddlebags.

And now at last,
Comes Traveller and his master. Look at them well.
The horse is an iron-grey, sixteen hands high,
Short back, deep chest, strong haunch, flat legs, small head,
Delicate ear, quick eye, black mane and tail,
Wise brain, obedient mouth.
                                        Such horses are   40
The jewels of the horseman's hands and thighs,

187

They go by the word and hardly need the rein.
They bred such horses in Virginia then,
Horses that were remembered after death
And buried not so far from Christian ground
That if their sleeping riders should arise
They could not witch them from the earth again
And ride a printless course along the grass
With the old manage and light ease of hand.
The rider, now.
                            He too, is iron-grey,   10
Though the thick hair and thick, blunt-pointed beard
Have frost in them.
                            Broad-foreheaded, deep-eyed,
Straight-nosed, sweet-mouthed, firm-lipped, head cleanly set,
He and his horse are matches for the strong
Grace of proportion that inhabits both.
They carry nothing that is in excess
And nothing that is less than symmetry,
The strength of Jackson is a hammered strength,
Bearing the tool marks still. This strength was shaped   20
By as hard arts but does not show the toil
Except as justness, though the toil was there.
—And so we get the marble man again,
The head on the Greek coin, the idol-image,
The shape who stands at Washington's left hand,
Worshipped, uncomprehended and aloof,
A figure lost to flesh and blood and bones,
Frozen into a legend out of life,
A blank-verse statue—
                            How to humanize   30
That solitary gentleness and strength
Hidden behind the deadly oratory
Of twenty thousand Lee Memorial days,
How show, in spite of all the rhetoric,
All the sick honey of the speechifiers,
Proportion, not as something calm congealed
From lack of fire, but ruling such a fire
As only such proportion could contain?

The man was loved, the man was idolized,
The man had every just and noble gift.   40
He took great burdens and he bore them well,

188

Believed in God but did not preach too much,
Believed and followed duty first and last
With marvellous consistency and force,
Was a great victor, in defeat as great,
No more, no less, always himself in both,
Could make men die for him but saved his men
Whenever he could save them—was most kind
But was not disobeyed—was a good father,
A loving husband, a considerate friend:
Had little humor, but enough to play   10
Mild jokes that never wounded, but had charm,
Did not seek intimates, yet drew men to him,
Did not seek fame, did not protest against it,
Knew his own value without pomp or jealousy
And died as he preferred to live—sans phrase,
With commonsense, tenacity and courage,
A Greek proportion—and a riddle unread.
And everything that we have said is true
And nothing helps us yet to read the man,
Nor will he help us while he has the strength   20
To keep his heart his own.
                              For he will smile
And give you, with unflinching courtesy,
Prayers, trappings, letters, uniforms and orders,
Photographs, kindness, valor and advice,
And do it with such grace and gentleness
That you will know you have the whole of him
Pinned down, mapped out, easy to understand—
And so you have.
                    All things except the heart.   30
The heart he kept himself, that answers all.
For here was someone who lived all his life
In the most fierce and open light of the sun,
Wrote letters freely, did not guard his speech,
Listened and talked with every sort of man,
And kept his heart a secret to the end
From all the picklocks of biographers.

He was a man, and as a man he knew
Love, separation, sorrow, joy and death.
He was a master of the tricks of war,   40
He gave great strokes and warded strokes as great.

189

He was the prop and pillar of a State,
The incarnation of a national dream,
And when the State fell and the dream dissolved
He must have lived with bitterness itself—
But what his sorrow was and what his joy,
And how he felt in the expense of strength,
And how his heart contained its bitterness,
He will not tell us.
        We can lie about him,
Dress up a dummy in his uniform   10
And put our words into the dummy's mouth,
Say "Here Lee must have thought," and "There, no doubt,
By what we know of him, we may suppose
He felt—this pang or that—" but he remains
Beyond our stagecraft, reticent as ice,
Reticent as the fire within the stone.

Yet—look at the face again—look at it well—
This man was not repose, this man was act.
This man who murmured "It is well that war
Should be so terrible, if it were not   20
We might become too fond of it—" and showed
Himself, for once, completely as he lived
In the laconic balance of that phrase;
This man could reason, but he was a fighter,
Skilful in every weapon of defence
But never defending when he could assault,
Taking enormous risks again and again,
Never retreating while he still could strike,
Dividing a weak force on dangerous ground
And joining it again to beat a strong,   30
Mocking at chance and all the odds of war
With acts that looked like hairbreadth recklessness
—We do not call them reckless, since they won.
We do not see him reckless for the calm
Proportion that controlled the recklessness—
But that attacking quality was there.
He was not mild with life or drugged with justice,
He gripped life like a wrestler with a bull,
Impetuously. It did not come to him
While he stood waiting in a famous cloud,   40
He went to it and took it by both horns

And threw it down.
                    Oh, he could bear the shifts
Of time and play the bitter loser's game,
The slow, unflinching chess of fortitude,
But while he had an opening for attack
He would attack with every ounce of strength.
His heart was not a stone but trumpet-shaped
And a long challenge blew an anger through it
That was more dread for being musical
First, last, and to the end.   10
                    Again he said
A curious thing to life.
"I'm always wanting something."
                              The brief phrase
Slides past us, hardly grasped in the smooth flow
Of the well-balanced, mildly-humorous prose
That goes along to talk of cats and duties,
Maxims of conduct, farming and poor bachelors,
But for a second there, the marble cracked
And a strange man we never saw before   20
Showed us the face he never showed the world
And wanted something—not the general
Who wanted shoes and food for ragged men,
Not the good father wanting for his children,
The patriot wanting victory—all the Lees
Whom all the world could see and recognize
And hang with gilded laurels—but the man
Who had, you'd say, all things that life can give
Except the last success—and had, for that,
Such glamor as can wear sheer triumph out,   30
Proportion's son and Duty's eldest sword
And the calm mask who—wanted something still,
Somewhere, somehow and always.
                              Picklock biographers,
What could he want that he had never had?

He only said it once—the marble closed—
There was a man enclosed within that image.
There was a force that tried Proportion's rule
And died without a legend or a cue
To bring it back. The shadow-Lees still live.   40
But the first-person and the singular Lee?

191

The ant finds kingdoms in a foot of ground
But earth's too small for something in our earth,
We'll make a new earth from the summer's cloud,
From the pure summer's cloud.

                              It was not that,
It was not God or love or mortal fame.
It was not anything he left undone.
—What does Proportion want that it can lack?
—What does the ultimate hunger of the flesh
Want from the sky more than a sky of air?   10

He wanted something. That must be enough.

Now he rides Traveller back into the mist.

IX. *Transition*

Continual guns, be silent for a moment,
Be silent, now.
We know your thirst. We hear the roll of your wheels
Crushing down tangled June,
Virginia June,
With tires of iron, with heavy caissons creaking,
Crushing down maidenhair and wilderness-seal,
Scaring the rabbit and the possum-children,
Scaring the redbird and the mockingbird   20
As McClellan's army moves forward.
We know your bloody thirst so soon to be slaked
With the red burst-grape juices.
But now, we would have you silent, a little moment,
We would have you hold your peace and point at the moon
For when you speak, we can hear no sound but your sound,
And we would hear the voices of men and women
For a little while.

Jake Diefer, the barrel-chested Pennsylvanian,
Shippy, the little man with the sharp rat-eyes,   30
Luke Breckinridge, the gawky boy from the hills,
Clay Wingate, Melora Vilas, Sally Dupré,
The slaves in the cabins, ragged Spade in the woods,
We have lost these creatures under a falling hammer.

We must look for them now, again.

JAKE DIEFER is with the assault that comes from the ships,
He has marched, he has fought at Fair Oaks, but he looks the
    same:
A slow-thought-chewing Clydesdale horse of a man
Who doesn't think much of the way that they farm down here.
The sun may be good, if you like that sort of sun,
But the barns and the fields are different, they don't look right,
They don't look like Pennsylvania.
                            He spits and wonders.   10
Whenever he can, he reads a short, crumpled letter
And tries to puzzle out from the round, stiff writing
How things are back on the farm.
                        The boy's a good boy
But the boy can't do it all, or the woman either.
He knows too much about weather and harvest-hands
—It's all right fighting the Rebels to save the Union
But they ought to get through with it quicker, now they've
    begun,
They don't take the way the crops are into account,   20
You can't go off and leave a farm like a store,
And you can't expect a boy to know everything,
Or a hired man. No, sir.
                   He walks along like an ox.
—He'd like to see the boy and the woman again,
Eat pancakes and sleep in a bed and look at the hay—
This business comes first but after it's finished up—
He can't say he's bothered exactly most of the time.
The weather bothers him more than anything.
He knows it's not the same sort of weather down here,   30
But every day when he wakes, he looks at the sky
And tries to figure out what it's like back home.

SHIPPY, the little man with the sharp rat-eyes,
Creeps into an old house in beleaguered Richmond
And meets a woman dressed in severe black silk
With a gentle voice, soft delicate useless hands,
A calm, smooth, faded, handsome mask of a face
And an incredible secret under her brooches.
You would picture her with ivory crochet-needles
Demurely tatting, demurely singing mild hymns   40

To an old melodeon before a blurred mirror.
She is to live in Richmond throughout the war,
A Union spy, never caught, never once suspected,
And when she dies, she dies with a shut prim mouth
Locked on her mystery.
                           Shippy is afraid.
She gives him instructions, he tries to remember them.
But his hands are sweating, his eyes creep around the floor.
He is afraid of the rustle of the black silk.
He wishes he were back in Pollet's Hotel   10
With Sophy, the chambermaid.
                           The woman talks
And he listens, while the woman looks through and through him.

MELORA VILAS, rising by crack of dawn,
Looked at herself in the bottom of her tin basin
And wished that she had a mirror.
                           She thought dully,
"He's been gone two months. I can't get used to it yet.
I've got to get used to it. Maybe I'll die instead.
No, I'd know if he'd died."   20

SALLY DUPRÉ was tired of scraping lint
But her hands kept on. The hours, sunbonneted women,
Passed and passed. "If he ever comes back to me!"
She finished her scraping and wondered how to make coffee
Out of willow-bark and life from a barren stick. . . .
SPADE the fugitive stared at the bleak North Star. . . .
LUKE BRECKINRIDGE, on picket out in the woods,
Remembered a chambermaid at Pollet's Hotel.
And wanted a fight. He hadn't been lucky, of late.
Jim, his cousin, was lucky, out in the West,   30
Riding a horse and capturing Yankee scouts.
But his winter here had been nothing but work and mud,
He'd nearly got courtmartialed a dozen times,
Though they knew how he could shoot.
                           The chambermaid's name
Was SOPHY. She was little and scared and thin,
But he liked her looks and he liked the size of her eyes,
He'd like to feed her up and see how she looked,
If they ever got through with fighting the Yankees here.
The Yankees weren't all Kelceys. He knew that now,   40

194

But he always looked for Kelceys whenever he fought. . . .
CLAY WINGATE slept in his cloak and dreamed of a girl
With Sally's face and Lucy Weatherby's mouth
And waked again
To know today there would be continual guns.

Continual guns, silent so brief a moment,
Speak again, now,
For now your ignorance
Drowns out the little voices of human creatures.
Jackson slips from the Valley where he has played   10
A dazzling game against Banks and Shield and Frémont
And threatened the chess-game-king of Washington
Till strong pieces meant to join in McClellan's game
Are held to defend that king.
                              And now the two,
Jackson and Lee, strike hard for Seven Days
At the host come up from its ships, come up from the sea
To take the city set on a deck of land,
Till the deck is soaked and red with a bloody juice.
And the host goes back.   20
                    You can read in the histories
How the issue wavered, the fog of tiny events,
How here, at one dot, McClellan might have wrung
A victory, perhaps, with his larger force,
And there, on the other hand, played canny and well;
How Jackson, for once, moved slowly, how Porter held,
And the bitter, exhausted wrestling of Malvern Hill.
What we know is this.
                    The host from the ships went back,
Hurt but not broken, hammered but undestroyed,   30
To find a new base far up the crook of the James
And rest there, panting.
                    Lincoln and Halleck come.
The gaunt, plain face is deeper furrowed than ever,
The eyes are strained with looking at books of tactics
And trying to understand.
                    There is so much
For one man to understand, so many lies,
So much half-truth, so many counselling voices,
So much death to be sown and reaped and still no end.   40
The dead of the Seven Days. The four months dead

Boy who used to play with a doll named Jack,
Was a bright boy as boys are reckoned and now is dead.
The doll named Jack was sometimes a Union soldier,
Sometimes a spy.
                    The boy and his brother held
A funeral in the White House flower-beds
After suitably executing the doll named Jack
But then they thought of a different twist to the game.
The gaunt man signed a paper.
                                      "The doll named Jack   10
Is pardoned. By order of the President.
A. Lincoln."
              So Jack was held in honor awhile
But next day the boy and his brother forgot the pardon
And the doll named Jack was shot and buried once more.
So much death to be sown and reaped.
                                        So much death to be sown
By one no sower of deaths.
                            And still no end.

The council is held. The chiefs and captains debate.   20
McClellan clings to his plan of storming the deck
From the water ways. He is cool now. He argues well.
He has written Lincoln "From the brink of eternity"
—A strained, high-flown, remarkable speech of a letter
Of the sort so many have written and still will write—
Telling how well he has done in saving his army,
No thanks to the Government, or to anything else
But the pith of his fighting-men and his own craft.
Lincoln reads and pockets the speech and thanks him.
There had been craft and courage in that retreat   30
And much was due to McClellan.
                                  The others speak.
Some corps commanders agree and some demur,
The Peninsula-stroke has failed and will fail again.
Elbow-rubbing Halleck, newly-made chief of staff,
Called "Old Brains," for reasons that history
Still tries to fathom, demurs. He urges withdrawal.
Washington must be defended first and last—
Withdraw the army and put it in front of Washington.
Lincoln listens to all as he tries to sift   40
The mustardseed from the twenty barrels of chaff

196

With patient hands.
                    There has been a growth in the man,
A tempering of will in these trotting months
Whose strong hoofs striking have scarred him again and again.
He still rules more by the rein than by whip or spur
But the reins are fast in his hands and the horses know it.
He no longer says "I think," but "I have decided."
And takes the strength and the burden of such decision
For good or bad on himself.
                              He will bear all things   10
But lack of faith in the Union and that not once.
Now at last he decides to recall McClellan's army
For right or wrong.
                    We see the completed thing,
Long afterward, knowing all that was still to come,
And say "He was wrong."
                         He saw the incomplete,
The difficult chance that might turn a dozen ways
And so decided.
                Be it so. He was wrong.   20

So the deck is cleared and the host goes back to its ships.
The bells in the Richmond churches, clanging for Sunday,
Clang as if silver were mixed in their sweet bell-metal,
The dark cloud lifts, the girls wear flowers again.
Virginia June,
Crushed under cannon, under the cannon ruts,
The trampled grass lifts up its little green guidons,
The honeysuckle and the eglantine
Blow on their tiny trumpets,
Blow out "Dixie,"   30
Blow out "Lorena," blow the "Bonnie Blue Flag"
—There are many dead, there are many too many dead,
The hospitals are crowded with broken dolls—
But cotton has won again, cotton is haughty,
Cotton is mounting again to a sleepy throne,
Wheat and iron recoil from the fields of cotton,
The sweet grass grows over them, the cotton blows over them,
One more battle and free, free, free forever.
Cotton moves North in a wave, in a white-crested
Wave of puff-blossoms—in a long grey coil   40
Of marching men with tongues as dry as cotton.

197

Cotton and honeysuckle and eglantine
Move North in a drenching wave of blossom and guns
To wash out wheat and iron forever and ever.
There will be other waves that set toward the North,
There will be a high tide,
But this is the high hour.
Jackson has still three hammerstrokes to strike,
Lee is still master of the attacking sword,
Stuart still carries his black feather high.
Put silver in your bell-metal, Richmond bells,   10
The wave of the cotton goes North to your sweet ringing,
The first great raiding wave of the Southern dream.

X. *Jack Ellyat in a Confederate prison*

JACK ELLYAT, in prison deep in the South,
Gaunt, bearded, dirty old man with the captive eyes,
Lay on his back and stared at the flies on the wall
And tried to remember, through an indifferent mist,
A green place lost in the woods and a herd of black swine.
They came and went and the mist moved round them again.
The mist was not death. He was used to death by now,
But the mist still puzzled him, sometimes.   20
It was curious—being so weak and yet used to death.
When you were strong, you thought of death as a strong
Rider on a black horse, perhaps, or at least
As some strong creature, dreadful because so strong.
But when you were weak and lived in a place like this,
Things changed. There was nothing strong about death any more.
He was only the gnawed rat-bone on the dirty floor,
That you stumbled across and hardly bothered to curse.
That was all.
        The two Michigan men had died last night.   30
The Ohio brothers were going to die this week,
You got pretty soon so you knew when people would die,
It passed the time as well as carving bone-rings,
Playing checkers with straws or learning Italian nouns
From the lanky schoolteacher-sergeant from Vermont.
Somewhere, sometime, in a tent, by a red loud noise,
Under a dirty coat and a slab of tobacco,
He had lost a piece of himself, a piece of life.

He couldn't die till he got that piece of him back
And felt its ragged edges fit in his heart.
Or so he thought. Sometimes, when he slept, he felt
As if he were getting it back—but most of the time
It was only the mist and counting the flies that bothered him.
He heard a footstep near him and turned his head.
"Hello, Charley," he said, "Where you been?"

                            Bailey's face looked strange,
The red, hot face of a hurt and angry boy,
"Out hearing the Rebs," he said. He spat on the floor   10
And broke into long, blue curses. When he was through,
"Did you hear them?" he asked. Jack Ellyat tried to remember
A gnat-noise buzzing the mist. "I guess so," he said.
"What was it? Two-bottle Ed on another tear?"
"Hell," said Bailey. "They cheered. They've licked us again.
The news just come. It happened back at Bull Run."
"You're crazy," said Ellyat. "That was the start of the war.
I was in that one."
                 "Oh, don't be a fool," said Bailey,
"They licked us again, I tell you, the same old place.   20
Pope's army's ruined."
                   "Who's he?" said Ellyat wearily.
"Aw, we had him out West—he's God Almighty's pet horse,
He came East and told all the papers how good he was,
'Headquarters in the saddle'!" Bailey snickered.
"Well, they snaffled his saddle and blame near snaffled him,
Jackson and Lee—anyhow they licked us again."

"What about Little Mac?"
                   "Well, Gawd knows what's happened to *him*,"
Said Bailey, flatly, "Maybe he's captured, too,   30
Maybe they captured Old Abe and everyone else.
I don't know—you can't tell from those lyin' Rebs."

There was a silence. Ellyat lay on his back
And watched the flies on the wall for quite a long time.
"I wish I had a real newspaper," said Bailey,
"Not one of your Richmond wipers. By God, you know, Jack,
When we get back home, I'll read a newspaper, sometimes.
I never was much at readin' the newspaper
But I'd like to read one now, say once in a while."
Ellyat laughed.   40

"You know, Charley," he said at last.
"We've got to get out of this place."
Bailey joined in the laugh.
Then he stopped and stared at the other with anxious eyes.
"You don't look crazy," he said, "Stop countin' those flies."
Ellyat raised himself on one arm.
"No, honest, Charley,
I mean it, damn it. We've got to get out of here.
I know we can't but we've got to. . . ."
He swallowed dryly.   10
"Look here—" he said, "It just came over me then.
I've got a girl and she doesn't know where I am.
I left her back in a tent—no, that wasn't a girl—
And you say we got licked again. But that's just it, Charley.
We get licked too much. We've got to get out of here."

He sank back to the floor and shut his ghost-ridden eyes.
Bailey regarded him for a long, numb moment.
"You couldn't walk a mile and a half," he muttered,
"And, by God, I couldn't carry you twenty feet,
And, by God, if we could, there ain't no way to get out,   20
But all the same—"
"If there was any use tryin',"
He said, half-pleadingly, half-defiantly,
"I tell you, Jack, if there was any use tryin'—"
He stopped. Ellyat's eyes were shut. He rose with great care.
"I'll get you some water," he muttered. "No, let you sleep."
He sat down again and stared at the sleeping face.
"He looks bad," he thought. "I guess I look bad myself.
I guess the kid's goin' to die if we don't get out.
I guess we're both goin' to die. I don't see why not."   30
He looked up at the flies on the ceiling and shook his fist.
"Listen, you dirty Rebs," he said, under his breath,
"Flap your goddam wings—we're goin' to get out of here!"

XI. *Refrain*

John Brown lies dead in his grave and does not stir,
It is nearly three years since he died and he does not stir,
There is no sound in his bones but the sound of armies
And that is an old sound.

He walks, you will say, he walks in front of the armies,
A straggler met him, going along to Manassas,
With his gun on his shoulder, his phantom-sons at heel,
His eyes like misty coals.

A dead man saw him striding at Seven Pines,
The bullets whistling through him like a torn flag,
A madman saw him whetting a sword on a Bible,
A cloud above Malvern Hill.

But these are all lies. He slumbers. He does not stir.
The spring rains and the winter snows on his slumber   10
And the bones of his flesh breed armies and yet more armies
But he himself does not stir.

It will take more than cannon to shake his fortress,
His song is alive and throbs in the tramp of the columns,
His song is smoke blown out of the mouth of a cannon,
But his song and he are two.

The South goes ever forward, the slave is not free,
The great stone gate of the Union crumbles and totters,
The cotton-blossoms are pushing the blocks apart,
The roots of cotton grow in the crevices,   20
John Brown's body lies a-mouldering in the grave.
Soon the fight will be over, the slaves will be slaves forever.
John Brown's body lies a-mouldering in the grave.
You did not fight for the Union or wish it well,
You fought for the single dream of a man unchained
And God's great chariot rolling. You fought like the thrown
Stone, but the fighters have forgotten your dream.
John Brown's body lies a-mouldering in the grave.
You fought for a people you did not comprehend,
For a symbol chained by a symbol in your own mind,   30
But, unless you arise, that people will not be free.
Are there no seeds of thunder left in your bones
Except to breed useless armies?
John Brown's body lies a-mouldering in the grave.
Arise, John Brown,
Call up your sons from the ground,
In smoky wreaths, call up your sons to heel,
Call up the clumsy country boys you armed

With crazy pikes and a fantastic mind.
Call up the American names,
Kagi, the self-taught scholar, quiet and cool,
Stevens, the cashiered soldier, bawling his song,
Dangerfield Newby, the freed Scotch-mulatto,
Watson and Oliver Brown and all the hard-dying.
Call up the slug-riddled dead of Harper's Ferry
And cast them down the wind on a raid again.
This is the dark hour,
This is the ebb-tide,   10
This is the sunset, this is the defeat.
The cotton-blossoms are growing up to the sky,
The great stone gate of the Union sinks beneath them,
And under the giant blossoms lies Egypt's land,
The dark river,
The ground of bondage,
The chained men.
If the great gate falls, the cotton grows over your dream.
Find your heart, John Brown,
A-mouldering in the grave.   20
Call your sons and get your pikes,
A-mouldering in the grave.
Your song goes on, but the slave is still a slave,
And all Egypt's land rides Northward while you moulder in the
    grave!
Rise up, John Brown,
A-mouldering in the grave.
Go down, John Brown,
Against all Egypt's land
Go down, John Brown,   30
Go down, John Brown,
Go down, John Brown, and set that people free!

BOOK FIVE:

The Soul Begins to March

Through Lincoln's eyes we see the progress of the war, the brief flashes of hope and despair—terrible victory, terrible defeat—after eighteen months of strife. We follow his thoughts as the resolution crystallizes to save the Union by whatever means his hands can find under the Constitution, and hear his solemn promise that if Antietam spells victory, his proclamation shall go out to set the slaves "from this next year, then and forever free."

Meanwhile Spade, the runaway slave, hungry and spent, glimpses freedom across the river; Melora Vilas, looking back to her brief time of happiness and forward to the child which, out of that happiness, is to be born, watches the slow seasons pass; and Jack Ellyat, through an exchange of Northern and Southern prisoners, gains freedom for a second time.

I. *Through Lincoln's eyes*

It was still hot in Washington, that September,
Hot in the city, hot in the White House rooms,
Desiccate heat, dry as a palm-leaf fan,
That makes hot men tuck cotton handkerchiefs
Between their collars and their sweaty necks,
And Northern girls look limp at half-past-four,
Waiting the first cool breath that will not come
For hours yet.
                The sentinel on post
Clicks back and forth, stuffed in his sweltering coat,   **10**
And dreams about brown bottles of cold beer
Deep in a cellar.
               In the crowded Bureaus
The pens move slow, the damp clerks watch the clock.
Women in houses take their corsets off
And stifle in loose gowns.
                    They could lie down
But when they touch the bed, the bed feels hot,
And there are things to do.
                   The men will want   **20**
Hot food when they come back from work.
                        They sigh
And turn, with dragging feet, to the hot kitchens.

Sometimes they pause, and push a window up
To feel the blunt, dry buffet of the heat
Strike in the face and hear the locust-cry
Of shrilling newsboy-voices down the street,
"News from the army—extra—ter-ble battle—
Terr-r-ble vic'try—ter-r-ble defeat—
Lee's army trapped invading Maryland—   **30**
McClellan—Sharpsburg—fightin'—news from the front—"
The women at the windows sigh and wonder
"I ought to buy a paper—No, I'll wait
Till Tom gets home—I wonder if it's true—
Terrible victory—terrible defeat—
They're always saying that—when Tom gets home
He'll have some news—I wonder if the army—
No, it's too hot to buy a paper now—"

A hot, spare day of waiting languidly
For contradictory bits of dubious news.

It was a little cooler, three miles out,
Where the tall trees shaded the Soldiers' Home.
The lank man, Abraham Lincoln, found it so,
Glad for it, doubtless, though his cavernous eyes
Had stared all day into a distant fog
Trying to pierce it.
                              "General McClellan
Is now in touch with Lee in front of Sharpsburg   10
And will attack as soon as the fog clears."

It's cleared by now. They must be fighting now.

We can't expect much from the first reports.
Stanton and Halleck think they're pretty good
But you can't tell. Nobody here can tell.
We're all too far away.
                              You get sometimes
Feeling as if you heard the guns yourself
Here in the room and felt them shake the house
When you keep waiting for the news all day.   20
I wish we'd get some news.
                              Bull Run was first.
We got the news of Bull Run soon enough.
First that we'd won, hands down, which was a lie,
And then the truth.
                              It may be that to-day.
I told McClellan not to let them go,
Destroy them if he could—but you can't tell.
He's a good man in lots of different ways,
But he can't seem to finish what he starts   30
And then, he's jealous, like the rest of them,
Lets Pope get beaten, wanted him to fail,
Because he don't like Pope.
                              I put him back
Into command. What else was there to do?
Nobody else could lick those troops in shape.
But, if he wins, and lets Lee get away,
I'm done with him.
                              Bull Run—the Seven Days—

Bull Run again—and eighteen months of war—
And still no end to it.
                    What is God's will?

They come to me and talk about God's will
In righteous deputations and platoons,
Day after day, laymen and ministers.
They write me Prayers From Twenty Million Souls
Defining me God's will and Horace Greeley's.
God's will is General This and Senator That,
God's will is those poor colored fellows' will,   10
It is the will of the Chicago churches,
It is this man's and his worst enemy's.
But all of them are sure they know God's will.
I am the only man who does not know it.

And, yet, if it is probable that God
Should, and so very clearly, state His will
To others, on a point of my own duty,
It might be thought He would reveal it me
Directly, more especially as I
So earnestly desire to know His will.   20

The will of God prevails. No doubt, no doubt—
Yet, in great contests, each side claims to act
In strict accordance with the will of God.
Both may, one must be wrong.
                    God could have saved
This Union or destroyed it without war
If He so wished. And yet this war began,
And, once begun, goes on, though He could give
Victory, at any time, to either side.
It is unfathomable. Yet I know   30
This, and this only. While I live and breathe,
I mean to save the Union if I can,
And by whatever means my hands can find
Under the Constitution.
                    If God reads
The hearts of men as clearly as He must
To be Himself, then He can read in mine
And has, for twenty years, the old, scarred wish
That the last slave should be forever free

207

Here, in this country.
                              I do not go back
From that scarred wish and have not.
                                              But I put
The Union, first and last, before the slave.
If freeing slaves will bring the Union back
Then I will free them; if by freeing some
And leaving some enslaved I help my cause,
I will do that—but should such freedom mean
The wreckage of the Union that I serve   10
I would not free a slave.
                              O Will of God,
I am a patient man, and I can wait
Like an old gunflint buried in the ground
While the slow years pile up like moldering leaves
Above me, underneath the rake of Time,
And turn, in time, to the dark, fruitful mold
That smells of Sangamon apples, till at last
There's no sleep left there, and the steel event
Descends to strike the live coal out of me   20
And light the powder that was always there.

That is my only virtue as I see it,
Ability to wait and hold my own
And keep my own resolves once they are made
In spite of what the smarter people say.
I can't be smart the way that they are smart.
I've known that since I was an ugly child.
It teaches you—to be an ugly child.
It teaches you—to lose a thing you love.
It sticks your roots down into Sangamon ground   30
And makes you grow when you don't want to grow
And makes you tough enough to wait life out,
Wait like the fields, under the rain and snow.

I have not thought for years of that lost grave
That was my first hard lesson in the queer
Thing between men and women we call love.
But when I think of it, and when I hear
The rain and snow fall on it, as they must,
It fills me with unutterable grief.

We've come a good long way, my hat and I,
Since then, a pretty lengthy piece of road,
Uphill and down but mostly with a pack.
Years of law-business, years of cracking jokes,
And watching Billy Herndon do his best
To make me out, which seemed to be a job;
Years trying how to learn to handle men,
Which can be done, if you've got heart enough,
And how to deal with women or a woman
And that's about the hardest task I know.   10
For, when you get a man, you've got the man
Like a good big axehandle in your fist,
But you can't catch a woman like an axe.
She'll run like mercury between your hands
And leave you wondering which road she went,
The minute when you thought you knew her ways.

I understand the uses of the earth,
And I have burned my hands at certain fires
Often enough to know a use for fire,
But when the genius of the water moves,   20
And that's the woman's genius, I'm at sea
In every sense and meaning of the word,
With nothing but old patience for my chart,
And patience doesn't always please a woman.

Bright streams of water, watering the world,
Deep seas of water that all men must sail
Or rest half-men and fill the narrow graves,
When will I understand or comprehend
Your salt, sweet taste, so different from the taste
Of Sangamon russets, weighing down the bough?   30
You can live with the water twenty years
And never understand it like the earth
But that's the lesson I can't seem to learn.

"Abraham Lincoln, his hand and pen,
He will be good, but God knows when."
He will be wise, but God knows when.

It doesn't matter. If I had some news—
News from that fog—

I'll get the hypo, sure,
Unless I watch myself, waiting for news.
I can't afford to get the hypo now,
I've got too much to do.
                              Political years,
Housekeeping years of marrying and begetting
And losing, too, the children and the town,
The wife, the house, the life, the joy and grief,
The profound wonder still behind it all.

I had a friend who married and was happy.   10
But something haunted him that haunted me
Before he did, till he could hardly tell
What his own mind was, for the brooding veil
And immaterial horror of the soul
Which colors the whole world for men like that.

I do not know from whence that horror comes
Or why it hangs between us and the sun
For some few men, at certain times and days,
But I have known it closer than my flesh,
Got up with it, lain down and walked with it,   20
Scotched it awhile, but never killed it quite,
And yet lived on.
                              I wrote him good advice,
The way you do, and told him this, for part,
"Again you fear that that Elysium
Of which you've dreamed so much is not to be.
Well, I dare swear it will not be the fault
Of that same black-eyed Fanny, now your wife.
And I have now no doubt that you and I,
To our particular misfortune, dream   30
Dreams of Elysium far exceeding all
That any earthly thing can realize."

I wrote that more than twenty years ago,
At thirty-three, and now I'm fifty-three,
And the slow days have brought me up at last
Through water, earth and fire, to where I stand,
To where I stand—and no Elysiums still.

No, no Elysiums—for that personal dream
I dreamt of for myself and in my youth

Has been abolished by the falling sledge
Of chance and an ambition so fulfilled
That the fulfillment killed its personal part.

My old ambition was an iron ring
Loose-hooped around the live trunk of a tree.
If the tree grows till bark and iron touch
And then stops growing, ring and tree are matched
And the fulfillment fits.
                                    But, if by some
Unlikely chance, the growing still keeps on,   10
The tree must burst the binding-ring or die.

I have not once controlled the circumstances.
They have controlled me. But with that control
They made me grow or die. And I have grown.
The iron ring is burst.
                                    Three elements,
Earth, water and fire. I have passed through them all,
Still to find no Elysium for my hands,
Still to find no Elysium but growth,
And the slow will to grow to match my task.   20

Three elements. I have not sought the fourth
Deeply, till now—the element of air,
The everlasting element of God,
Who must be there in spite of all we see,
Who must be there in spite of all we bear,
Who must exist where all Elysiums
Are less than shadows of a hunter's fire
Lighted at night to scare a wolf away.

I know that wolf—his scars are in my hide
And no Elysiums can rub them out.   30
Therefore at last, I lift my hands to You
Who Were and Are and Must Be, if our world
Is anything but a lost ironclad
Shipped with a crew of fools and mutineers
To drift between the cold forts of the stars.

I've never found a church that I could join
Although I've prayed in churches in my time

And listened to all sorts of ministers
Well, they were good men, most of them, and yet—
The thing behind the words—it's hard to find.
I used to think it wasn't there at all
Couldn't be there. I cannot say that, now.
And now I pray to You and You alone.
Teach me to know Your will. Teach me to read
Your difficult purpose here, which must be plain
If I had eyes to see it. Make me just.

There was a man I knew near Pigeon Creek   10
Who kept a kennel full of hunting dogs,
Young dogs and old, smart hounds and silly hounds.
He'd sell the young ones every now and then,
Smart as they were and slick as they could run.
But the one dog he'd never sell or lend
Was an old half-deaf foolish-looking hound
You wouldn't think had sense to scratch a flea
Unless the flea were old and sickly too.
Most days he used to lie beside the stove
Or sleeping in a piece of sun outside.   20
Folks used to plague the man about that dog
And he'd agree to everything they said,
"No—he ain't much on looks—or much on speed—
A young dog can outrun him any time,
Outlook him and outeat him and outleap him,
But, Mister, that dog's hell on a cold scent
And, once he gets his teeth in what he's after,
He don't let go until he knows he's dead."

I am that old, deaf hunting-dog, O Lord,
And the world's kennel holds ten thousand hounds   30
Smarter and faster and with finer coats
To hunt your hidden purpose up the wind
And bell upon the trace you leave behind.
But, when even they fail and lose the scent,
I will keep on because I must keep on
Until You utterly reveal Yourself
And sink my teeth in justice soon or late.
There is no more to ask of earth or fire
And water only runs between my hands,
But in the air, I'll look, in the blue air,   40

212

The old dog, muzzle down to the cold scent,
Day after day, until the tired years
Crackle beneath his feet like broken sticks
And the last barren bush consumes with peace.

I should have tried the course with younger legs,
This hunting-ground is stiff enough to pull
The metal heart out of a dog of steel;
I should have started back at Pigeon Creek
From scratch, not forty years behind the mark.
But you can't change yourself, and, if you could,   10
You might fetch the wrong jack-knife in the swap.
It's up to you to whittle what you can
With what you've got—and what I am, I am
For what it's worth, hypo and legs and all.
I can't complain. I'm ready to admit
You could have made a better-looking dog
From the same raw material, no doubt,
But, since You didn't, this'll have to do.

Therefore I utterly lift up my hands
To You, and here and now beseech Your aid.   20
I have held back when others tugged me on,
I have gone on when others pulled me back
Striving to read Your will, striving to find
The justice and expedience of this case,
Hunting an arrow down the chilly airs
Until my eyes are blind with the great wind
And my heart sick with running after peace.
And now, I stand and tremble on the last
Edge of the last blue cliff, a hound beat out,
Tail down and belly flattened to the ground,   30
My lungs are breathless and my legs are whipped,
Everything in me's whipped except my will.
I can't go on. And yet, I must go on.

I will say this. Two months ago I read
My proclamation setting these men free
To Seward and the rest. I told them then
I was not calling on them for advice
But to hear something that I meant to do.
We talked about it. Most of them approved

The thing, if not the time. Then Seward said
Something I hadn't thought of, "I approve
The proclamation—but, if issued now
With our defeats in everybody's mouth
It may be viewed as a last shriek for help
From an exhausted, beaten government.
Put it aside until a victory comes,
Then issue it with victory."

                                    He was right.
I put the thing aside—and ever since   10
There has been nothing for us but defeat,
Up to this battle now—and still no news.

If I had eyes to look to Maryland!
If I could move that battle with my hands!
No, it don't work. I'm not a general.
All I can do is trust the men who are.

I'm not a general, but I promise this,
Here at the end of every ounce of strength
That I can muster, here in the dark pit
Of ignorance that is not quite despair   20
And doubt that does but must not break the mind!
The pit I have inhabited so long
At various times and seasons, that my soul
Has taken color in its very grains
From the blind darkness, from the lonely cave
That never hears a footstep but my own
Nor ever will, while I'm a man alive
To keep my prison locked from visitors.

What if I heard another footstep there,
What if, some day—there is no one but God,   30
No one but God who could descend that stair
And ring his heavy footfalls on the stone.
And if He came, what would we say to Him?

That prison is ourselves that we have built,
And, being so, its loneliness is just,
And, being so, its loneliness endures.
But, if another came,
                              What would we say?
What can the blind say, given back their eyes?

No, it must be as it has always been.
We are all prisoners in that degree
And will remain so, but I think I know
This—God is not a jailor . . . .
                  And I make
A promise now to You and to myself.
If this last battle is a victory
And they can drive the Rebel army back
From Maryland, back over the Potomac,
My proclamation shall go out at last   10
To set those other prisoners and slaves
From this next year, then and forever free.

So much for my will. Show me what is Yours!

That must be news, those footsteps in the hall,
Good news, or else they wouldn't come so fast.

What is it, now? Yes, yes, I'm glad of that.
I'm very glad. There's no mistake this time?
We have the best of them? They're in retreat?
This is a great day, Stanton. . . . .
. . . . .If McClellan   20
Can only follow up the victory now!

Lord, I will keep my promise and go on,
Your will, in much, still being dark to me,
But, in this one thing, as I see it, plain.

And yet—if Lee slips from our hands again
As he well may from all those last reports
And the war still goes on—and still no end—
Even after this Antietam—not for years—

I cannot read it but I will go on,
Old dog, old dog, but settled to the scent   30
And with fresh breath now from this breathing space,
Almighty God.
             At best we never seem
To know You wholly, but there's something left,
A strange, last courage.
               We can fail and fail,

But, deep against the failure, something wars,
Something goes forward, something lights a match,
Something gets up from Sangamon County ground
Armed with a bitten and a blunted axe
And after twenty thousand wasted strokes
Brings the tall hemlock crashing to the ground.

II. *Spade sees Freedom's land*

Spade saw the yellow river rolling ahead
His sore, cracked lips curled back in a death's head grin
And his empty belly ceased to stick to his sides.
He sat on the bank a minute to rest his legs   10
And catch his breath. He had lived for the last three days
On a yam, two ears of horse-corn and the lame rabbit
That couldn't run away when he threw the stick.

He was still a big man but the ribs stuck into his skin
And the hard, dry muscles were wasted to leather thongs.
"Boy, I wisht we had a good meal," he thought with a dull
Fatigue. "Dat's Freedom's lan' ovah dere fer sho',
But how we gwine to swim it without a good meal?
I wisht we had even a spoonful of good hot pot-licker
Or a smidgin' of barbecued shote.   20
                                Dat river's cold.
Colder'n Jordan. I wisht we had a good meal."

He went down to the river and tested it with his hand.
The cold jumped up his arm and into his heart,
Sharp as the toothache. His mouth wried up in a queer
Grimace. He felt like crying. "I'se tired," he said.
"Flow easy, river," he said.
                                Then he tumbled in.
The hard shock of the plunge took his breath away.
So stinging at first that his arms and legs moved fast,   30
But then the cold crept into his creaking bones
And he rolled wild eyes.
                                "Oh, God," he thought as he struggled,
"I'se weak as a cat. I ust to be a strong man."

The yellow flood sucked round him, pulling him down,
The yellow foam had a taste like death in his mouth,

"We ought to of had a good meal," he thought with a weak
Wonder, as he fought weakly. "A good hot meal.
Dis current, she's too strong for a hungry mouth.
We'se done our best, but she fights like a angel would
Like wrestlin' with a death-angel."

                                    He choked and sank
To come up gasping and staring with bloodshot eyes.
His brain had a last, clear flash. "You're drowned," said the brain.
Then it stopped working.

                        But the black, thrashing hands   10
Caught hold of something solid and hard and rough
And hung to it with a last exhausted grip.
—He had been fighting an angel for seven nights
And now he hung by his hands to the angel's neck,
Lost in an iron darkness of beating wings.
If he once let go, the angel would push him off
And touch him across the loins with a stony hand
In the last death-trick of the wrestle.

                                He moaned a little.
The blackness began to lighten. He saw the river   20
Rolling and rolling. He was clutched to a log
Like a treetoad set afloat on a chip of wood,
And the log and he were rushing downstream together,
But the current pulled them both toward the freedom side.

He hunched up a little higher. An eddy took
The log and him and spun them both like a top
While he prayed and sickened.

                          Then they were out of the eddy
And drifting along more slowly, straight for the shore.
He hauled himself up the bank with enormous care,   30
Vomited and lay down.

                    When he could arise
He looked at his hands. They were still hooked into a curve.
It took quite a time to straighten them back again.

He said a prayer as he tried to dry his clothes,
Then he looked for a stone and threw it into the river.
"You'se a mean and hungry river," he said. "You is.
Heah's a present for you. I hope it busts up your teef.
Heah's a present fum Mistah Spade."

                        He felt better then,   40

But his belly started to ache. "Act patient," he said,
Rubbing it gently, "We'se loose in Freedom's land,
Crossed old Jordan—bound to get vittles now."

He started out for the town. The town wasn't far
But he had to go slow. Sometimes he fell on the way.
The last time he fell was in front of a little yard
With a white, well-painted fence. A woman came out.
"Get along," she said. "You can't get sick around here.
I'm tired of you nigger tramps. You're all of you thieves."
Spade rose and said something vague about swimming rivers   10
And vittles. She stamped her foot. "Get along!" she said,
"Get along or I'll call the dog and——"
                                        Spade got along.

The next house, the dog was barking out in the yard,
He went by as fast as he could, but when he looked back
A man had come out with a hostile stick in his hand.
Spade shook his head. "Freedom's land," he thought to himself,
"They's some mighty quick-actin' people in Freedom's land,
Some mighty rash-tempered dogs."
                                        He swayed as he walked.   20
Here was another house. He looked for the dog
With fright in his eyes. Then a swimming qualm came over him,
A deathly faintness. His hands went out to the fence.
He gripped two palings, hung, and stared at his shoes.
Somebody was talking to him. He tried to move on
But his legs wouldn't walk. The voice was a woman's voice.

She'd be calling the dog in a minute. He shivered hard.
"Excuse me ma'am, but I'se feelin' poorly," he said.
"I just crossed over—I'll go as soon as I kin."
A man's voice now. They were taking him under the arms.   30
He didn't care what they did. He let himself walk.

Then he was sitting up in a bentwood chair
In a tidy kitchen that smelt of frying and ham;
The thick, good smell made him strangely sick at first
But it soon passed off. They fed him little by little
Till at last he could tell his tale and ask about them.

They were churchgoing people and kind to runaway slaves.
She wore a blue dress. They had two sons in the war.

That was all that he knew and all that he ever knew.
But they let him sleep in the garret and gave him some shoes
And fifty cents when he left.
                                    He wanted to stay
But times were bad and they couldn't afford to keep him.
The town was tired of runaway negroes now.

All the same, when he left, he walked with a different step.
He went down town. He was free. He was Mister Spade.
The President had written a letter about it
And the mule and the coal-black gal might come any day.   10

He hummed a tuneless whistle between his teeth
And fished a piece of paper out of his pants,
They'd written him down a boss's name and address
But he'd have to get somebody to read it again.
He approached a group of three white men on a corner
Holding the paper.
                    " 'Scuse me, boss, can you tell me——"
The white men looked at him with hard, vacant eyes.
At last one of them took the paper. "Oh, Hell," he said,
Spitting, and gave Spade a stare. Then he seemed to think   20
Of something funny. He nudged the other two men.
"Listen, nigger," he said. "You want Mr. Braid.
You'll find him two blocks down at the Marshal's office,
Tell him Mr. Clarke sent you there—Mr. William Clarke—
He'll fix you up all right."
                            The other men grinned,
Adding directions. Spade thanked them and went away.
He heard them laugh as he went.
                                Another man took him
To a red-faced person who sat in a tilted chair,   30
Reading a paper, his feet cocked up on his desk.
He looked at Spade and his feet came down with a slam.
"Take that God damn smile off," he said. "Who let you come in?
You contraband niggers think that you own this town
And that all you've got to do is cross over here
For people to feed you free the rest of your lives.
Well it don't go down with me—just understand that."

Spade brought out his paper, dumbly. The man looked at it.
"Hell, this ain't for me," he said.
                                Spade started to go.   40

"Come back here, nigger," ordered the red-faced man.
"Hey, Mike!" he yelled, "Here's another of Lincoln's pets.
Send him out with the rest of the gang."
                                        "But, boss——" said Spade.
"Don't get lippy with me," said the man, "Mike, take him along."
The pimply boy named Mike jerked a sallow thumb.
"Come on, black beauty," he said. "We got you a job."
Spade followed him, dazed.
                        When they were out in the street
The boy turned to him. "Now, nigger, watch out," he said,   10
Patting a heavy pistol swung at his belt,
With puppy-fierceness, "You don't get away from me.
I'm a special deputy, see?"
                        "All right, boss," said Spade.
"I ain't aimin' to get away from nobody now,
I just aims to work till I gets myself a good mule."
The boy laughed briefly. The conversation dropped.
They walked out of the town till they came to a torn-up road
Where a gang of negroes was working.
                                "Say, boss—" said Spade. 20
The boy cut him off. "Hey, Jerry," he called to the foreman,
"Here's another one."
                        The foreman looked up and spat.
"Judas!" he said, "Can't they keep the bastards at home?
I'd put a gun on that river if I was Braid.
Well, come along, nig, get a move on and find a shovel.
Don't stand lookin' at me all day."
                                The boy went away.
Spade found a shovel and started work on the road.
The foreman watched him awhile with sarcastic eyes,   30
Spade saw that he, too, wore a pistol.
                        "Christ," said the foreman,
Disgustedly, "Try and put some guts in it there.
You're big enough. That shovel'll cost five dollars.
Remember that—it comes out of your first week's pay.
You're a free nigger now."
                        He chuckled. Spade didn't answer
And, after a while, the foreman moved away.

Spade turned to the gingerskinned negro who worked beside him.
"You fum de Souf?" he mouthed at him.   40
                        Ginger nodded.

"I been here a month now. They fotched me here the first day.
Got any money?"
                    "Nuthin' but fifty cents."
"You better give it to him," said Ginger, stealing
A glance at the foreman. "He'll treat you bad if you don't.
He's a cranky man."
                    Spade's heart sank into his boots.
"Don't we uns get paid? We ain't none of us slaves no more,
The President said so. Why we wuhkin' like dis?"
Ginger snickered. "Sho' we uns get paid," he said,   10
"But we got to buy our stuff at de company sto'
And he sells his old shovels a dozen times what dey's wuth.
I only been here a month but I owes twelve dollars.
Dey ain't no way to pay it except by wuhk,
And de more you wuhk de more you owe at the sto.'
I kain't figure it out exactly but it's dat way."
Spade worked for a while, revolving these things in his mind.
"I reckoned I sho' was gwine to be sassy and free
When I swum dat river," he said.
                              Ginger grinned like a monkey,   20
"Swing your shubbel, boy, and forget what you ain't.
You mought be out on de chain-gang, bustin' up rocks,
Or agin, you mought be enlisted."
                         "Huh?" said Spade.

"Sho', dey's gwine to enlist us all when we finish dis road.
All excep' me. I got bad sight in my eyes
And dey knows about it."
                         "Dey kain't enlist me," said Spade.
"I ain't honin' to go an' fight in no white-folks war,
I ain't bust loose into Freedom's land fer dat,   30
All I want is a chance to git me a gal and a mule.
If I'se free, how kin dey enlist me, lessen I want?"

"You watch 'em," said Ginger. They worked on for a time.
The foreman stood on the bank and watched them work,
Now and then he drank from a bottle.
                         Spade felt hungry.

THE SEASONS PASS

      Autumn is filling his harvest-bins
         With red and yellow grain,

Fire begins and frost begins
    And the floors are cold again.

Summer went when the crop was sold,
    Summer is piled away,
Dry as a faded marigold
    In the dry, long-gathered hay.

It is time to walk to the cider-mill
    Through air like apple wine
And watch the moon rise over the hill,
    Stinging and hard and fine.   10

It is time to cover your seed-pods deep
    And let them wait and be warm,
It is time to sleep the heavy sleep
    That does not wake for the storm.

Winter walks from the green, streaked West
    With a bag of Northern Spies,
The skins are red as a robin's breast,
    The honey chill as the skies.

III. *Melora dreams*

Melora Vilas walked in the woods that autumn
And heard the dry leaves crackle under her feet,   20
Feeling, below the leaves, the blunt heavy earth.
"It's getting-in time," she thought. "It's getting-in time,
Time to put things in barns and sit by the stove,
Time to watch the long snow and remember your lover.

He isn't dead. I know that he isn't dead.
Maybe they've changed his body into a tree,
Maybe they've changed his body into a cloud
Or something that sleeps through the Winter.
                        But I'll remember.
I'll sleep through the Winter, too. We all sleep then   30
And when the Spring freshet drums in the narrow brooks
And fills them with a fresh water, they'll let him come
Out of the cloud and the tree and the Winter-sleep.

The Winter falls and we lie like beleaguered stones
In the black, cramped ground.
                              And then you wake in the morning
And the air's got soft and you plant the narrow-edged seeds,
They grow all Summer and now we've put them in barns
To sleep again for a while.
I am the seed and the husk. I have sown and reaped.
My heart is a barn full of grain that my work has harvested.
My body holds the ripe grain. I can wait my time."

She walked on farther and came to the lip of the spring,   10
The brown leaves drifted the water. She watched them drift.

"I am satisfied," she thought, "I am satisfied.
I can wait my time in spite of Mom being sad
And Pop looking fierce and sad when he sees me walk
So heavy and knows I'll have to walk heavier still
Before my time comes. I'm sorry to make them sad,
I'm sorry I did a bad thing if it was a bad thing;
But I'm satisfied.
                    We cut the heart on the tree.
I've got my half of the dime and he's got his,   20
He'll come back when Winter's over or else I'll find him,
When you can push up the windows, when the new colts
Come out in the Spring, when the snake sheds his winter coat,
When the old, shed coat of Winter lies on the ground
Grey as wasp-paper under the green, slow rain,
When the big barn door rolls open.
I was worried to death at first and I couldn't tell.
But as soon as I knew what it was—it was different then—
It made things all right.
                          I can't tell why it did that."   30

She awkwardly stooped and put her hand on the ground,
Under the brittle leaves the soil was alive,
Torn with its harvest, turned on its side toward sleep,
But stripped for battle, too, for the unending
Battle with Winters till the Spring is born
Like a tight green leaf uncurling, so slightly, so gently,
Out of the husk of ice and the blank, white snows.

The wind moved over it, blowing the leaves away,
Leaving the bare, indomitable breast.

She felt a wind move over her heavy body,
Stripping it clean for war.
                        She felt the blind-featured
Mystery move, the harmonics of the quick grain,
The battle and the awakening for battle,
And the salt taste of peace.

A flight of geese passed by in a narrow V,
Honking their cry.
                        That cry was stuck in her heart
Like a bright knife.   10
                        She could have laughed or wept
Because of that cry flung down from a moving wing,
But she stood silent.
                        She had touched the life in the ground.

MELORA'S SONG

Love came by from the riversmoke,
   When the leaves were fresh on the tree,
But I cut my heart on the blackjack oak
   Before they fell on me.

The leaves are green in the early Spring,
   They are brown as linsey now,   20
I did not ask for a wedding-ring
   From the wind in the bending bough.

Fall lightly, lightly, leaves of the wild,
   Fall lightly on my care,
I am not the first to go with child
   Because of the blowing air.

I am not the first nor yet the last
   To watch a goosefeather sky,
And wonder what will come of the blast
   And the name to call it by.   30

Snow down, snow down, you whitefeather bird,
   Snow down, you winter storm,
Where the good girls sleep with a gospel word
   To keep their honor warm.

The good girls sleep in their modesty,
    The bad girls sleep in their shame,
But I must sleep in the hollow tree
    Till my child can have a name.

I will not ask for the wheel and thread
    To spin the labor plain,
Or the scissors hidden under the bed
    To cut the bearing-pain.

I will not ask for the prayer in church
    Or the preacher saying the prayer,   10
But I will ask the shivering birch
    To hold its arms in the air.

Cold and cold and cold again,
    Cold in the blackjack limb
The winds of the sky for his sponsor-men
    And a bird to christen him.

Now listen to me, you Tennessee corn,
    And listen to my word,
This is the first child ever born
    That was christened by a bird.   20

He's going to act like a hound let loose
    When he comes from the blackjack tree,
And he's going to walk in proud shoes
    All over Tennessee.

I'll feed him milk out of my own breast
    And call him Whistling Jack.
And his dad'll bring him a partridge nest,
    As soon as his dad comes back.

IV.   John Brown's soul begins to march

John Brown's raid has gone forward, the definite thing is done,
Not as we see it done when we read the books,   30
A clear light burning suddenly in the sky,
But dimly, obscurely, a flame half-strangled by smoke,

225

A thing come to pass from a victory not a victory,
A dubious doctrine dubiously received.
The papers praise, but the recruiting is slow,
The bonds sell badly, the grind of the war goes on—
There is no sudden casting off of a chain,
Only a slow thought working its way through the ground,
A slow root growing, touching a hundred soils,
A thousand minds—no blossom or flower yet.

It takes a long time to bring a thought into act
And when it blossoms at last, the gardeners wonder—   10
There have been so many to labor this patch of ground,
Garrison, Beecher, a dozen New England names,
Courageous, insulting Sumner, narrow and strong,
With his tongue of silver and venom and his wrecked body,
Wendell Phillips, Antinous of Harvard—
But now that the thought has arisen, they are not sure
It was their thought after all—it is good enough—
The best one could expect from a man like Lincoln,
But this and that are wrong, are unshrewdly planned,
We could have ordered it better, we knew the ground,   20
It should have been done before, in a different way,
And our praise is grudging.
                              Pity the gardeners,
Pity Boston, pity the pure in heart,
Pity the men whom Time goes past in the night,
Without their knowledge. They worked through the heat of the
    day.

Let us even pity
Wendell Phillips, Antinous of Harvard,
For he was a model man and such men deserve   30
A definite pity at times.
                          He too did his best.
Secure in his own impenetrable self-knowledge,
He seldom agreed with Lincoln or thought him wise;
He sometimes thought that a stunning defeat would give
A needed lesson to the soul of the nation,
And, before, would have broken the Union as blithely as Yancey
For his own side of abolition, speaking about it
In many public meetings where he was heckled
But usually silenced the hecklers sooner or later   40

226

With his mellifluous, masculine, well-trained accents.
War could hardly come too soon for a man like that
And when it came, he was busy. He did his part,
Being strong and active, blessed with a ready mind,
And the cause being one to which he professed devotion,
He spoke. He spoke well, with conviction, and frequently.

So much for the banner-bearers of abolition,
The men who carried the lonely flag for years
And could bear defeat with the strength of the pure in heart
But could not understand the face of success.   10

The other dissenters are simpler to understand.
They are ready to fight for the Union but not for niggers,
They don't give a damn for niggers and say so now
With a grievous cry.
               And yet the slow root-thought works
Gradually through men's minds.
                    The Lancashire spinners,
Thrown out of work because no cotton can come
To feed their mills through the choking Union blockade,
Yet hold starvation meetings and praise the Union.   20
The tide has begun to turn in some English minds,
The watchers overseas feel their hands grow numb,
Slidell and Mason and Huse still burrow and argue,
But a cold breath blows through the rooms with the chandeliers.
A door is beginning to close.
                  Few men perceive
The turn of the tide, the closing of the door.
Lincoln does not perceive it. He sees alone
The grind of the war, the lagging of the recruits,
Election after election going against him,   30
And Lee back safe in Virginia after Antietam
While McClellan sticks for five weeks and will not move.
He loses patience at last and removes McClellan.
Burnside succeeds him—
              and the grimly bewildered
Army of the Potomac has a new rider,
Affable, portly, whiskered and self-distrusting,
Who did not wish the command and tried to decline it,
Took it at last and almost wept when he did.
A worried man who passes like a sad ghost   40

Across November, looking for confidence,
And beats his army at last against stone walls
At Fredericksburg in the expected defeat
With frightful slaughter.
                              The news of the thing comes back.
There are tears in his eyes. He never wanted command.
"Those men over there," he groans, "Those men over there"
—They are piled like cordwood in front of the stone wall—

He wants to lead a last desperate charge himself,
But he is restrained.   10
                              The sullen army draws back,
Licking its wounds. The night falls. The newspapers rave.
There are sixty-three hundred dead in that doomed attack
That never should have been made.
                              His shoulders are bowed.
He tries a vain march in the mud and resigns at last
The weapon he could not wield.
                              Joe Hooker succeeds him.
The winter clamps down, cold winter of doubt and grief.

ELEGY

        The sun shines, the wind goes by,   20
        The prisoners and captives lie
        In a cell without an eye.

        Winter will not touch them more
        Than the cold upon a sore
        That was frozen long before.

        Summer will not make them sweet
        Nor the rainy Springs refresh
        That extremity of heat
        In the self-corrupting flesh.

        The band blares, the bugles snort,   30
        They lose the fort or take the fort,
        Someone writes a wise report.

        Someone's name is Victory.
        The prisoners and captives lie
        Too long dead before they die.

228

V. *Prison reports*

For all prisoners and captives now,
For the dark legion,
The Andersonvillers, the Castle Thunder men,
The men who froze at Camp Morton and came from the dungeons
With blood burst out on their faces.
The men who died at Salisbury and Belle Isle,
Elmira, St. Louis, Camp Douglas—the Libby tunnellers—
The men in the fetid air.

There are charges back and forth upon either side,   10
Some true, some false.
                    You can read the official reports,
The dozen thick black-bound volumes of oaths and statements,
A desert of type, a dozen black mummy-cases
Embalming the long-forgotten, building again
The cumbrous machine of guards and reports and orders,
"Respectfully submitted" . . . "I beg to state" . . .
"State of kitchen—good." . . . "Food, quality of—quite good." . . .
"Police of hospital—good except Ward 7" . . .
"Remarks—we have ninety-five cases of smallpox now." . . .   20
"Remarks—as to general health of prisoners, fair." . . .
"Remarks" . . . "Remarks" . . . "Respectfully submitted" . . .
Under this type are men who used to have hands
But the creaking wheels have respectfully submitted them
Into a void, embalmed them in mummy-cases,
With their chills and fever, their looks and plans of escape.
They called one "Shorty," they called another "The Judge,"
One man wore the Virgin's medal around his neck,
One had a broken nose and one was a liar,
"Respectfully submitted—"   30
                    But, now and then,
A man or a scene escapes from the mummy-cases,
Like smoke escaping, blue smoke coiling into pictures,
Stare at those coils—
                    and see in the hardened smoke,
The triple stockade of Andersonville the damned,
Where men corrupted like flies in their own dung
And the gangrened sick were black with smoke and their filth.
There were thirty thousand Federal soldiers there

Before the end of the war.
                    A man called Wirtz,
A Swiss, half brute, half fool, and wholly a clod,
Commanded that camp of spectres.
                              One reads what he did
And longs to hang him higher than Haman hung,
And then one reads what he said when he was tried
After the war—and sees the long, heavy face,
The dull fly buzzing stupidly in the trap,
The ignorant lead of the voice, saying and saying,
"Why, I did what I could, I was ordered to keep the jail.
Yes, I set up deadlines, sometimes chased men with dogs,
Put men in torturing stocks, killed this one and that,
Let the camp corrupt till it tainted the very guards
Who came there with mortal sickness.
But they were prisoners, they were dangerous men,
If a hundred died a day—how was it my fault?
I did my duty. I always reported the deaths.
I don't see what I did different from other people.
I fought well at Seven Pines and was badly wounded.
I have witnesses here to tell you I'm a good man
And that I was really kind. I don't understand.
I'm old. I'm sick. You're going to hang me. Why?"

Crush out the fly with your thumb and wipe your hand,
You cannot crush the leaden, creaking machine,
The first endorsement, the paper on the desk
Referred by Adjutant Feeble to Captain Dull
For further information and his report.

Some men wish evil and accomplish it
But most men, when they work in that machine,
Just let it happen somewhere in the wheels.
The fault is no decisive, villainous knife
But the dull saw that is the routine mind.

Why, if a man lay dying on their desk
They'd do their best to help him, friend or foe,
But this is merely a respectfully
Submitted paper, properly endorsed
To be sent on and on, and gather blood.

Stare at the smoke again for a moment's space
And see another live man in another prison.

A colored trooper named Woodson was on guard
In the prison at Newport News, one night around nine.
There was a gallery there, where the privy was,
But prisoners weren't allowed in it after dark.

The colored soldier talked with the prisoners
At first, in a casual, more or less friendly way;
They tried to sell him breastpins and rings they had
And bothered him by wanting to go to the privy.   10

At last, he fired on a man
Who went in the gallery, but happened to miss him.
A lieutenant came down to ask the cause of the shot.
Woodson told him.
                    A second prisoner went
On the same errand, a shadow slipping through shadows.
Woodson halted him twice but he kept on moving.
"There's a man in the gallery now," said the young lieutenant.
"Well, I reckon it's one of the men makin' water again,"
Said Woodson, uneasily. The lieutenant stiffened.   20
He was officer of the guard and orders were orders.
"Why don't you use the bayonet on him?" he said.
Woodson jumped forward. The bayonet hunched and struck.
The man ran into the privy and fell like a log. . . . .
A prisoner said "You've killed him dead," in a voice.
"Yes, by God!" said Woodson, cleaning his bayonet,
"They buried us alive at Fort Pillow."
                                    The court
Found the sentry a trifle hasty, but on the whole
Within his instructions, the officer's orders lawful;   30
One cannot dispute the court.
                            And yet the man
Who went to the privy is inconveniently dead.
It seems an excessive judgment for going there.

The little pictures wreathe into smoke again.
The mummy-cases close upon the dark legion.
The papers are filed away.
                            If they once were sent

To another court for some last word of review,
They are back again. It seems strange that such tidy files
Of correspondence respectfully submitted
Should be returned from God with no final endorsement.

VI. *Prisoners for exchange*

The slow carts hitched along toward the place of exchange
Through a bleak wind.

                         It was not a long wagon train,
Wagons and horses were too important to waste
On prisoners for exchange, if the men could march.
Many did march and some few died on the way   10
But more died up in the wagons, which was not odd.
If a man was too sick to walk, he was pretty sick.

They had been two days on the road.

                                        Jack Ellyat lay
Between a perishing giant from Illinois
Who raved that he was bailing a leaky boat
Out on the Lakes, and a slight, tubercular Jew
Who raved that he was bailing a leaky boat
Bailey marched. He still was able to march
But his skin hung on him. He hummed to the Weaver's tune.   20

They got to the river at last.

                                 Jack Ellyat saw
A yellow stream and slow boats crossing the stream.
Bailey had helped him out. He was walking now
With his arm around Bailey's neck. Their course was a crab's.
The Jew was up and staring with shoe-button eyes
While his cough took him. The giant lay on a plank,
Some men were trying to lift him.

                                     The wind blew
Over a knife of frost and shook their rags.   30
The air was a thawing ice of most pure, clear gold.
They stared across the river and saw the flag
And the tall, blue soldiers walking in thick, warm coats
Like strong, big men who fed well. And then they cheered,
A dry thin cheer, pumped up from exhausted lungs
And yet with a metal vibrance.

                                 The bright flag flapped.

232

Who muttered like a sick duck when the
wagon jounced.

"I can smell 'em frying meat," said the coughing Jew.
He sniffed, "Oh God, I hope it ain't ham," he said
With his mouth puckered. A number of scarecrows laughed.
And then they heard the echo of their own cheer
Flung back at them, it seemed, in a high, shrill wail
With that tongue of metal pulsing its feebleness.
But it did not end like an echo, it gathered and rose,
It was the Confederate sick on the other side,
Cheering their own.

     The two weak crowd-voices met 10
In one piping, gull-like cry.

       Then the boats began
To take the weak men on board.

         Jack Ellyat walked
To his boat on stuffless legs. "Keep quiet," he thought,
"You're not through yet—you won't be through till you land.
They can jerk you back, even now, if you look too pleased.
Look like a soldier, damn you, and show them how."
The thought was childish but it stiffened his back
And got him into the boat.   20

       In the midst of the stream
They passed a boat with Confederate prisoners
So near they could yell at each other.

         "Hello there, Yank."
"Hello Reb" . . . "You look pretty sick—don't we feed you
 good?" . . .
"You don't look so damn pretty, yourself" . . . "My, ain't that a
 shame!" . . .
"You'll look a lot sicker when Hooker gets after you." . . .
"Hell, old Jack'll take Hooker apart like a coffee-pot" . . . 30
"Well, good-by, Yank" . . . "Good-by, Reb" . . . "Get fat if you
 kin."

So might meet and pass, perhaps, on a weedier stream
Other boats, no more heavily charged, to a wet, black oar.
Bailey watched the boat move away with its sick grey men
Still yelling stingless insults through tired lips.
He cupped his hands to his mouth. "Oh——" he roared,
Then he sank back, coughing.

       "They look pretty bad," he said,
"They look glad to get back. They ain't such bad Rebs at that." 40

The boat's nose touched the wharf. It swung and was held.
They got out. They didn't move toward the camp at first.
They looked back at the river first and the other side,
Without saying words. They stood there thus for a space
Like a row of tattered cranes at the edge of a stream,
Blinking at something.

"All right, you men," said an officer. "Come along."
Jack Ellyat's heart made a sudden lump in his chest.
It was a blue officer. They were back in their lines,
Back out of prison.   10
                    Bailey whirled out his arm
In a great wheel gesture. "Hell," he said in a low,
Moved voice, thumbed his nose across at the Stars and Bars
And burst into horrible tears. Jack Ellyat held him.
"Captain, when do we eat?" said the Jew in a wail.

BOOK SIX:
The Crowded Third Act

Christmas comes to Wingate Hall—not the bountiful Christmas such as Cudjo remembers—but still, in spite of hard times, a gallant effort to be festive.

Sally Dupré and Wingate, separated by distance and their own confused hearts, cannot help thinking of each other.

Finding the New England winter not at all changed from his remembrance, Jack Ellyat, home on sick leave, lets his eyes rest on familiar scenes but finds that the image of Melora cannot be dimmed.

Among the hiders, the pride of John Vilas fights with his love for his daughter, and his heart is torn with pity and with anger as Melora's child is born.

Spring calls the leaders and the soldiers out of winter quarters; it brings a turn in the fortunes of Shippy, the spy, of Luke Breckinridge and Sophy; it fosters the self-love of Lucy; it is a crowded third act. Against these small lives, we learn also of The Wilderness where Stonewall Jackson, the right arm of General Lee, lies dying.

I. *Cudjo finds conjurings can't cure*

Cudjo breathed on the silver urn
And rubbed till his hand began to burn,
With his hoarded scrap of chamois-skin.
The metal glittered like bright new tin
And yet, as he labored, his mouth was sad—
"Times is gettin' almighty bad.
Christmas a-comin', sure and swif',
But no use hollerin' 'Christmas Gif'!'
No use keepin' the silver fittin',
No use doin' nothin' but sittin'.   10
Old Marse Billy stayin' away,
Yankees shootin' at Young Marse Clay,
Grey hairs in Miss Mary's brush,
And a-whooin' wind in de berry-bush,
Dat young red setter done eat her pups,
We was washin' de tea set an' bust two cups,
Just come apart in Liza's han'—
Christmas, where has you gwine to, man?
Won't you never come back again?
I feels like a cat in de outdoors rain."   20
Christmas used to come without fail,
A big old man with a raccoon tail,
So fine and bushy it brushed the ground
And made folks sneeze when he waltzed around.
He was rolling river and lucky sun
And a laugh like a double-barrelled gun,
And the chip-straw hat on his round, bald head
Was full of money and gingerbread.
"Come in, Christmas, and have a cheer!
But, if he's comin', he won't stop here,   30
He likes folks cheerful and dinners smokin'
And famblies shootin' off caps and jokin',
But he won't find nothin' on dis plantation,
But a lot of grievin' conversation.

Dey's tooken de carpets and window-weights
To go and shoot at de Yankee States,
Dey's tooken Nelly, de cross-eye mule,
And whoever took her was one big fool;
Dey's tooken dis an' dey's tooken dat,

Till I kain't make out what dey's drivin' at.
But if Ole Marse Billy could see dis place
He'd cuss all Georgia blue in de face.
To see me wuhkin with dis ole shammy
Like a field-hand-nigger fum Alabammy,
And Ole Miss wearin' a corn-husk hat,
Dippin' ole close in de dyein' vat,
Scrapin' her petticoats up for lint
An' bilin' her tea out of julep-mint.

Young Marse Clay he'd feel mighty sad   10
If he'd seed de weddin' his sisters had.
De grooms was tall and de brides was fine,
But dey drunk de health in blackberry wine,
And supper was thu at half-past-nine.

Weddin's ust to last for a week,
But now we's rowin' up Hard Times Creek.
Somethin's conjured dis white-folks' South.
Somethin' big with a hongry mouth,
Eatin' an' eatin'—I done my bes',
Scattered de fedders and burnt de nes',   20
Filled de bottle an' made de hand
An' buried de trick in Baptis' land,
An' dat trick's so strong, I was skeered all night,
But, somehow or udder, it don' wuhk right.
Ef I got me a piece of squinch-owl's tail
An' some dead-folks' yearth fum de county jail,
It mout wuhk better—but I ain't sho',
And de wind keeps scrabblin' under de do',
Scratchin' and scratchin' his buzzard-claws,
Won't nuthin' feed you, hongry jaws?   30

Field hands keeps on hoein' de corn,
Stupidest niggers ever born,
All dey's good for is gravy-lickin',
Ram-buttin' and cotton-pickin';
Dey don't hear de wind in de slew,
But dat wind's blowin' over 'em too,
An' dat wind's res'less an' dat wind's wile,
An' dat wind aches like a motherless chile,
Won't nuthin' feed you, achin' wind?"

238

The hand stopped rubbing. The spoons were shined.
He put them back in the flannel bag
And stared at his scrap of chamois-rag.
War was a throat that swallowed things
And you couldn't cure it with conjurings.

II. Sally's heart

Sally Dupré watched over her dyeing pots,
Evening was setting in with a light slow rain
That marched like a fairy army—there being nothing
From the white fog on the hill to the soaked door-stone
But a moving grey and silver hurry of lances,   10
Distinct yet crowded, thin as the edge of the moon,
Carried in no fleshed hand.

                  She thought to herself,
"I have stained my arms with new colors, doing this work,
The red is pokeberry-juice, the grey is green myrtle,
The deep black is queen's delight.

                  If he saw me now
With my hands so parti-colored he would not know them.
He likes girls' hands that nothing has stained but lotions,
This is too fast a dye.   20
                  I will dye my heart
In a pot of queen's delight, in the pokeberry sap,
I will dye it red and black in the fool's old colors
And send it to him, wrapped in a calico rag,
To keep him warm through the rain.

                  It will keep him warm.
And women in love do better without a heart.
What fools we are to wait the wheel of the year,
The year will not help our trouble.

                  What fools we are   30
To give our parti-colored hearts to the rain.

I am tired of the slogans now and tired of the saving,
I want to dance all night in a brand-new dress
And forget about wars and love and the South and courage.

The South is an old high house full of charming ladies,
The war is a righteous war full of gallant actions,
And love is a white camellia worn in the hair.

But I am tired of talking to charming ladies
And the smell of the white camellia, I will dye
My hands twice as black as ink in the working waters
And wait like a fool for bitter love to come home.

He was wounded this year. They hurt him. They hurt you,
    darling.
I have no doubt she came with a bunch of flowers
And talked to your wound and you like a charming lady.
I have no doubt that she came.

Her heart is not parti-colored. She'll not go steeping   10
Her gentle hands in the pulp and the dead black waters
Till the crooked blot lies there like a devil's shadow,
And the heart is stained with the stain.

If I came to the bed where you lay sick and in fever,
I would not come with little tight-fisted flowers
But with the white heron's plume that lay in the forest
Till it was cooler than sleep.

The living balm would touch on your wound less gently,
The Georgia sun less fierce than my arms to hold you,
The steel bow less stubborn than my curved body   20
Strung against august death.

They hurt you, darling, they hurt you and I not with you,
I nowhere there to slit the cloth from your burning,
To find the head of the man who fired the bullet
And give his eyes to the crows.

House, house, house, it is not that my friend was wounded,
But that you kept him from me while he had freedom,
You and the girl whose heart is a snuffed white candle—
Now I will curse you both.

Comely house, high-courteous house of the gentle,   30
You must win your war for my friend is mixed in your quarrel,
But then you must fall, you must fall, for your walls divide us,
Your worn stones keep us apart.

I am sick of the bland camellias in your old gardens,
Your pride and passion are not my pride and my passion,

I am strangling to death in your cables of honeysuckle,
Your delicate lady-words.

I would rather dig in the earth than learn your patience,
I have need of a sky that never was cut for dresses
And a rough ground to tear my hands on like lion's clothing,
And a hard wheel to move.

The low roof by the marches of rainy weather,
The sharp love that carries the fool's old colors,
The bare bed that is not a saint's or a lady's,
The strong death at the end.   10

They hurt you, darling, they hurt you, and I not with you,
I nowhere by to see you, to touch my darling,
To take your fever upon me if I could take it
And burn my hands at your wound.

If I had been there—oh, how surely I would have found you,
How surely killed your foe—and sat by your bedside
All night long, like a mouse, like a stone unstirring,
Only to hear your slow breath moving the darkness,
Only to hear, more precious than childish beauty,
The slow tired beat of your heart."   20

III. *Wingate remembers*

Wingate sat by a smoky fire
Mending a stirrup with rusty wire.
His brows were clenched in the workman's frown,
In a day or a week they'd be back in town,
He thought of it with a brittle smile
That mocked at guile for its lack of guile
And mocked at ease for its lack of ease.
It was better riding through rainy trees
And playing tag with the Union spies
Than telling ladies the pleasant lies,   30
And yet, what else could you do, on leave?

He touched a rent in his dirty sleeve,
That was the place that the bullet tore
From the blue-chinned picket whose belt he wore,

The man who hadn't been quick enough,
And the powder-burn on the other cuff
Belonged to the fight with the Yankee scout
Who died in Irish when he went out.
He thought of these things as a man might think
Of certain trees by a river-brink,
Seen in a flash from a passing train,
And, before you could look at them, gone again.
It was more important to eat and drink
Than give the pain or suffer the pain   10
And life was too rapid for memory.

"There are certain things that will cling to me,
But not the things that I thought would cling,
And the wound in my body cannot sting
Like the tame black crow with the bandaged wing,
The nervous eye and the hungry craw
That picked at the dressing-station straw
Till I was afraid it would pick my eyes
And couldn't lift hand to beat it off.
I can tell the ladies the usual lies   20
Of the wild night-duels when two scouts clash
And your only light is his pistol-flash;
But I remember a watering-trough
Lost in a little brushwood town
And the feel of Black Whistle slumping down
Under my knees in the yellow air,
Hit by a bullet from God knows where . . .
Not the long, mad ride round the Union lines
But the smell of the swamp at Seven Pines,
The smell of the swamp by Gaines's Mill,   30
And Lee in the dusk before Malvern Hill,
Riding along with his shoulders straight
Like a sending out of the Scæan Gate,
The cold intaglio of war. *carved in opposite of cameo*
'This is Virginia's *Iliad*,'
But Troy was taken nevertheless—
I remember the eyes my father had
When we saw our dead in the Wilderness—
I cannot remember any more—

Lucy will wear her English gown   40
When the Black Horse Troop comes back to town,

242

Pin her dress with a silver star
And tell our <u>shadows</u> how brave we are.   *false front*
Lucy I like your white-and-gold—"

He blew on his hands for the day was cold,
And the damp, green wood gave little heat:
There was something in him that matched the sleet
And washed its hands in a rainy dream,
Till the stirrup-strap and the horses' steam
And Shepley and Bristol behind his back,
Playing piquet with a dog-eared pack   10
And the hiss of the sap in the smoky wood
Mixed for a moment in something good,
Something outside of peace or war
Or a fair girl wearing a silver star,
Something hardly as vain as pride
And gaunt as the men he rode beside.
It made no comments but it was there,
Real as the color of Lucy's hair
Or the taste of Henry Weatherby's wine.
He thought "These people are friends of mine.   20
And we certainly fooled the Yanks last week,
When we caught those wagons at Boiling Creek,
I guess we're not such a bad patrol
If we never get straight with the muster-roll,
I guess, next Spring, we can do it again—"

Bristol threw down a flyspecked ten,
"Theah," he said, in the soft, sweet drawl
That could turn as hard as a Minie-ball,
"This heah day is my lucky day,
And Shepley nevah could play piquet."   30
He stretched his arms in a giant yawn,
"Gentlemen, when are we movin' on?
I have no desire for a soldier's end,
While I still have winnin's that I can spend
And they's certain appointments with certain ladies
Which I'd miss right smart if I went to Hades,
Especially one little black-eyed charmer
Whose virtue, one hopes, is her only armor,
So if Sergeant Wingate's mended his saddle
I suggest that we all of us now skedaddle,   40

243

To employ a term that the Yankees favor—"
He tasted his words, for he liked the flavor.
"And yet, one dreads to be back," said he,
"One knows how tippled one well may be
If one meets with the oppor-tun-ity.
And even the charmers can likewise raise
Unpleasant doubts that may last for days—
And as one," he sighed, "of our martial lads,
I'd rather be chargin' Columbiads,
Than actin' sweet to some old smooth-bore   10
When he tells me how he could win the War
By burnin' the next Yank crossroads-store.
The Yanks aren't always too blame polite,
But they fight like sin when they've got to fight,
And after they've almost nailed your hide
To your stinkin' saddle in some ole ride,
It makes you mad when some nice home-guard
Tells you they nevah could combat hard.
I have no desire to complain or trouble
But I'd find this conflict as comfortable   20
As a big green pond for a duck to swim in,
If it wasn't for leave, and the lovin' women."

IV. Jack Ellyat home on furlough

The snow lay hard on the hills. You could burn your eyes
By too-long-looking into the cold ice-lens
Of infinite, pure, glittering, winter air.
It was as cold as that, as sparkling as that,
Where the crystal trees stood up like strange, brittle toys
After the sleet storm passed, till the setting sun
Hung the glass boughs with rainbows frozen to gems
And the long blue shadows pooled in the still hill-hollows.   30

The white and the purple lilacs of New England
Are frozen long, they will not bloom till the rains,
But when you look from the window, you see them there,
A great field of white lilacs.
                    A gathered sheaf
Of palest blossoms of lilac, stained with the purple evening.

Jack Ellyat turned away from the window now,
The frosty sleighbell of winter was in his ears,
He saw the new year, a child in a buffalo-robe,
Dragged in a sleigh whose runners were polished steel
Up the long hill of February, into chill light.
The child slept in the robe like a reindeer-colt,
Nuzzled under the winter. The bright bells rang.

He warmed his hands at the stove and shivered a little
Hearing that ice-sweet chime.

                    He was better now,   10
But his blood felt thin when he thought of skating along
Over black agate floors in the bonfire light
Or beating a girl's red mittens free of the snow,
And he slept badly at times, when his flesh recalled
Certain smells and sights that were prison.

He stared at the clock where Phaëton's horses lunged
With a queer nod of recognition. The rest had altered,
People and winter and nightmares and Ellen Baker,
Or stayed in a good dimension that he had lost,
But Phaëton was the same. He said to himself,   20
"I have met you twice, old, drunken charioteer,
Once in the woods, and once in a dirty shack
Where Death was a coin of spittle left on the floor.
I suppose we will meet again before there's an end,
Well, let it happen.

              It must have been cold last year
At Fredericksburg. I'm glad I wasn't in that.
Melora, what's happened to you?"

                        He saw Melora
Walking down from the woods in the low spring light.   30
His body hurt for a minute, but then it stopped.
He was getting well. He'd have to go back pretty soon.
He grinned, a little dryly, thinking of chance,
Father had seen the congressman after all,
Just before Shiloh. So now, nearly ten months later,
The curious wheels that are moved by such congressmen
Were sending him back to the Army of the Potomac,
Back with the old company, back with the Eastern voices,
Henry Fairfield limping along with his sticks,
Shot through both hips at Antietam.   40

                                          He didn't care,
Except for losing Bailey, which made it tough.
He tried to puzzle out the change in his world
But gave it up. Things and people looked just the same,
You could love or like or detest them just the same way,
But whenever you tried to talk of your new dimension
It didn't sound right, except to creatures like Bailey.
"I have met you twice, old, drunken charioteer,
The third time you may teach me how to be cool."

Ned, asleep by the stove, woke up and yawned,   10
"Hello Ned," said his master, with a half-smile,
"I told a girl about you, back in a wood,
You'd like that girl. She'd rub the back of your ears.
And Bailey'd like you too. I wish Bailey was here.
Want to go to war, Ned?" Ned yawned largely again.
Ellyat laughed. "You're right, old fella," he said,
"You get too mixed up in a war. You better stay here.
God, I'd like to sleep by a stove for a million years,
Turn into a dog and remember how to stand cold."
The clock struck five. Jack Ellyat jumped at the sound   20
Then he sank back. "No, fooled you that time," he said,
As if the strokes had been bullets.
                                          Then he turned
To see his mother, coming in with a lamp,
And taste the strange tastes of supper and quietness.

              V. *Fruit of the wilderness-stone*

John Vilas heard the beating of another
Sleet at another and a rougher wall
While his hands knotted together and then unknotted.
Each time she had to moan, his hands shut down,
And now the moans were coming close together,   30
Close as bright streaks of hail.
                                          The younger children
Slept the uneasy sleep of innocent dogs
Who know there's something strange about the house,
Stranger than storms, and yet they have to sleep,
And someone has to watch them sleeping now.

                           246

"Harriet's right and Harriet's upstairs,
And Harriet cried like this when she gave birth,
Eighteen years back, in that chintz-curtained room,
And her long cry ran like an icicle
Into my veins. I can remember yet
The terrible old woman with the shawl
Who sat beside me, like deserted Fate,
Cursing me with those eyes each time she cried,
Although she must, one time, have cried like that
And been the object of as wild a cry,   10
And so far back,—and on—and always that,
The linked, the agonizing chain of cries
Brighter than steel, because earth will be earth
And the sun strike it, and the seed have force.
And yet no cry has touched me like this cry.

Harriet's right and Harriet's upstairs
And Harriet would have kept her from today,
And now today has come, I look at it,
Under the icicle, and wish it gone,
Because it hurts me to be sitting here,   20
Biting my fingers at my daughter's cry
And knowing Harriet has the harder task
As she has had for nearly twenty years.
And yet, what I have sought that I have sought
And cannot disavouch for my own pang,
Or be another father to the girl
Than he who let her run the woods alone
Looking for stones that have no business there.
For Harriet sees a dozen kinds of pain.
And some are blessed, being legitimate,
And some are cursed, being outside a law: 30
But she and I see only pain itself
And are hard-hearted with our epitaphs,
And yet I wish I could not hear that cry.
I know that it will pass because all things
Pass but the search that only ends with breath,
And, even after that, my daughter and I
May still get up from bondage, being such
Smoke as no chain of steel-bright cries can chain
To walk like Indian Summer through the woods   40

247

And be the solitaries of the wind
Till we are sleepy as old clouds at last.

She has a lover and will have a child
And I'm alone. I had forgotten that,
Though you'd not think it easy to forget.
No, we'll not go together.
                The cries beat
Like hail upon the cold panes of my heart
Faster and faster, till they crack the glass
And I can know at last how old I am.   10

That is my punishment and my defence,
My ecstasy and my deep-seated bane.
I prayed to life for life once, in my youth,
Between the rain and a long stroke of cloud
Till my soaked limbs felt common with the sky
And the black stone of heaven swung aside,
With a last clap of water, to reveal
Lonely and timid, after all that wrath,
The small, cold, perfect flower of the new moon
And now, perhaps, I'll pray again tonight,   20
Still to the life that used me as a man
Uses and wears a strong and riotous horse,
Still to the vagrants of no fortunate word.

Men who go looking for the wilderness-stone,
Eaters of life who run away from bread
And are not satisfied with lucky days!
Robbers of airy gold, skin-changing men
Who find odd brothers when the moon is full,
Stray alchemics who entertain an imp
And feed it plums within a hollow tree   30
Until its little belly is sufficed,
Men who have seen the bronze male-partridge beat
His drum of feathers not ten feet away,
Men who have listened to wild geese at night
Until your hearts were hollowed with that sound,
Moth-light and owl-light and first-dayspring men,
Seekers and seldom-finders of the woods,
But always seekers till your eyes are shut;
I have an elder daughter that I love

And, having loved from childhood, would not tame
Because I once was tamed.
                              If you're my friends,
Then she's your friend.
                              I do not ask for her
Refusal or compunction or the safe
Road between little houses and old gates
Where Death lies sleepy as a dog in the sun
And the slow cows come home with evening bells
Into the tired peace that's good for pain.   10
Those who are never tired of eating life
Must immolate themselves against a star
Sooner or late, as she turns crucified
Now, on that flagellating wheel of light
Which will not miss one revolution's turn
For any anguish we can bring to it,
Because it is our master and our stone,
Body of pain, body of sharpened fire,
Body of quenchless life, itself, itself,
That safety cannot buy or peddlers sell   20
Or the rich cowards leave their silly sons.
But, oh,
She's tired out, she's broken, she's athirst.
Wrap her in twilights now, she is so torn,
And mask again the cold, sweat-runnelled mask
With the deep silence of a leafy wood
So cool and dim its birds are all asleep
And will not fret her. Wipe her straining hands
With the soft, gleaming cobwebs April spins
Out of bright silver tears and spider silk   30
Till they are finer than the handkerchiefs
Of a young, wild, spear-bearing fairy-queen.
Soothe her and comfort her and let her hear
No harshness but the mumbling peaceful sound
The fed bee grumbles to his honey-bags
In the red foxglove's throat.
                              Oh, if you are
Anything but lost shadows, go to her!"

Melora did not make such words for herself,
Being unable, and too much in pain.   40
If wood-things were beside her, she did not see them,

249

But only a lamp, and hands.
                    The pains came hard now,
A fist that hardly opened before it shut,
A red stair mounting into an ultimate
Flurry of misty conflict, when it seemed
As if she fought against the earth itself
For mere breath and something other than mere breath.
She heard the roar of the tunnel, drowned in earth.
Earth and its expulsive waters, tearing her, being born.
Then it was yellow silence and a weak crying.   10

After the child was washed, they showed her the child,
Breakable, crumpled, breathing, swathed and indignant,
With all its nails and hands that moved of themselves—
A queer thing to come out of that, but then it was there.
"Looks healthy enough," said her mother in a tired voice.
Melora stared. "He's got blue eyes," she said finally.
Her mother sniffed. "A lot of 'em start out blue."
She looked at the child as if she wanted to tell it,
"You aren't respectable. What are you doing here?"
But the child began wailing. She rocked it mechanically.   20
The rain kept on through the night but nobody listened.
The parents talked for a while, then they fell asleep.
Even the new child slept with its fists tight shut.
Melora heard the rain for a single moment
And then deep, beautiful nothing. "Over," she thought.
She slept, handfasted to the wilderness-stone.

VI. A new spring

Now the earth begins to roll its wheel toward the sun,
The deep mud-gullies are drying.
                              The sluggish armies
That have slept the bear-months through in their winter-camps,   30
Begin to stir and be restless.
                    They're tired enough
Of leaky huts and the rain and punishment-drill.
They haven't forgotten what it was like last time,
But next time we'll lick 'em, next time it won't be so bad,
Somehow we won't get killed, we won't march so hard.
"These huts looked pretty good when we first hit camp

But they look sort of lousy now—we might as well git—
Fight the Rebs—and the Yanks—and finish it up."
So they think in the bored, skin-itching months
While the roads are drying. "We're sick of this crummy place,
We might as well git, it doesn't much matter where."
But when they git, they are cross at leaving the huts,
"We fixed up ours first rate. We had regular lamps.
We knew the girls at the Depot. It wasn't so bad.
Why the hell do we have to git when we just got fixed?
Oh, well, we might as well travel."   10
                                        So they go on,
The huts drop behind, the dry road opens ahead . . . .

Fighting Joe Hooker feels good when he looks at his men.
A blue-eyed, uncomplex man with a gift for phrase.
"The finest army on the planet," he says.
The phrase is to turn against him with other phrases
When he is beaten—but now he is confident.
Tall, sandy, active, sentimental and tart,
His horseman's shoulder is not yet bowed by the weight
Of knowing the dice are his and the cast of them,   20
The weight of command, the weight of Lee's ghostly name.
He rides, preparing his fate.
                            In the other camps,
Lee writes letters, is glad to get buttermilk,
Wrings food and shoes and clothes from his commissariat,
Trusts in God and whets a knife on a stone.
Jackson plays with his new-born daughter, waiting for Spring,
His rare laugh clangs as he talks to his wife and child.
He is looking well. War always agrees with him,
And this, perhaps, is the happiest time of his life.   30
He has three months of it left.
                            By the swollen flood
Of the Mississippi, stumpy Grant is a mole
Gnawing at Vicksburg. He has been blocked four times
But he will carry that beaver-dam at last.
There is no brilliant lamp in that dogged mind
And no conceit of brilliance to shake the hand,
But hand and mind can use the tools that they get
This long way out of Galena.
                            Sherman is there   40
And Sherman loves him and finds him hard to make out,

251

In Sherman's impatient fashion—the quick, sharp man
Seeing ten thousand things where the slow sees one
And yet with a sort of younger brother awe
At the infinite persistence of that slow will
—They make a good pair of hunting dogs, Grant and Sherman,
The nervous, explosive, passionate, slashing hound
And the quiet, equable, deadly holder-on,
Faded-brown as a cinnamon-bear in Spring—
See them like that, the brown dog and the white dog,
Calling them back and forth through the scrubby woods   10
After the little white scut of Victory,
Or see them as elder brother and younger brother,
But remember this. In their time they were famous men
And yet they were not jealous, one of the other.
When the gold has peeled from the man on the gilded horse,
Riding Fifth Avenue, and the palm-girl's blind;
When the big round tomb gapes empty under the sky,
Vacant with summer air, when it's all forgotten,
When nobody reads the books, when the flags are moth-dust,
Write up that. You won't have to write it so often.   20
It will do as well as the railway-station tombs.

So with the troops and the leaders of the bear-armies,
The front-page-newspaper-things.
                                   Tall Lincoln reviews
Endless columns crunching across new snow.
They pass uncheering at the marching-salute.
Lincoln sits on his horse with his farmer's seat,
Watching the eyes go by and the eyes come on.
The gaunt, long body is dressed in its Sunday black,
The gaunt face, strange as an omen, sad and foreboding.   30
The eyes look at him, he looks back at the eyes;
They pass and pass. They go back to their camps at last.
"So that was him," they say. "So that's the old man.
I'm glad we saw him. He isn't so much on looks
But he looks like people you know. He looks sad all right,
I never saw nobody look quite as sad as that
Without it made you feel foolish. He don't do that.
He makes you feel—I dunno—I'm glad we could see him.
He was glad to see us but you could tell all the same
This war's plumb killin' him. You can tell by his face.   40

252

I never saw such a look on any man's face.
I guess it's tough for him. Well, we saw him, for once."

That day in Richmond, a mob of angry women
Swarm in the streets and riot for bread or peace.
They loot some shops, a few for the bread they need,
A few for thieving, most because they are moved
By discontent and hunger to do as the rest.
The troops are called out. The troops are about to fire,
But Davis gets on a wagon and calms the crowd
Before the tumbled bodies clutter the street.   10
He never did a better thing with his voice
And it should be told. Next day they riot again,
But this time the fire is weaker. They are dispersed,
A few arrested. Bread grows dearer than ever.
The housewives still go out with their market-baskets,
But coffee's four dollars a pound and tea eleven.
They come back with a scraping of this and a scrap of that
And try to remember old lazy, lagnappe days,
The slew-foot negro chanting his devilled crabs
Along the street, and the market-women piling   20
The wicker baskets with everything good and fresh;
Topping it off with a great green fist of parsley
That you used to pretty the sides of the serving-dish
And never bothered to eat.
                              They improvise dishes,
"Blockade pudding" . . . "Confederate fricassee,"
Serve hominy grits on the Royal Derby china
And laugh or weep in their cups of willow-bark tea.

Davis goes back from the riot, his shoulders stooped,
The glow of speech has left him and he feels cold.   30
He eats a scant meal quickly and turns to the endless
Papers piled on his desk, the squabbles and plans.
A haggard dictator, fretting the men he rules
And being fretted by them.
                              He dreams, perhaps,
Of old days, riding wild horses beside his wife
Back in his youth, on a Mississippi road.
That was a good time. It is past. He drowns in his papers.

The curtain is going up on that battlesmoked,
Crowded third act which is to decide this war
And yet not end it for years.
                              Turn your eyes away
From these chiefs and captains, put them back in their books.
Let the armies sleep like bears in a hollow cave.
War is an iron screen in front of a time,
With pictures smoked upon it in red and black,
Some gallant enough, some deadly, but all intense.
We look at the pictures, thinking we know the time,   10
We only know the screen.
                         Look behind it now
At the great parti-colored quilt of these patchwork States.
This part and that is vexed by a battle-worm,
But the ploughs go ahead, the factory chimneys smoke,
A new age curdles and boils in a hot steel caldron
And pours into rails and wheels and fingers of steel,
Steel is being born like a white-hot rose
In the dark smoke-cradle of Pittsburg—
                                   a man with a crude   20
Eye of metal and crystal looks at a smear *research work*
On a thin glass plate and wonders—   *bacteriology*
                              a shawled old woman
Sits on a curbstone calling the evening news.
War, to her, is a good day when papers sell
Or a bad day when papers don't. War is fat black type.
Anything's realer than war.
                           By Omaha
The valleys and gorges are white with the covered wagons
Moving out toward the West and the new, free land.   30
All through the war they go on.
                               Five thousand teams
Pass Laramie in a month in the last war-year,
Draft-evaders, homesteaders, pioneers,
Old soldiers, Southern emigrants, sunburnt children. . . .
Men are founding colleges, finding gold,
Selling bad beef to the army and making fortunes,
Ploughing the stone-cropped field that their fathers ploughed.
(Anything's realer than war.)
                             A moth of a woman,   40
Shut in a garden, lives on scraps of Eternity
With a dog, a procession of sunsets and certain poems

Emily Dickinson

254

She scribbles on bits of paper. Such poems may be
Ice-crystals, rubies cracked with refracted light,
Or all vast death like a wide field in ten short lines.
She writes to the tough, swart-minded Higginson
Minding his negro troops in a lost bayou,
"War feels to me like an oblique place."
                                        A man
Dreams of a sky machine that will match the birds
And another, dusting the shelves of a country store,
Saves his pennies until they turn into dimes.   10
(Anything's realer than war.)
                        A dozen men
Charter a railroad to go all across the Plains
And link two seas with a whistling iron horse.
A whiskered doctor stubbornly tries to find
The causes of childbed-fever—and, doing so,
Will save more lives than all these war-months have spent,
And never inhabit a railway-station tomb.
All this through the war, all this behind the flat screen. . . .

A SONG OF BREATH

I heard the song of breath   20
Go up from city and country,
The even breath of the sleeper,
The tired breath of the sick,
The dry cough in the throat
Of the man with the death-sweat on him,
And the quiet monotone
We breathe but do not hear.

The harsh gasp of the runner,
The long sigh of power
Heaving the weight aloft,   30
The grey breath of the old.
Men at the end of strength
With their lungs turned lead and fire,
Panting like thirsty dogs;
A child's breath, blowing a flame.

The breath that is the voice,
The silver, the woodwinds speaking,

The dear voice of your lover,
The hard voice of your foe,
And the vast breath of wind,
Mysterious over mountains,
Caught in pines like a bird
Or filling all hammered heaven.

I heard the song of breath,
Like a great strand of music,
Blown between void and void,
Uncorporal as the light.
The breath of nations asleep,
And the piled hills they sleep in,
The word that never was flesh
And yet is nothing but life.

What are you, bodiless sibyl,
Unseen except as the frost-cloud
Puffed from a silver mouth
When the hard winter's cold?
We cannot live without breath,
And yet we breathe without knowledge,
And the vast strand of sound
Goes on, eternally sighing,
Without dimension or space,
Without beginning or end.

I heard the song of breath
And lost it in all sharp voices,
Even my own voice lost
Like a thread in that huge strand,
Lost like a skein of air,
And with it, continents lost
In the great throat of Death.
I trembled, asking in vain,
Whence come you, whither art gone?
The continents flow and melt
Like wax in the naked candle,
Burnt by the wick of time—
Where is the breath of the Chaldees,
The dark, Minoan breath?
I said to myself in hate,

256

Hearing that mighty rushing,
Though you raise a new Adam up
And blow fresh fire in his visage,
He has only a loan of air,
And gets but a breathing-space.
But then I was quieted.

I heard the song of breath,
The gulf hollow with voices,
Fused into one slow voice
That never paused or was faint.   10
Man, breathing his life,
And with him all life breathing,
The young horse and the snake,
Beetle, lion and dove,
Solemn harps of the fir,
Trumpets of sea and whirlwind
And the vast, tiny grass
Blown by a breath and speaking.
I heard these things. I heard
The multitudinous river.   20
When I came back to my life,
My voice was numb in my ears,
I wondered that I still breathed.

VII. Sophy

Sophy, scared chambermaid in Pollet's Hotel,
Turned the cornhusk mattress and plumped the pillow
With slipshod hands.
           Then she picked the pillow up
And sniffed it greedily.
               Something in it smelt sweet.
The bright, gold lady had slept there the night before—   30
Oh, her lovely, lovely clothes! and the little green bottle
That breathed out flowers when you crept into the room
And pulled out the silver stopper just far enough
To get the sweetness, not far enough to be caught
If anyone came.
           It made her thin elbows ache
To think how fine and golden the lady was

And how sweet she smelled, how sweet she looked at the men,
How they looked at her.
                         "I'd like to smell sweet," she thought,
"Smell like a lady."
                     She put the hard pillow back.
The lady and the green bottle had gone away.
—If only you had clever hands—after the next sleeper—
—You could steal green bottles—the room would smell stale again—
Hide it somewhere under your dress—as it always did—
Stale cigars and tired bodies—or even say   10
When they reached to give you the tip, "Don't give me a tip,
Just give me"—unwashed men with their six-weeks' beards,
Trying to hold you back when—"that little green bottle,
I want it so."—but the lady would never do it.
Ladies named Lucy. Lucy was a good name,
Flower-smelling. Sophy was just a name.

She took up her broom and swept ineffectively,
Thinking dim thoughts.
                        The ladies named Lucy came,
Sometimes in the winter, and then all the men got shaved   20
And you could look through the door at the people dancing.
But when battles drew near, the ladies went home to stay.
It was right they should. War wasn't a thing for ladies.
                         She sighed and dabbed with her broom.

Shippy, the little man with the sharp rat-eyes,
Came behind her and put his hands on her waist.
She let him turn her around. He held her awhile
While his eyes tried to look at her and over his shoulder
At once and couldn't.

"What do you want, next time I come back?" he said.   30
Her face was sharper. "You bring me a bottle, Charley,
The kind that lady had, with the Richmond scent.
Hers has got a big silver stopper."
                         He pursed his mouth.
"I don't know," he said. "I'll try. I'd like to all right.
You be a good girl now, Soph. Do you love me, Sophy?"
"Uh-huh," she said, in a tired voice, thinking of pitchers.

"Well, I—you're a good girl, Soph." He held her again.
"I'm late," he muttered. She looked at him and felt mean.

258

He was skimpy like her. They ought to be nice to each other.
She didn't like him much but she sort of loved him.
"You be a good girl till Charley comes back," he mumbled
Kissing her nervously. "I'll bring you the scent."

"It's got a name called French Lilies," she said. "Oh, Charley!"
They clung together a moment like mournful shadows.
He was crying a little, the wet tears fell on her chin,
She cried herself when he'd gone, she didn't know why,
But when she thought of the scent with the silver stopper
She felt more happy. She went to make the next bed.   10

VIII. *Death of a spy*

Luke Breckinridge, washing his shirt in a muddy pool,
Chewed on a sour thought.
                              Only yesterday
He had seen the team creak by toward Pollet's Hotel
With that damn little rat-eyed peddler driving his mules
As if he was God Almighty.
                              He conjured up
A shadow-Shippy before him to hate and bruise
As he beat his shirt with a stone.
                              "If we-uns was home,   20
I could just lay for him and shoot him out of the bresh,
Goin' to see my girl with his lousy mules.
Tryin' to steal my girl with his peddler's talk!"

But here, in the war, you could only shoot at the Yanks,
If you shot other folks, they found out about it and shot you,
Just like you was a spyer or something mean
Instead of a soldier. There wasn't no sense to it.
"Teach him to steal my girl—if I had him home,
Back in the mountains—I told her straight the last time,
You be a good girl, Soph, and I'll buy you a dress—   30
We can fix the cabin up fine—and if we have kids
We'll get ourselves married. Couldn't talk fairer than that,
And she's a good girl—but women's easy to change—
God-damn peddler, givin' her Richmond trash,
And we-uns movin' away to scrimmage the Yanks
Before I git a chance to see her agin

And find out if she's been good—He'll come back this way,
Drivin' his mules—plumb easy to lay for him,
But they'd catch me, shore."

                       His mouth had a bitter twist,
His slow mind grubbed for a plan to settle his doubts.
At last he dropped his stone with a joyous whoop.
"Hey, Billy," he called to his neighbor. "Got your shirt dry?
Well, lend it here for a piece until mine's wrung out,
I got to go see the Captain."

                       Billy demurred.   10
"I got friends enough in this shirt," he said with a drawl.
"I ain't hankerin' after no visitors out of yours.
I'm a modest man and my crawlies is sort of shy,
They don't mix well with strangers. They's Piedmont crawlies.
Besides, this shirt, she's still got more shirt than hole,
Yours ain't a shirt—it's a doughnut."

                       They swore for a while
But finally Luke went off with the precious shirt,
Whistling the tuneless snatch of a mountain jig,
"Gawd help you, peddler," he thought, as he looked for the 20
    Captain.

Shippy drove his rattletrap cart along
Through the dusty evening, worried and ill at ease.
He ought to have taken the other road by the creek
But he'd wasted too much time at Pollet's Hotel
Looking for Sophy—and hardly seen her at that—
And now she wanted a bottle of scent.

                       His soul
Shivered with fear like a thin dog in the cold,
Raging in vain at the terrible thing called Life.   30
—There must be a corner somewhere where you could creep,
Curl up soft and be warm—but he'd never found it.
The big boys always stole his lunch at the school
And rubbed his nose in the dirt—and when he grew up
It was just the same.

                   There was something under his face,
Something that said, "Come, bully me—I won't bite."
He couldn't see it himself, but it must be there.
He was always going places and thinking, "This time,
They won't find out." But they always did find out   40
After a while.

It had been that way at the store,
That way in the army, that way now as a spy.
Behind his eyes he built up a super-Shippy
Who ordered people around, loved glittering girls,
Threw out his chest and died for a bloody flag
And then revived to be thanked by gilt generals,
A schoolboy Shippy, eating the big boys' lunch.
It was his totem. He visioned that Shippy now,
Reckless Shippy with papers sewed in his boots,
Slyly carrying fate through the Rebel lines   10
To some bright place where—

                        The off mule stumbled and brayed.
He cursed it whimperingly and jerked at the reins,
While his heart jerked, too. The super-Shippy was gone.
He was alone and scared and late on the road.
My God, but he was scared of being a spy
And the mute-faced woman in Richmond and war and life!
He had some papers sewn in his boots all right
And they'd look at the papers while he stood sweating before
    them,   20
Crumple them up and bully him with cross speech,
"Couldn't you even find out where Heth's men are?
Can't you draw a map? You don't know about Stonewall Jackson?
Why don't you know it? What's this ford by the church?
My God, man, what do you think you are out there for?
You'll have to do better next time, I can tell you that.
We'll send you over Route 7. We had a man there,
But he's been reported killed—"

                        He shuddered in vain,
Seeing a rope and a tree and a dangling weight   30
And the mute-faced woman sending a paper off
In somebody's else's boots, and somebody saying
In an ice-cream voice to another scared little man.
"Next time, you'll try Route 7. We had a man there,
But he's been reported killed—"

                      Oh, there is a hole
Somewhere deep in the ground where the rabbits hide,
But I've never found it—

                  They stuck up signs and a flag
And it was war and you went and got scared to death   40
By the roar and the yells and the people trying to kill you

Till anything else seemed better—and there you were,
Driving mules with papers sewn in your boots,
But people still wanting to kill you—and no way out.
If you deserted, the mute-faced woman would know
And that would be the worst—and if you went back,
It would be Bull Run and yelling and all that blood
When it made you sick to your stomach. Even at school
You always had to fight. There was no way out.

Sophy was sweet and Sophy was a good girl
And Sophy was the warm earth where the rabbits hide   10
Away from danger, letting their hearts go slow,
But you couldn't stay with Sophy, you couldn't stay,
And she'd say she'd be a good girl—
                                    but, in spite of himself,
He saw a big boy tearing a cardboard box
Apart, with greedy hands, in a bare school-yard,
Where a Shippy whimpered—
                            "Oh, Soph, I'll get you the scent,
Honest I will! Oh God, just let me get through,
Just this one time—and I'll pray—I'll be good—oh God,   20
Make these papers something they want!"

                                    He clucked to his mules.
Another mile and he'd be out on the pike
And pretty safe for a while.
                            His spirit returned
To building the super-Shippy from dust again.
His head began to nod with the sway of the cart. . . .
Half a dozen men rode out from a little clearing
And casually blocked the road. He pulled up his mules,
Staring around. He saw a face that he knew,   30
Now queer with triumph—Sophy filling a pail
And that gangling fellow lounging against the pump,
Hungry-eyed—
            It happened too fast to be scary.
You got stopped such a lot. It was only some new patrol.
"All the boys know me," he said. "Yes, I got my pass."
They took the pass but they did not give it back.
There was a waver shaking the dusty air,
The feel of a cord grown tauter. How dry his throat was!
He'd be driving on in a minute. "Well boys?" he said,   40

"Well, fellers?"

      They didn't answer or look at him.
"I tell you that's the man," said the mountaineer.

The sergeant-feller looked dubiously at the rest,
Gentlemanly he looked like, a nice young feller
With his little black moustache and his thin, brown face,
He wouldn't do anything mean. It would be all right.
Another man was paring his nails with a knife,
His face was merry and reckless—nice feller, too,
Feller to stand you a drink and talk gay with the girls,   10
Not anybody to hurt you or twist your wrist.
They were all nice fellers except for the mountaineer.

They were searching him now, but they didn't do it mean.
He babbled to them all through it.

                     "Now boys, now boys,
You're making a big mistake, boys. They all know me,
They all know Charley the peddler."

                      The sergeant looked
Disgusted now—wonder why. Go ahead and look,
You'll never find it—Sophy—bottle of scent—   20

A horrible voice was saying, "Pull off his boots,"
He fought like a frightened rat then, weeping and biting,
But they got him down and found the papers all right.
Luke Breckinridge observed them with startled eyes,
"Christ," he thought, "so the skunk's a spy after all.
Well, I told 'em so—but I didn't reckon he was.
Little feist of a peddler, chasin' my girl,
Wanted to scare him off so he wouldn't come back—
Hell, they ought to make me a corporal now."
He was pleased.   30

        Clay Wingate looked at the writhing man,
"Get up!" he said, in a hard voice, feeling sick.
But they had to drag it up before it would stand
And even then it still babbled.

                   His throat was dry
But that was all right—it was going to be all right—
He was alive—he was Shippy—he knew a girl—
He was going to buy her a bottle of first-class scent.
It couldn't all stop. He wasn't ready to die.

He was willing enough to be friends and call it a joke.
Let them take the mules and the cart and hurt him a lot
Only not that—it was other spies who were hung,
Not himself, not Shippy, not the body he knew
With the live blood running through it, making it warm.
He was real. He wore clothes. He could make all this go away
If he shut his eyes. They'd turn him loose in a minute.
They were all nice fellers. They wouldn't treat a man mean.
They couldn't be going to hang him.

But they were.   10

IX. *Vanity*

Lucy Weatherby spread out gowns on a bed
And wondered which she could wear to the next levee.
The blue was faded, the rose brocade had a tear,
She'd worn the flowered satin a dozen times,
The apricot had never gone with her hair,
And somebody had to look nice at the evening parties.
But it was hard. The blockade runners of course—
But so few of them had space for gowns any more
And, really, they charged such prices!

Of course it is   20

The war, and, of course, when one thinks of our dear, brave
   boys—
But, nevertheless, they like a girl to look fresh
When they come back from their fighting.

When one goes up

To the winter-camps, it doesn't matter so much,
Any old rag will do for that sort of thing.
But here, in Richmond . . .

She pondered, mentally stitching,

Cutting and shaping, lost in a pleasant dream.   30

Fighting at Chancellorsville and Hooker beaten
And nobody killed that you knew so terribly well
Except Jo Frear's second brother—though it was sad
Our splendid general Jackson's lost his arm,
Such an odd man but so religious.

She hummed a moment

"That's Stonewall Jackson's way" in her clear cool voice.

264

"I really should have trained for nursing," she thought.
She heard a voice say. "Yes, the General's very ill,
But that lovely new nurse will save him if anyone can.
She came out from Richmond on purpose."

                              The voice stopped speaking.

She thought of last month and the boys and the Black Horse
   Troop,
And the haggard little room in Pollet's Hotel
Whose slipshod chambermaid had such scared, round eyes
She was just as glad they were fighting now, after all,   10
Huger had been so jealous and Clay so wild,
It was quite a strain to be engaged to them both
Especially when Jim Merrihew kept on writing
And that nice Alabama major—

                        She heard the bells
Ring for a wedding—but who was the man beside her?
He had a face made up of too many faces.
And yet, a young girl must marry—

                        You may dance,
Play in the sun and wear bright gowns to levees,   20
But soon or late, the hands unlike to your hands
But rough and seeking, will catch your lightness at last
And with strange passion force you. What is this passion,
This injury that women must bear for gowns?
It does not move me or stir me. I will not bear it.
There are women enough to bear it. If I have sweetness,
It is for another service. It is my own.
I will not share it. I'll play in the heat of the sun.
And yet, young girls must marry—what am I thinking?

She stepped from her hoops to try on the rose brocade,   30
But let it lie for a moment, while she stood up
To look at the bright ghost-girl in the long dark mirror,
Adoringly.

          "Oh, you honey," she thought. "You honey!
You look so pretty—and nobody knows but me.
Nobody knows."

                She kissed her little white shoulders,
With fierce and pitying love for their shining whiteness,
So soft, so smooth, so untarnished, so honey-sweet.
Her eyes were veiled. She swayed in front of the mirror.   40
"Honey, I love you," she whispered, "I love you, honey.

Nobody loves you like I do, do they, sugar?
Nobody knows but Lucy how sweet you are.
You mustn't get married, honey. You mustn't leave me.
We'll be pretty and sweet to all of them, won't we, honey?
We'll always have beaus to dance with and tunes to dance to,
But you mustn't leave me, honey. I couldn't bear it.
You mustn't ever leave me for any man."

X. *Lee's right arm*

In the dense heart of the thicketed Wilderness,
Stonewall Jackson lies dying for four long days.
They have cut off his arm, they have tried such arts as they know, 10
But no arts now can save him.
                              When he was hit
By the blind chance bullet-spatter from his own lines,
In the night, in the darkness, they stole him off from the field
To keep the men from knowing, but the men knew.
The dogs in the house will know when there's something wrong.
You do not have to tell them.
                              He marched his men
That grim first day across the whole Union front
To strike a sleepy right wing with a sudden stone   20
And roll it up—it was his old trick of war
That Lee and he could play like finger and thumb!
It was the last time they played so.
                              When the blue-coated
Unprepared ranks of Howard saw that storm,
Heralded by wild rabbits and frightened deer,
Burst on them yelling, out of the whispering woods,
They could not face it. Some men died where they stood,
The storm passed over the rest. It was Jackson's storm,
It was his old trick of war, for the last time played.   30
He must have known it. He loosed it and drove it on,
Hearing the long yell shake like an Indian cry
Through the dense black oaks, the clumps of second-growth pine,
And the red flags reel ahead through the underbrush.
It was the hour he did not stop to taste,
Being himself. He saw it and found it good,
But night was falling, the Union centre still held,
Another attack would end it. He pressed ahead

266

Through the dusk, pushing Little Sorrel, as if the horse
Were iron, and he were iron, and all his men
Not men but iron, the stalks of an iron broom
Sweeping a dire floor clean—and yet, as he rode,
A canny captain, planning a ruthless chess
Skilfully as night fell. The night fell too soon.
It is hard to tell your friend from your enemy
In such a night. So he rode too far in advance
And, turning back toward his lines, unrecognized,
Was fired upon in the night, in the stumbling darkness,   10
By his own men. He had ridden such rides before
Often enough and taken the chance of them,
But this chance was his bane.
                              He lay on the bed
After the arm had been lopped from him, grim and silent,
Refusing importunate Death with terrible eyes.
Death was a servant and Death was a sulky dog
And Death crouched down by the Lord in the Lord's own time,
But he still had work to finish that Death would spoil.
He would live in spite of that servant.   20
                                   Now and then
He spoke, with the old curt justice that never once
Denied himself or his foe or any other
The rigid due they deserved, as he saw that due.
He spoke of himself and his storm. "A successful movement.
I think the most successful I ever made."
—He had heard that long yell shake like an Indian cry
Through the ragged woods and seen his flags go ahead.
Later on, they brought him a stately letter from Lee
That said in Lee's gracious way, "You have only lost   30
Your left arm, I my right."
                           The dour mouth opened.
"Better ten Jacksons should fall than one Lee," it said
And closed again, while the heart went on with its task
Of beating off foolish, unnecessary Death.

The slow time wore. They had to tell him at last
That he must die. The doctors were brave enough,
No doubt, but they looked awhile at the man on the bed
And summoned his wife to do it. So she told him.
He would not believe at first. Then he lay awhile   40
Silent, while some slow, vast reversal of skies

267

Went on in the dying brain. At last he spoke.
"All right," he said.
                              She opened the Bible and read.
It was Spring outside the window, the air was warm,
The rough, plank house was full enough of the Spring.
They had had a good life together, those two middle-aged
Calm people, one reading aloud now, the other silent.
They had passed hard schools. They were in love with each other
And had been for many years. Now that tale was told.
They had been poor and odd, found each other trusty,   10
Begotten children, prayed, disliked to be parted,
Had family-jokes, known weather and other matters,
Planned for an age: they were famous now, he was dying.

The clock moved on, the delirium began.
The watchers listened, trying to catch the words;
Some awed, one broken-hearted, a few, no doubt,
Not glad to be there precisely, but in a way
Glad that, if it must happen, they could be there.
It is a human emotion.
                              The dying man   20
Went back at first to his battles, as soldiers do.
He was pushing a new advance
With the old impatience and skill, over tangled ground,
A cloudy drive that did not move as he willed
Though he had it clear in his mind. They were slow today.
"Tell A. P. Hill to push them—push the attack—
Get up the guns!"
                              The cloudy assault dispersed.
There were no more cannon. The ground was plain enough now.

He lay silent, seeing it so, while the watchers listened.   30
He had been dying once, but that was a dream.
The ground was plain enough now.
He roused himself and spoke in a different voice.
"Let us cross the river," he said, "and rest under the shade of
    the trees."

BOOK SEVEN:

Road to Appomattox

The ripples caused by the stone that fell in the pool that April of 1861 continue to spread. The South plans to invade the North for the second time. Lee has beaten back McClellan, Burnside, Hooker at Chancellorsville, Pope at the second Manassas, Banks in the Valley, but the Confederate resources are terribly depleted. The Union army hears the rumor of Lee's advance and starts to move. On June 30, 1863, the day before the Battle of Gettysburg, the Confederate army lies west of Gettysburg; the Union army, south. In the morning a Confederate brigade advances toward Gettysburg looking for supplies. At the same time General Buford advances and encamps the Union troops on Seminary Ridge.

We follow the course of the three days of furious fighting, meeting again Jake Diefer, who comes home to find his peaceful fields the terrain of war; Jack Ellyat and Clay Wingate, both of whom are wounded; seeing the leaders on both sides advancing, retreating, forcing their troops up the steep hills of the section, to the bitter moment when General Lee watches the remnants of his army return across the fields and General Meade hears his victorious troops rejoicing.

The war is not over, but Gettysburg has turned the tide.

I. *Picture of Gettysburg*

They came on to fish-hook Gettysburg in this way, after this fashion.
Over hot pikes heavy with pollen, past fields where the wheat was high.
Peaches grew in the orchards; it was a fertile country,
Full of red barns and fresh springs and dun, deep-uddered kine.

A farmer lived with a clear stream that ran through his very house-room,
They cooled the butter in it and the milk, in their wide, stone jars;
A dusty Georgian came there, to eat and go on to battle;
They dipped the milk from the jars, it was cold and sweet in his mouth.

10

He heard the clear stream's music as the German housewife served him,
Remembering the Shenandoah and a stream poured from a rock;
He ate and drank and went on to the gunwheels crushing the harvest.
It was a thing he remembered as long as any guns.

Country of broad-backed horses, stone houses and long, green meadows,
Where Getty came with his ox-team to found a steady town
And the little trains of my boyhood puffed solemnly up the Valley
Past the market-squares and the lindens and the Quaker meeting-house.

20

Penn stood under his oak with a painted sachem beside him,
The market-women sold scrapple when the first red maples turned;
When the buckeyes slipped from their sheaths, you could gather a pile of buckeyes,
Red-brown as old polished boots, good to touch and hold in the hand.

30

The ice-cream parlor was papered with scenes from *Paul and Virginia*,

The pigs were fat all year, you could stand a spoon in the cream.
—Penn stood under his oak with a feathered pipe in his fingers,
His eyes were quiet with God, but his wits and his bargain sharp.

So I remember it all, and the light sound of buckeyes falling
On the worn rose-bricks of the pavement, herring-boned, trodden
   for years;
The great yellow shocks of wheat and the dust-white road
   through Summer,
And, in Fall, the green walnut shells, and the stain they left for
   a while.   10

So I remember you, ripe country of broad-backed horses,
Valley of cold, sweet springs and dairies with limestone-floors;
And so they found you that year, when they scared your cows
   with their cannon,
And the strange South moved against you, lean marchers lost
   in the corn.

II. *Lee sets his fate on the odds*

Two months have passed since Jackson died in the woods
And they brought his body back to the Richmond State House
To lie there, heaped with flowers, while the bells tolled,
Two months of feints and waiting.   20
                     And now, at length,
The South goes north again in the second raid,
In the last cast for fortune.
                  A two-edged chance
And yet a chance that may burnish a failing star;
For now, on the wide expanse of the Western board,
Strong pieces that fought for the South have been swept away
Or penned up in hollow Vicksburg.
                  One cool Spring night
Porter's ironclads run the shore-batteries   30
Through a velvet stabbed with hot flashes.
                    Grant lands his men.
Drives the relieving force of Johnston away
And sits at last in front of the hollow town
Like a huge brown bear on its haunches, terribly waiting.
His guns begin to peck at the pillared porches,
The sleepy, sun-spattered streets. His siege has begun.

Forty-eight days that siege and those guns go on
Like a slow hand closing around a hungry throat,
Ever more hungry.
                    The hunger of hollow towns,
The hunger of sieges, the hunger of lost hope.
As day goes by after day and the shells still whine
Till the town is a great mole-burrow of pits and caves
Where the thin women hide their children, where the tired men
Burrow away from the death that falls from the air
And the common sky turned hostile—and still no hope,   10
Still no sight in the sky when the morning breaks
But the brown bear there on his haunches, steadfastly waiting,
Waiting like Time for the honey-tree to fall.

The news creeps back to the watchers oversea.
They ponder on it, aloof and irresolute.
The balance they watch is dipping against the South.
It will take great strokes to redress that balance again.
There will be one more moment of shaken scales
When the Laird rams almost alter the scheme of things,
But it is distant.   20
                    The watchers stare at the board
Waiting a surer omen than Chancellorsville
Or any battle won on a Southern ground.

Lee sees that dip of the balance and so prepares
His cast for the surer omen and his last stroke
At the steel-bossed Northern shield. Once before he tried
That spear-rush North and was halted. It was a chance.
This is a chance. He weighs the chance in his hand
Like a stone, reflecting.
                    Four years from Harper's Ferry—   30
Two years since the First Manassas—and this last year
Stroke after stroke successful—but still no end.

He is a man with a knotty club in his hand
Beating off bulls from the breaks in a pasture fence
And he has beaten them back at each fresh assault,
McClellan—Burnside—Hooker at Chancellorsville—
Pope at the Second Manassas—Banks in the Valley—
But the pasture is trampled; his army needs new pasture.
An army moves like a locust, eating the grain,

273

And this grain is well-nigh eaten. He cannot mend
The breaks in his fence with famine or starving hands,
And if he waits the wheel of another year
The bulls will come back full-fed, shaking sharper horns
While he faces them empty, armed with a hunger-cracked
Unmagic stick.
              There is only this thing to do,
To strike at the shield with the strength that he still can use
Hoping to burst it asunder with one stiff blow
And carry the war up North, to the untouched fields   10
Where his tattered men can feed on the bulls' own grain,
Get shoes and clothes, take Washington if they can,
Hold the fighting-gauge in any event.
                        He weighs
The chance in his hand. I think that he weighed it well
And felt a high tide risen up in his heart
And in his men a high tide.
                  They were veterans,
They had never been beaten wholly and blocked but once,
He had driven four Union armies within a year   20
And broken three blue commanders from their command.
Even now they were fresh from triumph.
                      He cast his stone
Clanging at fortune, and set his fate on the odds.

Lincoln hears the rumor in Washington.
They are moving North.
                The Pennsylvania cities
Hear it and shake, they are loose, they are moving North.
Call up your shotgun-militia, bury your silver,
Shoulder a gun or run away from the State,   30
They are loose, they are moving.
                  Fighting Joe Hooker has heard it.
He swings his army back across the Potomac,
Rapidly planning, while Lee still visions him South.
Stuart's horse should have brought the news of that move
But Stuart is off on a last and luckless raid
Far to the East, and the grey host moves without eyes
Through crucial days.
             They are in the Cumberland now,
Taking minor towns, feeding fat for a little while,   40
Pressing horses and shoes, paying out Confederate bills

To slow Dutch storekeepers who groan at the money.
They are loose, they are in the North, they are here and there.
Halleck rubs his elbows and wonders where,
Lincoln is sleepless, the telegraph-sounders click
In the War Office day and night.

                     There are lies and rumors,
They are only a mile from Philadelphia now,
They are burning York—they are marching on Baltimore—

Meanwhile, Lee rides through the heart of the Cumberland.
A great hot sunset colors the marching men,   10
Colors the horse and the sword and the bearded face
But cannot change that face from its strong repose.
And—miles away—Joe Hooker, by telegraph
Calls for the garrison left at Harper's Ferry
To join him. Elbow-rubbing Halleck refuses.
Hooker resigns command—and fades from the East
To travel West, fight keenly at Lookout Mountain,
Follow Sherman's march as far as Atlanta,
Be ranked by Howard, and tartly resign once more
Before the end and the fame and the Grand Review,   20
To die a slow death, in bed, with his fire gone out,
A campfire quenched and forgotten.

                     He deserved
A better and brusquer end that marched with his nickname,
This disappointed, hot-tempered, most human man
Who had such faith in himself except for once,
And the once, being Chancellorsville, wiped out the rest.
He was often touchy and life was touchy with him,
But the last revenge was a trifle out of proportion.
Such things will happen—Jackson went in his strength,   30
Stuart was riding his horse when the bullet took him,
And Custer died to the trumpet—Dutch Longstreet lived
To quarrel and fight dead battles. Lee passed in silence.
McClellan talked on forever in word and print.
Grant lived to be President. Thomas died sick at heart.

So Hooker goes from our picture—and a spent aide
Reaches Meade's hut at three o'clock in the morning
To wake him with unexpected news of command.
The thin Pennsylvanian puts on his spectacles
To read the order. Tall, sad-faced and austere,   40

275

He has the sharp, long nose of a fighting-bird,
A prudent mouth and a cool, considering mind.
An iron-grey man with none of Hooker's panache, *plume*
But resolute and able, well skilled in war;
They call him "the damned old goggle-eyed snapping-turtle"
At times, and he does not call out the idol-shout
When he rides his lines, but his prudence is a hard prudence,
And can last out storms that break the men with panache,
Though it summons no counter-storm when the storm is done.

His sombre schoolmaster-eyes read the order well.   10
It is three days before the battle.
                              He thinks at first
Of a grand review, gives it up, and begins to act.

That morning a spy brings news to Lee in his tent
That the Union army has moved and is on the march.
Lee calls back Ewell and Early from their forays
And summons his host together by the cross-roads
Where Getty came with his ox-cart.
                              So now we see
These two crab-armies fumbling for each other,   20
As if through a fog of rumor and false report,
These last two days of sleepy, hay-harvest June.
Hot June lying asleep on a shock of wheat
Where the pollen-wind blows over the burnt-gold stubble
And the thirsty men march past, stirring thick grey dust
From the trodden pikes—till at last, the crab-claws touch
At Getty's town, and clutch, and the peaches fall
Cut by the bullets, splashing under the trees.

That meeting was not willed by a human mind,
When we come to sift it.   30
                              You say a fate rode a horse
Ahead of those lumbering hosts, and in either hand
He carried a skein of omen. And when, at last,
He came to a certain umbrella-copse of trees
That never had heard a cannon or seen dead men,
He knotted the skeins together and flung them down
With a sound like metal.
                              Perhaps. It may have been so.
All that we know is—Meade intended to fight

Some fifteen miles away on the Pipe Creek Line
And where Lee meant to fight him, if forced to fight,
We do not know, but it was not there where they fought.
Yet the riding fate,
Blind and deaf and a doom on a lunging horse,
Threw down his skeins and gathered the battle there.

III. *Through the eyes of a child*

The buttercup-meadows
Are very yellow.
A child comes there
To fill her hands.
The gold she gathers   10
Is soft and precious
As sweet new butter
Fresh from the churn.

She fills her frock
With the yellow flowers,
The butter she gathers
Is smooth as gold,
Little bright cups
Of new-churned sunshine   20
For a well-behaved
Hoop-skirted doll.

Her frock's full
And her hands are mothy
With yellow pollen
But she keeps on.
Down by the fence
They are even thicker.
She runs, bowed down with
Buttercup-gold.   30

She sees a road
And she sees a rider.
His face is grey
With a different dust.
He talks loud.

277

He rattles like tinware.
He has a long sword
To kill little girls.

He shouts at her now,
But she does not answer.
"Where is the town?"
But she will not hear.
There are other riders
Jangling behind him.
"We won't hurt you, youngster!" 10
But they have swords.

The buttercups fall
Like spilt butter.
She runs away.
She runs to her house.
She hides her face
In her mother's apron
And tries to tell her
How dreadful it was.

IV. *Before the attack*

Buford came to Gettysburg late that night 20
Riding West with his brigades of blue horse,
While Pettigrew and his North Carolinians
Were moving East toward the town with a wagon-train,
Hoping to capture shoes.
                    The two came in touch.
Pettigrew halted and waited for men and orders.
Buford threw out his pickets beyond the town.

The next morning was July first. It was hot and calm.
On the grey side, Heth's division was ready to march
And drive the blue pickets in. There was still no thought 30
Of a planned and decisive battle on either side
Though Buford had seen the strength of those two hill-ridges
Soon enough to be famous, and marked one down
As a place to rally if he should be driven back.

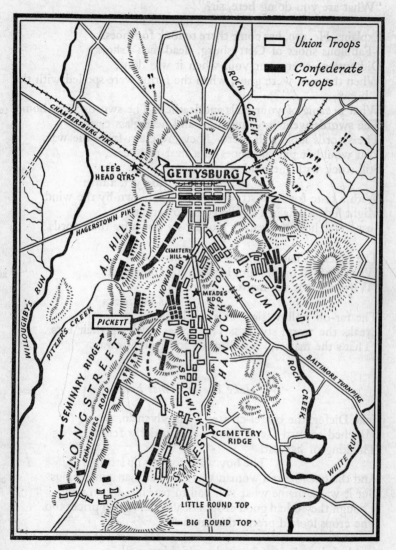

Gettysburg—The Third Day

He talks with his staff in front of a tavern now.
An officer rides up from the near First Corps.
"What are you doing here, sir?"
                                    The officer
Explains. He, too, has come there to look for shoes.
—Fabulous shoes of Gettysburg, dead men's shoes,
Did anyone ever wear you, when it was done,
When the men were gone, when the farms were spoiled with the
      bones,
What became of your nails and leather? The swords went home, 10
The swords went into museums and neat glass cases,
The swords look well there. They are clean from the war.
You wouldn't put old shoes in a neat glass case,
Still stuck with the mud of marching.
                                    And yet, a man
With a taste for such straws and fables, blown by the wind,
Might hide a pair in a labelled case sometime
Just to see how the leather looked, set down by the swords.

The officer is hardly through with his tale
When Buford orders him back to his command.   20
"Why, what is the matter, general?"
                                    As he speaks
The far-off hollow slam of a single gun
Breaks the warm stillness. The horses prick up their ears.
"That's the matter," says Buford and gallops away.

V.   *Jake Diefer comes home*

Jake Diefer, the barrel-chested Pennsylvanian,
Marched toward Getty's town past orderly fences,
Thinking of harvest.
                                    The boy was growing up strong
And the corn-haired woman was smart at managing things   30
But it was a shame what you had to pay hired men now
Though they'd had good crops last year and good prices too.
The crops looked pretty this summer.
                                    He stared at the long
Gold of the wheat reflectively, weighing it all,
Turning it into money and cows and taxes,
A new horse-reaper, some first-class paint for the barn,

Maybe a dress for the woman.
                                    His thoughts were few,
But this one tasted rough and good in his mouth
Like a spear of rough, raw grain. He crunched at it now.
—And yet, that wasn't all, the paint and the cash,
They were the wheat but the wheat was—he didn't know—
But it made you feel good to see some good wheat again
And see it grown up proper.
                              He wasn't a man
To cut a slice of poetry from a farm.   10
He liked the kind of manure that he knew about
And seldom burst into tears when his horses died
Or found a beautiful thought in a bumble-bee,
But now, as he tramped along like a laden steer,
The tall wheat, rustling, filled his heart with its sound.

Look at that column well, as it passes by,
Remembering Bull Run and the cocksfeather hats,
The congressmen, the raw militia brigades
Who went to war with a flag and a haircloth trunk
In bright red pants and ideals and ignorance,   20
Ready to fight like picture-postcard boys
While fighting still had banners and a sword
And just as ready to run in blind mob-panic. . . .
These men were once those men. These men are the soldiers,
Good thieves, good fighters, excellent foragers,
The grumbling men who dislike to be killed in war
And yet will hold when the raw militia break
And live where the raw militia needlessly die,
Having been schooled to that end.
                                    The school is not   30
A pretty school. They wear no cocksfeather hats.
Some men march in their drawers and their stocking feet.
They have handkerchiefs round their heads, they are footsore
    and chafed,
Their faces are sweaty leather.
                                And when they pass
The little towns where the people wish them godspeed,
A few are touched by the cheers and the crying women
But most have seen a number of crying women,
And heard a number of cheers.   40
                          The ruder yell back

To the sincere citizens cool in their own front yards,
"Aw, get a gun and fight for your home yourself!"
They grin and fall silent. Nevertheless they go on.
Jake Diefer, the barrel-chested Pennsylvanian,
The steer-thewed, fist-plank-splitter from Cumberland,
Came through the heat and the dust and the mounting roar
That could not drown the rustle of the tall wheat
Making its growing sound, its windrustled sound,
In his heart that sound, that brief and abiding sound,
To a fork and a road he knew.   10
                                        And then he heard
That mixed, indocile noise of combat indeed
And as if it were strange to him when it was not strange.
—He never took much account of the roads they went,
They were always going somewhere and roads were roads.
But he knew this road.
                                        He knew its turns and its hills,
And what ploughlands lay beyond it, beyond the town,
On the way to Chambersburg.
                                        He saw with wild eyes   20
Not the road before him or anything real at all
But grey men in an unreal wheatfield, tramping it down,
Filling their tattered hats with the ripe, rough grain
While a shell burst over a barn.
                                        "Grasshoppers!" he said
Through stiff dry lips to himself as he tried to gauge
That mounting roar and its distance.
                                        "The Johnnies is there!
The Johnnies and us is fighting in Gettysburg,
There must be Johnnies back by the farm already,   30
By Jesus, those damn Johnnies is on my farm!"

VI.   The battle of the first day

That battle of the first day was a minor battle
As such are counted.
                                        That is, it killed many men.
Killed more than died at Bull Run, left thousands stricken
With wounds that time might heal for a little while
Or never heal till the breath was out of the flesh.
The First Corps lost half its number in killed and wounded.

The pale-faced women, huddled behind drawn blinds
Back in the town, or in apple-cellars, hiding,
Thought it the end of the world, no doubt.
                                    And yet,
As the books remark, it was only a minor battle.
There were only two corps engaged on the Union side,
Longstreet had not yet come up, nor Ewell's whole force,
Hill's corps lacked a division till evening fell.
It was only a minor battle.
                          When the first shot   10
Clanged out, it was fired from a clump of Union vedettes
Holding a farm in the woods beyond the town.
The farmer was there to hear it—and then to see
The troopers scramble back on their restless horses
And go off, firing, as a grey mass came on.

He must have been a peaceable man, that farmer.
It is said that he died of what he had heard and seen
In that one brief moment, although no bullet came near him
And the storm passed by and did not burst on his farm.
No doubt he was easily frightened. He should have reflected   20
That even minor battles are hardly the place
For peaceable men—but he died instead, it is said.
There were other deaths that day, as of Smiths and Clancys,
Otises, Boyds, Virginia and Pennsylvania,
New York, Carolina, Wisconsin, the gathered West,
The tattered Southern marchers dead on the wheat-shocks.
Among these deaths a few famous.
                                Reynolds is dead,
The model soldier, gallant and courteous,
Shot from his saddle in the first of the fight.   30
He was Doubleday's friend, but Doubleday has no time
To grieve him, the Union right being driven in
And Heth's Confederates pressing on toward the town.
He holds the onrush back till Howard comes up
And takes command for a while.
                              The fighting is grim.
Meade has heard the news. He sends Hancock up to the field.
Hancock takes command in mid-combat. The grey comes on.
Five color-bearers are killed at one Union color,
The last man, dying, still holds up the sagging flag.   40
The pale-faced women creeping out of their houses,

Plead with retreating bluecoats, "Don't leave us boys,
Stay with us—hold the town." Their faces are thin,
Their words come tumbling out of a frightened mouth.
In a field, far off, a peaceable farmer puts
His hands to his ears, still hearing that one sharp shot
That he will hear and hear till he dies of it.
It is Hill and Ewell now against Hancock and Howard
And a confused, wild clamor—and the high keen
Of the Rebel yell—and the shrill-edged bullet song
Beating down men and grain, while the sweaty fighters   10
Grunt as they ram their charges with blackened hands.

Till Hancock and Howard are beaten away at last,
Outnumbered and outflanked, clean out of the town,
Retreating as best they can to a fish-hook ridge,
And the clamor dies and the sun is going down
And the tired men think about food.
                                        The dust-bitten staff
Of Ewell, riding along through the captured streets,
Hear the thud of a bullet striking their general.
Flesh or bone? Death-wound or rub of the game?   20
"The general's hurt!" They gasp and volley their questions.
Ewell turns his head like a bird, "No, I'm not hurt, sir,
But, supposing the ball had struck you, General Gordon,
We'd have the trouble of carrying you from the field.
You can see how much better fixed for a fight I am.
It don't hurt a mite to be shot in your wooden leg."

So it ends. Lee comes on the field in time to see
The village taken, the Union wave in retreat.
Meade will not reach the ground till one the next morning.

So it ends, this lesser battle of the first day,   30
Starkly disputed and piecemeal won and lost
By corps-commanders who carried no magic plans
Stowed in their sleeves, but fought and held as they could.
It is past. The board is staked for the greater game
Which is to follow—The beaten Union brigades
Recoil from the cross-roads town that they tried to hold,
And so recoiling, rest on a destined ground.
Who chose that ground?
                                        There are claimants enough in the books.
Howard thanked by Congress for choosing it   40

As doubtless, they would have thanked him as well had he
Chosen another, once the battle was won,
And there are a dozen ifs on the Southern side,
How, in that first day's evening, if one had known,
If Lee had been there in time, if Jackson had lived,
The heights that cost so much blood in the vain attempt
To take days later, could have been taken then.
And the ifs and the thanks and the rest are all true enough
But we can only say, when we look at the board,
"There it happened. There is the way of the land.   10
There was the fate, and there the blind swords were crossed."

VII.   *The shrine of Gettysburg*

You took a carriage to that battlefield.
Now, I suppose, you take a motor-bus,
But then, it was a carriage—and you ate
Fried chicken out of wrappings of waxed paper,
While the slow guide buzzed on about the war
And the enormous, curdled summer clouds
Piled up like giant cream puffs in the blue.
The carriage smelt of axle-grease and leather
And the old horse nodded a sleepy head   20
Adorned with a straw hat. His ears stuck through it.
It was the middle of hay-fever summer
And it was hot. And you could stand and look
All the way down from Cemetery Ridge,
Much as it was, except for monuments
And startling groups of monumental men
Bursting in bronze and marble from the ground,
And all the curious names upon the gravestones. . . .

So peaceable it was, so calm and hot,
So tidy and great-skied.   30
                        No men had fought
There but enormous, monumental men
Who bled neat streams of uncorrupting bronze,
Even at the Round Tops, even by Pickett's boulder,
Where the bronze, open book could still be read
By visitors and sparrows and the wind:
And the wind came, the wind moved in the grass,
Saying . . . while the long light . . . and all so calm . . .

285

>   "Pickett came
>   And the South came
>   And the end came,
>   And the grass comes
>   And the wind blows
>   On the bronze book
>   On the bronze men
>   On the grown grass,
>   And the wind says
>   'Long ago
>   Long
>   Ago.'"

Then it was time to buy a paperweight
With flags upon it in decalcomania
And hope you wouldn't break it, driving home.

VIII. *The site of the battle*

Draw a clumsy fish-hook now on a piece of paper,
To the left of the shank, by the bend of the curving hook,
Draw a Maltese cross with the top block cut away.
The cross is the town. Nine roads star out from it
East, West, South, North.   20
                         And now, still more to the left
Of the lopped-off cross, on the other side of the town,
Draw a long, slightly-wavy line of ridges and hills
Roughly parallel to the fish-hook shank.
(The hook of the fish-hook is turned away from the cross
And the wavy line.)
                         There your ground and your ridges lie.
The fish-hook is Cemetery Ridge and the North
Waiting to be assaulted—the wavy line
Seminary Ridge whence the Southern assault will come.   30

The valley between is more than a mile in breadth.
It is some three miles from the lowest jut of the cross
To the button at the far end of the fish-hook shank,
Big Round Top, with Little Round Top not far away.
Both ridges are strong and rocky, well made for war.
But the Northern one is the stronger shorter one.
Lee's army must spread out like an uncoiled snake

286

Lying along a fence-rail, while Meade's can coil
Or halfway coil, like a snake part clung to a stone.
Meade has the more men and the easier shifts to make,
Lee the old prestige of triumph and his tried skill.
His task is—to coil his snake round the other snake
Halfway clung to the stone, and shatter it so,
Or to break some point in the shank of the fish-hook line
And so cut the snake in two.
                                 Meade's task is to hold.

That is the chess and the scheme of the wooden blocks   10
Set down on the contour map.
                                 Having learned so much,
Forget it now, while the ripple-lines of the map
Arise into bouldered ridges, tree-grown, bird-visited,
Where the gnats buzz, and the wren builds a hollow nest
And the rocks are grey in the sun and black in the rain,
And the jacks-in-the-pulpit grow in the cool, damp hollows.
See no names of leaders painted upon the blocks
Such as "Hill," or "Hancock," or "Pender"—
                                 but see instead   20
Three miles of living men—three long double miles
Of men and guns and horses and fires and wagons,
Teamsters, surgeons, generals, orderlies,
A hundred and sixty thousand living men
Asleep or eating or thinking or writing brief
Notes in the thought of death, shooting dice or swearing,
Groaning in hospital wagons, standing guard
While the slow stars walk through heaven in silver mail,
Hearing a stream or a joke or a horse cropping grass
Or hearing nothing, being too tired to hear.   30
All night till the round sun comes and the morning breaks,
Three double miles of live men.
Listen to them, their breath goes up through the night
In a great chord of life, in the sighing murmur
Of wind-stirred wheat.
                                 A hundred and sixty thousand
Breathing men, at night, on two hostile ridges set down.

IX. *The battle through Jack Ellyat's eyes*

Jack Ellyat slept that night on the rocky ground
Of Cemetery Hill while the cold stars marched,

And if his bed was harder than Jacob's stone
Yet he could sleep on it now and be glad for sleep.

He had been through Chancellorsville and the whistling wood,
He had been through this last day. It is well to sleep
After such days.
            He had seen, in the last four months,
Many roads, much weather and death, and two men fey
Before they died with the prescience of death to come,
John Haberdeen and the corporal from Millerstown.
Such things are often remembered even in sleep.   10
He thought to himself, before he lay on the ground,
"We got it hot today in that red-brick town
But we'll get it hotter tomorrow."
                        And when he woke
And saw the round sun risen in the clear sky,
He could feel that thought steam up from the rocky ground
And touch each man.
               One man looked down from the hill,
"That must be their whole damn army," he said and whistled,
"It'll be a picnic today, boys. Yes, it'll be   20
A regular basket-picnic." He whistled again.

"Shut your trap about picnics, Ace," said another man,
"You make me too damn hungry!"
                   He sighed out loud.
"We had enough of a picnic at Chancellorsville,"
He said. "I ain't felt right in my stummick since.
Can you make 'em out?"
                "Sure," said Ace, "but they're pretty far."

"Wonder who we'll get? That bunch we got yesterday
Was a mean-shootin' bunch."   30
                 "Now don't you worry," said Ace,
"We'll get plenty."
             The other man sighed again.
"Did you see that darky woman selling hot pies,
Two days ago, on the road?" he said, licking his lips,
"Blackberry pies. The boys ahead got a lot
And Jake and me clubbed together for three. And then
Just as we were ready to make the sneak,
Who comes up with a roar but the provost-guard?

Did we get any pies? I guess you know if we did.
I couldn't spit for an hour, I felt so mad.
Next war I'm goin' to be provost-guard or bust."

A thin voice said abruptly, "They're moving—lookit—
They're moving. I tell you—lookit—"
                                        They all looked then.
A little crackling noise as of burning thornsticks
Began far away—ceased wholly—began again—
"We won't get it awhile," thought Ellyat. "They're trying the
   left.   10
We won't get it awhile, but we'll get it soon.
I feel funny today. I don't think I'm going to be killed
But I feel funny. That's their whole army all right.
I wonder if those other two felt like this,
John Haberdeen and the corporal from Millerstown?
What's it like to see your name on a bullet?
It must feel queer. This is going to be a big one.
The Johnnies know it. That house looks pretty down there.

(Phaëton, charioteer in your drunken car,
What have you got for a man that carries my name?)   20

We're a damn good company now, if we say it ourselves,
And the Old Man knows it—but this one's bound to be tough.
I wonder what they're feeling like over there.

(Charioteer, you were driving yesterday,
No doubt, but I did not see you. I see you now.
What have you got today for a man with my name?)"

X. *The guns all speak*

The firing began that morning at nine o'clock,
But it was three before the attacks were launched.
There were two attacks, one a drive on the Union left
To take the Round Tops, the other one on the right.   30
Lee had planned them to strike together and, striking so,
Cut the Union snake in three pieces.
                                It did not happen.
On the left, Dutch Longstreet, slow, pugnacious and stubborn,

289

Hard to beat and just as hard to convince,
Has his own ideas of the battle and does not move
For hours after the hour that Lee had planned,
Though, when he does, he moves with pugnacious strength.
Facing him, in the valley before the Round Tops,
Sickles thrusts out blue troops in a weak right angle,
Some distance from the Ridge, by the Emmettsburg pike.
There is a peach orchard there, a field of ripe wheat
And other peaceable things soon not to be peaceful.

They say the bluecoats, marching through the ripe wheat,   10
Made a blue-and-yellow picture that men remember
Even now in their age, in their crack-voiced age.
They say the noise was incessant as the sound
Of all wolves howling, when that attack came on.
They say, when the guns all spoke, that the solid ground
Of the rocky ridges trembled like a sick child.
We have made the sick earth tremble with other shakings
In our time, in our time, in our time, but it has not taught us
To leave the grain in the field.
                                    So the storm came on   20
Yelling against the angle.
                        The men who fought there
Were the tried fighters, the hammered, the weather-beaten,
The very hard-dying men.
                        They came and died
And came again and died and stood there and died,
Till at last the angle was crumpled and broken in,
Sickles shot down, Willard, Barlow and Semmes shot down,
Wheatfield and orchard bloody and trampled and taken,
And Hood's tall Texans sweeping on toward the Round Tops   30
As Hood fell wounded.
                        On Little Round Top's height
Stands a lonely figure, seeing that rush come on—
Greek-mouthed Warren, Meade's chief of engineers.
—Sometimes, and in battle even, a moment comes
When a man with eyes can see a dip in the scales
And, so seeing, reverse a fortune. Warren has eyes
And such a moment comes to him now. He turns
—In a clear flash seeing the crests of the Round Tops taken,
The grey artillery there and the battle lost—   40
And rides off hell-for-leather to gather troops

And bring them up in the very nick of time,
While the grey rush still advances, keening its cry.
The crest is three times taken and then retaken
In fierce wolf-flurries of combat, in gasping Iliads
Too rapid to note or remember, too obscure to freeze in a song.
But at last, when the round sun drops, when the nun-footed night,
Dark-veiled walker, holding the first weak stars
Like children against her breast, spreads her pure cloths there,
The Union still holds the Round Tops and the two hard keys of
    war.   10

Night falls. The blood drips in the rocks of the Devil's Den.
The murmur begins to rise from the thirsty ground
Where the twenty thousand dead and wounded lie.
Such was Longstreet's war, and such the Union defence,
The deaths and the woundings, the victory and defeat
At the end of the fish-hook shank.
                                And so Longstreet failed
Ere Ewell and Early struck the fish-hook itself
At Culp's Hill and the Ridge and at Cemetery Hill,
With better fortune, though not with fortune enough   20
To plant hard triumph deep on the sharp-edged rocks
And break the scales of the snake.
                              When that last attack
Came, with its cry, Jack Ellyat saw it come on.

XI.—The last attack

They had been waiting for hours on that hard hill,
Sometimes under fire, sometimes untroubled by shells.
A man chewed a stick of grass and hummed to himself.
Another played mumbledeypeg with a worn black knife.
Two men were talking girls till they got too mad
And the sergeant stopped them.   30
                              Then they waited again.

Jack Ellyat waited, hearing that other roar
Rise and fall, be distant and then approach.
Now and then he turned on his side and looked at the sky
As if to build a house of peace from that blue,
But could find no house of peace there.

Only the roar,
The slow sun sinking, the fey touch at his mind. . . .

He was lying behind a tree and a chunk of rock
On thick, coarse grass. Farther down the slope of the hill
There were houses, a rough stone wall, and blue loungy men.
Behind them lay the batteries on the crest.

He wondered if there were people still in the houses.
One house had a long, slant roof. He followed the slant
Of the roof with his finger, idly, pleased with the line.

The shelling burst out from the Southern guns again.   10
Their own batteries answered behind them. He looked at his
    house
While the shells came down. I'd like to live in that house.
Now the shelling lessened.
                    The man with the old black knife
Shut up the knife and began to baby his rifle.
They're coming, Jack thought. This is it.
                                    There was an abrupt
Slight stiffening in the bodies of other men,
A few chopped ends of words scattered back and forth,   20
Eyes looking, hands busy in swift, well-accustomed gestures.
This is it. He felt his own hands moving like theirs
Though he was not telling them to. This is it. He felt
The old familiar tightness around his chest.
The man with the grass chewed his stalk a little too hard
And then suddenly spat it out.
                            Jack Ellyat saw
Through the falling night, that slight, grey fringe that was war
Coming against them, not as it came in pictures
With a ruler-edge, but a crinkled and smudgy line   30
Like a child's vague scrawl in soft crayon, but moving on
But with its little red handkerchiefs of flags
Sagging up and down, here and there.
                                It was still quite far,
It was still like a toy attack—it was swallowed now
By a wood and came out larger with larger flags.
Their own guns on the crest were trying to break it up
—Smoking sand thrown into an ant-legged line—
But it still kept on—one fringe and another fringe

292

And another and—
                    He lost them all for a moment
In a dip of ground.
                    This is it, he thought with a parched
Mind. It's a big one. They must be yelling all right
Though you can't hear them. They're going to do it this time,
Do it or bust—you can tell from the way they come—
I hope to Christ that the batteries do their job
When they get out of that dip.
                    Hell, they've lost 'em now,   10
And they're still coming.
                    He heard a thin gnat-shrieking
"Hold your fire till they're close enough, men!"
                    The new lieutenant.
The new lieutenant looked thin. "Aw, go home," he muttered,
"We're no militia—What do you think we are?"

Then suddenly, down by his house, the low stone wall
Flashed and was instantly huge with a wall of smoke.
He was yelling now. He saw a red battleflag
Push through smoke like a prow and be blotted out   20
By smoke and flash.
                    His heart knocked hard in his chest.
"Do it or bust," he mumbled, holding his fire
While the rags of smoke blew off.
                    He heard a thick chunk
Beside him, turned his head for a flicker of time.
The man who had chewed on the grass was injuredly trying
To rise on his knees, his face annoyed by a smile.
Then the blood poured over the smile and he crumpled up.
Ellyat stretched out a hand to touch him and felt the hand   30
Rasped by a file.
                    He jerked back the hand and sucked it.
"Bastards," he said in a minor and even voice.

All this had occurred, it seemed, in no time at all,
But when he turned back, the smoky slope of the hill
Was grey—and a staggering red advancing flag
And those same shouting strangers he knew so well,
No longer ants—but there—and stumblingly running—
And that high, shrill, hated keen piercing all the flat thunder.

His lips went back. He felt something swell in his chest
Like a huge, indocile bubble.

                              "By God," he said,
Loading and firing, "You're not going to get this hill,
You're not going to get this hill. By God, but you're not!"
He saw one grey man spin like a crazy dancer
And another fall at his heels—but the hill kept growing them.
Something made him look toward his left.

                                        A yellow-fanged face
Was aiming a pistol over a chunk of rock.   10
He fired and the face went down like a broken pipe
While something hit him sharply and took his breath.
"Get back, you suckers," he croaked, "Get back there, you
    suckers!"
He wouldn't have time to load now—they were too near.
He was up and screaming. He swung his gun like a club
Through a twilight full of bright stabbings, and felt it crash
On a thing that broke. He had no breath any more.
He had no thoughts. Then the blunt fist hit him again.

He was down in the grass and the black sheep of night ran over 20
    him . . .

XII.   *Bent comes out of hiding*

That day, Melora Vilas sat by the spring
With her child in her arms and felt the warm wind blow
Ruffling the little pool that had shown two faces
Apart and then clung together for a brief while
As if the mouths had been silver and so fused there. . . .

The wind blew at the child's shut fists but it could not open
    them.
The child slept well. The child was a strong, young child.

"Wind, you have blown the green leaf and the brown leaf   30
And in and out of my restless heart you blow,
Wakening me again.

                    I had thought for a while
My heart was a child and could sleep like any child,
But now that the wind is warm, I remember my lover,
Must you blow all summer, warm wind?"

294

"Divide anew this once-divided flesh
Into twelve shares of mercy and on each
Bestow a fair and succourable child,
Yet, in full summer, when the ripened stalks
Bow in the wind like golden-headed men,
Under the sun, the shares will reunite
Into unmerciful and childless love."

She thought again, "No, it's not that, it's not that,
I love my child with an 'L' because he's little,
I love my child with an 'S' because he's strong.   10
With an 'M' because he's mine.
                              But I'm restless now.
We cut the heart on the tree but the bark's grown back there.
I've got my half of the dime but I want his.
The winter-sleep is over."

The shadows were longer now. The child waked and cried.
She rocked and hushed it, feeling the warm wind blow.
"I've got to find him," she said.

About that time, the men rode up to the house
From the other way. Their horses were rough and wild.   20
There were a dozen of them and they came fast.
Bent should have been out in the woods but he had come down
To mend a split wagon-wheel. He was caught in the barn.
They couldn't warn him in time, though John Vilas tried,
But they held John Vilas and started to search the place
While the younger children scuttled around like mice
Squeaking "It's drafters, Mom—it's the drafters again!"
Even then, if Bent had hidden under the hay
They might not have found him, being much pressed for time,
But perhaps he was tired of hiding.   30
                              At any rate
When Melora reached the edge of the little clearing,
She saw them there and Bent there, up on a horse,
Her mother rigid as wood and her father dumb
And the head man saying, gently enough on the whole,
"Don't you worry, ma'am—he'll make a good soldier yet
If he acts proper."
                    That was how they got Bent.

On the crest of the hill, the sweaty cannoneers,
The blackened Pennsylvanians, picked up their rammers
And fought the charge with handspikes and clubs and stones,
Biting and howling. It is said that they cried
Wildly, "Death on the soil of our native state
Rather than lose our guns." A general says so.
He was not there. I do not know what they cried
But that they fought, there was witness—and that the grey
Wave that came on them fought, there was witness too.
For an instant that wheel of combat—and for an instant   10
A brief, hard-breathing hush.

               Then came the hard sound
Of a column tramping—blue reinforcements at last,
A doomsday sound to the grey.

               The hard column came
Over the battered crest and went in with a yell.
The grey charge bent and gave ground, the grey charge was
   broken.
The sweaty gunners fell to their guns again
And began to scatter the shells in the ebbing wave.   20

Thus ended the second day of the locked bull-horns
And the wounding or slaying of the twenty thousand.
And thus night came to cover it.

               So the field
Was alive all night with whispers and words and sighs,
So the slow blood dripped in the rocks of the Devil's Den.
Lincoln, back in his White House, asks for news.
The War Department has little. There are reports
Of heavy firing near Gettysburg—that is all.
Davis, in Richmond, knows as little as he.   30
In hollow Vicksburg, the shells come down and come down
And the end is but two days off.

               On the field itself
Meade calls a council and considers retreat.
His left has held and the Round Tops still are his.
But his right has been shaken, his centre pierced for a time,
The enemy holds part of his works on Culp's Hill,
His losses have been most stark.

                          He thinks of these things
And decides at last to fight it out where he stands.

                    XIV.   Jack Ellyat is wounded

Ellyat lay upon Cemetery Hill.
His wounds had begun to burn.
                                   He was rising up
Through cold and vacant darknesses into faint light,
The yellow, watery light of a misty moon.
He stirred a little and groaned.
                                   There was something cool
On his face and hands. It was dew. He lay on his back   10
And stared at a blowing cloud and a moist, dark sky.
"Old charioteer," he thought.
                           He remembered dully
The charge. The charge had come. They had beaten the charge.
Now it was moist dark sky and the dew and his pain.

He tried to get his canteen but he couldn't reach it.
That made him afraid.
                           "I want some water," he said.
He turned his head through stiff ages.
                                   Two feet away   20
A man was lying quietly, fast asleep,
A bearded man in an enemy uniform.
He had a canteen. Ellyat wet his lips with his tongue.
"Hey Johnnie, got some water?" he whispered weakly.
Then he saw that the Johnnie had only half a head,
And frowned because such men could not lend canteens.

He was half-delirious now, and it seemed to him
As if he had two bodies, one that was pain
And one that lay beyond pain, on a couch of dew,
And stared at the other with sober wondering eyes.   30
"Everyone's dead around here but me," he thought,
"And as long as I don't sing out, they'll think that I'm dead
And those stretcher-bearers won't find me—there goes their lan-
    tern
No, it's the moon—Sing out and tell 'em you're here."
The hot body cried and groaned. The cool watched it idly.

The yellow moon burst open like a ripe fruit
And from it rolled on a dark, streaked shelf of sky
A car and horses, bearing the brazen ball
Of the unbearable sun, that halted above him
In full rush forward, yet frozen, a motion congealed,
Heavy with light.
                Toy death above Gettysburg.
He saw it so and cried out in a weak, thin voice
While something jagged fitted into his heart
And the cool body watched idly.   10
                      And then it was
A lantern, bobbing along through the clumped dead men,
That halted now for an instant. He cried again.
A voice said, "Listen, Jerry, you're hearing things,
I've passed that feller twice and he's dead all right,
I'll bet you money."
                Ellyat heard himself piping,
"I'm alive, God damn you! Can't you hear I'm alive?"

Something laughed, quite close now.
                      "All right, Bub," said a cloud, 20
"We'll take your word for it. My, but the boy's got language!
Go ahead and cuss while we get you up on the stretcher—
It helps some—easy there, Joe."
                  Jack Ellyat fell
Out of his bodies into a whispering blackness
Through which, now and then, he could hear certain talking
    clouds
Cough or remark.
                One said. "That's two and a half
You owe me, Joe. You're pickin' 'em wrong tonight."   30
"Well, poor suckers," said Joseph. "But all the same,
If this one doesn't last till the dressing station
The bet's off—take it slower, Jerry—it hurts him."

XV. *Longstreet and Lee disagree*

Another clear dawn breaks over Gettysburg,
Promising heat and fair weather—and with the dawn
The guns are crashing again.
                It is the third day.

The morning wears with a stubborn fight at Culp's Hill
That ends at last in Confederate repulse
And that barb-end of the fish-hook cleared of the grey.

Lee has tried his strokes on the right and left of the line.
The centre remains—that centre yesterday pierced
For a brief, wild moment in Wilcox's attack,
But since then trenched, reinforced and alive with guns.

It is a chance. All war is a chance like that.
Lee considers the chance and the force he has left to spend
And states his will.   10
                  Dutch Longstreet, the independent,
Demurs, as he has demurred since the fight began.
He had disapproved of this battle from the first
And that disapproval has added and is to add
Another weight in the balance against the grey.
It is not our task to try him for sense or folly,
Such men are the men they are—but an hour comes
Sometimes, to fix such men in most fateful parts,
As now with Longstreet who, if he had his orders
As they were given, neither obeyed them quite   20
Nor quite refused them, but acted as he thought best,
So did the half-thing, failed as he thought he would,
Felt justified and wrote all of his reasons down
Later in controversy.
                We do not need
Such controversies to see that pugnacious man
Talking to Lee, a stubborn line in his brow
And that unseen fate between them.
                      Lee hears him out
Unmoved, unchanging.   30
                "The enemy is there
And I am going to strike him," says Lee, inflexibly.

XVI. *The Black Horse Troop comes into the fight*

Wingate cursed with an equal stress
The guns in the sky and his weariness,
The nightmare riding of yesterday
When they slept in the saddle by whole platoons

And the Pennsylvania farmer's grey
With hocks as puffy as toy balloons,
A graceless horse, without gaits or speed,
But all he had for his time of need.
"I'd as soon be riding a Jersey cow."
But the Black Horse Troop was piebald now
And the Black Horse Troop was worn to the blade
With the dull fatigue of this last, long raid.
Huger Shepley rode in a tense
Gloom of the spirit that found offence   10
In all things under the summer skies
And the recklessness in Bristol's eyes
Had lost its color of merriment.
Horses and men, they were well-nigh spent.
Wingate grinned as he heard the "Mount,"
"Reckon we look sort of no-account,
But we're here at last for somebody's fight."
They rode toward the curve of the Union right.

XVII. Third day's attack

At one o'clock the first signal-gun was fired
And the solid ground began to be sick anew.   20
For two hours then that sickness, the unhushed roar
Of two hundred and fifty cannon firing like one.

By Philadelphia, eighty-odd miles away,
An old man stooped and put his ear to the ground
And heard that roar, it is said, like the vague sea-clash
In a hollow conch-shell, there, in his flowerbeds.
He had planted trumpet-flowers for fifteen years
But now the flowers were blowing an iron noise
Through earth itself. He wiped his face on his sleeve
And tottered back to his house with fear in his eyes.   30

The caissons began to blow up in the Union batteries. . . .

The cannonade fell still. All along the fish-hook line,
The tired men stared at the smoke and waited for it to clear;
The men in the centre waited, their rifles gripped in their hands,
By the trees of the riding fate, and the low stone wall, and the
    guns.

These were Hancock's men, the men of the Second Corps,
Eleven States were mixed there, where Minnesota stood
In battle-order with Maine, and Rhode Island beside New York,
The metals of all the North, cooled into an axe of war.

The strong sticks of the North, bound into a fasces-shape,
The hard winters of snow, the wind with the cutting edge,
And against them came that summer that does not die with the
    year,
Magnolia and honeysuckle and the blue Virginia flag.

Tall Pickett went up to Longstreet—his handsome face was 10
    drawn.
George Pickett, old friend of Lincoln's in days gone by with the
    blast,
When he was a courteous youth and Lincoln the strange shawled
    man
Who would talk in a Springfield street with a boy who dreamt of
    a sword.

Dreamt of a martial sword, as swords are martial in dreams,
And the courtesy to use it, in the old bright way of the tales.
Those days are gone with the blast. He has his sword in his hand. 20
And he will use it today, and remember that using long.

He came to Longstreet for orders, but Longstreet would not
    speak.
He saw Old Peter's mouth and the thought in Old Peter's mind.
He knew the task that was set and the men that he had to lead
And a pride came into his face while Longstreet stood there
    dumb.

"I shall go forward, sir," he said and turned to his men.
The commands went down the line. The grey ranks started to
    move.   30
Slowly at first, then faster, in order, stepping like deer,
The Virginians, the fifteen thousand, the seventh wave of the
    tide.

There was a death-torn mile of broken ground to cross,
And a low stone wall at the end, and behind it the Second Corps,

And behind that force another, fresh men who had not yet
  fought.
They started to cross that ground. The guns began to tear them.

From the hill they say that it seemed more like a sea than a wave,
A sea continually torn by stones flung out of the sky,
And yet, as it came, still closing, closing and rolling on,
As the moving sea closes over the flaws and rips of the tide.

You could mark the path that they took by the dead that they
  left behind,
Spilled from that deadly march as a cart spills meal on a road, 10
And yet they came on unceasing, the fifteen thousand no more,
And the blue Virginia flag did not fall, did not fall, did not fall.

They halted but once to fire as they came. Then the smoke closed
  down
And you could not see them, and then, as it cleared again for a
  breath,
They were coming still but divided, gnawed at by blue attacks,
One flank half-severed and halted, but the centre still like a tide.

Cushing ran down the last of his guns to the battle-line.
The rest had been smashed to scrap by Lee's artillery fire.   20
He held his guts in his hand as the charge came up the wall
And his gun spoke out for him once before he fell to the ground.

Armistead leapt the wall and laid his hand on the gun,
The last of the three brigadiers who ordered Pickett's brigades,
He waved his hat on his sword and "Give 'em the steel!" he cried,
A few men followed him over. The rest were beaten or dead.

A few men followed him over. There had been fifteen thousand
When that sea began its march toward the fish-hook ridge and
  the wall.
So they came on in strength, light-footed, stepping like deer,   30
So they died or were taken. So the iron entered their flesh.

Lee, a mile away, in the shade of a little wood,
Stared, with his mouth shut down, and saw them go and be slain,
And then saw for a single moment, the blue Virginia flag
Planted beyond the wall, by that other flag that he knew.

The two flags planted together, one instant, like hostile flowers.
Then the smoke wrapped both in a mantle—and when it had
    blown away,
Armistead lay in his blood, and the rest were dead or down,
And the valley grey with the fallen and the wreck of the broken
    wave.

Pickett gazed around him, the boy who had dreamt of a sword
And talked with a man named Lincoln. The sword was still in
    his hand.
He had gone out with fifteen thousand. He came back to his lines 10
    with five.
He fought well till the war was over, but a thing was cracked in
    his heart.

XVIII.   *Wingate is wounded*

Wingate, waiting the sultry sound
That would pour the troop over hostile ground,
Petted his grey like a loving son
And wondered whether the brute would run
When it came to fighting, or merely shy
There was a look in the rolling eye
That he knew too well to criticize   20
Having seen it sometimes in other eyes.
"Poor old Fatty," he said, "Don't fret,
It's tough, but it hasn't happened yet
And we may get through it if you behave,
Though it looks just now like a right close shave.
There's something funny about this fight—"

He thought of Lucy in candlelight,
White and gold as the evening star,
Giving bright ribbons to men at war.
But the face grew dimmer and ever dimmer,   80
The gold was there but the gold was fainter,
And a slow brush streaked it with something grimmer
Than the proper tint of a lady's painter
Till the shadow she cast was a ruddy shadow.
He rubbed his eyes and stared at the meadow. . . .

"There was a girl I used to go with,
  Long ago, when the skies were cooler,

There was a tree we used to grow with
   Marking our heights with a stolen ruler.

There was a cave where we hid and fought once.
   There was a pool where the wind kept writing.
There was a possum-child we caught once.
   Caged it awhile, for all its biting.

There was a gap in a fence to see there,
   Down where the sparrows were always wrangling.
There was a girl who used to be there,
   Dark and thin, with her long braids dangling.   10

Dark and thin in her scuffled brown slippers
   With a boy's sling stuck in her apron-pocket,
With a sting in her tongue like a gallinipper's
   And the eyes of a ghost in a silver locket.

White and gold, white and gold,
You cannot be cold as she was cold,
Cold of the air and the running stream
And cold of the ice-tempered dream.

Gold and white, gold and white,
You burn with the heat of candlelight.   20
But what if I set you down alone
Beside the burning meteor-stone?

Blow North, blow South, blow hot, blow cold,
My body is pledged to white and gold,
My honor given to kith and kin,
And my doom-clothes ready to wrap me in
For the shut heart and the open hand
As long as Wingate Hall shall stand
And the fire burn and the water cool
And a fool beget another fool—   30

But now, in the hour before this fight,
I have forgotten gold and white.
I will remember lost delight.
She has the Appleton mouth, it seems,
And the Appleton way of riding,

But if she quarrels or when she gleams,
Something comes out from hiding.

She can sew all day on an Appleton hem
And look like a saint in plaster,
But when the fiddles begin to play,
And her feet beat fast but her heart beats faster,
An alien grace is alive in them
And she looks like her father, the dancing-master,
The scapegrace elegant, 'French Dupré.' "

Then the word came and the bugle sang   10
And he was part of the running clang,
The rush and the shock and the sabres licking
And the fallen horses screaming and kicking.
His grey was tired and his arm unsteady
And he whirled like a leaf in a shrieking eddy
Where every man was fighting his neighbor
And there was no room for the tricks of sabre
But only a wild and nightmare sickling.
His head felt burnt—there was something trickling
Into his eyes—then the new charge broke   20
The eddy apart like scattered smoke;
The cut on his head half made him blind.
If he had a mind, he had lost that mind.

He came to himself in a battered place,
Staring at Wainscott Bristol's face,
The dried blood made it a ferret's mask.

"What happened?" he croaked.
                              "Well, you can ask,"
Said Bristol, drawling, "But don't ask me,
For any facts of the jamboree.   30
I reckon we've been to an Irish wake
Or maybe cuttin' a johnny-cake
With most of the Union cavalry-corps.
I don't know yet, but it was a war.
Are you crazy still? You were for a piece.
You yelled you were Destiny's long-lost niece
And wanted to charge the whole Yank line
Because they'd stolen your valentine.

You fought like a fool but you talked right wild.
You got a bad bump, too."
                              Wingate smiled
"I reckon I did, but I don't know when.
Did we win or what?"
                              "And I say again,"
Said Bristol, heavily, "don't ask me.
Inquire of General Robert Lee.
I know we're in for a long night ride
And they say we got whipped on the other side.   10
What's left of the Troop are down by the road.

We lost John Leicester and Harry Spode
And the Lawley boys and Ballantyne.
The Major's all right—but there's Jim Divine
And Francis Carroll and Judson White—
I wish I had some liquor tonight."

Wingate touched the cut on his head.
It burned, but it no longer bled.
"I wish I could sleep ten years," he said.

XIX. *Confederate retreat*

The night of the third day falls. The battle is done.   20
Lee entrenches that night upon Seminary Ridge.
All next day the battered armies still face each other
Like enchanted beasts.
                              Lee thinks he may be attacked,
Hopes for it, perhaps, is not, and prepares his retreat.

Vicksburg has fallen, hollow Vicksburg has fallen,
The cavedwellers creep from their caves and blink at the sun.
The pan of the Southern balance goes down and down.
The cotton is withering.

Army of Northern Virginia, haggard and tattered,   30
Tramping back on the pikes, through the dust-white summer,
With your wounds still fresh, your burden of prisoners,
Your burden of sick and wounded,
"One long groan of human anguish six miles long."

You reach the swollen Potomac at long last,
A foe behind, a risen river in front,
And fording that swollen river, in the dim starlight,
In the yellow and early dawn,
Still have heart enough for the tall, long-striding soldiers
To mock the short, half swept away by the stream.
"Better change our name to Lee's Waders, boys!"
"Come on you shorty—get a ride on my back."
"Aw, it's just we ain't had a bath in seven years
And General Lee, he knows we need a good bath."   10

So you splash and slip through the water and come at last
Safe, to the Southern side, while Meade does not strike;
Safe to take other roads, safe to march upon roads you know
For two long years. And yet—each road that you take,
Each dusty road leads to Appomattox now.

BOOK EIGHT:

The Arms Are Stacked

It is the aftermath of Gettysburg. Two more years pass with matters too bitter for any thought of treaty. Luke is one of many deserters from the Confederate Army.

We must gather up the threads of our story. We see John Vilas returning to his early home in the East, accompanied by his daughter and her child. They have become a legend in the land as they pass from town to town searching for Melora's lover. The magic of the wilderness-stone is great indeed when out of all the world Melora finds him.

General Sherman fulfills his boast of marching from Atlanta to the sea. In his path is Wingate Hall, which, after his passing, lies in ruins.

Yet out of the fall of Wingate glory will later blossom the happiness of Sally Dupré and Clay.

In a house at Appomattox, two generals—Grant and Lee— meet to bring about a formal close to hostilities.

First of the new order, Spade, the runaway slave, becomes a "hired man" to Jake Diefer.

Abraham Lincoln finds his dream fulfilled and dies at the hand of an assassin. With his death, the era of the Civil War ends. Much must happen before North and South can feel even a semblance of amity, but with the issue of slavery settled, the soul of John Brown can rest.

I. *Aftermath of Gettysburg*

It is over now, but they will not let it be over.

It was over with John Brown when the sun rose up
To show him the town in arms and he did not flee,
Yet men were killed after that, before it was over,
And he did not die until November was cool
—Yellow leaves falling through a blue-grey dusk,
The first winds of November whirl and scatter them—
So now, the Confederacy,
Sick with its mortal sickness, yet lives on
For twenty-one falling months of pride and despair,   10
Half-hopes blown out in the lighting, heroic strokes
That come to nothing, and death piled hard upon death.

Follow that agony if you must and can
By the brushwood names, by the bloody prints in the woods,
Cold Harbor and Spottsylvania and Yellow Tavern
And all the lost court-houses and country stores
In the Wilderness, where the bitter fighting passed,
(No fighting bitterer)—follow the rabbit-runs
Through the tangled wilds where the hair of the wounded men
Caught fire from the burning trees, where they lay in the swamps 20
Like half-charred logs—find the place they called "Hell's Half
    Acre."
Follow the Indian names in the Indian West,
Chickamauga and Chattanooga and all the words
That are sewn on flags or cut in an armory wall.
My cyclorama is not the shape of the world
Nor even the shape of this war from first to last,
But like a totem carved, like a totem stained
With certain beasts and skies and faces of men
That would not let me be too quiet at night   30
Till they were figured.
                        Therefore now, through the storm,
The war, the rumor, the grinding of the machine,
Let certain sounds, let certain voices be heard.

A Richmond lady sits in a Richmond square
Beside a working-girl. They talk of the war,
They talk of the food and the prices in low-pitched voices

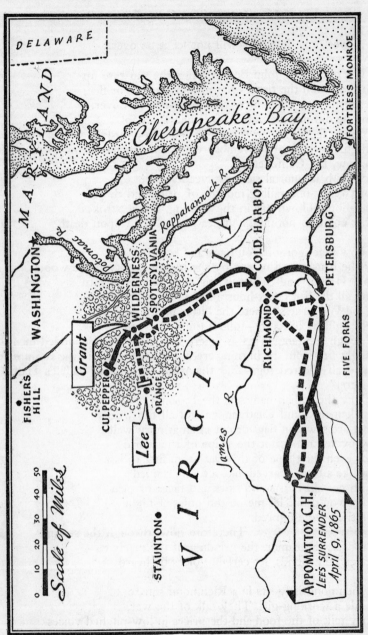

Battles Culminating in the Surrender at Appomattox C. H.

With hunger fretting them both. Then they go their ways.
But, before she departs, the lady has asked a question—
The working-girl pulls up the sleeve of her dress
And shows the lady the sorry bone of her arm.

Grant has come East to take up his last command
And the grand command of the armies.
                                          It is five years
Since he sat, with a glass, by the stove in a country store,
A stumpy, mute man in a faded Army overcoat,
The eldest-born of the Grants but the family-failure,   10
Now, for a week, he shines in the full array
Of gold cord and black-feathered hat and superb blue coat,
As he talks with the trim, well-tailored Eastern men.
It is his only moment of such parade.
When the fighting starts, he is chewing a dead cigar
With only the battered stars to show the rank
On the shoulderstraps of the private's uniform.

It is sullen Cold Harbor. The Union attack has failed,
Repulsed with a ghastly slaughter. The twilight falls.
The word goes round the attack will be made again   20
Though all know now that it cannot be made and win.
An anxious officer walks through his lines that night.
There has been no mutiny yet, throughout all these years,
But he wonders now. What are the men doing now?
He sees them there. They are silently writing their names
On bits of rag and sewing the scraps of cloth
To their jackets while they can, before the attack.
When they die, next morning, somebody may read the names.

Pickett's son is born on a night of mid-July
While the two armies face each other, and Pickett's men   30
Light bonfires of celebration along his lines.
The fire is seen from the tents of the other camp.
The news goes back to Grant and his chief of staff.

"Haven't we any wood for the little Pickett?" says Grant,
And the Union bonfires are lighted for Pickett's son.
—All night those two lines of brush-fire, facing each other—
Next day they send the baby a silver service.
Next week or so they move upon Pickett's works.

On a muddy river, little toy boats go out.
The soldiers are swapping coffee for rank tobacco,
A Northern badge for a Southern souvenir,
A piece of white-flour bread for a hunk of corn-pone.
A Northern lieutenant swims the river at night
To go to a Southern dance at a backwoods store,
Joke with the girls, swim back, and fight the next day
With his hosts of the night before.

                       On disputed ground,
A grey-clad private worms his way like a snake,   10
The Union sentries see him and start to fire.
"Aw, shut up, Yank," he calls in a weary voice,
"I just skun out to salvage the chaplain's hat,
It's the only one he's got and it just blew off."
The firing stops.
               "All right, Johnny," the sentries call,
"Get your hat, but be quick about it. We won't hurt you
But you better be back by the time our relief gets here."

A Southern sharpshooter crouched in a blue-gum tree
Drills a tiny blue-coated figure between the eyes   20
With a pea-ball fired from a smooth-bore squirrel-rifle.
The dead man's brother waits three days for his shot,
Then the sharpshooter crashes down through the breaking boughs
Like a lumpy bird, spread-eagled out of his nest.

The desolate siege of Petersburg begins.
The grain goes first, then the cats and the squeaking mice,
The thin cats stagger starving about the streets,
Die or are eaten. There are no more cats
In Petersburg—and in Charleston the creeping grass
Grows over the wharves where the ships of the world came in. 30
The grass and the moss grow over the stones of the wharves.
A Georgia belle eats sherbet near Andersonville   *Rebel prison*
Where the Union prisoners rot. Another is weeping
The death of her brother, killed in a Union raid.

In the North, the factory chimneys smoke and fume;
The minstrels have raised their prices, but every night
Bones and Tambo play to a crowded house.
The hotels are full. The German Opera is here.

The ladies at Newport drive in their four-in-hands.
The old woman sells her papers about the war
The country widows stitch on a rusty black.

In the Shenandoah Valley, the millwheels rot.
(Sheridan has been there.) Where the houses stood,
Strong houses, built for weather, lasting it out,
The chimneys stand alone. The chimneys are blackened.
(Sheridan has been there.) This Valley has been
The granary of Lee's army for years and years.
Sheridan makes his report on his finished work.   10
"If a crow intends to fly over the Valley now
He'll have to carry his own provisions," says Sheridan.

The lonely man with the chin like John Calhoun's   *Jeff Davis*
Knows it is over, will not know it is over.
Many hands are turning against him in these last years.
He makes mistakes. He is stubborn and sick at heart.
He is inflexible with fate and men.
It is over. It cannot be. He fights to the end,
Clinging to one last dream—of somehow, somewhere,
A last, miraculous battle where he can lead   20
One wing of the Southern army and Lee the other
And so wrench victory out of the failing odds.
Why is it a dream? He has studied grand strategy,
He was thought a competent soldier in Mexico,
He was Secretary of War once—
                              He is the rigid
Scholar we know and have seen in another place,
Lacking that scholar's largeness, but with the same   *Wilson*
Tight mouth, the same intentness on one concept,
The same ideal that must bend all life to its will   30
Or break to pieces—and that is the best of him.
The pettiness is the pettiness of a girl
More than a man's—a brilliant and shrewish girl,
Never too well in body yet living long.
He has that unforgiveness of women in him
And women will always know him better than men
Except for a few, in spite of Mexican wars,
In spite of this last, most desolate, warlike dream.
Give him the tasks that other scholar assumed,
He would not have borne them as greatly or with such skill,   40

315

And yet—one can find a likeness.

                       So now he dreams
Hopelessly of a fight he will never fight
And if worst comes to worst, perhaps, of a last
Plutarch-death on a shield.

                     It is not to be.
He will snatch up a cloak of his wife's by accident
In the moment before his capture, and so be seen,
The proud man turned into farce, into sorry farce
Before the ignorant gapers.

                     He shades his eyes   **10**
To rest them a moment, turns to his work again.

The gaunt man, Abraham Lincoln, lives his days.
For a while the sky above him is very dark.
There are fifty thousand dead in these last, bleak months
And Richmond is still untaken.

                     The papers rail,
Grant is a butcher, the war will never be done.
The gaunt man's term of office draws to an end,
His best friends muse and are doubtful. He thinks himself   **20**
For a while that when the time of election comes
He will not be re-elected. He does not flinch.
He draws up a paper and seals it with his own hand.
His cabinet signs it, unread.

                     Such writing might be
A long historic excuse for defeated strength.
This is very short and strict with its commonsense.
"It seems we may not rule this nation again.
If so, we must do our best, while we still have time,
To plan with the new rulers who are to come   **30**
How best to save the Union before they come,
For they will have been elected upon such grounds
That they cannot possibly save it, once in our place."

The cloud lifts, after all. They bring him the news.
He is sure of being President four years more.
He thinks about it. He says, "Well, I guess they thought
They'd better not swap horses, crossing a stream."
The deserters begin to leave the Confederate armies. . . .

Luke Breckinridge woke up one sunshiny morning
Alone, in a roadside ditch, to be hungry again,
Though he was used to being hungry by now.
He looked at his rifle and thought, "Well, I ought to clean it."
He looked at his feet and he thought, "Well, I ought to get
Another bunch of rags if we-uns is goin'
To march much more—these rags is down to my hide."
He looked at his ribs through the tears in his dirty shirt
And he thought, "Well, I sure am thin as a razorback.
Well, that's the way it is. Well, I ought to do somethin'.   10
I ought to catch up with the boys. I wish I remembered
When I had to quit marchin' last night. Well, if I start now,
I reckon I'm bound to catch 'em."
                                        But when he rose
He looked at the road and saw where the march had passed
—Feet going on through the dust and the sallow mud,
Feet going on forever—
                          He saw that track.
He was suddenly very tired.
He had been tired after fighting often enough   20
But this was another weariness.

He rubbed his head in his hands for a minute or so,
As if to rub some slow thought out of his mind
But it would not be rubbed away.
                                  "I'm near it," he thought,
"The hotel ain't a mile from here if Sophy's still there.
Well, they wouldn't give me a furlough when I ast.
Well, it's been a long time."
                              On the way to the plank hotel
He still kept mumbling, "I can catch up to the boys."   30
But another thought too vague to be called a thought
Washed over the mumble, drowning it, forcing it down.

The grey front door was open. No one was there.
He stood for a moment silent, watching the sun
Fall through the open door and pool in the dust.
"Sophy!" he called. He waited. Then he went in.
The flies were buzzing over the dirty plates
In the dining room and nobody there at all.

It made him feel tired. He started to climb the stairs.
"Hey, Sophy!" he called and listened. There was a creak
From somewhere, a little noise like a dusty rat
Running across a dusty, sun-splattered board.
His hands felt stronger.
                        He was on the second floor
Slamming the doors of empty room after room
And calling "Sophy!" At last he found the locked door.
He broke it down with his shoulder in a loud noise.
She was lying in bed with the covers up to her chin   10
And her thin hands clutching the covers.
                                    "Well, Soph," he said.
"Well, it's you," she said.
                        They stared at each other awhile.

"The rest of 'em's gone," she said. "They went off last night.
We haven't had no business. The nigger said
The Yanks were coming. They didn't have room in the cart.
They said I could stay for a while and take care of things
Or walk if I wanted. I guess Mr. Pollet's crazy.
He was talking things to himself all the time they went.   20
I never slept in a bed like this before.
I didn't know you could sleep so soft in a bed."

"Did they leave any shoes?" said Luke.
                                    She shook her head.
"I reckon you could maybe tear up a quilt.
I reckon they wouldn't mind."
                            Luke grinned like a wolf.
"I reckon they hadn't better," he said. "Not much.
Got anything to eat? I'm hungry as hell."

They ate what food she could find and she washed his feet   30
And bound them up in fresh rags.
                            He looked at the rags.
"Do for a while," he said. "Well, come along, Soph.
We got a long way to go."
                        Her eyes were big at him.
"The Yanks were comin'," she said. "You mean the war's over?"

He said, "I ain't had shoes for God knows how long."
He said, "If it was all Kelceys, you wouldn't mind.

318

Now I'm goin' to get me some shoes and raise me a crop,
And when we get back home, we'll butcher a hog.
There's allus hogs in the mountains."
                                        "Well," she said.
"Well, you get your duds," he said.
                                    She didn't have much.
They went along two days without being stopped.
She walked pretty well for a thin sort of girl like that.
He told her she'd get fatter when they were home.

The third day, they were tramping along toward dusk,   10
On a lonely stretch of road, when she heard the horse-hoofs.
Luke had heard them before and shifted his rifle then.

The officer came in sight. He was young and drawn.
His eyes were old in their sockets. He reined his horse.
"You're goin' the wrong way, soldier. What's your regiment?"

Luke's eyes grew little. "—th Virginia," he drawled,
"But I'm on furlough."
                        "H'm," said the officer,
"Where are your furlough-papers?"
                                    Luke's hand slid down   20
By his trigger guard. "This here's my furlough," he said,
Resting the piece in the palm of the other hand.
The officer seemed to debate a thing in his mind
For a long instant. Then he rode on, in silence.
Luke watched him out of sight. When he was quite gone,
The hand slid back, the rifle was shouldered again.

III.   Lee through the eyes of his aide-de-camp

The night had fallen on the narrow tent.
—Deep night of Virginia summer when the stars
Are burning wax in the near, languid sky
And the soft flowers hardly close all night   30
But bathe in darkness, as a woman bathes
In a warm, fragrant water and distill
Their perfume still, without the fire of the sun.
The army was asleep as armies sleep.
War lying on a casual sheaf of peace

For a brief moment, and yet with armor on,
And yet in the child's deep sleep, and yet so still.
Even the sentries seemed to walk their posts
With a ghost-footfall that could match that night.

The aide-de-camp knew certain lines of Greek
And other such unnecessary things
As birds and music, that are good for peace
But are not deemed so serviceable for war.
He was a youth with an inquisitive mind
And doubtless had a failing for romance,   10
But then he was not twenty, and such faults
May sometimes be excused in younger men
Even when such creatures die, as they have done
At one time or another, for some cause
Which we are careful to point out to them
Much later, was no cause worth dying for,
But cannot reach them with our arguments
Because they are uneconomic dust.

So, when the aide-de-camp came toward the tent,
He knew that he was sleepy as a dog,   20
And yet the starlight and the gathered scents
Moved in his heart—like the unnecessary
Themes of a music fallen from a cloud
In light, upon a dark water.
                                        And though he had
Some bitterness of mind to chew upon,
As well as messages that he must give
Before he slept, he halted in his tracks.

He saw, imprinted on the yellow light
That made the tent a hollow jack-o'-lantern,   30
The sharp, black shadow of a seated man,
The profile like the profile on a bust.
Lee in his tent, alone.
He had some shadow-papers in his hand,
But you could see he was not reading them,
And, if he thought, you could not read his thoughts,
Even as shadows, by any light that shines.

"You'd know that face among a million faces,"
Thought the still watcher, "and yet, his hair and beard

320

Have quite turned white, white as the dogwood-bloom
That blossomed on the way to Chancellorsville
When Jackson was alive and we were young
And we were winning and the end was near.
And now, I guess, the end is near enough
In spite of everything that we can do,
And he's alone tonight and Jackson's dead.

I saw him in the Wilderness that day
When he began to lead the charge himself
And the men wouldn't let him.   10
                         Gordon spoke
And then the men themselves began to yell
"Lee to the rear—General Lee to the rear!"
I'll hear that all my life. I'll see those paws
Grabbing at Traveller and the bridle-rein
And forcing the calm image back from death.

Reckon that's what we think of you, Marse Robert,
Reckon that's what we think, what's left of us,
The poor old devils that are left of us.
I wonder what he thinks about it all.   20
He isn't staring, he's just sitting there.
I never knew a man could look so still
And yet look so alive in his repose.

It doesn't seem as if a cause could lose
When it's believed in by a man like that.
And yet we're losing.
                      And he knows it all.
No, he won't ever say it. But he knows.

I'd feel more comfortable if he'd move.

We had a chance at Spottsylvania,   30
We had some chances in the Wilderness.
We always hurt them more than we were hurt
And yet we're here—and they keep coming on.

What keeps us going on? I wish I knew.
Perhaps you see a man like that go on
And then you have to follow.

There can't be
So many men that men have followed so.

And yet, what is it for? What is it for?
What does he think?
His hands are lying there
Quiet as stones or shadows in his lap.
His beard is whiter than the dogwood bloom,
But there is nothing ruined in his face,
And nothing beaten in those steady eyes.
If he's grown old, it isn't like a man,   10
It's more the way a river might grow old.

My mother knew him at old dances once.
She said he liked to joke and he was dark then,
Dark and as straight as he can stand today.
If he would only move, I could go forward.

You see the faces of spear-handling kings
In the old books they taught us from at school;
Big Agamemnon with his curly beard,
Achilles in the cruelty of his youth,
And Œdipus before he tore his eyes.   20

I'd like to see him in that chariot-rank,
With Traveller pulling at the leader-pole.
I don't think when the winged claws come down
They'll get a groan from him.
So we go on.
Under the claws. And he goes on ahead.

The sharp-cut profile moved a fraction now,
The aide-de-camp went forward on his errand.

IV. *Requiem*

The years ride out from the world like couriers gone to a throne
That is too far for treaty, or, as it may be, too proud;   30
The years marked with a star, the years that are skin and bone.
The years ride into the night like envoys sent to a cloud.

Perhaps they dismount at last, by some iron ring in the skies,
Dismount and tie their stallions and walk with an armored tread
Where an outlaw queen of the air receives strange embassies
Under a tree of wisdom, between the quick and the dead.

Perhaps they are merely gone, as the white foam flies from the bit,
But the sparkling noise of their riding is ever in our ears.—
The men who came to the maze without foreknowledge of it,
The losers and the finders, under the riding years.

They pass, and the finders lose, the losers find for a space.
There are love and hate and delusion and all the tricks of the 10
   maze.
There are always losers and finders. There is no abiding-place
And the years are unreturning. But, here and there, there were
   days.

Days when the sun so shone that the statue gave its cry
And a bird shook wings or a woman walked with a certain mirth,
When the staff struck out a spring from the stones that had long
   been dry,
And the plough moved on from the hilltop, but its share had
   opened the earth.   20

So the bird is caught for an instant, and so the bird escapes.
The years are not halted by it. The losers and finders wait.
The years move on toward the sunset, the tall, far-trafficking
   shapes,
Each with a bag of news to lay at a ghostly gate.

Riders shaking the heart with the hoofs that will not cease,
Will you never lie stretched in marble, the hands crossed over the
   breast,
Some with hounds at your feet to show that you passed in peace,
And some with your feet on lions?   30
                        It is time that you were at rest.

V. John Vilas's odyssey

John Vilas clucked to the scurvy rack of bones
Between the shafts. The rickety cart moved on
Like a tired insect, creaking through the dust.

There was another day behind them now
And any number of such days ahead
Unrolling like a long block-printed cloth
Pattered with field and stream and snake-rail fence,
And now and then, a flash of cavalry
Fording a backwoods creek; a big, slow star
Mounting in silver over lonely woods
While the fire smelled of pine and a cougar cried;
A warm barn, full of the sweet milky breath
Of cows; a lank-haired preacher on a mule;   10
A red-cheeked woman who rushed after them
Armed with a hot and smoking apple-pie
And would not take a penny from the old man
Who held the mended reins as if they were
The vast, slow-sweeping scythe of Time himself
—Old Time and the last children of his age,
Drawn in a rattling cart, too poor to thieve,
By a gaunt horse, too ancient to die,
Over a rutted road, day after day,
Returning to the East from whence he came.   20

It was a portent in the little towns.
The time had bred odd voyagers enough;
Disbanded soldiers, tramping toward the West
In faded army blouses, singing strange songs,
Heroes and chickenthieves, true men and liars,
Some with old wounds that galled them in the rains
And some who sold the wounds they never had
Seven times over in each new saloon;
Queer, rootless families, plucked up by war
To blow along the roads like tumbleweed,   30
Who fed their wild-haired children God knows how
But always kept a fierce and cringing cur,
Famished for scraps, to run below the cart;
Horsedealers, draft-evaders, gipsymen;
Crooked creatures of a thousand dubious trades
That breed like gnats from the débris of war;
Half-cracked herb-doctor, patent-medicine man
With his accordeon and his inked silk hat;
Sellers of snake-oil balm and lucky rings
And the old, crazy hatless wanderer   40
Who painted "God is Love" upon the barns

324

And on the rocks, "Prepare to Meet Thy God"
Lost tribes and maverick nations of the road—
The shiftless people, who are never still
But blow before the wind unquietly
And will so blow, until the last starved cur
Yaps at the last fat farmer, and lies down
With buckshot tearing at his ravening heart,
For the slow years to pick his carcass clean
And turn the little chapel of his bones
Into a dust so sifted by the wind   10
No winds that blow can sift it any more.

There were unquiet people on the road,
There were outlandish strays and travellers,
Drifting the little towns from day to day,
Stopping to mend a wheel or patch a shoe,
Beg, steal or sleep or write God's judgments out
And then pass on.
                        And yet, when these three came,
John Vilas and his daughter and her child,
Like snail-drawn Time, along the dusty track,   20
The story had gone on ahead of them.
And there was something in the rickety cart
Or the gaunt horse or in his driver's eyes
That made a fable of their journeying,
Until you heard John Vilas was that same
Lost Jew that wanders after every war
But cannot die in any, being curst.
He was the skipper, who first brought the slaves.
He was John Brown, arisen from his stone.
He was the drummer who had lost his way   30
At Valley Forge and frozen in the snow,
To rove forevermore, a dread old man
Beating a phantom drum across the wind.
He was a dozen such uncanny fetches,
And, while one must not talk with him too long,
There was no luck at all in crossing him,
Because, and in the end, the man was Time;
White-headed Time, stoop-shouldered on his scythe,
Driving a daughter and a daughter's son
Beyond the war, to some wrought-iron gate   40
Where they would drop their heavy load at last

—Load of all war and all misfortune's load—
On the green grass of a New England grave
Set on the sea-cliffs, looking toward the sea.

While, for the other tale, the woman's tale,
The heart-faced girl with the enormous eyes,
Roving from little town to little town
Still looking for her soldier—it became
Mixed with each story of such fortune told
Behind drawn blinds, by women, in the dusk,
Until she too grew fabulous as a song   10
Sung to a beechwood fiddle, and all the old
Barely-recorded chants that are the land
And no one poet's or musician's
—"Old Dan Tucker," "The Belle of Albany,"
The girl who died for love in the high woods
And cruel Barbara Allen in her pride.

So she became a concertina tune
Played in plank taverns by a blind, old man,
A jew's-harp strain, a comb-and-banjo song,
The music of a soapbox violin   20
Shrilled out against the tree-toads and the crickets
Through the hot nights of June. So, though she passed
Unknowing, yet she left the legend-touch
Bright as a splash of sumach still behind
Wherever the gaunt horse pulled on his load.
Till, later, those who knew no more of her
Living, than they might know of such removed
And singable creations as "Lord Randall,"
"Colombo," "Little Musgrave," or "Jay Gould's Daughter"
Yet knew enough of her to sing about   30
And fit her name, Melora, to the same
Slow-dropping minor of the water and earth—
The minor of the country barber-shops
That keens above the grave of Jesse James
And the lone prairie where the cowboy died,
The desolate minor of the jail-bird's song,
Luscious with sorrow, and the minor notes
That tell about the tragic end of such
As loved too well to have such cruel fathers
But were so loving, even in the dust,   40

A red-rose brier grew out of their dead hearts
And twined together in a lover's knot
For all the county people to admire,
And every lost, waif ballad we have made
And, making, scorned because it smelt of the earth,
And now would seek, but cannot make again—
So she became a legend and a name.

John Vilas, moving always toward the East,
Upon his last adventure, felt the sun
Strike at his bones and warm them like the last   10
Heat of the wood so long within the fire
That long ago the brightness ate its heart
And yet it lies and burns upon the iron
Unready still to crumble and be cool
The white, transmuted log of purest ash
Still glowing with a late and borrowed flame.

"This is the sun of age," he thought, "and so
We enter our last journeys with that sun
Which we have watched sink down ten thousand times
Knowing he would arise like Dedalus   20
On the first wings of morning, and exult
Like our own youth, fresh-risen from its bed
And inexhaustible of space and light.
But now the vessel which could not be filled
By violence or desire or the great storm,
Runs over with its weight of little days
And when this sun sinks now, we'll sink with him
And not get up again.
                      I find it fit
That I, who spent the years of my desire   30
In the lost forest, seeking the lost stone,
With little care for Harriet or the rest,
With little trust in safety or the world,
Should now retrace at last, and in my age,
The exact highway of my youth's escape
From everything that galled it and take on,
Like an old snake resuming his cast skins,
The East I fled, the little towns I mocked,
The dust I thought was shaken from my shoes,
The sleepiness from which I ran away.   40

327

Harriet's right and Harriet is just
And Harriet's back in that chintz-curtained room
From which I took her, twenty years ago,
With all the children who were always hers
Because I gave them nothing but my seed
And hardly heard their laughter or their tears
And hardly knew their faces or their names,
Because I listened for the wind in the bough,
Because my daughters were the shooting-stars,
Because my sons were the forgotten streams   10
And the wild silvers of the wilderness.

Men who go looking for the wilderness-stone
And find it, should not marry or beget,
For, if they do so, they may work a wrong
Deeper than any mere intent of pain.
And yet, what I have sought that I have sought
And cannot disavouch, although it is
The double knife that cuts the giver's hand
And the unwilling taker's.
                                        So I took   20
My wife, long since, from that chintz-curtained room
And so she has gone back to it again
After these years, with children of those years,
And, being kind, she will not teach them there
To curse me, as I think, though if she did
She could find reason in her neighbor's eyes,
And, being Harriet, she will bring them up
As all such children should and must be reared
In all such houses, till the end of time,
As if she had not been away at all.   30
And so, at last, she'll get the peace she should.
And yet, some time, a child may run away.

We have had sons and daughters, she and I,
And, of them all, one daughter and one son
In whom our strange bloods married with the true
Marriage that is not merely sheath and sword.
The rest are hers. Those two were partly mine.

I taught my son to wander in the woods
Till he could step the hidden paths with me

328

Light as a whisper, indolent as Spring.
I would not tame his sister when I might,
I let her follow patterans of leaves,
Looking for stones rejected by the wise.
I kept them by me jealously and long.

And yet, the day they took him, when he sat
There on his horse, before they all rode off,
It was his mother who looked out of him
And it was to his mother that he looked.

That is my punishment and my offence   10
And that is how it was. And he is dead.
Dead of a fever, buried in the South,
Dead in this war I thought a whirligig
For iron fools to play with and to kill
Other men's sons, not mine. He's buried deep.
I kept him by me jealously and long.
Well, he walked well, alive. He was my son.
I'll not make tags of him.
                                We got the news.
She could not stay beside me after that.   20
I see so clearly why she could not stay.

So I retrace the hard steps of my youth
Now with this daughter, in a rattling cart
Drawn by a horse as lean as famine's self,
And am an omen in the little towns—
Because this daughter has too much of me
To be content with bread made out of wheat.
To be in love and give it up for rest,
To live serene without a knife at heart.

Such is the manner and the bound escape   30
Of those a disproportion drives unfed
From the world's table, without meat or grace,
Though both are wholesome, but who seek instead
Their solitary victual like the fox.
And who at last return as I return
In the ironic wagon of the years,
Back to the pasture that they found too green,
Broken of every knowledge but the last

329

Knowledge of how escape is not a door
But a slow-winding road whose hundred coils
Return upon each other, soon or late
—And how and when and under what cold stars
The old wound bleeds beneath the armored mind.

And yet, this journey is not desolate
Nor am I desolate in it, as we crawl
Slowly from little town to little town
Always against the sun, and the horse nods,
And there's my daughter talking, and her child   10
Sleeping or waking, and we stop awhile
And then go on awhile, and I can feel
The slow sun creeping through me summerlong.
Until, at times, I fall into a doze
Awake, a daydream without apparitions
And, falling so, inhabit for a space
A second childhood, calmer than the first,
But wise in the same fashion, and so touch
For a long, drowsy hour of afternoon,
The ripened thing, the autumn at the heart,   20
The one full star of evening that is age.

Yes, I must be a second child sometimes,
For as we pass and as they watch us pass,
It seems to me their eyes make stories of us
And I can hear those stories murmuring
Like pigeons in a loft when I'm asleep,
Till sometimes I must wonder for a while
If I've not changed myself for someone else
Or grown a story without knowing it,
And, with no intermediary death,   30
Stepped out of flesh and taken on a ghost.

For at such times, it almost seems to me
As if I were no longer what I am
But the deluded shade of Peter Rugg
Still looking for his Boston through the storm,
Or the strange spook of Johnny Appleseed,
Crept out of heaven on a windless night
To see if his wild orchards prosper still
And leave a heap of Baldwins and sweet russets

—Moonglittered, scrubbed with rags of silver cloud
And Indian magic—by the lucky doors
Of such good people as take care of them—
While for my daughter, though I know she's real,
She and her story, yet, in the waking dream
She mixes with that song I used to know
About the Spanish lady of old days
Who loved the Englishman and sought for him
All through green England in her scarlet shoes,
Knowing no word of English but his name.   10

I hear her voice, where the guitar is mixed
With the sweet, jangling mule-bells of Castile,
I see her face under its high shell-comb
—And then it is my daughter's—and I wake—
And yet know, even in waking, that we are
Somewhere between a story and a dream.
And so, you see, I find a kind of peace
In this last foray, will not rail at the sun,
Eat, drink and sleep, in spite of what is past,
Talk with my daughter, watch the turning skies.   20
The Spanish lady found her Englishman.
Well, we may find this boy I've half-forgot,
Although our story is another story.

So life works in us for a little while
And then the ferment's quiet.
                         So we do
Wrongs much beyond intent, and suffer them.
So we go looking for the wilderness-stone.

I shall smell lilac in Connecticut
No doubt, before I die, and see the clean   30
White, reticent, small churches of my youth,
The gardens full of phlox and mignonette,
The pasture-bars I broke to run away.

It was my thought to lie in an uncropped
And savage field no plough had ever scored,
Between a bee-tree and a cast deer-horn.
It was my thought to lie beside a stream
Too secret for the very deer to find,

331

Too solitary for remembrance.
It was a dream. It does not matter now.

Bury me where the soldiers of retreat
Are buried, underneath the faded star,
Bury me where the courtiers of escape
Fall down, confronted with their earth again.
Bury me where the fences hold the land
And the sun sinks beyond the pasture-bars
Never to fall upon the wilderness-stone.

And yet I have escaped, in spite of all."   10

VI. Safety

Lucy Weatherby smoothed out clothes in a trunk
With a stab at her heart.
                    The trunk was packed to the lid.
There wasn't an empty corner anywhere,
Pack as she would—but the blue dress wouldn't go in.

Of course she'd be getting a lot of new dresses soon
And the blue was old—but she couldn't leave it behind.
If only Henry wasn't so selfish, at times!
But Henry was like all brothers and like all men,
Expecting a lady to travel to Canada   20
With just one trunk and the boxes!
                    It was too bad.
He had a trunk of his own for razors and shirts,
And yet she couldn't take two—and there were the hoops;
He kept on fussing because she wouldn't leave them
When she knew he was hoping to take all those silly books,
As if you couldn't buy books wherever you went!

She pinched her cheek and stared at the trunk again.
The green could come out, of course, and the blue go in,
But she couldn't bear the idea of leaving the green.   30

The war, of course, and one thinks so much of the war,
And those terrible Yankees actually at our gates,
In spite of our fine, brave boys and poor Mr. Davis,
In spite of wearing old dresses for two whole years
And sending the servants out to work at the forts,

332

In spite of the cheers and the songs and the cause and the right.
Only, one must not be selfish. One must be brave.
One must think about Henry's health and be sensible,
And Henry actually thinks we can get away. . . .

The blue or the green? She couldn't decide it yet,
And there were all those letters to write tonight.
She'd simply have to write to Clay and Huger
About Henry's health—and how it just breaks my heart,
But one cannot leave one's sick brother—and afterwards,
One can always send one's address—and I'm sure if they do   10
We'll give them a real, old-fashioned Richmond welcome,
Though they say that the British leftenants are simply sweet
And every Southern girl is an absolute belle.
They play the "Bonnie Blue Flag" at the dances there,
And Sara Kenefick is engaged to an earl.
She saw herself, for an instant, walking the safe
Street of a calm and British-looking town.
She had on a new dress. Her shoes and her hat were new.
A white-haired, dim-faced man in a British coat
Walked beside her and looked and was listening,   20
While she told him all about it, and hearing the guns,
And how they'd actually lived without butcher's meat
For weeks and weeks—and the wounded—and General Lee—
And only Henry's health had forced them at last
To leave the dear South. She choked. He patted her hand.
He hoped they would stay in Canada for a while.

The blue or the green? It was dreadfully hard to choose,
And with all the letters to write—and Jim Merrihew
And that nice Alabama Major—
                          She heard the bells   30
Ring for a wedding, but this was a different groom,
This was a white-haired man with stars on his coat,
This was an Order wrapped in an English voice.

Honey, sugar-lump honey I love so dearly,
You have eluded the long pursuit that sought you,
You have eluded the hands that would so enclose you
And with strange passion force you.
                          What was this passion?
We do not know, you and I, but we would not bear it

And are gone free.
            So at last, if fair girls must marry,
As young girls should, it is after another fashion
And not with youth but wisely.
            So we are ransomed,
And I am yours forever and you are mine,
Honey, sugar-lump honey.
            So we attain,
The white-haired bridegrooms with the stars on their coats
And yet have the beaus to dance with, for we like dancing,   10
So all the world finds our wifely devotion charming,
So we play all day in the heat of the sun.

She held the blue dress under her chin once more
And smoothed it with one white hand. Then she put it down
Smiling a little. No, it couldn't go in,
But she would see if she couldn't help Henry pack,
And if she did, the blue could go with his shirts.
It hardly mattered, leaving some shirts behind.

VII. *Sherman's march to the sea*

Sherman's buzzin' along to de sea,
Jubili, Jubilo!   20
Sherman's buzzin' along to de sea,
Like Moses ridin' on a bumblebee,
Settin' de prisoned and de humble free!
Hit's de year of Jubilo!

Massa was de whale wid de big inside,
Jubili, Jubilo!
Massa was de lion and de lion's hide.
But de Lord God smacked him in his hardheart pride,
And de whale unswallered, and de lion died!
Hit's de year of Jubilo!   30

Oh, hit don't matter if you's black or tan,
Jubili, Jubilo!
Hit don't matter if you's black or tan,
When you hear de noise of de freedom-ban'
You's snatched baldheaded to de Promise Lan',
Hit's de year of Jubilo!

Oh, hit don't matter if you pine or ail,
Jubili, Jubilo!
Hit don't matter if you pine or ail,
Hit don't matter if you's been in jail,
De Lord's got mercy for your mumblin' tale!
Hit's de year of Jubilo!

Every nigger's gwine to own a mule,
Jubili, Jubilo!
Every nigger's gwine to own a mule,
An' live like Adam in de Golden Rule,   10
An' send his chillun to de white-folks' school!
In de year of Jubilo!

Fall down on your knees and bless de Lord,
Jubili, Jubilo!
Fall down on your knees and bless de Lord,
Dat chased old Pharaoh wid a lightnin'-sword,
And rose up Izzul fum de withered gourd,
Hit's de year of Jubilo!

Shout thanksgivin' and shout it loud!
Jubili, Jubilo!   20
Shout thanksgivin' and shout it loud,
We was dead and buried in de Lazrus-shroud,
But de Lord came down in a glory-cloud,
An' He gave us Jubilo!

So Sherman goes from Atlanta to the sea
Through the red-earth heart of the land, through the pine-smoke
    haze
Of the warm, last months of the year.
                        In the evenings
The skies are green as the thin, clear ice on the pools   30
That melts to water again in the heat of noon.
A few black trees are solemn against those skies.
The soldiers feel the winter touching the air
With a little ice.
            But when the sun has come up,
When they halt at noonday, mopping their sweaty brows,
The skies are blue and soft and without a cloud.

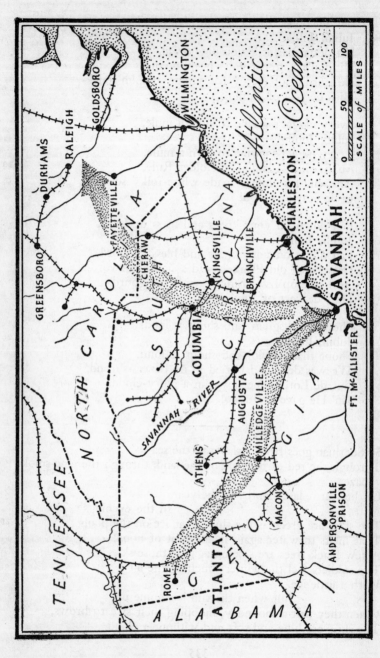

Sherman's March to the Sea (Gray arrows indicate route of Sherman's troops)

Strange march, half-war, half trooping picnic-parade,
Cutting a ruinous swathe through the red-earth land;
March of the hardy bummers and coffee-coolers
Who, having been told to forage, loot as they can
And leave a wound that rankles for sixty years.
March of the honest, who did not loot when they could
And so are not remembered in Southern legend.
Rough-bearded Sherman riding the red-earth roads,
Writing home that his rascals are fat and happy,
Saying or else not saying that war is hell,   10
Saying he almost trembles himself to think
Of what will happen when Charleston falls in the hands
Of those same rascals—and yet, when we read that march
Hardly the smoking dragon he has been called,
But the mere rough-handed man who rode with a hard
Bit through the land, unanxious to spare his foe
Nor grimly anxious to torture for torture's sake,
Smashing this and that,—and yet, in the end,
Giving such terms to the foe struck down at last
That the men in Washington disavow them and him   20
For over-kindness.
                        So now, through the pine-smoke Fall,
The long worm of his army creeps toward Savannah
Leaving its swathe behind.
                              In the ruined gardens
The buried silver lies well hid in the ground.
A looter pocks bullet-marks in an old oil-portrait.
A woman wails and rages against the thieves
Who carry her dead child's clothes on their drunken bayonets.
A looter swings from a pine tree for thefts too crude.   30
A fresh-faced boy gets scars he will carry long
Hauling a crippled girl from a burning house,
But gets no thanks but hate from the thing he saved,
And everywhere,
A black earth stirs, a wind blows over black earth,
A wind blows into black faces, into old hands
Knotted with long rheumatics, cramped on the hoe,
Into old backs bent double over the cotton,
The wind of freedom, the wind of the jubilo.

They stray from the lost plantations like children strayed,   40
Grinning and singing, following the blue soldiers,

337

They steal from the lonesome cabins like runaways
Laden with sticks and bundles and conjur-charms;
A huge black mother carries her sucking child
Wrapped in a quilt, a slim brown girl and her lover
Wander November woods like Adam and Eve,
Living on roots and rabbits and liberty,
An old grey field hand dimly plods through the mud,
Looking for some vague place he has heard about
Where Linkum sits at a desk in his gold silk hat
With a bag of silver dollars in either hand   10
For every old grey field hand that comes to him,
All God's chillun got shoes there and fine new clothes,
All God's chillun got peace there and roastin'-ears,
Hills of barbecue, rivers of pot-licker,
Nobody's got to work there, never no more.

His feet are sore with the road but he stumbles on,
A hundred, a thousand others stumble as he,
Chanting, dizzied, drunken with a strange fever,
A child's delight, a brightness too huge to grasp,
The hidden nation, untaught, unrecognized,   20
Free at last, but not yet free with the free,
Ignorant, joyful, wronged, child-minded and searching,
Searching the army's road for this new wild thing
That means so much but can't be held in the hand,
That must be there, that yet is so hard to find,
This dream, this pentecost changing, this liberty.

Some wander away to strange death or stranger life,
Some wander awhile and starve and come back at last,
Some stay by the old plantation but will not work
To the great disgust of masters and mistresses,   30
Sing idly, gamble, sleep through the lazy hours,
Waiting for friendly heaven to rain them down
The mule and the forty acres of their desire.
Some, faithful beyond the bond that they never signed,
Hold to that bond in ruin as in the sun,
Steal food for a hungry mistress, keep her alive,
Keep the house alive, try to pick the weeds from the path,
Gather the wood and chop it and make the fire,
With pitying scorn for the runaway sheep of freedom,
Freedom's a ghost and freedom's a foolish talk,   40

338

What counts is making the fire as it should be made. . . .
Oh, blackskinned epic, epic with the black spear,
I cannot sing you, having too white a heart,
And yet, some day, a poet will rise to sing you
And sing you with such truth and mellowness,
—Deep mellow of the husky, golden voice
Crying dark heaven through the spirituals,
Soft mellow of the levee roustabouts,
Singing at night against the banjo-moon—
That you will be a match for any song   10
Sung by old, populous nations in the past,
And stand like hills against the American sky,
And lay your black spear down by Roland's horn.

Meanwhile, in Georgia, the scythe of the march mows on,
The Southern papers discount it as best they can.
Lincoln is anxious, Davis more anxious still.
The war is in its last winter of strife and pain.

VIII. *Wingate Hall prepares for the invaders*

Cudjo buried the silverware
On a graveyard night of sultry air
While the turned sods smelled of the winter damp   20
And Mary Lou Wingate held the lamp.
They worked with a will. They did not speak.
The light was yellow. The light was weak.
A tomb-light casting a last, brief flame
Over the grave of Wingate fame.
The silver bowl of the Wingate toasts,
The spoons worn hollow by Wingate ghosts,
Sconce and ladle and bead-rimmed plate
With the English mark and the English weight,
The round old porringer, dented so   30
By the first milk-teeth of the long ago,
And the candlesticks of Elspeth Mackay
That she brought with her youth on her wedding-day
To light the living of Wingate Hall
While the mornings break and the twilights fall
And the night and the river have memories. . . .

There was a spook in Cudjo's eyes
As he lowered the chests where they must lie

And patted the earth back cunningly.
He knew each chest and its diverse freight
As a blind man knows his own front gate
And, decade by decade and piece by piece,
With paste and shammy and elbow-grease,
He had made them his, by the pursed-up lips
And the tireless, polishing fingertips,
Till now as he buried them, each and all,
What he buried was Wingate Hall,
Himself and the moon and the toddy-sippers,   10
The river mist and the dancing-slippers,
Old Marse Billy and Mary Lou
And every bit of the world he knew,
Master and lady and house and slave,
All smoothed down in a single grave.
He was finished at length. He shook his head.
"Mistis, reckon we's done," he said.
They looked at each other, black and white,
For a slow-paced moment across the light.

Then he took the lamp and she smoothed her shawl   20
And he lit her back to the plundered Hall,
To pray, with her old serene observance
For the mercy of God upon faithful servants
And a justice striking all Yankees dead
On her cold, worn knees by the great carved bed,
Where she had lain by a gentleman's side,
Wife and mother and new-come bride,
Sick with the carrying, torn with the borning,
Waked by the laughter on Christmas morning,
Through love and temper and joy and grief,   30
And the years gone by like the blowing leaf.

She finished her prayer with Louisa's child,
And, when she had risen, she almost smiled.
She struck her hand on the bedstead head,
"They won't drive me from my house," she said,
As the wood rang under her wedding-ring.
Then she stood for a moment, listening,
As if for a step, or a gentleman's name,
But only the gnats and the echoes came.

340

Cudjo, being less fortified,
Covered his ears with his hands and tried
To shut the noise of the risen wind
Out of the trouble of his mind.
He thought, "Ain't right for dat wind to blow.
She wasn't blowing awhile ago.
Jus' riz up fum de earth somewhere
When we buried dat orphan silver dere.
Got to hide it, and so we tried,
But silver like dat don't like to hide,   10
Silver's ust to be passed aroun'
Don't like lyin' in lonesome groun',
Wants to come back to de Hall, all right.
Silver, I always shone you bright,
You could see yo'self in de shine—
Silver, it wasn't no fix of mine!
Don't you come projeckin' after me!"

His eyes were shut but he still could see
The slow chests rising out of the ground
With an ominous clatter of silver sound,   20
The locks undoing, the bags unfastening,
And every knife and platter and spoon
Clinking out of the grave and hastening
Back to the Hall, in the witches' moon;
And the wind in the chimney played such tricks
That it was no wind, be it soft or loud,
But Elspeth seeking her candlesticks
All night long in her ruffled shroud,
The deep voice haunting the ocean-shell
To give her judgment and weave her spell,   30
"*Thrift and love for the house and the chief*
And a scone on the hob for the son of grief,
But a knife in the ribs for the pleasant thief."

Cudjo heard it, and Cudjo shook,
And Cudjo felt for the Holy Book,
And the wind blew on without peace or rest,
Blowing the straws from the dried-up nest.

IX. *Bailey comes to Wingate Hall*

Bailey, tramping along with Sherman's bummers,
Grumbled and found life pleasant and hummed his tune.

He was well, the blood ran in him, he ate for ten,
He and the gang had salvaged a wall-eyed nig
To fix their victuals—and if the captain was on,
The captain had a blind eye.
                         Last night it was turkey,
The night before it was duck—well, you couldn't expect
Such things to keep on forever, but while they did
It was pretty soft—it was war like it ought to be.
The Old Man marched 'em hard, but that was all right,
The Old Man knew his job and the nig was a buster   1&
And the gang was as good a gang as you'd hope to find,
None of your coffee-coolers and straggle-tails
But a regular gang that ran like an eight-day clock.
Oh it was gravy, it was the real duck soup,
Marchin' into Atlanta after the fight
And then this marchin'—well, they were due for it,
And he was a sergeant now.

He mused a moment, thinking of Ellyat now.
There was another kid and a crazy kid,
Sort of missed him, hope he's gettin' it soft,   20
Must have got a banger at Gettysburg,
Wrote me a letter a couple of months ago,
Maybe six, I dunno, I sort of forget.
Ought to give him his old spread-eagle now,
Darn good kid, but done enough for his pay.
Hope he finds that girl he was talkin' about,
Sounds like a pretty good piece for a storm-and-strife,
Skinny, though—we like 'em more of a weight,
Don't we, Carrots?
                         Well, it's all in a life.   30
Ought to write him sometime if we get a chance,
Wish we was West—we'd have him out to the weddin',
Me and Bessie, show him the Cairo girls,
Hand him the fireman's grip and give him a time.

His heart was overflowing with charity,
But his throat was dry as the bottom of his canteen.
There was a big, white house, some way from the road. . . .

He found his captain, saluted and put his question.
The captain's eyes were satiric but not displeased.

342

"All right, Sergeant, take your detail and forage,
We're running low on bacon, it seems to me,
And if you happen to find a pigeon or two
Remember the Colonel's penchant for pigeon-pie.
But don't waste time and don't put your hopes too high,
The Nth Corps must have gone by there hours ago
And they're the biggest thieves in this whole, wide army.
You'll be back, in ranks, all sober, in just two hours
Or you won't have stripes. And if I find one more man
Trying to take a pet with him on this march,   10
I don't care if it's only a treetoad, I'll skin him alive."

So Bailey came to the door of Wingate Hall,
With the high wind blowing against him and gave his orders
"Make it quick now, boys—don't cut any monkeyshines,
But be sure and get the pigeons if they're around.
Clark, you and Ellis stay with me by the door,
I'm going to talk to the house if there's anyone left."

He knocked and called. There was a long, heavy silence.
"Hey you, the house!" The silence made him feel queer.
He cursed impatiently and pushed at the door.   20
It swung wide open. He turned to Ellis and Clark.
"I'm goin' in," he said. "If you hear me yell
Come in bilin'."
                    They watched him with mocking eyes.
"Wish to hell they'd make me a sergeant, Clark,"
"A three-stripe souvenir sergeant."
                                      "Aw, hell," said Clark,
"Bailey's all right. He'll let us in on the juice
If there's any lawful juice that a man could get."
"Sure he's all right. Who says that he ain't all right!"   30
"But all the same, he's a sergeant."
                                      Bailey, meanwhile
Was roving like a lost soul through great, empty rooms
And staring at various objects that caught his eye.
Funny old boy with a wig, hung up on the wall,
Queer sort of chairs, made your hands feel dirty to touch 'em
Though they were faded.
                          Everything faded and old
And quiet—and the wind blowin'—he moved as on tiptoe
Though he couldn't say why he did.   40

343

                                    Old workbasket there.
He opened it idly—most of the things were gone
But there was a pair of little, gold-mounted scissors
Made like a bird, with the blades the beak of the bird.
He picked it up and opened and shut the blades.
Hadn't rusted—sort of handsome and queer—
Bessie would certainly like it—
                            He held it a minute.
Wouldn't take up any room. Then he frowned at the thing.
"Aw hell," he said, "I got enough souvenirs.   10
I ain't no damn coffee-cooler."

He started to put the scissors back in the case
And turned to face a slight grey-headed old woman
Dressed in black, with eyes that burned through his skin
And a voice that cut at his mind like a rawhide whip,
Calling him fifty different kinds of a thief
And Yankee devil and liar and God knows what,
Tearing the throat of her dress with her thin old hands
And telling him he could shoot her down like a dog
But he'd steal her children's things over her dead body.   20
My God, as if you went around shootin' old women
For fun, my God!
                    He couldn't even explain.
She was like all of 'em, made him sick in his lunch.
"Oh hell," he yelled. "Shut up about your damn scissors,
This is a war, old lady!"
                            "That's right," she said,
"Curse a helpless female, you big, brave soldier."
Well, what was a man to do?
                                He got out of the house,   30
Sore and angry, mean as a man could feel,
But her voice still followed, reviling, making him burn.
Now, where in hell was that detail?
                                    He saw them now,
All except Clark and Ellis, gathered around
A white-polled nigger wringing his hands and weeping.
One man had a neck-wrung pigeon stuffed in his blouse.
Well, that was something.
                            He laid his hand on the nigger.
"Hey, Uncle, where's the well? You folks got a well?"   40
But the nigger just kept on crying like an old fool.

"He thinks we're goin' to scalp him," said one of the men,
"I told him twict that he's free but the shine won't listen.
I give him some money, too, but he let it drop.
The rest of 'em run away when the army came."

"Well, tell him he's safe and make him rustle some water,
I'm dry as a preacher's tongue. Where's Ellis and Clark?"

He found Clark solemnly prodding the hard dirt floor
Of a negro cabin, while Ellis lighted the task
With a splinter of burning pine.
                                    His rage exploded   10
In boiling lava. They listened respectfully.
"And next time, I give you an order," he ended up,
"Why you—— —— ——"
                        Clark wiped his face with his sleeve.
"Sorry, Sergeant," he said in an awed, low voice.
"Well you better be! What the hell do you think you're at,
Playin' tit-tat-toe or buryin' somebody's dog?"
"Well, Sergeant," said Ellis, humbly, "I allus heard
They buried stuff, sometimes, under these here cabins.
Well, I thought we could take a look—well—"   26
                        "Huh?" said Bailey.
He seized the torch and looked at the trodden floor
For an instant. Then his pride and his rage returned.
"Hell's fire!" he said, and threw the splinter aside,
"That's just about what you would think, you and Clark!
Come out of there on the double! Yes, I said you!"
They were halfway down the driveway when Ellis spoke.
"Sergeant," he said. "There's somethin' on fire back there."
Bailey stopped—looked back—a smoke-puff climbed in the sky
And the wind was high.   30
                        He hesitated a moment.
The cabin must have caught from the burning splinter.
Then he set his jaw. Well, suppose the cabin had caught?
—Damned old woman in black who called him a thief.
Serve her right if all her cabins burnt up.
The house wouldn't catch—and here they were, losing time—

"Oh well," he said. "That nigger'll put it out.
It ain't our detail—mosey along with it there—

345

The Cap won't mind if we run it on him a little,
Now we got the Colonel's squab, but we better step."

They hurried along. The smoke rose higher behind them.
The wind blew the burning flakes on Wingate Hall.

X. *Fall of Wingate glory*

Sally Dupré stared out of her bedroom window
As she had stared many times at that clump of trees.
And saw the smoke rise out of it, thick and dark.

They hadn't had much trouble at Appleton.
It was too far off the main road—and, as for the slaves,
Those who straggled after the troops were better away.   10
The aunts complained, of course—well, the aunts complained.
They were old, and, at least, they had a man in the house,
Even if the man were but crippled old Uncle Paul.
It was the end of the world for him and the aunts.
It wasn't for her.
                    The years had worn on her youth,
Much had worn, but not the crook from her smile
Nor the hidden lightness out of her narrow feet.

She looked at the smoke again, and her eyes were grey
And then they were black as that smoke. She felt the fire   20
Run on her flesh. "It's Wingate Hall and it's burning?
House that married my lover before he saw me,
You are burning, burning away in a little smoke,
Burning the wall between us with your fierce burning,
Burning the strife between us in your black flame,
Burning down."
                    She trod for an instant there
A light glass floor of omen, brighter than sleet
Over a hurtless fire.
                    Then she caught her breath.   30
The flesh was cool, the blackness died from her eyes.
"We'll have to get the slaves if the slaves will go.
I know Ned will. I'm not sure about Bob or Jim.
Uncle Paul must give me his pistol. I'll have to start them.
They won't go without me. The aunts won't be any use.
Why wouldn't she come over here when we all first heard?

346

I know why she wouldn't. I never liked her so much.
Hurry, Sally!"
                    She ran downstairs like the wind.

They worked at the Hall that night till the dawn came up,
Two smoke-stained women, Cudjo and Bob and Ned,
But when the dawn had risen, the Hall was gone
And Elspeth's candles would not light it again.

XI.   *The last of the Black Horse Troop*

Wingate wearily tried to goad
A bag of bones on a muddy road
Under the grey and April sky   10
While Bristol hummed in his irony
"If you want a good time, jine the cavalry!
Well, we jined it, and here we go,
The last event in the circus-show,
The bareback boys in the burnin' hoop
Mounted on cases of chicken-croup,
The rovin' remains of the Black Horse Troop!
Though the only horse you could call real black
Is the horsefly sittin' on Shepley's back,
But, women and children, do not fear,   20
They'll feed the lions and us, next year.
And, women and children, dry your eyes,
The Southern gentleman never dies.
He just lives on by his strength of will
Like a damn ole rooster too tough to kill
Or a brand-new government dollar-bill
That you can use for a trousers-patch
Or lightin' a fire, if you've got a match,
Or makin' a bunny a paper collar,
Or anythin' else—except a dollar.   30

Old folks, young folks, never you care,
The Yanks are here and the Yanks are there,
But no Southern gentleman knows despair.
He just goes on in his usual way,
Eatin' a meal every fifteenth day
And showin' such skill in his change of base

347

That he never gets time to wash his face
While he fights with a fury you'd seldom find
Except in a Home for the Crippled Blind,
And can whip five Yanks with a palmleaf hat,
Only the Yanks won't fight like that.

Ladies and gentlemen, here we go!
The last event in the minstrel show!
Georgia's genuine gamboliers,
(Ladies and gentlemen, dry those tears!)
See the sergeant, eatin' the hay   10
Of his faithful horse, in a lifelike way!
See the general, out for blood,
And try to tell the man from the mud!
See the platoon in its savage lair,
A half-grown boy on a wheezy mare.
Ladies and gentlemen, pass the hat!
We've got one trick that you won't forget,
'The Vanishin' Commissariat'
And nobody's found the answer yet!
Here we go, here we go,   20
The last parade of the circus-show,
Longstreet's orphans, Lee's everlastin's
Half cast-iron and half corn-pone,
And if gettin' to heaven means prayer and fastin's
We ought to get there on the fasts alone.

Here we go with our weddin' bells,
Mr. Davis's immortelles,
Mr. Lincoln's Thanksgivin' turkey,
Run right ragged but actin' perky,
Chased right handsome, but still not carved,   30
—We had fleas, but the fleas all starved.
We had rations and new recruits,
Uniforms and cavalry-boots,
Must have mislaid, for we can't find 'em.
They all went home with their tails behind 'em.
Here we are, like the old man's mutton,
Pretty well sheared, but not past buttin',
Lee's last invalids, heart and hand,
All wropped up in a woolen band,
Oh, Dixie land. . . . oh, Dixie land! . . ."   40

348

He tossed his hat and caught it again
And Wingate recalled, without grief or pain
Or any quietus but memory
Lucy, under another sky,
White and gold as a lily bed,
Giving toy ribbons to all her dead.
She had been pretty and she was gone,
But the dead were here—and the dead rode on,
Over a road of mud and stones,
Each one horsed on a bag of bones.   10

Lucy, you carried a golden head,
But I am free of you, being dead.
Father's back in that cluttered hall
Where the beds are solid from wall to wall
And the scrubbed old floor has a rusty stain.
He'll never ride with the dogs again,
Call Bathsheba or Planter's Child
In the old, high quaver that drives them wild
—Rocketing hounds on a red-hot scent—
After such wounds, men do not ride.   20
I think that his heart was innocent.
I know he rode by the riverside,
Calling Blue Ruin or Georgia Lad
With the huntsman's crotchet that sets them mad.
His face was ruddy—his face is white—
I wonder if Father died last night?
That cloud in the sky is a thunderhead.
The world I knew is a long time dead.

Shepley looks like a knife on guard,
Reckon he's taking it mighty hard,   30
Reckon he loved her and no mistake,
Glad it isn't my wedding cake,
Wainscott oughtn't to plague him so,
Means all right but he doesn't know.
"Here we go, here we go,
The last events of the minstrel-show!"

Shepley suddenly turned his head.
"Mr. Bristol's funny," he said.
The voice was flat with an injury.

349

Bristol stared at him, puzzledly.
"What's the matter with you, Huger?
Lost your dog or your rosy cheeks?
Haven't been human for weeks and weeks.
I'll sing you a hymn, if you're so inclined,
But the rest of the boys don't seem to mind.
Are you feelin' poorly or just unkind?"

Shepley looked at him with the blind
Eyes of a man too long at war
And too long nursing a secret sore.   10
"Mr. Bristol's funny," said he,
In a level voice of enmity.
Bristol laughed, but his face grew red.
"Well, if you take it like that—" he said.

"Here we go, here we go,
The old Confederate minstrel-show!"
His mouth was merry, he tossed his hat,
"Belles skedaddled and left us flat—"

Shepley leaned from his swaying hips
And flicked him over the singing lips.   20
"Will you take it?" he said, "or let it go?
You never could sing for shucks, you know."
The color drained out of Bristol's face.
He bowed with an odd, old-fashioned grace.
"Name your people and choose your land,
I don't take a slap from God's own hand.
Mr. Shepley, your servant, sir."

They stared at each other across a blur.
The troop stared with them, halted and still.
A rider lunged from the top of the hill,   30
Dusty man with a bandaged hand
Spilling his orders.
                    "Who's in command?
Well, it doesn't signify, more or less.
You can hold the Yanks for a while, I guess.
Make 'em think you're the whole rear guard
If you can do it—they're pressin' hard
And somebody's got to lose some hair.
Keep 'em away from that bend down there

350

As long as a horse or a man can stand.
You might give 'em a charge, if you think you can,
And we'll meet sometime in the Promised Land,
For I can't spare you another man."

Bristol whistled, a shrill, sweet slur.
"Beg to acknowledge the orders, sir.
Boys, we're booked for the shivaree.
Give our regards to the infantry
And tell Marse Robert, with fortitude,
We stacked up pretty as hickory-wood.   10
While might I ask, while bein' polite,
How many Yank armies we aim to fight?"

"Well," said the other, "about a corps.
Roughly speakin'—there may be more."

"Thank you," said Bristol, "that's mighty sweet,
You will not remain at the mourner's seat?
No sir? Well, I imagined not,
For from this time hence it will be right hot."
He turned to Shepley with his punctilious
Air of the devil turned supercilious   20
When the damned display a vulgar nettlement.
"Sir, I regret that our little settlement
Must be postponed for a fitter season,
But war and necessity know no reason,
And should we survive in this comin' fracas
I'll do you the honors—you damned old jackass!"

Shepley grinned at his sometime friend.
They took the cover they must defend.
Wingate, fighting from tree to tree,
Felt a red-hot skewer surgeon his knee   30
And felt his shoulder hitting the ground.
He rolled on his side and made a sound,
Dimly seeing through failing sight
The last brief passion of his last fight.
One Cotter dying, the other dead
With the brains run out of his shattered head.
Stuart Cazenove trying to squirm
His way to the road like a scythe-cut worm,
Weakly humming "Cadet Rousselle",

351

Shot through the belly and half in hell,
While Shepley croaked through a bloody spray,
"Come on, you bastards, and get your pay.
We've fought you mounted and fought you standin'
And I got a hole I could put my hand in—
And they're comin', Wayne—and it hurts my head—"
Bristol looked at him, lying dead.
"Got the start of me, Shep," he said.
"Dirty welchers, killin' Huger
Before we could settle up properly." 10
He stooped to the body and took its pistol
And Wingate saw, through a rising mist,
The last, cold madness of Wainscott Bristol,
Walking out like a duellist
With his torn coat buttoned up at the throat
As if it were still the broadcloth coat
Duellists button to show no fleck
Of telltale white at the wrists or neck.
He stepped from his cover and dropped his hat.
"Yanks, come get it!" he said and spat 20
While his pistols cracked with a single crack,
"Here we go on the red dog's back!
High, low, jack and the goddam game."
And then the answering volley came.

Wingate waked from a bloodshot dream.
They were touching his leg and he heard his scream.
A blue-chinned man said a word or two.
"Well now, Johnny, you ought to do
Till the sawbones comes with his movin'-van,
And you're lucky you're livin', little man. 30
But why the hell did you act so strict,
Fightin' like that when you know you're licked,
And where's the rest of your damn brigade?"
The voice died out as the ripples fade
Into the flow of the running stream,
And Wingate sank to the bloodshot dream.

XII. *It is over now*

Richmond is fallen—Lincoln walks in its streets,
Alone, unguarded, stops at George Pickett's house,

Knocks at George Pickett's door. George Pickett has gone
But the strange, gaunt figure talks to George Pickett's wife
A moment—she thinks she is dreaming, seeing him there—
"Just one of George Pickett's old friends, ma'am."

                                    He turns away.

She watches him down the street with wondering eyes.
The red light falls upon him from the red sky.
Houses are burning, strange shadows flee through the streets.
A gang of loafers is broaching a liquor-barrel
In a red-lit square. The liquor spills on the cobbles.   10
They try to scoop it up in their dirty hands.

A long, blue column tramps by, shouting "John Brown's Body."
The loafers scatter like wasps from a half-sucked pear,
Come back when the column is gone.

                                A half-crazy slave

Mounts on a stoop and starts to preach to the sky.
A white-haired woman shoos him away with a broom.
He mumbles and reels to the shadows.

                             A general passes,

His escort armed with drawn sabres. The sabres shine   20
In the red, low light.

                   Two doors away, down the street,

A woman is sobbing the same long sob all night
Beside a corpse with crossed hands.

                          Lincoln passes on.

On the way to Appomattox, the ghost of an army
Staggers a muddy road for a week or so
Through fights and weather, dwindling away each day.
For a brief while Davis is with them and then he goes
To be tracked by his private furies into the last   30
Sad farce of his capture, and, later, to wear his chains.
Benjamin is with them for some few days,
Still sleek, still lively, still impeccably dressed,
Taking adversity as he took success
With the silk-ribbed fan of his slight, unchangeable smile.
Behind that fan, his mind weighs war and defeat
In an old balance.

                   One day he is there and smiling.

The next he is gone as if he had taken fernseed
And walked invisible so through the Union lines.   40

You will not find that smile in a Northern prison
Though you seek from now till Doomsday. It is too wise.
You will find the chief with the chin like John Calhoun's,
Gadfly-stung, tormented by hostile fate,
You will find many gallant blockheads and tragic nobles
But not the black-eyed man with life in his eyes.

So this week, this death-march, these final, desperate strokes,
These last blood-spots on the harvest—until, at length,
The battered grey advance guard, hoping to break
A last, miraculous hole through the closing net,   10
Sees Ord's whole corps as if risen out of the ground
Before them, blocking all hope.
                                    The letters are written,
The orders given, while stray fighting goes on
And grey men and blue men die in odd clumps of ground
Before the orders can reach them.
                                    An aide-de-camp
Seeks a suitable house for the council from a chance farmer.
The first one found is too dirty to please his mind,
He picks another.   20
                    The chiefs and the captains meet,
Lee erect in his best dress uniform,
His dress-sword hung at his side and his eyes unaltered.
Chunky Grant in his mudsplashed private's gear
With the battered stars on his shoulders.
                                    They talk a while
Of Mexico and old days.
                        Then the terms are stated.
Lee finds them generous, says so, makes a request.
His men will need their horses for the spring-ploughing.   30
Grant assents at once.
                        There is no parade of bright swords
Given or taken. Grant saw that there should not be.
It is over, then. . . .
                        Lee walks from the little room.
His face is unchanged. It will not change when he dies.
But as he steps on the porch and looks toward his lines
He strikes his hands together once with a sound. . . .

In the room he has left, the blue men stare at each other
For a space of heartbeats, silent. The grey ride off.   40
They are gone—it is over. . . .

The room explodes like a bomb, they are laughing and shouting,
Yelling strange words, dragging chairs and tables outdoors,
Bearded generals waltzing with one another
For a brief, wild moment, punching each others' ribs,
Everyone talking at once and nobody listening,
"It's over—it's done—it's finished!"
                                                    Then, order again.
The grey ghost-army falls in for the last time,
Marching to stack its arms.
                                        As the ranks move forward   10
The blue guns go to "Present." Gordon sees the gesture.
He sweeps his sabre down in the full salute.
There are no cheers or words from blue lines or grey.
Only the sound of feet. . . .
It is over, now. . . .
                            The arms are stacked from the war.
A few bronzed, tattered grey men, weeping or silent,
Tear some riddled bits of cloth from the color-staffs
And try to hide them under their uniforms.

XIII.   *Hired man*

JAKE DIEFER, ploughing, a day of the early Spring,   20
Smelt April steam from the ground as he turned it up
And wondered how the new forty would do this year.

The stump of his left arm ached in the living wind.
It was not a new pain.
                              When he got back to the house
The woman would ease it some with her liniments
But there wasn't much you could do.
                                                  The boy had been smart.
The boy had fixed the jigger so he could plough.
It wasn't an arm you could show to company   36
With a regular-looking hand, but it did the work.
The woman still hankered after the varnished one
They'd seen that day in the Philadelphia store
—Well, he'd tried it on, and it was a handsome arm,
And, if the new forty did well—
                                            Meanwhile, the huge
Muscles of his right shoulder bulged with the strain

As the plough sheared on.
                              Sometimes, the blade of the plough
Still turned up such odd harvest as bullets leave,
A spoilt canteen, the brass of a cartridge-pouch,
An eyeless skull, too white for the grin it wore.
But these were rarer now.
                              They had cleaned the well.
They could drink from the well again.
                                        The earth was in plough.

He turned his team and started the backward furrow.   10
He was clumsy still, in some matters, but he could manage.
This year he'd see his own wheat.
                              He thought to himself:
"You ain't the feller you was but the ground looks good.
It smells like good plantin' weather. We cleaned the well.
Maybe some time we'll get you that varnished arm,
For Sundays, maybe. It'd look good on Sundays."
He gazed ahead.
                    By the end of the farther fence
A ragamuffin-something leaned on the rail,   20
Regarding him and his team.
                              "Tramp feller," he thought,
"Colored man, too—well, he can't hang around this farm,
Him or no other tramps. I wish I could get
An honest to God cheap hired man."
                              The team drew near.
The negro did not move.
                    Jake halted the team.
They stared at each other. One saw a crippled ox,
The other a scar-faced spectre with haunted eyes   30
Still dressed in the rags of a shoddy uniform.
"Well, feller?" said Jake.
                    The negro said " 'Scuse me, Sarjun."
He scratched his head with the wreck of a forage-cap.
His eyes remembered a darkness.
                              "Huh!" said Jake,
Sharply, "Where did you get it?"
                    The negro shrank.
"I was in de Crater, boss," he said with a dull
Stain in his voice. "You mebbe heard about us.   40

356

You mebbe heard of de Crater at Petersburg.
I doan' like thinkin' about it. You need a fiel'-han'?"

Jake thought for a moment. "Crater," he said at last.
"Yuh, I heard about that Crater."
                              The wind blew on,
Hurting his arm. "I wasn't to there," he said.
"I knew some boys that was there."
                         The negro said,
"I'd work for my keep, boss, honest. I knows a team.
I knows how to work. I got hurt bad in de Crater   10
But I knows how to work a farm."
                         He coughed and was dumb.
Jake looked at him as he might have looked at a horse,
Measuringly.
            "I ain't runnin' a hospital,"
He said, in an aggrieved voice. "You was to the Crater.
I seen the way you colored folks farm down South.
It ain't no way to farm. You ought to be et.
We'll eat you up to the house when it's mealin'-time.
I don't know where we'll sleep you. How do I know   20
You can work your keep?"
                    The negro said nothing at all.
His eyes had resumed their darkness.
                         "Huddup!" said Jake,
As the team swung round.
                    "Dat's ploughin'!" the negro said.

Jake spat. "The woman'll fix you a snack to eat
If you holler the house."
                    The negro shook his head.
"I'll wait till you's done furrowin', boss," he said.   30
"Mebbe I kin help you unhitch when it's time for dat."

"Well," said Jake, "I ain't payin' a hired man much."

"Dey call me Spade," said the negro.
                         The plough went on.
The negro watched it, cutting the furrow clean.

357

JACK ELLYAT, an old cudgel in his fist,
Walked from the town, one day of melting ice,
Past fields still patched with old snow but warm in the sun,
His heart and mind being something like those fields. . . .
Behind him, in the town, the spangled flags
Still fluttered or hung limp for fallen Richmond,
And here or there, in corners, you could see
The burst firecracker-cases, rotten with rain,
The guttered stumps of torches flung away
And other odds and ends of celebration   10
Not yet swept up.
          The old cannon in the Square
Still had a blackened mouth from its salutes,
The little boys would not be good all week
And everything wore airs of Monday morning. . . .

Jack Ellyat, remembering it all,
Was glad enough when he got past the houses
And could see nothing but the road ahead
Going up hills and down.
          "It's over now.   20
Finished for good. Well, I was part of it.
Well, it is over."
          When he reached the crest
Of the Long Hill, he paused and felt the wind
Blow on his face, and leaned upon his stick,
Gazing at troubled Spring.
          He carried still
Wounds of a sort, some healed into the scars
And some that hardly would be healed awhile,
Being in stuff few surgeries can reach,   30
But he was well enough, although the wind
Felt colder than it had in other Springs.

"Oh, yes," he thought, "I guess that I'm all right.
I guess I'm lucky. I remember once
Coming along this road with poor old Ned
Before they fired on Sumter. Well, it's over.
I was a part of it."
          He flipped a stone

Down toward the hill and watched it strike and strike
And then lie quiet, while his mind recalled
The long, white, bloodless months of getting well
And the strange feel of first civilian clothes.
Well, that was over, too, and he was back,
And everybody knew he'd settled down,
Only he couldn't stand it any more.

He had a picture of Melora's face,
Dim with long looking-at, a carried image,
He tried to see it now, but it was faint.   10
He'd tried to find her but he couldn't find her.
Couldn't get any news while he was sick,
And then, at last, the news that they were gone—
That and no more—and nobody knew where.

He saw the clock upon the mantelpiece
Back in the house, ticking its fettered time
To fettered Phaëton.
                         "I'll settle down.
I will forget. I'll wear my riddled coat
Fourth of Julys and have boys gape at me.   20
I'll drink and eat and sleep, marry a girl;
Be a good lawyer, wear the hunger out.
I hardly knew her. It was years ago.
Why should the hunger stay? A dozen men
Might find a dozen girls and lose them so
And never once think of it, but perhaps
As a dim fragrance, lost with their first youth,
A seashell in a box of cedarwood,
A silver mist that vanished with the day.

It was such years ago. She must have changed.   30
I know that I have changed.
                         We find such things
And lose them, and must live in spite of it.
Only a fool goes looking for the wind
That blew across his heartstrings yesterday,
Or breaks his hands in the obscure attempt
To dig the knotted roots of Time apart,
Hoping to resurrect the golden mask
Of the lost year inviolate from the ground.
Only a fool drives horses in the sky."   40

And here he was, out walking on this road
For no more reason than a crazy yarn
Just heard, about some gipsy travellers
Going through towns and looking for a soldier.
And even and supposing it were she . . .

He saw Melora walking down from the wood
With the sun behind her, low in the western cloud.
He saw the long shadow that her slight body made.

The fetters fell like straws from the clock of time.
The horses moved from the gate.   10
                          This life, this burning,
This fictive war that is over, this toy death,
These were the pictures of Phaëton.
                          This is Phaëton.
He cast a final look down at the town.
Another at the fields still patched with snow.
The wind blew on his face. He moved away
Out toward the crossroads, where the wagons pass,
And when he got there, waited patiently
Under a windbreak of three twisted elms   20
Half-hidden from the road.
                          "Find her," he said.
"I guess we'll go back West then. Well, that's that."
The wind burned at his flesh. He let it burn,
Staring at a lost year.
                          So he perceived
A slow cart creaking up a slope of hill,
Drawn by a horse as gaunt as poverty
And driven by a woman with great eyes.

XV. *For a lost cause*

Edmund Ruffin, old Secessionist,   30
Firer of the first gun that rang against Sumter,
Walks in his garden now, in the evening-cool,
With a red, barred flag slung stiffly over one arm
And a silver-butted pistol in his right hand.
He has just heard of Lee's surrender and Richmond's fall
And his face is marble over his high black stock.

For a moment he walks there, smelling the scents of Spring,
A gentleman taking his ease, while the sun sinks down.
Now it is well-nigh sunken. He smiles with the close,
Dry smile of age. It is time. He unfolds the flag,
Cloaks it around his shoulders with neat, swift hands,
Cocks the pistol and points it straight at his heart.
The hammer falls, the dead man slumps to the ground.
The blood spurts out in the last light of the sun
Staining the red of the flag with more transient red.

XVI. *Madman's bullet*

The gaunt man, Abraham Lincoln, woke one morning   10
From a new dream that yet was an old dream
For he had known it many times before
And, usually, its coming prophesied
Important news of some sort, good or bad,
Though mostly good as he remembered it.

He had been standing on the shadowy deck
Of a black formless boat that moved away
From a dim bank, into wide, gushing waters—
River or sea, but huge—and as he stood,
The boat rushed into darkness like an arrow,   20
Gathering speed—and as it rushed, he woke.

He found it odd enough to tell about
That day to various people, half in jest
And half in earnest—well, it passed the time
And nearly everyone had some pet quirk,
Knocking on wood or never spilling salt,
Ladders or broken mirrors or a Friday,
And so he thought he might be left his boat,
Especially now, when he could breathe awhile
With Lee surrendered and the war stamped out   30
And the long work of binding up the wounds
Not yet begun—although he had his plans
For that long healing, and would work them out
In spite of all the bitter-hearted fools
Who only thought of punishing the South
Now she was beaten.

But this boat of his.
He thought he had it.
                    "Johnston has surrendered.
It must be that, I guess—for that's about
The only news we're waiting still to hear."
He smiled a little, spoke of other things.
That afternoon he drove beside his wife
And talked with her about the days to come
With curious simplicity and peace.
Well, they were getting on, and when the end   10
Came to his term, he would not be distressed.
They would go back to Springfield, find a house,
Live peaceably and simply, see old friends,
Take a few cases every now and then.
Old Billy Herndon's kept the practice up,
I guess he'll sort of like to have me back.
We won't be skimped, we'll have enough to spend,
Enough to do—we'll have a quiet time,
A sort of Indian summer of our age.

He looked beyond the carriage, seeing it so,   20
Peace at the last, and rest.

They drove back to the White House, dressed and ate,
Went to the theatre in their flag-draped box.
The play was a good play, he liked the play,
Laughed at the jokes, laughed at the funny man
With the long, weeping whiskers.
                                 The time passed.
The shot rang out. The crazy murderer
Leaped from the box, mouthed out his Latin phrase,
Brandished his foolish pistol and was gone.   30
Lincoln lay stricken in the flag-draped box.
Living but speechless. Now they lifted him
And bore him off. He lay some hours so.
Then the heart failed. The breath beat in the throat.
The black, formless vessel carried him away.

XVII.   Sally sees a new future

Sally, waiting at Appleton
On an autumn day of clear, bright sun,

362

Felt her heart and body begin to burn
As she hummed the lesson she had to learn.
"Yellow cornmeal and a jackass colt
And a door that swings on a broken bolt.
Comfort the old and pity the wise
And see your lover with open eyes.
Mend the broken and patch the frayed
And carry the sorrow undismayed
When your lover limps in the falling rain,
Never quite to be whole again.   16
Clear the nettle and plant the corn
And keep your body a hunting-horn.
Succor your love at fire and frost
When your lover remembers the blood he lost,
And break your hands on the hard-moved wheel
Till they are tougher than hands of steel,
Till the new grass grows on the barren plain
And the house is built from the dust again,
With thrift and love for the house and the chief,
A scone on the hob for the son of grief,   20
A knife in the ribs for the pleasant thief,
While the night and the river have memories . . ."
She stared at the future with equal eyes.
And yet, in her glance, there was something still
Not to be ground by Wingate will
Or under the honor of Elspeth's name,
A dancing flicker that went and came
But did not falter for joy or grief
Or the years gone by with the blowing leaf.
—French Dupré with his alien grace   30
Always turning the buried ace.
French Dupré in his dancer's pride,
Leading a reel with his stolen bride—
She smiled a little and turned to see
A weed-grown path and a scarlet tree
And Wingate coming there, painfully.

XVIII. The soul rests

John Brown's body lies a-mouldering in the grave.
Spread over it the bloodstained flag of his song,
For the sun to bleach, the wind and the birds to tear,

The snow to cover over with a pure fleece
And the New England cloud to work upon
With the grey absolution of its slow, most lilac-smelling rain,
Until there is nothing there
That ever knew a master or a slave
Or, brooding on the symbol of a wrong,
Threw down the irons in the field of peace.
John Brown is dead, he will not come again,
A stray ghost-walker with a ghostly gun.
Let the strong metal rust   10
In the enclosing dust
And the consuming coal
That was the furious soul
And still like iron groans,
Anointed with the earth,
Grow colder than the stones
While the white roots of grass and little weeds
Suck the last hollow wildfire from the singing bones.

Bury the South together with this man,
Bury the bygone South.   20
Bury the minstrel with the honey-mouth,
Bury the broadsword virtues of the clan,
Bury the unmachined, the planters' pride,
The courtesy and the bitter arrogance,
The pistol-hearted horsemen who could ride
Like jolly centaurs under the hot stars.
Bury the whip, bury the branding-bars,
Bury the unjust thing
That some tamed into mercy, being wise,
But could not starve the tiger from its eyes   30
Or make it feed where beasts of mercy feed.
Bury the fiddle-music and the dance,
The sick magnolias of the false romance
And all the chivalry that went to seed
Before its ripening.

And with these things, bury the purple dream
Of the America we have not been,
The tropic empire, seeking the warm sea,
The last foray of aristocracy
Based not on dollars or initiative   40

364

Or any blood for what that blood was worth
But on a certain code, a manner of birth,
A certain manner of knowing how to live,
The pastoral rebellion of the earth
Against machines, against the Age of Steam,
The Hamiltonian extremes against the Franklin mean,
The genius of the land
Against the metal hand,
The great, slave-driven bark,
Full-oared upon the dark,   10
With gilded figurehead,
With fetters for the crew
And spices for the few,
The passion that is dead,
The pomp we never knew,
Bury this, too.

Bury this destiny unmanifest,
This system broken underneath the test,
Beside John Brown and though he knows his enemy is there
He is too full of sleep at last to care.   20

He was a stone, this man who lies so still,
A stone flung from a sling against a wall,
A sacrificial instrument of kill,
A cold prayer hardened to a musket-ball:
And yet, he knew the uses of a hill,
And he must have his justice, after all.

He was a lover of certain pastoral things,
He had the shepherd's gift.
When he walked at peace, when he drank from the watersprings,
His eyes would lift   30

To see God, robed in a glory, but sometimes, too,
Merely the sky,
Untroubled by wrath or angels, vacant and blue,
Vacant and high.

He knew not only doom but the shape of the land,
Reaping and sowing.

He could take a lump of any earth in his hand
And feel the growing.

He was a farmer, he didn't think much of towns,
The wheels, the vastness.
He liked the wide fields, the yellows, the lonely browns,
The black ewe's fastness.

Out of his body grows revolving steel,
Out of his body grows the spinning wheel
Made up of wheels, the new, mechanic birth,
No longer bound by toil   10
To the unsparing soil
Or the old furrow-line,
The great, metallic beast
Expanding West and East,
His heart a spinning coil,
His juices burning oil,
His body serpentine.
Out of John Brown's strong sinews the tall skyscrapers grow,
Out of his heart the chanting buildings rise,
Rivet and girder, motor and dynamo,   20
Pillar of smoke by day and fire by night,
The steel-faced cities reaching at the skies,
The whole enormous and rotating cage
Hung with hard jewels of electric light,
Smoky with sorrow, black with splendor, dyed
Whiter than damask for a crystal bride
With metal suns, the engine-handed Age,
The genie we have raised to rule the earth,
Obsequious to our will
But servant-master still,   30
The tireless serf already half a god—

Touch the familiar sod
Once, then gaze at the air
And see the portent there,
With eyes for once washed clear
Of worship and of fear:
There is its hunger, there its living thirst,
There is the beating of the tremendous heart
You cannot read for omens.

366

Stand apart
From the loud crowd and look upon the flame
Alone and steadfast, without praise or blame.
This is the monster and the sleeping queen
And both have roots struck deep in your own mind,
This is reality that you have seen,
This is reality that made you blind.

So, when the crowd gives tongue
And prophets, old or young,
Bawl out their strange despair   10
Or fall in worship there,
Let them applaud the image or condemn
But keep your distance and your soul from them.
And, if the heart within your breast must burst
Like a cracked crucible and pour its steel
White-hot before the white heat of the wheel,
Strive to recast once more
That attar of the ore
In the strong mold of pain
Till it is whole again,   20
And while the prophets shudder or adore
Before the flame, hoping it will give ear,
If you at last must have a word to say,
Say neither, in their way,
"It is a deadly magic and accursed,"
Nor "It is blest," but only "It is here."

NOTES

Page 3

line
13-14. *I set my sorry / And mortal snare:* The poet endeavors to portray the diversity of the great country which is to be the background of his epic.
20. *Shropshire:* A county in England.
22. *Garden of the Gods:* A national park in Colorado.

Page 4

11. *English song:* The words of "My Country, 'Tis of Thee" are set to the music of the British national anthem, "God Save the King."
17-18. *Thames . . . Mississippi:* The original English heritage was merged with the character of the New World.
25. *regicide:* One who kills a king; a term applied to the judges who pronounced sentence of execution on Charles I of England. One of these later fled to America.
28. *Versailles:* A city near Paris where the court of the kings of France was situated.
County Clare: A county in Ireland.
31. *These were your lovers:* The various people who came to explore and settle America were of all ranks and conditions.
buckskin-youth: Pioneer days.

Page 5

10. *riposting:* A returning thrust of a sword.
15. *Never the running stag:* As difficult as it is to capture the stag running, or imprison the gull on the wing, so it is for the poet to put in words the spirit that is America.
16. *And yet at moments:* Occasionally when an experience or a memory has deeply moved him, the poet feels sure that he has caught the secret of what America and the American way really are. In the following stanzas the poet re-creates some typically American scenes which have moved him.

Page 6

17. *sea-lion's tusk:* A walrus's tooth is a sort of charm to a sailor; holding it in his hand he can summon pictures of the sea.

369

line

26. *No nation . . . Art:* Possibly the people are right who say that Art
    should be universal and not simply national. But the poet cannot help
    writing as he does, and although Art may transcend the bounds of
    nationality, nevertheless all he has known and felt as a human being
    and a member of a nation goes into it.

Page 7

1. *This flesh:* The poet himself is truly American in his heritage, a product of Pennsylvania, Kentucky, California, and New England.
6. *alien moon:* The poet wrote the poem *John Brown's Body* while living in France.
8. *half-forgotten battle-tune:* A song popular during the Civil War,
   "John Brown's Body Lies a-Mouldering in the Grave." The poet tries
   to picture and interpret the events and passions of the Civil War.
11. *Long House:* The council room of the Indian tribes; hence, typically
    American.
20. *receive it there . . .:* The poet realizes that his efforts fall short of his
    dream, and of his inspiration. But still he hopes that in some measure
    his words re-create America. If not, they may still spur other poets
    to this high purpose.

PRELUDE

In 1619 the first cargo of Negro slaves landed on the shores of North
America. For almost two hundred years slave trade continued. During the
Revolutionary period, however, all Southern states except South Carolina
and Georgia prohibited the trade, and in 1808 all slave trade was prohibited
by Congress.

Page 11

33. *"Damn cheating Arabs!":* Arab traders from the Mediterranean went
    down the Gold Coast—the west coast of Africa in the vicinity of the
    section that we know as Dakar today—and made deals with the
    chieftains of the tribes to sell their captives for trinkets that they had
    brought from the Mediterranean. The Arabs encouraged them to
    make forays into the interior in quest of able-bodied men, women,
    and children, who later would be sold as slaves to the traders.

Page 14

14. *Back in the twenties:* The captain is thinking back to his own youth.
33. *chanty:* A song sung by sailors and other laborers while at work.

Page 15

30. *Oh Lordy Je-sus:* Note the plaintive tone of the spiritual.

Page 16

20. *From Salem to the Guinea Coast:* From the seaport of Salem, Massa-
    chusetts, to the slave coast of Africa.

370

BOOK ONE

Page 19

line

16–17. *like a beggared sachem . . . tanager:* A sachem is a hereditary chief of the highest rank in some North American Indian tribes. His ceremonial dress features the feathers of birds of bright plumage like the tanager. Now reduced to nominal sovereignty, he still keeps the tattered show of rank.

Page 20

32. *winged stallions:* Symbolic of war, ridden by the four horsemen, War, Famine, Pestilence, and Death.

Page 21

20. *hickory tough:* The nickname "Old Hickory," testifying to his physical toughness and sturdiness, was given to Andrew Jackson, later seventh President of the United States (1829–37), by his soldiers in 1813.

26. *scuppernong-wine:* Wine made from a green fox grape grown in the southeastern part of the United States, near the Scuppernong River in North Carolina.

Page 22

27. *tomahawk . . . buried in prairie-sod:* The tomahawk was the chief weapon used by the Indians. The line means that peace now marks the relations between the whites and the Indians.

29. *the new States:* New states were later formed from the territory known as the Louisiana Purchase, and from the Northwest Territory.

39. *bowie-knife:* A knife much used by hunters. It is named after its inventor, Colonel James Bowie, a Texas hero who died at the Alamo.

Page 23

3. *vaquero gods:* The gods, or objects of veneration, of the herdsman or cowboy, called a *vaquero* in the southwestern part of the United States.

6. *spayed:* Made sterile.

12. *Uncle Toms:* A reference to the faithful negro slave in the novel *Uncle Tom's Cabin,* who was known for his piety and patient suffering.

14. *Topsies:* The amusing and mischievous young slave girl in *Uncle Tom's Cabin* by Harriet Beecher Stowe.

22. *Swanee river:* Made famous by the popular plantation song which begins "'Way down upon the Swanee River." Its composer was Stephen Foster.

27. *God-damn Yankee:* A descriptive phrase applied so frequently in the South to the term Yankee that it is often written in small letters, as *damnyankee.* It may be traced to the hatred the rural South felt for the sharp traders of the industrial North and their widely divergent views on many questions.

line

36. *abolitionists:* A term given to those who favored the liberation of the slaves—the abolition of slavery. Most famous were William Lloyd Garrison, Wendell Phillips, John Greenleaf Whittier, and John Brown.

37. *Wendell Phillips:* The principal orator of the Antislavery party, a valued ally of William Lloyd Garrison. His eloquent address in Faneuil Hall in 1837 is ranked with Patrick Henry's oration at Williamsburg and with Lincoln's at Gettysburg.

37. *John Brown:* The American abolitionist (1800–1859) was born in 1800 in Torrington, Connecticut, the descendant of a Mayflower settler. At the age of eighteen he thought to prepare himself for the ministry, but became interested instead in land surveying, in sheep raising, and in trading. In 1849, having lived in Ohio, Pennsylvania, and Massachusetts, he moved to North Elba, N. Y., where he took up farming. In 1855, he went to Kansas where the violent conflict was raging between the "free-state" and proslavery settlers. John Brown, who had long hated slavery, soon became a leading figure. After a short time of service in the border warfare to make Kansas a "free" or a "slave" state, he returned East for the purpose of raising funds to arouse the people to the evil of slavery and to assist Kansas in the struggle.

In 1858–59 he took steps to carry out a project he had long contemplated—that of providing a stronghold for fugitive slaves in the mountains of Virginia, and of arming them for self-defense. At Chatham, Canada, with eleven white and thirty-five negro associates, he adopted a "Provisional Constitution and Ordinance for the People of the United States." John Brown was elected Commander-in-Chief, and members of Congress as well as a Secretary of War, of State, and of the Treasury were named from this group. Shortly thereafter with arms furnished by the Massachusetts-Kansas committee and with funds contributed by friends and associates, he went to live on a farm near Harper's Ferry, Virginia. It was his plan to capture the arsenal there as the first step in his larger plan.

His plans fell through, however, and he was forced to surrender. His imprisonment, trial, and execution followed swiftly, as did those of his men captured with him.

Page 24

6. *Emerson and Thoreau:* Ralph Waldo Emerson (1803-1882), known as the sage of Concord, and Henry David Thoreau (1817-1862), poet-naturalist of Walden, were famous philosophers and writers.

10. *Minister Higginson:* Thomas Wentworth Higginson (1823–1911), author, soldier, clergyman, and abolitionist entered vigorously in the movement against slavery. With Dr. Howe and other prominent New Englanders, he believed in fighting to secure abolition. This group financed John Brown's first step toward freedom.

Dr. Howe: Samuel Gridley Howe (1802–76), Boston philanthropist and physician, who edited the antislavery *Commonwealth*, assisted by his wife, Julia Ward Howe.

line

11. *Waited for news about a certain project:* The "project" referred to
was a plan to force abolition of slavery by resort to arms. John
Brown was the active leader of a small group of white men and colored who planned secretly to attack the arsenal at Harper's Ferry,
Virginia, and thus secure arms for an uprising of all slaves.

12. *Harper's Ferry:* Harper's Ferry, a town in what is now West Virginia, is situated at the junction of the Shenandoah and Potomac
rivers. On October 16, 1859, it was the scene of the outbreak of a
conspiracy of abolitionists and Negroes to incite a slave insurrection
in northern Virginia. John Brown, who had recently come there
from Kansas, was at the head of the enterprise. He was a man of
great intensity of character, of perseverance, and broad human sympathies. It is said that twenty years earlier he had decided upon the
course he took in 1859. Having recruited over several months a group
of twenty-two young men, five of whom were colored, and having
assembled some arms, he made a surprise attack on the arsenal and
overpowered the watchman. A shot fired at the relief watchman on
the bridge gave the alarm. For twenty hours Brown's men held the
arsenal. On Tuesday, October 18, 1859, a company of United States
marines demanded unconditional surrender. On being refused they
assaulted. Brown's son, Owen, and six others escaped. Brown himself was severely wounded. Taken prisoner, he was quartered in the
county jail at Charleston from October 19 until the conclusion of
his trial, October 31, 1859. He was indicted on three counts: for
conspiring with Negroes to produce insurrection; for treason to the
Commonwealth of Virginia; for murder. He was found guilty and
hanged, December 2, 1859. His execution aroused bitter factional
strife. In the North he was popularly regarded as a martyr.

17. *Taliaferro . . . Huger:* Names of prominent well-born Southern
families. Pronounce *Tolliver, You-jee.*

18. *Maryland Carroll:* The Carrolls of Maryland were a distinguished
family, Charles Carroll being one of the signers of the Declaration
of Independence.

18. *Virginia Lee:* The Lees of Virginia were another prominent family.

19. *Albemarle:* George Monk, first Duke of Albemarle, was instrumental
in restoring the Stuarts to the English throne and was high in Charles
II's favor.

20. *second Charles:* The monarch of the Restoration, Charles II, exer-
cising his royal prerogative, gave grants of Crown lands in America
to friends and followers. The Wingate right to lands thus went back
to the late seventeenth century.

28. *Monmouth:* The Duke of Monmouth was reputedly one of the king's
illegitimate sons, and his favorite.

Page 25

6. *Stuart:* Charles I and II, as descendants of James I (son of Mary
Stuart of Scotland), belonged to the House of Stuart. These references
indicate that there is a strain of royal blood in the Wingates.

16. *tartan:* A woolen cloth with a plaid pattern worn in the Scottish Highlands, each clan having its distinctive tartan pattern. *Her wit was a tartan of colored weather* implies that it was vivid, suited to changes of mood, and a protective covering to softness of heart.
31. *painted Death:* The Indian on the warpath painted himself hideously.
33. *fief:* Land holdings.
36. *sigil:* Seal or mark.

Page 26

19-22. *the last to feel . . . arms won under the bastard's star:* Clay Wingate was the last to reveal the Stuart traits, as inherited from Monmouth, illegitimate son of Charles II.

Page 27

20. *pot-pourri:* A mixture of dried and spiced flower petals, usually kept in jars.

Page 28

15-16. *unseen cavalry / Riding the wind:* A reference to the four horsemen, suggesting the coming disaster of war.

Page 29

34. *Pottawattomie:* Kansas, then a territory, was the scene of bloody disturbances created by those who wished it to be a slave state and those who were determined that it be free. At Pottawattomie, Kansas, occurred the massacre of five proslavery settlers, by men under Brown's orders, in retaliation for the murder, a short time before, of five "free-state" settlers.

Page 30

7. *my hardy sons:* John Brown, twice married, was the father of twenty children. His sons aided him in all his undertakings.
17. *Joshua's sword:* Successor to Moses, Joshua led the Israelites in their invasion and settlement of Canaan.
30. *Oliver Brown:* One of John Brown's sons who died in the attack on Harper's Ferry.

Page 32

11. *bearded faces:* It was the convention for men in the Civil War period to wear beards.
12. *old daguerreotypes:* The pictures taken by an early method of photography which utilized silver-coated plates.

374

line
26. *fabulous sword* (of Washington): According to legend this sword was the gift of Frederick the Great to George Washington. There was also a pistol presented to Washington by Lafayette. With these weapons John Brown wished to strike the first blow for the freedom of a race.

Page 33

3. *Old Testament eyes:* John Brown's religious intensity and fanaticism were apparent in his eyes.

Page 34

38. *Nat Turner:* In 1831 Nat Turner with a group of Negroes attacked and killed a large number of whites, alarming the proslavery group.

Page 35

2. *Jefferson Guards:* The militia from Charlestown.
6. *blunderbuss:* An old-fashioned, short gun with a flaring muzzle.
34. *this:* The capture of the Potomac Bridge.

Page 40

1. *Light Horse Harry's son:* Robert E. Lee was the son of Henry Lee, an American general under George Washington, familiarly known as "Light Horse Harry."
22. *Stuart:* James Ewell Brown Stuart, later celebrated for his services to the Confederates. One of the most gallant and daring heroes of the war.

Page 41

9. *Ossawattomie:* Guerrilla warfare in Kansas gave to John Brown the title from a desperate defense which he made at that place against a group ten times stronger than his own.
28. *glissades:* Gliding steps to one side.
29. *splay-feet:* Unusual flatness, turned outward at the ankle.

Page 42

30. *conjur-bag:* A bag in which are carried articles supposed to have magical powers.
35. *The wind . . . news:* News picked up no one knew how.
37. *grapevine:* A secret system by which news was carried from person to person.

Page 43

31. *misalliance:* Marriage with someone socially inferior.

375

line
31. *I.O.U.'s:* A debtor's recognition of his indebtedness.
32. *elegized:* Wrote a lament.
40. *tag-line:* The end or catch word of an actor's speech; cue.

Page 45

7. *expunge:* Efface, wipe out.

Page 46

14. *ha'nts:* Ghosts.
15. *paterollers:* The planters in a district maintained patrollers who picked up runaway slaves or slaves who wandered away from their plantations after curfew or without permission.
23. *nacre:* Mother-of-pearl.
34. *Godey's Lady's Book:* A periodical founded in Philadelphia in 1830. It was the first American woman's magazine and dealt with fashions and etiquette.

Page 48

32. *Phaëton:* The son of Helios, the sun-god, Phaëton induced his father to permit him to drive the chariot of the Sun. To prevent his setting the world on fire, Zeus struck him down by a thunderbolt.
35. *black-marble sea:* The base of the clock.

Page 49

9. *broomstick witches of New England:* A reference to the witch-hunting episode in colonial New England.

Page 50

10. *they'll hang slavery:* Note the prophecy.

Page 51

11. *whickered:* Whinnied.

Page 53

14. *old task of sorting wool:* John Brown was engaged in sheep raising and the wool trade.
17. *the shepherd's gift:* Ability to identify different kinds and types of wool.
38. *eroded:* Worn away.
41. *Shubel Morgan:* One of the names John Brown assumed as the leader of a band in the guerrilla warfare in Kansas.

line
18. *mores:* Folkways, unwritten laws of conduct.
19. *Mansoul:* Spiritual essence.

Page 56

17. *Mrs. Russell:* Mrs. Thomas Russell. In an effort to raise funds and ammunition for his free-state band in Kansas, Brown made a trip to the East. He stayed for a week in Boston at the Russell's house. Judge Russell had never been conspicuous in abolitionist affairs and his home proved an excellent hiding-place for John Brown. At the time referred to in this passage Mrs. Russell visited the prisoner and repaired his coat.
18. *A sculptor:* Edwin A. Brackett, a sculptor of Boston, sketched John Brown from the door of his cell, as the first step toward the making of the bust.
20, 25. *Dr. Howe / Higginson:* Mentioned in the notes for page 24.
22. *Gerrit Smith:* A warm friend of Brown's from the northern part of New York who had formerly offered a large tract of land as a refuge for Negroes.

Page 57

17. *Hung fables:* The story of kissing the Negro child has been discredited.
27. *"I, John Brown . . . might be done,"* and *"This is a beautiful country"* (line 37): Both statements are quoted as authentic in Villard's biography. The second statement appeared December 3, 1859, in both the New York *Herald* and the New York *Tribune*.

Page 58

4. *T. J. Jackson:* Later known as "Stonewall" Jackson.
6. *Deploy:* To spread out in line of battle.
9. *fey:* Visionary, portentous.
12. *Calvin:* John Calvin (1509–64), Protestant theologian, founder of Presbyterianism.
17. *predestined cinder:* Theory of Calvin that men were preordained to be saved or damned.
20. *Blue Ridge Mountains:* Southeast range of Appalachian system near Harper's Ferry.

Page 59

7. *preparate:* Made ready.

Page 60

13–15. *Glory, Glory, Hallelujah:* From the "Battle Hymn of the Republic," written by Julia Ward Howe (1819–1910), an American poet and philanthropist.

BOOK TWO

Page 63

line

2. *Sumter:* The attack on Fort Sumter marks the opening of the Civil War. During the progress of secession all properties of the Federal government in the secession states were taken over by these states. On March 4, 1861, the Federal government still had in its control only four military posts in the seceded states. Of these posts, Fort Sumter, commanding Charleston, was most important. The Confederate States now regarded the Federal government as a foreign power. Consequently a fort under its control and situated in their territory was not to be tolerated. Lincoln was opposed to Seward's plan, advocated by many others, too, that the Federal government evacuate Sumter. Actually the fort was without food, reinforcements, and supplies, and for these reasons the commander offered to evacuate in three days if not provisioned or overruled by the Federal government.

8. *beau sabreur:* Gallant swordsman.

10. *Murat:* A French marshal who, under Napoleon, rose to the highest commands and married Napoleon's sister Caroline.

11. *Beauregard:* Pierre Gustave Toutant Beauregard (1818–93), Confederate general. Assigned command at Charleston, South Carolina, his aides began the war on April 12, 1861, by the bombardment of Fort Sumter. On July 21 he won the First Battle of Bull Run; was defeated, later, at Pittsburg Landing. In 1863 he defended Charleston and aided in the defense of Richmond.

Page 64

16. *Chancellorsville:* A prophecy of one of the fiercest battles of the Wilderness, which took place in May, 1863. The South achieved victory but lost its favorite leader, Stonewall Jackson.

25. *trick:* Shift, time on duty.

Page 65

8. *Judah P. Benjamin:* Attorney General, Secretary of War, later Secretary of State; Davis's friend and confidential adviser.

17. *Toombs:* General Robert Toombs, Secretary of State.

20. *Stephens:* Alexander H. Stephens, Vice-President of the Confederate States.

24. *Mallory:* Stephen R. Mallory, Secretary of the Navy.
Reagan: John H. Reagan, Postmaster General of the Confederate States.
Walker: General Leroy P. Walker, Secretary of War of the Confederate States.

Page 66

14. *cold, plain Franklin sense:* At the signing of the Declaration of Independence, July 4, 1776, Benjamin Franklin remarked: "We must all hang together, or assuredly we shall all hang separately."

378

20. *Their railsplitter:* Abraham Lincoln.

22. *Jefferson Davis* (1808–89): The President of the Confederate States during the Civil War. Born in Kentucky, he was a graduate of West Point, and came into political prominence first as a member of the House of Representatives and later of the United States Senate, representing Mississippi. He fought and won distinction in the Mexican War. During the presidency of Pierce he was appointed Secretary of War. He was not of the old "aristocratic" South; he represented a new Southern group.

26. *John Calhoun* (1782–1859): Vice-President under Adams and Jackson. Calhoun was a strong believer in state rights. In 1832 he resigned the vice-presidency and entered the United States Senate, becoming a leader in the state rights movement and a champion of the slave-holding states. Calhoun, Clay, and Webster are often called "the great triumvirate" of American political orators of their time.

35. *young black-haired girl with the Gentile-eyes:* His wife was a Creole (that is, of French parentage), the family having fled to New Orleans from St. Domingo. Mrs. Benjamin was a devout Catholic. The marriage between a Jew and a Catholic was not a happy one although Benjamin became a Catholic convert.

Page 67

5. *bayou:* Outlet of a lake; a term frequently applied to the sluggish waters of the deep South.

Page 68

8. *Hay:* John Hay (1858–1905) went to Washington as one of Lincoln's private secretaries.

10. *Plutarchan sentences:* Plutarch was a Greek moralist and biographer born in the first century A.D. He was well read in history and philosophy and a very careful writer.

18. *President now by the grace of luck:* Lincoln was nominated by the Republican party in 1856 during the acute slavery issue. His acceptance speech for United States senator, the famous "house-divided-against-itself" speech, revealed his stand, and during the ensuing campaign Lincoln met Stephen A. Douglas, his Democratic opponent, in a series of debates on slavery. Douglas's stand on the Dred Scott decision led to disruption in the Democratic party and destroyed his hopes of attaining the presidency. Although elected to the Senate through a majority in the legislature, Douglas received fewer popular votes than Lincoln. The latter became a figure of national importance and in 1860 was nominated as presidential candidate by the Republican party. He was elected, but before his inauguration seven states had formally seceded from the Union and inaugurated Jefferson Davis as their president. Lincoln, when he had been urged to seek the nomination, replied that men like Seward and Chase were entitled to take precedence and that "no such good luck" was in store for him.

22. *Cabinet:* Lincoln's Cabinet was composed of William H. Seward, Sec-- retary of State; Salmon P. Chase, Treasury; Simon Cameron, War, succeeded early in 1862 by Edward M. Stanton; Gideon Welles, Navy; Cable Smith, Interior; Edwin Bates, Attorney General; Montgomery Blair, Postmaster General; Hannibal Hamlin of Maine, Vice-President.

33. *Mollie:* Lincoln was married to Mary Todd. His children were Robert, Edward, William, and Thomas. William died during the presidency of Lincoln; the youngest, Thomas, is the one known as "Tad."

37. *Seward and Chase:* William H. Seward was Secretary of State under Lincoln; Salmon P. Chase was Secretary of the Treasury. Both men were brilliant and prominent members of the Republican party. Both found it hard to accept Lincoln as the President. The letter referred to contained Seward's no uncertain directions as to what he thought Lincoln should do. He was rebuffed and is quoted as saying: "I, who, by every right ought to have been chosen President, what am I now? Nothing but Abe Lincoln's little clerk!"

Page 69

13. *one pumpkin to bump in a sack:* In the Cabinet crisis after the Union defeat at Fredericksburg, enemies of Seward demanded his resignation. These people were also supporters of Chase, who also resigned as a result of the crisis. With these two resignations—which Lincoln refused to accept—he played one faction against the other and kept two valuable men in office.

Page 70

4. *seventy-five thousand volunteers:* The 75,000 were called for a three months' period. Probably their first service was "to repossess the forts, places, and property which have been seized from the Union." (The act of 1795 provided that the period of service of the militia could not be extended beyond thirty days after the next meeting of Congress.) This proclamation had the effect of pushing many of the border states into the Confederacy—Virginia, North Carolina, Arkansas, and Tennessee. Maryland, Kentucky, and Missouri, however, though with strong Southern sympathies, remained loyal to the Union.

5. *lanyard:* A strong cord with a hook at one end used in firing cannon.

Page 71

19. *Bull Run:* The First Battle of Bull Run was fought July 21, 1861. A Confederate army under Beauregard was stationed at Manassas Junction, Virginia, on a little stream called Bull Run, about thirty-five miles southwest of Washington. A second army, under General Johnston, was stationed in the Senandoah Valley across the Blue Ridge Mountains. The Union volunteers were sent forth to besiege the Southern capital, Richmond. Since the troops had signed up for three

line

months' enlistment only, it was necessary to hurry. According to the plan of attack General Patterson was to hold Johnston in check and General McDowell was to attack Beauregard. McDowell made the attack, but just as he was forcing a Southern retreat Johnston's army from the Shenandoah unexpectedly came up. The Union soldiers fled in disorder, reaching Washington in mob panic. The Confederates did not realize that victory was in their hands and were in almost as disorganized a condition. Consequently they did not follow up their advantage.

Page 72

21. *housewife:* Small sewing case for soldiers (pronounced *huzif*).

Page 75

32. *Meshuck:* Meshach. One of the three Hebrew youths—Meshach, Shadrach, and Abed-nego—who were thrown into the fiery furnace by Nebuchadnezzar but came out unharmed. (Daniel 3.)

Page 77

18. *de Jordan River:* A reference to the spiritual.

Page 78

1–2. *thunderstone . . . iron-filings:* The thunderstone is a lodestone or meteorite. Under the stress of war and conflict various people are pulled out of their ordinary lives and dragged together as iron-filings are pulled by a magnet.

Page 80

13. *ballad-English:* Old-fashioned language with an Elizabethan flavor that has not changed with the times.
16. *feud-temper:* Quick, sharp temper engendered by long-time enmity between neighbors.
feud-way: "Shoot on sight!"
37. *moonshiner:* One who distills liquor illegally.
39. *mail-order dress:* Dress selected from a catalogue, not made of "home-spun."

Page 83

11. *We'll hang Jeff Davis:* One of the popular war songs of the Union soldiers.
16. *On to Richmond!:* Union slogan in the first year of the war.
36. *three-months' men:* The volunteers were called for three months only.

381

line
6. *porcelain dolls:* The reference is to the traditionally dainty and delicate appearance of Southern women.
35. *Henry House:* Most of the Battle of Bull Run was fought on the plateau where the Henry House stood. See map.

Page 87

2. *cicada-saw:* The long, shrill note of the locust.
31. *La Haye Sainte:* The reference is to the Battle of Waterloo, June 18, 1814. The armies of England and the Netherlands occupied a semi-circle of hills in front of the village. The French occupied a ridge opposite. Between the British center and the French position stood the stone chateau of Hougoumont, held by the English. In front of Wellington's left center were the hamlet of Mont Saint Jean and the farm of La Haye Sainte, also held by the British. In this connection read the third canto of *Childe Harold's Pilgrimage* by Byron.
33. *Lexington:* Site of the surprise attack upon the British in the Revolutionary War, April 19, 1775. Paul Revere was the one who notified the townsmen of the arrival of the British.
35. *Blenheim:* A decisive battle in the War of the Spanish Succession, 1704, in which the English under Marlborough and the imperial forces under Prince Eugene defeated the French and broke the spell of victories of Louis XIV. Read in this connection *The Battle of Blenheim* by Robert Southey.

Page 88

4. *bivouac:* Camping in the open at night.
8. *Johnston:* General Joseph E. Johnston, Confederate general in charge of the troops in the Shenandoah.
9. *McDowell:* General Irwin McDowell in command of the Army of the Potomac.
36. *red-fezzed Fire-Zouaves:* At the beginning of the war a number of volunteer regiments assumed the garb or insignia of various foreign tribes.

Page 89

1. *Garibaldi Guards:* ⎱ At the beginning of the war a number of volun-
3. *Bedouin-caps:* ⎰ teer regiments assumed the garb or insignia of various foreign tribes.
5. *Sherman:* William T. Sherman (1820–91), Union colonel of infantry at this time.
Heintzelman: Samuel P. Heintzelman, under McDowell at Bull Run.
6–9. *Rickett . . . McDowell:* Union leaders.
37. *windrows:* A windswept line or row; a term applied to hay raked up to dry before being rolled or pitched into stacks. Later, of Antietam, Captain Noyes is reported to have said, "I saw bodies dressed in the rebel grey lying in ranks so regular that Death the reaper must have mowed them down."

39. *the stone-wall of Jackson:* General Bee of the Confederates, on seeing Jackson's brigade, rushed up to Jackson and cried, "They are beating us back!" "Well, sir, we will give them the bayonet," was the calm reply. Turning to his men, Bee shouted, "There's Jackson standing like a stone wall!"

Page 90

4. *Fighting Joe Hooker:* Joseph Hooker (1814-79), a graduate of West Point, had fought in the Florida and Mexican wars. When the Civil War began he entered the Union Army and was soon made major general. At this time he had been placed in command of the Army of the Potomac to relieve Burnside. His bravery in action brought him the nickname.
36. *Stone Bridge:* The first objective of the Battle of Bull Run.

Page 91

6. *Patterson:* General Robert Patterson in command of Union forces. He was supposed to block Johnson's army in the Shenandoah.
34. *Under a cupolaed gloom on Riverside Drive:* Grant's Tomb on Riverside Drive at 125th Street, New York City.

Page 93

2. *Cub Run:* See map.
   Cat Hairpin Bend: See map.
6. *an injured Napoleon:* General McClellan, placed in command of the Army of the Potomac at the close of the Battle of Bull Run, was popularly called "the Young Napoleon."
16. *sabretasche-War:* War of individuals in which sword and saber play could make heroes.
18. *Mitchell's ford:* See map.
28. *the Nelson-way:* Nelson's dying words to his flag-captain were, "Kiss me, Hardy." There is a comparison here between two fine fighters who were also warm-hearted.

Page 94

20. *Sudley Road:* See map.
26. *Centerville:* See map.

Page 95

1. *Warrentown pike:* See map.
25. *Young's Branch:* See map.
28. *Imboden:* John D. Imboden commanded the Staunton Artillery. On April 17, before the call to arms, together with the Monticello Guards and the Albemarle Rifles, he was sent to capture the works at Harper's Ferry.

29. *Parrotts:* Muzzle-loading, cast-iron, rifle guns, hurling heavy projectiles.
    howitzers: Small, light cannons.

Page 98

4. *the Scotch dominie:* General Johnston.
5. *hussar-sword:* Leader of the cavalry, Beauregard.
6. *his horse is shot under him:* Beauregard's horse.
9. *the odd, lemon-sucking ex-professor:* Jackson.
13. *the face they cut for him on Stone Mountain:* Outside Atlanta, Georgia, Gutzon Borglum (1871–1940), the sculptor, cut the memorial to the army of the Confederacy. Jackson is one of the figures. The original plan was to build, directly below the sculpture, a vast hall created in the solid rock bearing the inscription in six languages: "To the Valor of the Southern Soldiers."

Page 101

31–32. *Jefferson Davis . . . stranger:* "At the junction were a large number of men who had left the field in panic and who gave Davis graphic accounts of the defeat of the army. He asked a gray-bearded man whose calm face and composed demeanor inspired confidence, how the battle had gone. 'Our line was broken,' came the reply; 'all was confusion, the army routed, and the battle lost.' "—*History of the Civil War,* by James Ford Rhodes, p. 40.
34. *Plutarch death on a shield:* Warriors killed in battle were carried home on their shields.

Page 102

37. *Lord Randall:* Its first line begins, "O where have ye been, Lord Randall, my son?"

Page 105

21. *They tried . . . Centerville:* Seward's message to the President read: "General McDowell's army in full retreat through Centerville. The day is lost. Save Washington and the remnants of this army. . . . The routed troops will not reform."
32. *As dazed . . . defeat:* The Confederates made no effective pursuit nor did they follow up their advantage by entering Washington.

Page 106

23. *Pastor at Lexington:* The pastor at Lexington was eager to receive news. He received a letter from Jackson containing his vestry subscription—nothing more.

29. *Walt Whitman:* The American poet has included in his prose sketches, *Specimen Days in America,* full account of his personal experiences. A collection of his poems on Civil War themes is *Drum Taps.* See the poem "The Wound-Dresser"—"An old man bending I come upon new faces."

Page 107

12. *Horace Greeley:* His letter runs in part as follows: "This is my seventh sleepless night—Yours, too, doubtless—yet I think I shall not die, because I have no right to die. . . . You are not considered a great man, and I am a hopelessly broken one. If the rebels cannot be beaten—if our recent disaster is fatal—do not fear to sacrifice yourself to your country. . . . If it is best for the country and for mankind that we make peace with the rebels at once and on their own terms do not shrink even from that. . . ."—August 22, 1861.

Page 108

5. *"Evacuation" Lee:* Robert E. Lee. This nickname arose from the failure of Lee's first small campaign in West Virginia.

BOOK THREE

Page 111

1. *Pittsburg Landing:* In southwest Tennessee on the Tennessee River, about nine miles north of Savannah.
15. *mudsill:* A person of the lowest strata socially. A term of contempt colloquially used in the South.

Page 113

30. *Nine months have passed:* It is now April, 1862.

Page 115

28. *Halleck:* General H. W. Halleck was in command of the Army of the West, with headquarters at St. Louis. Under him was Grant.
    Frémont: General John C. Frémont was in command of the Union Army of the Mississippi. As presidential candidate he was defeated by Buchanan in the campaign of 1856.
30. *Fort Henry and Fort Donelson:* Commanding the two important gateways to the southwestern part of the Confederacy were Fort Henry on the Tennessee River and Fort Donelson on the Cumberland, the two rivers at this point being but eleven miles apart. Fort Henry was captured by the Union forces on February 6, 1862, and Grant said that he would take and destroy Fort Donelson two days later. After a desperate battle and a Union defeat, the Union army captured Fort Donelson on February 16, 1862. The capture of Fort Henry was the first important Union victory in the war.

33. *Major-General Grant:* Ulysses S. Grant (1822–85), eighteenth president of the United States, was born at Point Pleasant, Ohio. He was graduated from West Point, and served under General Taylor in the Mexican War. At the beginning of the Civil War Grant volunteered his services and was appointed colonel of an Illinois regiment. In August, 1861, he was appointed brigadier general and led an expedition on the Mississippi. In February, 1862, he distinguished himself in the capture of Fort Donelson and was made major-general. The poem here stops in its pen picture just before his victory at Pittsburg Landing, or Shiloh.

37. *one dogged letter:* "I would write you many particulars, but you are so imprudent that I dare not trust you with them; and while on this subject let me say a word. I have not an enemy in the world who has done me so much injury as you in your efforts in my defense. I require no defenders, and for my sake let me alone. . . . You are constantly denouncing the general officers, and the inference with people naturally is that you get your impressions from me. Do nothing to correct what you have already done, but for the future keep quiet on this subject."—Quoted in W. E. Woodward, *Meet General Grant* (New York, Horace Liveright, 1928), pp. 257–58.

Page 116

7. *contraband cotton:* Actually the exchange of cotton from the South for needed supplies was encouraged, and supervised, by the Federal government. But the illicit trade was much larger, for the profits in contraband cotton were enormous.

11. *Tom Tiddler's Ground:* In a children's game, a space marked off for the chief player, Tom Tiddler, and invaded, if chance permits, by the others, who then sing, "We're on Tom Tiddler's ground, picking up gold and silver." Hence any no man's land where pickings may be had without interference.

19. *A British steamer in the Bahama Channel:* On November 8, 1861, Mason and Slidell, envoys to England, were taken from the British royal mail packet *Trent* by Captain Wilkes of the United States war vessel, *San Jacinto*. This incident brought the United States and England to the verge of war, and colored the relations of the two countries throughout the conflict.

29–37. *The* Merrimac *and the* Monitor: The naval operations of the war were, for the most part, confined to the assistance of land forces by expeditions on the Atlantic Coast, in the Gulf, and on the rivers, and to the maintenance of the blockade of Southern ports. On March 9, 1862, however, occurred the most famous naval battle of the Civil War, to raise the blockade at the James and Elizabeth Rivers. Before this battle the Confederate *Merrimac*, commanded by Franklin Buchanan, destroyed the *Congress* and three smaller vessels, rammed and sank the *Cumberland*, but during the night the iron-clad *Monitor* arrived, and after a fight of six hours the tables were turned and the *Monitor* came off victor. The encounter is important also because it demonstrated the superiority of iron-clads over wooden warships.

The London *Times* of the period states: "There is not now a ship in the English navy apart from these two [*The Warrior* and *The Ironside*] that it would not be madness to trust to an engagement with that little *Monitor*."

39. *Temeraire:* A line-of-battle ship of 98 guns, called "The Fighting Temeraire," captured from the French at the Battle of the Nile, August 1, 1798. Also used at the Battle of Trafalgar, October 21, 1805, under Captain Harvey.

Victory: Nelson's flagship at Trafalgar.

Constellation: Vessel of the United States Navy built in 1798; under Commodore Truxton in 1799 it captured the French frigate *Insurgente*.

40. *Serapis:* This English vessel engaged the *Bon Homme Richard*.

Bon Homme Richard: Ship commanded by John Paul Jones in a naval battle off England during the Revolutionary War.

Golden Hind: Only ship of Drake's fleet to circumnavigate the world.

41. *Galleys of Antony:* The ships of Marc Antony. While one of the triumvirate in 40–37 B.C. Antony lived mostly in Alexandria. He led an expedition against Parthia; was defeated at Actium.

galleys of Carthage: Carthage, situated on the Mediterranean, was engaged in many naval battles with Rome. The name of Carthage in history is linked with the Punic Wars.

Page 117

1. *Galleons:* Stately sailing ships of the fifteenth and sixteenth centuries often having three or four decks.

galleasses: Vessels propelled by sails and oars and carrying heavy guns; used by nations of Southern Europe in the sixteenth and seventeenth centuries.

2. *galliots:* One-decked vessels propelled by sails and oars, used especially in the Mediterranean.

3. *Argos:* Argo, in mythology, was the fifty-oared ship built of pines from Pelion under the direction of Athena. The plural *Argos* might mean ships as powerful.

argosies: Merchant vessels of large size; a fleet of vessels.

Achaean pride: The pride of the Achaeans, who in Homer's time lorded it over the other Hellenes.

5. *ghost-flagship of the Ark:* The first wooden ship—the Ark—is here considered to carry the commander of the phantom fleet and fly his flag.

11. *Fiddler's Green:* The imagined Elysian field of sailors—the bottom of the sea.

12. *Davy Jones:* He is also called Duffy Jonah and Duppy Jonah; the spirit of the sea.

20. *A sallow-faced and puffy Emperor:* The French emperor during the Civil War was Napoleon III, who, acting upon the expectation that the republic of the United States would be disrupted, resolved to create a puppet monarchy in Mexico.

31. *Mr. Gladstone:* In his speech at Newcastle, October 7, 1862, Gladstone said: "We have our own opinions about slavery;—we may be for or against the South; but there is no doubt that Jefferson Davis and other leaders of the South have made an army; and they have made, what is more than either, they have made a nation. We may anticipate with certainty the success of the Southern states as far as their separation from the North is concerned."

33. *Palmerston:* Palmerston also thought the plan for mediation excellent and suggested that it be made to both belligerents at the same time.

34. *Henry Adams:* At that time Henry Adams was private secretary to his father, Charles Francis Adams, the Minister to London. As a private citizen young Adams wrote letters to English papers and to a few papers in the United States. The publication of one of these letters by the Boston *Courier* evoked a satirical attack from the London *Times* which discouraged Adams from being "useful" in this way to the Northern cause.

Page 118

30. *claymore:* A two-edged, two-handed sword used by Scottish Highlanders. Here the word is used as a figurative adjective to indicate the sharp, piercing quality of the eyes.

Page 120

1. *preux chevalier:* Valiant knight.

3. *Waverley-streak:* Similar to the romantic view of warriors depicted in the novels of Sir Walter Scott. *Waverley* is the name of the first of the series.

17. *a wound that should not have been mortal:* Johnston had left his attending surgeon behind to care for the wounded, many of them Union prisoners.

Page 124

22. *Vast fictive heroisms:* Imaginary deeds of great bravery.

Page 126

23. *cut from leaden foil with blunt shears:* A dream with no clear outlines; every movement was an effort.

31. *Harper's Weekly:* A magazine devoted to current events and satirical comment.

Page 127

8. *molasses-taffy voice:* Soft, sweet, blurred Southern accent.

line
3. *Nibelung Hall:* The home of the legendary beings in the great epic
   of medieval Germany—the *Nibelungenlied;* referring to the Burgundi-
   ans in the time of Attila.
6. *runes:* Magical symbols.
8. *Ygdrasil:* In Norse mythology the great ash tree symbolizing the
   universe.
12. *hawk-Valkyrie:* In Norse mythology the maidens of Odin who hover
    over the battlefield choosing those to be slain and carrying the worthy
    heroes to Valhalla.
13. *Valhalla:* In Norse mythology the hall of Odin into which he re-
    ceives the souls of heroes slain in battle.
36. *hiders:* Draft evaders.

Page 129

4. *Rising Sun and Roses of Sharon:* Favorite patterns for quilting.
15. *Free-Soilers:* Those who advocated the nonextension of slavery.
18. *a plague on both of your houses:* See Mercutio in *Romeo and Juliet,*
    Act III, Scene 1.
31. *white trash:* Poor people of the South without a plantation.
32. *Macbeth:* See Shakespeare's *Tragedy of Macbeth.*
    Beulah: A novel written by Augusta Jane Wilson and published in
    the middle of the last century.
    Oliver Twist: A novel by Charles Dickens.

Page 130

3. *recruiters:* Those who enlist soldiers.
21. *muscadines:* Grapes.
27. *Duncan:* The murdered king in *Macbeth.*
29. *Fagin:* Head of a band of thieves in *Oliver Twist.*
30. *Bill Sikes:* A burglar in *Oliver Twist.*
31. *Lady Macduff:* Macduff's wife, murdered by Macbeth.

Page 131

7. *Banquo:* Macbeth's friend murdered by Macbeth for fear his line
   would succeed that of Macbeth on the throne of Scotland.
9. *The Artful Dodger:* A young pickpocket in *Oliver Twist.*

Page 133

9. *great Norn:* A demigoddess in old mythology who presides over and
   determines the fates of both men and gods.
37. *Young Seward:* A character in *Macbeth.*
38. *Oliver:* The hero of *Oliver Twist.*

line
3. *hel-shoes:* In Norse mythology, shoes placed on the dead before burial to aid them on the rough road.

29. *Mercutio's curse:* "A plague o' both your houses!"—*Romeo and Juliet,* Act III, scene 1.
40. *skulk:* One who evades his duties.

26. *the weaver's tune:* The song that Bailey hummed.

13. *an old nursery-rhyme:* "Jack and Jill went up the hill. . . ."
18. *wilderness-stone:* Symbol for the desire to be untrammeled, free.
22. *Faustus:* A reference to the opera *Faust.*
29. *elixirs from a rock:* Moses struck the rock and the water rushed forth —to prove that his power was from God.

15. *touchstone:* A test to try one's qualities.
19. *weighted with a borrowed shield:* Guided by characteristics, virtues, ideas, not her own.
20. *chafferers:* Bargainers.
37. *half-oriole and half-fox:* Possessing characteristics of the native birds and the swift shyness of the fox.
38. *the man by Walden Pond:* Thoreau.

11. *arras:* Curtain, tapestry, or screen.

10. *corposant:* "St. Elmo's fire or light"; literally, from the patron saint of sailors. Here, flamelike receptacle or vehicle.

37. *little scooped dishes:* The scales that were to determine his fate.

6. *necktie-party:* A hanging.

BOOK FOUR

Page 151

14. *around the cape:* Cape of Good Hope, South Africa.
17. *supernacular:* First quality, finest.
24. *a white ribbon:* Badge of temperance.
25. *Haman:* See The Book of Esther. Haman was the chief minister of Ahasuerus. He hated the Jews and was hanged on the gallows which he had prepared for Mordecai, who saved the Jews.
29. *blockade-runner:* A ship smuggling contraband goods.
31. *bullion:* Metal in the mass.

Page 152

4. *Bayou City:* New Orleans.
5. *damn-the-torpedoes commodore:* Farragut ran his fleet past the forts guarding the city, captured New Orleans and, later, the forts.
29. *profiteers:* Those who took advantage of war conditions to make money.

Page 153

5. *They play at Manassas:* Reference to Bull Run.

Page 154

23. *Curious blossom . . . ground:* Strange combination of affection and loyalty which the slaves held for their masters when supposedly their lack of freedom would prevent any gentle feeling.
26. *anomaly:* Something out of keeping with accepted notions.

Page 155

13. *schisms:* Disagreements.
14. *phthisics* (pronounced *tiziks*): Any throat or lung affliction; obsolete for *phthisis.*
20. *calaboose:* Prison, jail.

Page 156

27. *Jael:* Jael was the wife of Heber the Kenite who offered shelter to Sisera as the latter fled from his enemies, and then killed him with a tent nail. (Judges 4, 5.)

Page 158

33. *conjur-stone:* A stone supposedly possessing qualities of magic.

Page 161

17. *sacque:* Jacket or little coat.

line
27–28. *I will make . . . bodkins:* Making an image (effigy) of a hated person
and burning it or sticking pins in it or otherwise defacing it was supposed to bring misfortune or death to the person represented.

15. *Manassas:* The Battle of Bull Run was fought July 21, 1861, on Manassas Plains near the stream of Bull Run in eastern Virginia.

8. *guidon-bearer:* One who carries the small flag which distinguishes the
unit.
23. *like our Virginia boys:* Lucy comes from Virginia.

3. *There is an Eastern game and a Western game:* The northern frontier
of the Confederacy was bounded by the mountains of West Virginia,
Kentucky, and Tennessee. The Kentucky, Tennessee, and Mississippi
rivers were strongly fortified. The Northern armies were concerned
with securing control of the Mississippi and of the railroad lines leading southward into Georgia and Alabama. The Union objectives were
finally accomplished through the capture of Vicksburg, July 4, 1863,
by Grant and the defeat of General Bragg in the battles of Chickamauga (September 19–20) and Chattanooga (November 23–25) the
same year. In the Eastern campaign the Northern objective was to
take Richmond. After General McDowell's failure at Bull Run he was
succeeded by General George B. McClellan, who proposed to take his
army to Fortress Monroe and then advance up the Peninsula between
the York and the James Rivers. His plans were interfered with by
Stonewall Jackson in the Shenandoah Valley.
6. *Buell:* General Don Carlos Buell. At this time (February 16, 1862) the
Union forces under Grant and Buell were commanding western
Tennessee. General Johnston had concentrated his forces at Corinth,
Mississippi, and was planning a surprise attack. He moved out of
Corinth and, as we have seen, successfully attacked Grant's army at
Shiloh on April 6. The next day, reinforced by Buell and Wallace,
Grant renewed the battle, and the Confederates retreated to the upper
Mississippi, later to surrender.
Grant: After the Battle of Chattanooga he was given entire command
of all the Union armies, east and west.
Bragg: Braxton Bragg, Confederate general after the fall of Corinth,
attempted to hold northeastern Tennessee and to march into Ken-
tucky with the hope that the Kentuckians would repudiate the Union.
Beauregard: Confederate general in the Battle of Bull Run.
9. *New Orleans is taken:* New Orleans surrendered, April 5, 1862.
10. *ambiguous Butler:* Benjamin Butler was in charge of the Army of the
Potomac in 1861. He was bitterly hated by the South, and various

tales of cruelty and looting were attached to his name. Mrs. Chestnut characterized him as "this hideous cross-eyed beast."—*A Diary from Dixie,* as written by Mary Boykin Chestnut, edited by Isabella D. Martin and Myrta L. Avary (1906).

21. *It has been disproved . . . spoons:* Despite such charges against him as that concerning the spoons, Butler's administration of New Orleans was harsh but efficient. He ordered the confiscation—*theft* to the Southern mind—of property of anyone fighting in the Confederate Army or of anyone whose acts were treasonable to the Union.

25-26. *Napoleon . . . De Staël:* Madame De Staël was considered one of the most intellectual women of the eighteenth century. She was the daughter of Necker, finance minister of Louis XVI. There existed a mutual dislike between Napoleon and Madame De Staël, a dislike so strong that she was forbidden to come within forty leagues of Paris. Her book, *Revolution,* gives vivid and lifelike pictures of her own time.

30. *Vicksburg:* A Confederate stronghold, the last great position left to the Confederates on the Mississippi. It surrendered to the Union forces on July 4, 1863.

31. *Sheridan:* In 1863 Sheridan defeated General Early in the Shenandoah Valley.
Sherman: On December 15, 1864, Sherman began his famous march from Atlanta to the sea.
Thomas: General George H. Thomas defeated the Confederates, November 23-25, 1863, in the Battle of Chattanooga. These three generals, as well as Grant, first won their spurs in the Western campaigns.

39. *"Bombproof":* A term of contempt used by the fighters for staff officers who did not fight or had desk jobs with the War Department.

Page 172

12. *Artemus Ward:* Pen name of Charles Farrar Browne, humorist.
Orpheus C. Kerr: Wrote under the title "Office Seeker." He and Robert H. Newell were contributors to the satirical weekly, *Vanity Fair.* Both regarded Lincoln with loyalty and affection and upheld the Union cause. Lincoln found relaxation and amusement in reading the quaint misspelled missives of Artemus Ward and the florid, decorated English of the "Office Seeker," both revealing the parlous state of affairs and the pettiness and pomp which attended wartime activities.

14. *He has lost a son:* William Lincoln, "Willie," died when he was a boy of eleven. In February, 1862, he caught cold riding on his pony in a chill rain.

18. *McClellan:* George Brinton McClellan (1826-85).

18-34. *McClellan comes . . . McClellan feels abused:* McClellan was a good soldier and a good organizer, but he lacked decision and was always quarreling with his superiors in Washington. He was indecisive and frequently overestimated the strength of the enemy.

line

11. *parvenu:* One who has risen above his station because of sudden wealth.

27. *Seven Pines:* Two of McClellan's corps were wiped out in the Battle of Seven Pines, or Fair Oaks, on May 31, 1862, although the Union positions were recaptured the next day.

28. *The lonely man:* Jefferson Davis.

Page 174

16–17. *He, too, is to lose / A child:* In 1864 Davis's son, Joe was killed by falling from a high porch to a brick pavement.

22. *In the prison . . . kept him:* After the fall of Richmond, in 1865, Davis was captured and imprisoned in Fort Monroe for two years.

37. *Totems:* Inanimate objects regarded by a primitive people as having relationship to a specific family group or associated group. Totems are usually *taboo* because they represent the clan's, or group's, ancestors.

   sorcery-stones: Magic charms.

39. *the third game:* The attitude of England and France. Until the spring of 1862 the government of Great Britain preserved the neutrality which had been declared at the beginning of war. But most of the great middle class engaged in commerce and manufacture desired that the war should come to an end so that England could again secure cotton and resume the export of her manufactured goods to America. France, too, wanted cotton for her manufacturing industries and so favored the Confederacy.

Page 175

2. *iron and wheat:* There was a great scarcity of iron in the South. The railroads began to deteriorate and could not do the work of transporting food, especially corn and wheat.

25. *Jubal Early:* General Jubal Early invaded Maryland and Pennsylvania; crossed the Potomac, July 5, 1864; defeated General Lew Wallace on the Monocacy; was overcome by Sheridan at Winchester. He was killed at Petersburg.

Page 176

1. *John Magruder:* The story goes that Magruder marched the same ten thousand men back and forth on a level of ground, into the woods and out again, suggesting to McClellan's observers that they were facing a vast horde.

9–10. *There was another force . . . deck of land:* The Greeks against Troy as related by Homer in *The Iliad;* a battle in which the gods took part and aided the Greeks.

19. *Sarpedon:* An ally of the Trojans slain by Patroclus.

22. *Scamander:* River in Asia Minor on which ancient Troy was situated. Legend has it that in the great battle it was so choked by the slain that it rose against Achilles, who was rescued by Hephaestus.

26. *Ajax:* One of the Greek heroes in *The Iliad.* He killed himself in anger because the armor of Achilles was awarded to Ulysses.
    Hector: One of the bravest of the Trojan leaders in *The Iliad.* He slew Patroclus, friend of Achilles, and was himself slain by Achilles.
31. *disparate:* Dissimilar; distinct in quality.

Page 177

4. *Confused, huge weapon:* Figurative description of the army.
9. *Good stallion:* Another figurative description of the army.
28. *the chunky man from the West:* Grant.
35. *sullen Cold Harbor:* Confederate victory, June 3, 1864.

Page 179

7. *ruin of Fredericksburg:* Confederate victory, December 13, 1862.
   wounds of Antietam: September 16–17, 1862, when Lee's invasion of the North was defeated.
8. *Chancellorsville:* Confederate victory, May 1–4, 1863.
9. *Chickahominy:* A river in Virginia. The reference is here made to the Confederate plan to station Jackson's men on the north bank of the Chickahominy River and overwhelm the Union forces.
20. *Let us read old letters:* Note the sense of reality and vividness which the poet gives to the poem by such a statement.
26. *Two brothers lay on the field:* Eugene and John Carter. For a description of their experience see Robert G. Carter, *Four Brothers in Blue* (Washington: Gibson Press, 1913), p. 200.

Page 180

19. *rising out . . . paper:* More excerpts from the letters.
34. *Clara Barton* (1821–1912): Remembered for her relief work on the battlefields of the Civil War and for her organized searches for missing men. She was the founder and organizer of the National Red Cross of the United States.
    Old Mother Bickerdyke: Mary Ann Ball Bickerdyke (1817–1901), a Civil War nurse and one of the most picturesque figures of the war. She worked in field hospitals, saw duty on several warships on the Mississippi, and was with Grant's army at the siege of Vicksburg.

Page 181

38. *diapason:* Entire compass of musical notes.

Page 182

15. *Box and Cox:* A farcical comedy, adapted from the French, by J. M. Morton. The humor lies in the renting of the same room by two men, one of whom works at night.

38. *Army of Northern Virginia:* Virginia was the chief battlefield of the war, and this Army's main duty was to protect Richmond. After General J. E. Johnston had been wounded at the Battle of Fair Oaks, General Robert E. Lee succeeded him in command.

Page 183

1. *pastorals:* Herdsmen.
12. *King's Mountain:* The reference is to an episode in the Revolutionary War. In May, 1780, Charleston was surrendered to the English; in August, Gates was routed at Camden, and although the invasion of North Carolina was checked at King's Mountain, by the end of that year South Carolina and Georgia were occupied by the military forces of the British.
14. *Aristo-democracy:* A mixture of aristocracy and democracy.
23. *Darwin:* Charles Robert Darwin (1809–82), English naturalist and biologist, created a sensation both in scientific circles and in the minds of laymen by his investigation *On the Origin of Species by Means of Natural Selection.*
  Victor Hugo (1802–85): French poet and novelist. *Les Miserables* is perhaps his best-known book.
34. *the mocking-bird . . . grave:* Like "Lorena," a popular song of the day—"Listen to the mocking-bird!"
41. *Petersburg:* June 15–18, 1864, a Confederate victory.

Page 185

5. *Marse Robert:* Robert E. Lee.
  Old Jack: Stonewall Jackson.
6. *march like Moses:* In the Book of Exodus (q.v.) Moses led the Jews out of Egypt to the land of Canaan.
10. *To the Wilderness:* Battle of the Wilderness, May 5–7, 1864.
11. *To Appomattox:* Surrender of the Confederates, April 9, 1865.
22. *Stuart of Laurel Hill:* James E. B. Stuart (1833–64) is celebrated for his services to the Confederates. Among his chief exploits are a night attack in August, 1862, when General Pope's papers were captured, and a raid across the Potomac in the same year. He was killed at Yellow Tavern near Richmond.
25. *panache:* Swagger.
36. *Sheridan:* Philip H. Sheridan, cavalry leader with Grant. He cut off Lee's further retreat at Appomattox Court House.
37. *Pelham's guns:* John C. Pelham, a young West Pointer with Jeb Stuart. He was with the artillery and was one of the bravest of the Confederate leaders.

Page 186

1. *A. P. Hill:* In June, 1862, Generals A. P. Hill and Longstreet crossed the Chickahominy and attacked the Union right at Mechanicsville. Hill was wounded at Chancellorsville and his command was taken by Stuart. He was killed at Petersburg in the last year of the war.

4. *"Dutch" Longstreet:* General James S. Longstreet, a Confederate leader throughout the war, was severely wounded at Antietam and in the Battle of the Wilderness, May, 1864. He recovered in time to direct the defense at Petersburg.

10. *D. H. Hill:* General Daniel H. Hill, Confederate general at Malvern Hill. His many comments and letters reveal his deep resentment at the fall of the Confederacy.
Fitzhugh Lee: Lee's nephew. He conducted an attack which forced Sheridan to retreat from Five Forks.

11. *Hood . . . empty sleeve:* General John Bell Hood supplanted John‑ston in the summer of 1864 and made a fierce attack upon Sherman as he was moving down to Atlanta. In December of the same year he was defeated by Thomas at Nashville.

13. *berserk:* Frenzied, enraged.

17. *Ney:* Marshal of France who earned from the army under Napoleon and from Napoleon himself the title of the bravest of the brave. He commanded the Old Guard at Waterloo.

22. *The Army of the Valley:* A reference to Jackson's forces in the Shenandoah in the spring of 1862. Jackson's mission there was to prevent the sending of reinforcements to the Army of the Potomac, then besieging Richmond. As a result of Jackson's victories in the Shenandoah Washington felt itself to be threatened. Jackson's sol‑diers, who frequently made forced marches of unusual distance, were spoken of as "foot cavalry."

32. *frumenty:* Wheat boiled with milk.

Page 187

2–3. *Cromwell's short / Bleak remedy:* Oliver Cromwell, Lord Protector of England, Ireland, and Scotland (1653) was not one to delay with traitors or malcontents. His remedy was death.

10. *It glitters in his last words:* "Let us cross the river," he said, "and rest under the shade of the trees."

15. *vicegerent:* One deputed by a superior (here, the Lord) to exercise authority.

32. *The Bible . . . Maxims:* Jackson carried both books with him always.

33. *magic lemon:* Jackson also carried lemons with him when he could, frequently sucking one in moments of action.

35. *Traveller:* In a letter after the war, Lee writes of Traveller: "Trav‑eller was a 'Confederate grey.' He carried me through the Seven Days' battle around Richmond, the second Manassas, at Sharpsburg, Fredericksburg, the last day at Chancellorsville, at Gettysburg, and bore me to the final days at Appomattox Court House."

Page 190

19. *It is well that war:* This remark was made at the Battle of Fredericks‑burg on December 13, 1862, when Burnside, attacking Lee's army, was beaten with terrible loss.

23. *laconic:* Concise, pointed.

Page 192

line

18. *caissons:* Ammunition wagons.

Page 193

4. *Clydesdale horse:* A breed of heavy draft horses originally from Clydesdale, Scotland. Here used figuratively.

Page 194

3. *A Union spy never caught:* Elizabeth L. Van Lew.

Page 195

16. *Seven Days:* McClellan had formed the design of returning to a point on the James River below Richmond. Before the movement could begin, Lee, on June 25, had struck the right wing of the Union Army at Oak Grove. The next day the tide turned and at Mechanicsville the Union Army was victorious. On the day following, Lee renewed the struggle at Gaines's Mill and came out victorious. On June 29, McClellan attacked at Savage's Station and again in the White Oak swamp. Following an attack at Frazier's Farm, the Union Army gathered for a final stand at Malvern Hill, twelve miles below Richmond. In the final battle on July 1—the end of the "seven days"— the Union forces retreated to Harrison's Landing unaware that the victory lay with them.

28. *Malvern Hill:* Lee attacked McClellan at Malvern Hill on July 1, 1862, and was driven back with severe losses.

33. *Halleck:* General H. W. Halleck was in command of the Army of the West, with headquarters at St. Louis. In 1862 he was called to Washington to aid the Army of the Potomac, and following McClellan's removal, was made commander in chief of the armies of the Union.

Page 196

23. *He has written Lincoln:* McClellan himself handed the letter to Lincoln when he reached Harrison's Landing. In it McClellan gave his ideas on how the country ought to be run. He wrote to his wife that he had written a strong, frank letter to the President. "If he acts upon it the country will be saved."

Page 197

12. *to recall McClellan's army:* On the night of November 7, 1862, a message was delivered to McClellan relieving him of command of the Army of the Potomac and ordering him to turn it over to Burnside.

Page 198

38. *He had lost a piece of himself:* This recalls his feeling at Shiloh.

line
16. *It happened at Bull Run:* Bailey reports the Second Battle of Bull Run. But to Ellyat, in prison camp, time has ceased to mean anything.
21. *Pope's army's ruined:* Pope, who was given command of McClellan's army after the Seven Days' Battle, was defeated by Lee and Jackson at the Second Battle of Bull Run and compelled to fall back on Washington.
28. *Little Mac:* McClellan.

Page 200

12. *I've got a girl:* Melora.
13. *I left her back in a tent:* Ellyat's regret for Melora and his feeling of "something lost" in himself become curiously confused here.

Page 202

7. *slug-riddled:* Pierced with many bullets.
28. *Go down, John Brown:* Note the suggestion of the spiritual:

> Go down, Moses
> Way down in Egypt's land
> Tell ole Pharoah
> To let my people go. . . .

BOOK FIVE

Page 205

1. *that September:* 1862.
3. *desiccate:* Shriveling heat, intensely dry.
30. *trapped invading Maryland:* Lee's army captured in succession Frederick and Hagerstown, Maryland. After these victories Lee suffered defeat at South Mountain. At Antietam Creek the outcome was a drawn battle, which forced Lee to withdraw from the field.

Page 206

10. *Sharpsburg:* McClellan's army took a strong position here, while Lee's army fell back to Antietam Creek.
14. *Stanton:* Edwin McMasters Stanton, Secretary of War in Lincoln's Cabinet.
   Halleck: Henry W. Halleck was at this time serving as general in chief of the whole land forces of the United States, with headquarters in Washington.
22. *Bull Run* (Virginia): The scene of terrible fighting on August 28-29, 1862, with the Confederates victorious.

line

7. *Prayers From Twenty Million Souls:* In the New York *Tribune* for August 19, 1862, Horace Greeley, speaking for twenty million people as he assumed, issued the Prayer of Twenty Million. It was the most dramatic scolding publicly given the President.
32. *I mean to save the Union:* These sentiments he expressed in his reply to Horace Greeley, dated August 22, 1862.

Page 208

18. *Sangamon:* The name of a county and a river in Illinois where Lincoln lived in 1832.
34. *that lost grave:* Grave of Ann Rutledge, Lincoln's first love.

Page 209

1. *my hat:* The famous stove-pipe hat.
5. *Billy Herndon:* Lincoln's close friend and law partner. Later his biographer.

Page 210

1. *hypo:* Short for "hypochondria." Lincoln referred to his fits of moodiness and dejection as "the hypo"—probably a well-known phrase at the time. Note its parallel with the English phrase, "I'm feeling hipped."
25. *Elysium:* State of ideal delight and happiness.

Page 211

16. *Three elements:* Early philosophers recognized four elements, earth, water, fire, and air, as the substances of which the physical universe is composed.

Page 212

29. *I am that old, deaf hunting-dog:* Compare the figure used here with that in Francis Thompson's poem, "The Hound of Heaven."

Page 213

34-35. *I read / My proclamation:* On August 22, 1862, Lincoln submitted to his Cabinet a draft of the Emancipation Proclamation substantially as it was later issued.

Page 214

4. *With our defeats in everybody's mouth:* May, June, July, and August, 1862, brought disaster and discouragement to the Union forces.

Page 215

line

7. *If this last battle is a victory:* The Battle of Antietam September 16–17, 1862, was a drawn battle, with terrific losses for both sides, but after it Lee retired from Maryland, recrossing the Potomac with his plans for invading Pennsylvania completely altered. On September 22, 1862, Lincoln issued a preliminary proclamation of emancipation.

20–21. *If McClellan / Can only follow up the victory now:* McClellan did not do so. Only on the imperative order of the President did the Union army cross the Potomac, six weeks after the Battle of Antietam. Its pursuit of Lee was slow. McClellan having lost the confidence of both the President and General Halleck, General Burnside was given the command of the Union forces.

Page 216

19. *pot-licker:* Liquid left from boiling a hog's jowl with greens.
20. *smidgin':* A tiny portion.
    shote: A young hog.

Page 219

10. *the mule and the coal-black gal:* This represents Spade's idea of happiness—a home of his own and the means to support it.

Page 223

26. *wasp-paper:* A wasps' nest resembles a plump bag of grayish paper. The insects often build their nests on the eaves or on the supports near a barn door.

Page 226

12. *Garrison, Beecher:* William Lloyd Garrison and Henry Ward Beecher were famous Abolitionists.
13. *Courageous . . . Sumner:* Charles Sumner (1811–74) was a statesman and orator ardently opposed to the extension of slavery in the territories. He was violently assaulted by a member of the Congress while at his desk in the Senate, and his health was enfeebled as a result.
15. *Wendell Phillips, Antinous of Harvard:* Wendell Phillips, a graduate of Harvard, was the principal orator of the Antislavery party. He was the loyal ally of Garrison in his support of Abolition. His eloquence as an orator ranked him with Clay, Webster, Patrick Henry. In being a "distinguished son" of Harvard with special gift of oratory he resembled the youth Antinous, favorite of the Emperor Hadrian, who raised him to the rank of a god, possessed of special attributes.
37. *Yancey:* William Lowndes Yancey (1814–63), Southern political leader who led the Southern withdrawal from the Democratic convention and split the party, thus permitting a Republican victory. A brilliant orator and an extremist in the cause of the South, he was potent in the secession movement.

Page 227

line

17. *Lancashire spinners:* Spinners of Lancashire, England, loyally supported Lincoln and the Union despite the misery occasioned by the Union blockade of Southern cotton.

23. *Slidell . . . Mason:* John Slidell and James M. Mason were commissioners from the Confederate States to Great Britain and France. They were the chief characters in the celebrated *Trent* affair.

    Huse: Major Caleb Huse, with James D. Bullock, was dispatched to England in 1861 to buy arms for the Confederacy. On two occasions he successfully ran the Union blockade.

24. *a cold breath blows through the rooms with the chandeliers:* See the note for page 117. Napoleon III begins to doubt the success of the Southern cause.

34. *Burnside:* Ambrose Everett Burnside was a graduate of West Point, commanded a brigade at Bull Run, and rendered important services at South Mountain and at Antietam. In November, 1862, he reluctantly superseded McClellan as general of the Army of the Potomac. He felt himself unfitted to take charge of such large numbers of men. In December, 1862, he crossed the Rappahannock and attacked Lee near Fredericksburg, but was defeated with a loss of 12,000 men. It was at this battle that the Confederate soldiers fired from behind a stone wall with such disastrous effect.

Page 228

18. *Joe Hooker:* A graduate of West Point, he fought under McClellan on the peninsula and in northern Virginia and Maryland. Known as "Fighting Joe Hooker," he was made commander of the Army of the Potomac in January, 1863.

Page 229

3. *Andersonvillers:*
   Castle Thunder men:
4. *Camp Morton:*
7. *Salisbury and Belle Isle:*
8. *Elmira . . . Libby tunnellers:*

These are references to the prisoners in Confederate and Union prisons. Libby Prison and Castle Thunder were in the city of Richmond. Tales of the hardships suffered by the prisoners were published serially in the Toledo *Blade*, 1879. See Walt Whitman, *Specimen Days in America* (Dutton ed., 1906), pp. 104-5.

Page 230

6. *Haman:* See note for page 151.

Page 233

33-34. *So might meet . . . oar:* Possibly boats on the River Styx.

BOOK SIX

Page 237

22. *A big old man with a raccoon tail:* The Southern Negro's counterpart of the Northern Santa Claus.
32. *shootin' off caps:* Christmas in the South is celebrated with firecrackers and fireworks.

Page 238

19. *"I done my bes'"*: Cudjo has resorted to all the conjuring tricks he knows to offset the evil that has come to the land he loves.

Page 242

33. *Like a sending out of the Scaean Gate:* The comparison is to the Trojan heroes going out to fight.
34. *intaglio* (in-tal-yo): An engraved or incised figure in stone or other hard material. The figure or design is depressed below the surface of the material; normal elevations of the design are hollowed out.
35-36. *Iliad . . . Troy:* Homer's Iliad is the story of the Trojan war, when for ten years Troy (Ilium) was besieged by the Greeks.
Virginia's Iliad: The story of the siege of Richmond, the protected city of the South. The aim of the Union forces was to effect the fall of Richmond; that of the Confederates, to defend the city against such an eventuality.

Page 243

10. *piquet:* A card game somewhat like euchre.
dog-eared pack: A much worn pack of cards.
28. *Minie-ball:* A kind of conical rifle bullet.

Page 244

9. *Columbiads:* A kind of cannon.

Page 248

29. *alchemics:* Men with powers to transform the commonplace into something precious.

Page 249

14. *flagellating:* Scourging.

Page 252

11. *scut:* The short, erect tail of a rabbit or a hare. Victory is here personified as the quarry pursued by the dogs.

line
15-16. *When the gold has peeled from the man on the gilded horse / Riding Fifth Avenue:* A reference to the commemorative statue of General Sherman on horseback on Fifth Avenue in New York City.
21. *railway-station tombs:* A reference to the type of memorial building which houses Grant's tomb on Riverside Drive, New York City. The story of two famous men who were too big for the petty jealousies which are only too common among men in public life would be a more fitting memorial to both Grant and Sherman, in the poet's opinion.

Page 253

18. *lagnappe* (lan-yap): In Louisiana, a trifling present given to customers by tradesmen; *lagnappe days*—days of plenty.

Page 254

33. *Laramie:* A town in Wyoming settled largely by people from New England, Michigan, Wisconsin, and Iowa in 1868.
40. *A moth of a woman shut in a garden:* Emily Dickinson, a recluse and a poet who lived in Amherst, Massachusetts.

Page 255

4. *Higginson:* See note for page 24. Higginson also served as a colonel of colored troops. It was he who first recognized Emily Dickinson's genius. He became her literary adviser and confidant.
7-8. *A man / Dreams of a sky machine:* Perhaps Darius Green, the hero of the humorous poem "Darius Green and His Flying Machine," written in 1869 by John T. Trowbridge.
13. *Charter a railroad:* During Lincoln's administration, the Union Pacific, the first transcontinental railroad, was chartered.
14. *iron horse:* The first steam locomotive was so called.
15. *whiskered doctor:* Dr. I. P. Semmelweis, of Vienna and Pest (1818–65), devoted his health and fortune to discovering the causes of puerperal fever. It was due to his efforts that the mortality rate of women in childbirth was reduced from 16 per cent to less than 1 per cent in the hospitals under his care.

Page 256

37. *the Chaldees:* The people of ancient Babylonia, famed for their magic and occult learnings.
38. *Minoan:* Pertaining to the people of ancient Crete, noted for their language written in a linear script which has not yet been satisfactorily deciphered.

Page 267

10-11. *fired upon in the night / By his own men:* Jackson was fatally wounded during the Battle of Chancellorsville in May, 1863, under the circumstances here recounted.
30. *Lee's gracious way:* Lee's tribute to General Jackson, his "right hand," most trusted and most brilliant subordinate.

404

BOOK SEVEN

Page 271

line

23. *my boyhood:* The boyhood of the poet, Stephen Vincent Benét.

27. *Penn stood under his oak:* William Penn (1644-1718), founder of Pennsylvania in 1682, entered into a treaty of perpetual friendship with the Indians.

sachem: A chief among the North American Indians. Paint was a sign of ceremonial dress.

34-35. *scenes from Paul and Virginia:* A romance written in 1788 by Bernardin de Saint-Pierre whose chief characters are a pair of innocent young lovers.

Page 272

4. *buckeyes:* A variety of the horse chestnut.

5. *herring-boned:* Arranged to resemble the spine of a herring—in rows of parallel lines which in any two successive rows slope in reverse directions.

37. *His siege has begun:* Grant's siege of Vicksburg was one of the great achievements of the Union forces. Begun on May 18, 1863, the siege ended with the surrender of Vicksburg on July 4, 1863.

Page 273

14. *watchers oversea:* England, France and Russia. There was a strong belief abroad that the Union cause could not triumph. The British vacillated between intervention and neutrality. The victories of Vicksburg and Gettysburg gave Europe pause, however.

19. *Laird rams almost alter the scheme of things:* The shipping firm of Lairds in England was building two steam iron-clad rams (warships) for the Confederates. Through the unremitting efforts of Charles Francis Adams, Minister to England from Washington, the British government, officially neutral, prevented the warships from sailing when once convinced that there was strong probability that these gunboats were intended "to carry on hostilities against the Federal government." The seizure of the rams by the British government before they could sail was a serious blow to the Confederate cause, since with them the Confederates could undoubtedly have broken the Union blockade.

30. *Four years from Harper's Ferry:* This makes the date 1863. The raid on Harper's Ferry took place on October 16, 1859.

Page 274

21. *broken three blue commanders:* Pope, after the Second Battle of Bull Run, September 2, 1862; Burnside, after Fredericksburg, December, 1862; Hooker, some time after Chancellorsville, June 27, 1863.

line
15. *Elbow-rubbing Halleck:* The epithet is used because of the habit of "scratching his elbows" General Halleck is said to have had.
18. *Sherman's march . . . to Atlanta:* With three armies Sherman set out on May 6 from Chattanooga, to make progress inch by inch through the heart of the enemy country to Atlanta.
19. *Be ranked by Howard:* Be superseded in rank by Howard.

Pages 275-6

36-5. *Reaches Meade's hut . . . "the damned old goggle-eyed snapping turtle":* General George A. Meade received the following letter from General-in-Chief Halleck: "You will receive with this the order of the President placing you in command of the Army of the Potomac." Meade did not want the place. General Schaff, a friend of Meade, wrote: "I have seen him so cross and ugly that no man dared speak to him." A medical officer complained to Meade that he wanted the soldiers stopped from calling him "old Pills." Meade clapped on his big eyeglasses, glared furiously, and snarled: "Well, what of it? How can I prevent it? Why, I hear that when I rode out the other day some of the men called me 'a damned old goggle-eyed snapping turtle'!"

Page 276

3. *panache:* Swagger.
33. *skein of omen:* The reference is to the yarn held in the hands of the three fates, symbolizing in mythology the span of man's life.
39. *Meade . . . fight:* It was an accidental encounter between Confederate and Union soldiers that precipitated the Battle of Gettysburg. General Meade had selected Pipe Creek, between Baltimore and Taneytown roads, about twelve miles to the south.

Page 278

20. *Buford:* Napoleon Buford, a Union general.
22. *Pettigrew:* A Confederate general whose brigade was practically wiped out after General Pickett's charge.
24. *Hoping to capture shoes:* It is stated authoritatively that in no single campaign could boots be supplied to all Lee's soldiers.
28. *The next morning was July first:* At five o'clock in the morning the Confederates advanced on the Chambersburg Pike and took their position on Herr's Ridge. The Union troops posted themselves on a ridge marked by Stone Avenue.
32. *hill-ridges:* Around Gettysburg were elevations—Herr's Ridge, Seminary Ridge, Cemetery Ridge, Little Round Top, Big Round Top, and Culp's Hill.

Page 282

28. *The Johnnies:* The Confederate soldiers.

Page 283

11. *vedettes:* Mounted sentinels stationed in advance of the pickets to give notice of danger.
28. *Reynolds:* General John F. Reynolds, who in dying urged his men forward.
37. *Hancock:* General Winfield S. Hancock.

Page 286

14. *decalcomania:* Transfer of pictures specially printed to cling to glass or marble surface.
16. *Draw a clumsy fish-hook:* See map.
28. *Cemetery Ridge:* See map.
30. *Seminary Ridge:* See map.
34. *Big Round Top . . . Little Round Top:* See map.

Page 288

7. *fey:* With foreknowledge of death.

Page 289

3. *provost-guard:* A police detail of soldiers under the authority of a provost marshal, an officer appointed to preserve order; the head of the military police.

Page 291

4. *in gasping Iliads:* A long series of attacks and counterattacks.

Page 299

12. *Demurs . . . fight began:* Longstreet differed with his commander and in a conversation at the close of the first day's fight he expressed his opinion that their troops should be placed at Meade's left. Such a position would force Meade to take the offensive because the Confederates would then be placed between the Union Army and Washington. Lee, however, was irritated by the suggestion and refused to consider the plan. "No," he said, "the enemy is there and I am going to attack him."

Page 301

5. *fasces-shape:* In Roman times the fasces was a bundle of rods having among them an ax with the blade projecting. It was borne before Roman magistrates as a symbol of authority.
12. *George Pickett:* General George E. Pickett, in charge of the Virginians under Longstreet's command, is described as a "tall arrow of a man, with his auburn hair flying as he galloped his horse." In his youth he studied law in Quincy, Illinois. There he remembered seeing daily men who tried cases "with the young attorney Abe Lincoln."

line
19. *Cushing:* Alonzo H. Cushing, a Lieutenant in the artillery brigade of the Second Army Corps.
23. *Armistead:* General Armistead in Pickett's charge is described as rushing forward with unyielding determination "to plant the Southern banner on the walls of the enemy."

12–13. *a thing was cracked in his heart:* Pickett's letters to his wife were published in 1913 under the title *The Heart of a Soldier*. His letters written after this engagement reveal his sorrow and despair at the slaughter of his men.

13. *gallinipper:* Mosquito or other stinging or biting insect.

18. *sickling:* A mowing down, as with a sickle, an agricultural implement with a curved metal blade mounted in a handle which sweeps in a half arc as the user wields it. The author means that there was no time for the niceties of warfare or military form.

BOOK EIGHT

15. *Cold Harbor . . . Tavern:* It is said that the fighting at Cold Harbor, two miles from Gaines's Mill, where the Confederates were repulsed in July, 1864, was the worst fighting of the war.
Spottsylvania: On May 17 and 18 the last effort made to force the Southern lines at Spottsylvania failed.
17. *In the Wilderness:* On May 3 the Army of the Potomac left its winter quarters and entered the Wilderness. It camped there a year and a day before Hooker met defeat. The battle between Lee and Grant began. It is said that the infantry of the two armies fought so close to one another and were so impeded by underbrush that there was no room for any military maneuvers and no possibility of using bayonets.
21–22. *Hell's Half Acre:* During the Battle of the Wilderness a fire broke out which burned several hundred helpless wounded.
26. *cyclorama:* Pictorial representation which encircles the spectator.

25. *The siege of Petersburg:* Lee had entered Petersburg at the end of June, 1864.

Page 315

line

4. *In the Shenandoah:* Because of constant raids from the Shenandoah Valley, Grant visited Hunter at Monocacy Bridge, Maryland, and ordered him to push up the valley. In doing so he was to see that "nothing should be left to invite the enemy to return." Hunter asked to be relieved and Sheridan was put in temporary command. "Do all the damage to railroads and crops you can," were Grant's orders. "If the war is to last another year we want the Shenandoah Valley to remain a barren waste." By October 6, 1864, Sheridan reported that he had destroyed over two thousand barns filled with wheat, hay, and farming implements, and over seventy mills filled with wheat and flour; moreover, not less than three thousand sheep had been killed and issued to the army.

Page 316

5. *Plutarch-death:* The death of a hero.
36–37. *Well, I guess they thought . . . crossing a stream:* Lincoln's comment at the news of his renomination.

Page 322

18. *Agamemnon:* King of Mycenae, brother of Menelaus, leader of the Greeks against Troy.
19. *Achilles:* Achilles, hero of *The Iliad,* stands for the Greek ideal of valor. In the opening scene of the epic he is sulking in his tent after a quarrel with Agamemnon.
20. *Œdipus:* It was prophesied that Œdipus of Thebes was to kill his father and marry his mother.

Page 324

8. *cougar:* Mountain lion or panther.

Page 325

2. *maverick:* Outside the herd; unbranded by the owner's mark—here used figuratively.
24. *a fable of their journeying:* Rumors of John Vilas made up by the country people.

Page 326

14–16. *"Old Dan Tucker" . . . cruel Barbara Allen:* Popular ballads.
28–29. *"Lord Randall" . . . "Jay Gould's Daughter":* Characters in popular ballads.
34. *keens:* Weeps, mourns.
grave of Jesse James: Of the many ballad characters mentioned in this passage perhaps the two best known are Barbara Allen and Jesse James:

Jesse James was a man, and he had a robber band
And he flagged down the eastern-bound train,
Robert Ford watched his eye, and he shot him on the sly
And they laid Jesse James in his grave.

In real life Jesse James was an American outlaw, born in Clay County,
Missouri, where his father, a Baptist preacher, owned a farm. The
family was Southern in its sympathies during the Civil War, and as
a consequence was most unpopular with the Union neighbors. Jesse
James joined Mantrell's guerrillas and soon earned a name for reckless daring. At the conclusion of the war he surrendered, and des-
perately wounded, returned to his old home. In 1866, however, he
was outlawed and from that time was pursued by the law. His
crimes were for the most part bank or train robberies. Two members
of his own band, Robert and Charles Ford, tempted by a reward
of ten thousand dollars for his capture, dead or alive, killed him.

Barbara Allen, a purely fictitious character, is sung in many ver-
sions:

In Scarlet Town, where I was born
There was a fair maid dwellin'
Made every youth cry well-a-way!
Her name was Barbara Allen.

line
35. *lone prairie:* The reference is to the familiar "Bury me . . . on the lone
prairie."

Page 327

4. *waif ballad:* Without "literary" parentage.
20-21. *Dedalus / On the first wings:* Dedalus and his son Icarus were confined in the Labyrinth near Cnosus because Dedalus had given
Ariadne the clue with which she guided Theseus through the maze.
The father and son succeeded in escaping on wings of wax and
feathers which Dedalus had made. Icarus approached too near the
sun, the wax melted, and he fell into the sea. Dedalus succeeded in
reaching Sicily.

Page 329

3. *patterans:* Colloquial for *patrins*—wood trails laid by the gypsies.

Page 330

34. *Peter Rugg:* He was driving a carriage and swore he'd get home with
or without the will of God. He is still driving. See the story by
William Austin.
36. *Johnny Appleseed:* The name by which John Chapman is known.
He lived from 1775 to 1843, and is remembered because he devoted
his life to scattering apple seeds through the Ohio Valley. Vachel
Lindsay and Edgar Lee Masters have both written poems about him.

line
7–10. *the Spanish lady . . . no word of English but his name:* The ballad,
from Percy's *Reliques,* begins:

Will you hear a Spanish lady,
How shee wooed an English man?

36. *Between a bee-tree and a cast deer-horn:* A bee tree is a hollow tree
in which honeybees have made a nest. The cast deerhorn suggests a
field where deer have roved at will.

Page 333

12. *leftenants:* Lieutenants.

Page 337

10. *Saying or else not saying that war is hell:* Although Sherman himself
denied ever saying that "war is hell," he is supposed to have used the
phrase on at least two occasions: in an address to a G.A.R. convention in 1880; and in speaking to the graduating class of the Michigan
Military Academy, 1879.

Page 339

28. *Sconce:* A bracket candlestick or group of candlesticks secured by a
plaque to the wall.
ladle: A large-sized cuplike spoon with a curved handle, used for
dipping.
29. *With the English mark . . . weight:* English mark is also called hall-
mark, and is the official mark of the Goldsmiths' Company stamped
on gold and silver articles at Goldsmiths' Hall in London to attest
to their purity.

Page 349

24. *crotchet:* A quarter note in music.

Page 351

7. *shivaree:* Colloquial for *charivari,* a mock serenade of discordant
noises.

Page 353

10–11. *The liquor spills on the cobbles:* Compare the poet's passage with a
similar scene in Dickens's *A Tale of Two Cities.*
26. *On the way to Appomattox:* The remnant of the Confederate Army
continues to fight in spite of the fact that the situation is hopeless.
31. *to wear his chains:* Davis was captured and imprisoned in Fortress
Monroe.

38–39. *One day . . . gone:* His biographer tells us that Benjamin went to London where he was, until his death, one of the most successful and respected of barristers.

39. *as if he had taken fernseed:* The old tradition is that anyone who eats fernseed or puts it in his shoes immediately becomes invisible.

Page 354

11. *Ord's whole corps:* General Ord was among those who attended Grant at Appomattox.

30. *His men will need their horses for the spring-ploughing:* The conversation between Grant and Lee is retold in Douglas Southall Freeman's *Biography of Robert E. Lee.*

Page 356

34. *forage-cap:* A small, low head covering of an officer or soldier, now called *service cap* or *service hat.*

39. *de Crater:* Spade is referring to an enormous dynamite mine sprung at Petersburg which shot some two hundred Confederate troops into the air and buried some of them alive. It demolished the Confederate trenches and left a huge crater into which Union troops marched. The Confederates made a quick recovery and soon had artillery at the crater's edge playing on a disordered, helpless mass of Union troops.

Page 360

30. *Edmund Ruffin:* Ruffin, an historical character, was wholeheartedly with the Confederate cause. When he knew that cause was lost he took his life.

Page 361

11. *an old dream:* Lincoln believed in dreams having validity for himself and others. In Carl Sandburg's *Abraham Lincoln: The War Years,* Vol. IV, pp. 243-45, Lincoln recounts an ominous dream of April, 1865. The dream of which Benét writes here is told in detail on p. 265 of Vol. IV. Lincoln said that this dream of the vessel, "moving with great rapidly toward an indefinite shore," had preceded many of the great events of the war.

26–27. *Knocking on wood . . . Friday:* Popular superstitions about luck which persist even today.

Page 362

3. *Johnston has surrendered:* Johnston surrendered to Sherman at Durham Station, North Carolina, April 26, 1865.

line

26. *centaurs:* A mythical race of Thessaly conceived as half man, half horse.

39. *foray:* A raid; a sudden incursion.

6. *The Hamiltonian extremes:* Alexander Hamilton (1757–1804) was an American statesman and financier, the leader of the Federalist party, whose adherents were in favor of centralized government.

the Franklin mean: Benjamin Franklin (1706–90) was one of the early American diplomats. It was he who induced the French to form an alliance with the colonies, an alliance which eventually was responsible for England's recognition of their independence. Franklin was of the opinion that two nations "would better throw dice than fight out a dispute."

QUESTIONS AND SUGGESTIONS

THE INVOCATION

1. Review briefly the history of the growth of the United States.
2. Show how the frontier was pushed farther and farther west.
3. What stanzas suggest the Colonial period? the Revolutionary period? modern America?
4. What different symbols are chosen to represent typical American scenes?
5. What does the poet mean by:

> "In your *Long House* there is an *attic-place* . . ."
> The *patchwork colors* . . ."
> "One slant ray of quick, American light . . ."

and the final couplet:

> "If not—the *dry bones* littered by the way
> May still point *giants* toward *their golden prey*."

6. Plan a pictorial map based on the Invocation, showing the chronological acquisition of territory, and indicating some of the characteristic features: Indian arrow, prairie schooners, skyscrapers, and the like.
7. Can you find other poems or prose passages which might aid you in understanding the American spirit? Carl Sandburg and James Truslow Adams may help you.

THE SLAVER

1. What characteristics of the captain are revealed? What of the mate?
2. What pictures of the "cargo" are given? What two slaves stand out in your mind?
3. Why does the captain speak of the Arabs as selling "pennyweight" kings?
4. Why was the mate reluctant to "take another 'look-see'"?
5. How could a few of the slaves know English?
6. In the conversation between the captain and the mate what biographical information do you gather? Where did each come from? How do you know?
7. Read the chanty aloud. What is the effect? Read the spiritual aloud. What contrast do you note in rhythm and tone?
8. In what way does the Prologue prepare you for the epic which follows? Does it set the tone? Is it informational?
9. With what feeling do you turn to the story which follows?

1. Note the abrupt way in which the story opens, yet how quickly you become acquainted with Jack Ellyat. What traits of character does he show? Do you like him? What is his attitude toward his dog? What is his frame of mind?
2. In what state does Jack Ellyat live? What time of year does the poet describe? What colorful pictures, what figures, what specific details are given to stir your imagination?
3. Compare this picture of the dog with russet paws, bewitched by the twilight, with a more detailed picture of a dog with silver paws, bewitched by the moonlight, in the poem "Silver" by Walter de la Mare.
4. What lines suggest coming disaster? How do we know that Jack Ellyat senses the storm which threatens?
5. Read carefully the little song of his thoughts.
6. What is the allegory of the thirteen sisters, the house they built, the black ghost that haunts it? What relation have the words in parentheses to the other lines in each stanza of the song? Select a classmate and try reading the poem aloud—one telling the story; the other reading the refrain.
7. As Jack continues his reflections, note the vivid images of the New West and the Old South that crowd his thoughts. What lines are especially rich in imagery?
8. What is his feeling toward abolition and a fight to secure it?
9. What is the force of the three "Meanwhiles"?
10. What pictures of the Wingate family and their ancestral home in Georgia are given? What characteristics distinguish the Wingates as a family? Note particularly the contrast between the characters of John the Second and Elspeth Mackay. What was Elspeth's contribution to Wingate fame? What traits of character did she bequeath to her son?
11. Characterize Clay Wingate. Which family traits reappear in him?
12. Note the picture of Georgia in autumn. What colorful pictures, figures, and details make the season vivid to Clay Wingate? Note how inseparable are horse and rider.
13. Clay, too, hears the footbeats of unseen cavalry riding the wind. What does this sensitivity signify? What does it tell you of the young man himself?
14. In your opinion, is this symbol of horses appropriate?
15. Two moving forces—Jack Ellyat from the North; Clay Wingate from the South—have been introduced, and their probable actions in the event of a clash over the issue of slavery have been hinted at. Now is introduced, the third moving force in the coming struggle—John Brown—first, through his prayer; second, through the raid at Harper's Ferry. What does his prayer reveal of his character, his aspirations, his attitude toward what he believes is destiny? The raid at Harper's Ferry is historic. Know the facts; then read the human account given here. What insight into the minds and motives and attitudes of the various people caught up in this crisis do the events of the raid afford us? Consider, for instance, Shepherd Heyward, Patrick Higgins, Dangerfield Newby, Fontaine Beckham, Mr. Brua, Lee of Virginia, John Brown, the slaves of Colonel Washington.

16. Characterize Cudjo. What special faculty had he as compensation for his inability to read and write? What qualities fit him to be major-domo of Wingate Hall?

17. What contrasting traits meet in the character of Sally Dupré? Do you like her? What is the attitude of the Appleton family toward Sue Appleton's daughter? What in her inheritance from her father do they fear?

18. What is Cudjo's feeling about the rumors he has heard about John Brown and the raid at Harper's Ferry?

19. As Sally and Clay sit out a dance for a few moments, each secretly ponders—across the snatches of light conversation—the attraction felt for the other. What do these secret comments and desires reveal of Sally and Clay?

20. What is the effect on Jack Ellyat of the humdrum scene in his family sitting room? What is his mood? To what extent can you understand and sympathize with it? What breaks the monotony of the routine of his home? Which lines express his realization of coming change? What is the reaction of the Ellyats to the news of the raid at Harper's Ferry and of John Brown's fate?

21. What vivid images, specific details, personal recollections does the poet give of market days and the courthouse in the square of a Southern town which he knew as a boy? In what way does the poet make this picture come alive for you? As a boy, what scenes within the courtroom did he perhaps witness from the courthouse windows? What held in check the "quiet men fit to turn mob" during some of the critical moments at a trial?

22. Against the unchanging background of the courtroom scene, place the details of the John Brown trial. What are the facts about his career known to all? To what extent is it true that "all he did consistently was fail"?

23. Explain:

> . . . whooped along to death
> By those who do not violence themselves
> But only buy the guns to have it done.

24. What can be said in his defense? What can be said against him?
25. Explain what the poet implies in the lines:

> You can weigh John Brown's body well enough,
> But how and in what balance weigh John Brown?

26. Read the last words of the prisoner at the bar. What impression of the man do they give? Which lines most vividly reveal his personality? What does his final statement regarding those who "had been induced to join him" reveal of him and of them?

27. What is the poet's opinion of Dr. Howe, Gerrit Smith, Dr. Higginson?

28. Why was it true that Brown was worth infinitely more to the cause "to die than to live"? In what way is it true that he knew how to die? What details of the ride to his execution are revealing of the man's caliber? Note the words, "This *is* a beautiful country."

29. Why did the North begin to deify John Brown? Contrast with this scene of John Brown's last moments the words of Colonel Preston.

30. The Prioress in *The Canterbury Tales* tells the story of a little boy who was murdered and cast into a pit. The mother sought for him vainly and finally found herself near the pit, drawn to it by the small clear voice of the murdered child singing. The murderers were punished according to the law and the child was buried in consecrated ground. From thence comes the legend of "the singing bones." What use of the old legend does the poet make here?

BOOK II

1. What qualities of Jefferson Davis are revealed through the discerning eyes of his Cabinet member, Judah P. Benjamin?
2. Why are Benjamin's feelings toward the South and Jefferson Davis peculiarly sympathetic? Why is he able to understand Davis so well?
3. Characterize the personality and character of Judah P. Benjamin. What lines suggest that he, too, like Wingate and Ellyat, has "second sight" and the gift of prophecy?
4. What details build an impression of the character of Abraham Lincoln? What strange contrasts are mentioned? What details are "homely" ones?
5. We see Lincoln's Cabinet through his own shrewd eyes. What is his estimate of Seward and of Chase? What is the particular contribution each made to Lincoln's Cabinet? What were Lincoln's personal relations to each? What does Lincoln's attitude toward these men reveal of his own character? What is the force of his musing about himself and Jefferson Davis?
6. Note the historic incidents which link the various episodes in this section. Give in each case a reason for the introduction. Begin to list the historic names. Some you will recognize immediately; others you must investigate. Know some fact about each which makes the inclusion necessary.
7. Note how the poet successfully pictures the groping on the part of Ellyat, Wingate, the slaves, Jake Diefer, and the Southern mountaineers to understand the underlying causes of the war and to reconcile war itself with their philosophies of life.
8. *Off to War—a kaleidoscope:* A company in blue marches to the train; Jack Ellyat goes to war. Comment on the poet's use of musings, snatches of conversation, flashes of imagery, to recapture the moment and spirit of a crisis.
9. Why are the three months' men at Centerville, Shippy, and Judith Henry introduced?
10. The battle rages around Henry House. Discuss briefly with diagrams the terrain, the plan of attack, the leaders, the attack itself, the outcome.
11. Contrast Jack Ellyat's thoughts, as the battle of Bull Run begins, with those of Luke Breckinridge.
12. Note how "Stonewall" Jackson earns his epithet.
13. Give a brief pen picture of the Georgia troops waiting to be picked up by Beauregard.
14. Contrast the two views of the battle from the eyes of Curly Hatton and Jack Ellyat.

15. *The Union Army in Retreat:* Which lines paint the "human" side of the retreat? Which are most successful in leaving an indelible impression of that far-off time on your mind?
16. Three important people react to the acid of defeat: Walt Whitman, Horace Greeley, Abraham Lincoln. What is the reaction of each one? What does it reveal of his character, his breadth of view, his sympathy, his power of constructive action? Comment upon the figurative language used in describing these three men. Which figures are appropriate, vivid, rich in association?
17. Interpret, in relation to the events in Book II, the line: "The stone falls in the pool; the ripples spread."

BOOK III

1. Where is Pittsburg Landing? What details describe the surrounding country?
2. Follow Jack Ellyat's fortunes since we last heard of him. What is the basis for his homesickness? What points of difference between him and his fellow soldiers from Illinois make him feel he is among aliens?
3. Note the pen pictures of generals whom Ellyat has known. What are the traits of character of Sherman? McClellan? Give a thumbnail sketch of the achievements of each in the Civil War.
4. What was the early history of Ulysses S. Grant? What was there ironic in his early military career?
5. Give briefly the facts of the part played in the war by Forts Henry and Donelson; the "brief siege"; the "unconditional surrender."
6. Explain what "lone hissing fuse" was lighted by Captain Wilkes. How and why did Lincoln and Seward stamp it out?
7. Note the brief history of the world's ships covered in fifteen lines by the poet. Compare the passage with Masefield's 'Cargoes." Note the beauty and force of the imagery which describes the last sailing of the phantom fleet.
8. Events in America find repercussions abroad. Explain more fully the brief notations given in the lines of the poem.
9. What is the significance of Ellyat's not dreaming of Grant or Lee or Lincoln, but dreaming only that he is at home again?
10. Locate on a map the chief places in the war in the West. Locate the opposing forces and give the objectives set by each.
11. Read carefully the pen picture of General Albert Sidney Johnston of the Confederate Army.
12. What in the account of Ellyat's being taken prisoner and his escape is noteworthy? Select lines which are most significant.
13. What is the background of Melora Vilas and her family? Why are they introduced into the narrative? What do the names given to the hogs reveal of this background?
14. Note the details of the picture of Melora hog-calling. What reference to classical mythology lies in the lines which describe the effect of Melora's "call" on Jack Ellyat?
15. What is dramatic about the meeting of Melora and Ellyat?
16. Select two or three of your classmates for a choral interpretation of the poem, "This is the hidden place that hiders know."

17. What characteristics of Melora's mother and father is the poet careful to give? Why? How do you reconcile the characteristics with the fact that these people are "hiders"? What traits in Melora are emphasized? Does it seem natural for Jack and Melora to fall in love?
18. How does it happen that Jack Ellyat is captured again?

BOOK IV

1. Note the recurrence of the rhythm associated with the Wingates and their fortunes.
2. The picture of life in the far South under blockade conditions is vividly drawn. What do you consider significant details?
3. Note how the rumors of war affect the Wingate slaves. What characteristics of the Wingate plantation Negroes are stressed in the lines expressing their interest on the return of Marse Billy?
4. The portrait of Aunt Bess, "the family-despot and the slave," epitomizes a relationship that was characteristic of the old South. Explain what this relationship was and account for it. What are Aunt Bess's chief traits of character?
5. Are Cudjo and Aunt Bess typical of the Southern Negro on the larger plantations? In what respects?
6. Write a brief pen picture of Mary Lou Wingate. Note that the poet depicts her in characteristic actions. Try not to miss the subtlety of some of the lines descriptive of the mistress of Wingate Hall.
7. Note the drama underlying Mary Lou's unawareness that the days of Wingate splendor are numbered and Clay's premonition that "there is only this hour and it goes fast—this is the last."
8. The conversation between Sally Dupré and Clay Wingate as they dance is most revealing. (So were another dance and conversation they had together.) What essential traits of their characters does each reveal in the lines spoken: the motive half revealed, the inconsequential remark hiding thought?
9. What is the basis for the attraction and repulsion they experience?
10. In what play has a modern playwright used this device successfully—portraying character by having the person's secret thoughts made known to the audience or reader at the same time that his words may convey a different impression?
11. Note the prophecy of the fall of Wingate Hall. How does the poet achieve a feeling of doom, and give this feeling reality?
12. Write a character sketch of Lucy Weatherby. Contrast her with Sally Dupré. Explain Lucy's attraction for Clay.
13. The runaway slave is well depicted. What specific details sketch his background, his reaction to the unrest of war, his hopes for the future? Which lines are richest in characterization?
14. The scene where Sally and Lucy bid farewell to the Black Horse Troop is full of hidden drama. Where does the conflict lie? What does Lucy reveal of herself in the conversation she holds with Sally after the men have ridden away?
15. What do Sally's musings and her resolve to make a waxen doll with Lucy's face and name portend?

16. The scene expands; we must look at it as a whole:
    a. Diagram the "Eastern game" and the "Western game."
    b. Characterize in well-rounded sketches the leaders on both sides.
    c. Read to see with discerning eye the details that build impressions of conditions in the North; in the South; the reaction of the people to a year of victories and losses.
    d. What picture is given of conditions of the prison camps?
    e. Note the descriptions of the ordeals of the various armies, both Union and Confederate.
17. Cull epithets that are noteworthy for their terse characterization of men and events.
18. The portraits of Grant and of Lee are remarkably full and vivid. Make a list of the salient traits in the character of each. Which lines are worth remembering?
19. Bring up to date events in the lives of people in whose fortunes we are interested: Jake Diefer, Shippy, Luke Breckinridge, Melora Vilas, Sally Dupré, Clay Wingate, Jack Ellyat.
20. There are scenes which reveal further the characters of McClellan and Lincoln. Discuss the characteristics revealed or corroborated.
21. Why is the influence of John Brown invoked in the last lines of Book IV? Of what at this point is John Brown a symbol?
22. In what sense was this "the dark hour . . . the ebb-tide"?

BOOK V

1. List the details that build an impression of enervating heat. Why does the poet take such pains to paint the background of the Washington scene?
2. What is the Washington scene? The mood of the people? The state of the armies?
3. The figure of Lincoln dominates this book. What trials has he had to endure? What petty vexations harass his days? What has been his guiding principle regarding abolition and the preservation of the Union? What is the immediate situation before him? What do his reflections reveal of his piety, his sympathy for his fellow man, his knowledge of self—his strength and his weakness? What evidence of humility do you find? Of lovableness? Of unselfishness? What evidence is there that Lincoln is a thinker? A practical man? A leader?
4. What bits of homely wisdom does he express?
5. What figures of speech seem most appropriate? Note the figure of the old hunting dog. Does the poet's idea, which this figure expresses, gain in strength and beauty through this comparison, or lose in effectiveness?
6. What news is brought him? How does he know it is good news before he hears it? What is the "if" that looms large in his plans for the future?
7. Spade, the runaway Negro, enters the story again. What other types of Negroes have we met so far? What is Spade's experience? What details appeal to your sense of reality, your fairness, your sympathy?
8. What conditions regarding the plight of "free Negroes" are revealed?
9. Write a character sketch of Spade.
10. What traits of Melora's character are stressed in this book? What lines emphasize that she has touched the "wilderness stone"?

11. The poet gives an "overview" of the period—brief epithets to describe or characterize the work or attitude of many well-known men. Do you agree that they are deserved, in the light of events as you know them?
12. What event was the "turn of the tide"?
13. Who is the new rider for the Army of the Potomac? Briefly give the facts of his career and tell the kind of man he is.
14. The picture of life in the prison camps is necessary to round out the panorama of the war. What impression is given the reader through the impersonal official reports?
15. How does the man or the scene which escapes from the "mummy case" differ from a scene as given in the official reports?
16. Characterize Wirtz as he pleads his own case.
17. What does the poet say is the cause of such conditions and of having such men as Wirtz in power? What excuse does he offer for the persistence of such conditions?
18. How does the scene of the exchange of prisoners make you feel? What details make it take on reality for you?

BOOK VI

1. Note the return to the fortunes of the Wingates and of Wingate Hall in Georgia. Do you recognize the characteristic rhythm? How has the war affected the plantation South, which Wingate Hall typifies? What details build the impression of conditions there?
2. What does the scene gain in vividness from being reported through Cudjo's eyes and words?
3. How has Sally Dupré changed since we first met her? How is she unchanged? What self-revealing remarks does she make?
4. What are the things that Clay Wingate remembers of his wartime experience? Are they what one would think he would remember most vividly?
5. Jack Ellyat at home on furlough looks out on a well-remembered and well-loved scene—winter in New England. What images etch the season in his memory? What comparisons or words are apt and picture-making? Select one especially well-drawn or well-suggested picture and share it with your classmates.
6. What gives the grumbling of the men in winter camps an air of reality?
7. Note the details that serve further to characterize Grant, Joe Hooker, Sherman. Contrast Grant and Serman as men, friends, leaders.
8. Lincoln reviewing troops is a picture that deepens impressions already formed by the reader. What details or instances serve to do so?
9. Describe the rioting in Richmond. What part did Jefferson Davis play on the occasion? What traits of his character are revealed here?
10. Note carefully the "parti-colored quilt of the patchwork States." Explain clearly what the phrase means. What makes the "overview" of the country impressive?
11. Read appreciatively the song of breath. Savor each word, each image, each symbol. What is the impression the poem makes upon you?
12. Shippy's last adventure is a sordid one. How does he conduct himself? At whose hands does he meet his death? What has been his part in the war?

13. Trace the various glimpses we have had of Lucy Weatherby from the time we first met her. What is the keynote to her character and personality? Write a well-rounded sketch of Lucy as she has shown herself to be throughout the war. Is she a type as well as an individual?

14. Review briefly Stonewall Jackson's military career. What was the secret of his success as soldier and general? What was the relationship between him and Lee? From this glimpse of his final hours, what impression do we gain of his character, his philosophy of life? Why was his death a great loss to the South? What is impressive about his final words?

BOOK VII

1. Study the map of the country around Gettysburg. What kind of country is it? What people settled it? What descriptive details as the poet gives them make it live for you?

2. "The South goes North again in the second raid, in the last cast for fortune." Give briefly the facts of the first campaign to invade the North. Why is this second raid a last cast for fortune? What "dip of the balance" does Lee see?

3. What were Lee's plans for attack?

4. How did it come about that the armies clashed at Gettysburg?

5. Follow carefully with a map the location of the opposing forces and the action of the three days of battle.

6. What was Longstreet's part in the battle? What was the Union defense?

7. Recount briefly the impressions of the battle as seen through Jack Ellyat's eyes.

8. What traits do Longstreet and Lee reveal on the third day of battle?

9. What is Pickett's part in the fight? What traits of character does he reveal in a crisis?

10. In Clay Wingate's moment of waiting for the attack to begin he reveals his real feelings for Lucy Weatherby and Sally Dupré. Have his feelings undergone change? What evidence is there that he has gained insight into another's personality?

11. Describe the onrush as Wingate experienced it. Wherein lies the humor of the scene between Bristol and Wingate?

12. Note the details that describe the condition of the Army of Northern Virginia. What is the temper of the men?

13. What foreshadowing is there in the final lines? Note the irony of the fact that the shadow of foreboding falls at the moment when the Southerners feel safest on the Southern side of the Potomac and most in luck— when Meade fails to follow up his advantage.

BOOK VIII

1. Note the plan of the final book. What names, places, events does the poet think it significant to mention? Give the reason for the attention accorded to each.

2. Which details of the bitter Wilderness fighting do you find most dramatic?

3. What is arresting about the details of the final picture of Jefferson Davis?

4. Contrast the popular feeling toward Davis and Lincoln.

423

5. Note the details which make the picture of Lee alone in his tent impressive to his aide-de-camp.
6. He compares Lee and his strong face to that of other leaders of old—Agamemnon, Achilles, Œdipus. What is the force of each comparison?
7. What made the journey of John Vilas and his daughter a fabulous one in the country through which they traveled back to their Eastern home? What was ironic about this return journey for one who had sought the "wilderness stone"? In what respects has his life been a success?
8. The joyous Negro song about Sherman's march tells us of some of the reactions to his historic campaign. What were other conditions that his march caused or heightened? In what sense was the march a "picnic-parade"? Can anything be said in extenuation of the conditions that attended the march from Atlanta to the sea, the cutting of a ruinous swathe?
9. What details help give reality and vividness to the scene from the spectators' points of view? From the Union soldiers'?
10. What has been the fate of Wingate Hall?
11. If you were to draw or paint the scene of Cudjo and Miss Mary Lou burying the family silver, what details would you emphasize? What mood do the lines create?
12. What eerie fantasy does Cudjo know? What incident gave rise to it? Note the introduction of the wind. It is an element with plot significance.
13. Describe the encounter between Bailey and Mary Lou Wingate. How is Mary Lou's attitude toward Bailey in part responsible for the destruction of Wingate Hall?
14. What is the significance for Sally Dupré of the burning of Wingate Hall?
15. What, in the lines which express Clay Wingate's random thoughts about his home, appeals to our sympathy?
16. What is tragic about the challenge to a duel between Shepley and Bristol?
17. What incident interrupts the course of the gentleman's code? What is dramatic about the orders given and the manner in which they are received by the Georgia men?
18. Describe the fighting "as long as a horse or a man can stand."
19. What elements of humor and banter mingle with the tragedy and grimness?
20. Is Wainscott Bristol's end in keeping with his character and background?
21. Describe the last events along the "road which leads to Appomattox"—and ends there: The last stand of the armies; the meeting between Grant and Lee; Lee's final gesture; the release of tension and the joy of the Union generals when it dawns upon them that the war is over at last; the grey ghost-army stacking its arms; the Union salute to a brave enemy; Confederate soldiers tearing bits of cloth from the color staffs and hiding them under their uniforms.
22. Gather up the threads of the story. Relate briefly the final fortunes of each of the men and women in whose destiny we have been interested. Comment upon the feelings of each as he or she "comes home" and accepts—or fails to do so—the necessary readjustment after the excitement of war.

23. Were you turning Melora into a "tale" or a legend, to what well-known story would you liken her?
24. What lines are noteworthy for their poetic beauty, the universal truth expressed, insight into character of individuals and of a people?
25. What is the final impression that the entire poem makes upon you? Has the poet succeeded in his aim to portray the "diverse heart" of America, to show that out of many there is one land and one people? What is John Brown's "justice, after all"?

GENERAL TOPICS FOR RESEARCH AND INVESTIGATION

1. The attitudes of the South toward its slaves.
2. "The South almost won because of its commanders; the North was victorious because of the multiplication of its troops." Can you support this statement with evidence? Do you wish to refute it?
3. The blockade runners.
4. Tales of personal heroism: North and South.
5. Jeb Stuart: romantic cavalry leader.
6. An evaluation of John Brown: a defense or an indictment.
7. Famous remarks attributed to Civil War heroes.
8. A picture of the deep South.
9. Songs and dances of Civil War days.
10. Pen pictures of Lee, Grant, Lincoln, Stonewall Jackson, or other officers.
11. As you read the Invocation, you will note how skillfully the poet portrays the "diverse heart" of the American scene—East and West, North and South. Analyze the descriptive phrases which evoke the scenes (1) of American history, (2) the distinctive character of a locality.
12. Discuss spirituals. Tell their origins and formation. Pick out a few famous ones for illustration. Study the epic *John Brown's Body* carefully. Pick out places where the spiritual influence is evident. Show how you would plan this material for choral work.
12. You have one chanty in the epic. Discuss chanties in similar fashion.
13. Walt Whitman was an eyewitness to many of the scenes mentioned and depicted by your poet. Of John Brown, he says:

> I would sing how an old man, tall, with white hair, mounted the scaffold in Virginia
>
> (I was at hand, silent I stood with teeth shut close, I watched
>
> I stood very near you, old man, when cool and indifferent, but trembling with age and your unheal'd wounds, you mounted the scaffold;)

Find similar instances cited by Whitman and develop a theme which shall bring out Whitman's personality, sympathies, intuition, and accuracy of fact.
14. "Not the Negro, not the saving of the Union, not a defense of States' rights but an economic issue" was the cause of the Civil War. If you believe this statement true, support it by factual evidence; if you disagree, present your own theory, supported by facts.
15. Analyze and show the poetic need for the lyrics in *John Brown's Body*: (1) their place in the narrative; (2) their contribution to the whole.
16. Note the freshness and aptness of the poet's imagery. Point out examples which appeal to you and discuss their poetic value.
17. Investigate the Southern mountaineer stock: our last frontier in (1) ancestry, (2) attitudes, (3) speech.

18. A study of the marching tunes of the Civil War.
19. Lincoln's Cabinet: (1) the personnel, (2) qualifications of members, (3) relationship to Lincoln as man and President, (4) hidden drama.
20. Interesting personalities in Davis's Cabinet.
21. The new era in shipping: Amplify with anecdote and illustration the passage from p. 117, lines 6-11:

> In such a swelling cloud of phantom sail
> They whitened Ocean—going down by the head,
> Green water seeping through the battened ports,
> Spreading along the scrubbed and famous decks,
> Going down—going down—going down—to mermaid-pools,
> To Fiddler's Green—to the dim barnacle-thrones, . . .

22. The shadows of coming events: Indicate somewhat in detail the poet's success and ingenuity in the device of foreshadowing.
23. Discuss the fiction people in the epic. Which ones seem real to you? Which ones shadowy? Point out the characteristic that is emphasized to make each a "story person."
24. The poet speaks of Jack Ellyat's mind-pictures of the conventional ideas of the South. Have you mind-pictures of any section of the United States? How did you get them? Mention stories or poems written about the section you have chosen to show how they support your ideas.
25. Discuss the idea of *epic*. What are some of the great epics? How do they throw light on the various countries which produced them? Suggest other periods or events in American history that have epic possibilities.

BOOKS FOR FURTHER READING

FICTION

Andrews, Mary R. S., *The Perfect Tribute* (New York: Charles Scribner's Sons, 1926).
Lincoln and the Southern soldier after the speech at Gettysburg.

Bacheller, Irving, *A Man for the Ages* (Indianapolis: The Bobbs-Merrill Company, 1919).
Biographical sketch of Lincoln in his youth—some description of the underground railroad.

Boyd, James, *Marching On* (New York: Charles Scribner's Sons, 1927).
The feelings and sentiments of the poor farming class of North Carolina before and during the Civil War.

Bradford, Roark, *Kingdom Coming* (New York: Harper & Brothers, 1933).
Occupation of New Orleans by Union soldiers—attitude of the freed Negroes toward freedom.

Churchill, Winston, *The Crisis* (New York: The Macmillan Company, 1930).
The attitude of the North—portraits of Lincoln, Sherman, Grant—love story of a Northern soldier and a Southern girl.

Colver, Anne, *Listen for the Voices* (New York: Farrar & Rinehart, Inc., 1939).
Story portraying Emerson, Thoreau, the Alcotts, and others of the Concord group.

Crane, Stephen, *The Red Badge of Courage* (New York: D. Appleton-Century Company, 1925).
Report of the Battle of Chancellorsville—reveals the fear and confusion felt by a soldier in his first military engagement.

De Forest, John William, *Miss Ravenal's Conversion from Secession to Loyalty* (New York: Harper & Brothers, 1939).
A novel of New Orleans during the Civil War.

Dowdey, Clifford, *Bugles Blow No More* (Boston: Little, Brown & Company, 1937).
Covers the years from secession to Appomattox with the setting, Richmond.

Ehrlich, Leonard, *God's Angry Man* (New York: Simon and Schuster, 1932).
A story built closely on the biography of John Brown.

Glasgow, Ellen, *The Battle-Ground* (New York: Doubleday, Doran & Company, 1929).
Life in Virginia before secession, following the course of the War.

Heyward, DuBose, *Peter Ashley* (New York: Farrar & Rinehart, Inc., 1932).
Life in Charleston in the 60's—a hero torn between the traditions of the South and his deep love of his country.

Holland, Rupert Sargent, *Sons of Seven Cities* (Philadelphia: Macrae, Smith Co., 1929).
  The story called "Keeper of the Light" throws light on Lincoln's life in Washington.
Johnston, Mary, *The Long Roll* (Boston: Houghton Mifflin Company, 1911).
  First years of the war, ending with the death of Stonewall Jackson.
Johnston, Mary, *Cease Firing* (Boston: Houghton Mifflin Company, 1912).
  Last years of the Civil War from the point of view of the South.
Kantor, MacKinlay, *Long Remember* (New York: Coward-McCann, Inc., 1934).
  Dramatic picture of the Battle of Gettysburg as seen by a noncombatant caught between the two armies.
Leech, Margaret, *Reveille in Washington: 1860-1865* (Boston: Little, Brown & Company, 1941).
  The day-to-day story of life in Washington during the years of the Civil War.
Mitchell, Margaret, *Gone With the Wind* (New York: The Macmillan Company, 1936).
  The story of Scarlett O'Hara, who, after the fall of Atlanta, returned to the plantation and saved her home.
Morrow, Honoré W., *Forever Free* (New York: William Morrow & Company, 1927).
———, *With Malice Toward None* (New York: William Morrow & Company, 1928).
———, *The Last Full Measure* (New York: William Morrow & Company, 1930).
  A trilogy of the Civil War with emphasis on Lincoln.
Scott, Evelyn, *The Wave* (London: Jonathan Cape, Ltd., 1929).
  "Clear facets through which are reflected, in North and South, wild mountain country, Mississippi flatlands, prim New England village, in home, camp, battlefield and hospital, the central fire which is the war itself—"
Twain, Mark (Samuel Clemens), *Life on the Mississippi* (New York: Harper & Brothers, any edition).
  Depicts the siege of Vicksburg.
Young, Stark, *Heaven Trees* (New York: Charles Scribner's Sons, 1926).
  A Mississippi plantation before the war.
Young, Stark, *So Red the Rose* (New York: Charles Scribner's Sons, 1934).
  At the same Mississippi plantation, carries further the pictures of Southern hospitality, touching the war years.

NONFICTION

Battles and Leaders of the Civil War (New York: The Century Company, 1884-87, 4 vols.).
  Contributions are by Union and Confederate officers.
Benét, Stephen Vincent, "Ode to Walt Whitman," in *Burning City* (New York: Farrar & Rinehart, Inc., 1936), p. 26.
  "Now comes Fourth Month and the early buds on the trees."

Bradford, Gamaliel, *Confederate Portraits* (Boston: Houghton Mifflin Company, 1914).
> Johnston, Stuart, Longstreet, Benjamin, Stephens, Toombs.

Bradford, Gamaliel, *Union Portraits* (Boston: Houghton Mifflin Company, 1916).
> McClellan, Hooker, Meade, Thomas, Sherman, Seward.

Bradford, Gamaliel, *Lee, the American* (Boston, Houghton Mifflin Company, 1927).

———, *Damaged Souls* (Boston: Houghton Mifflin Company, 1931).
> Portraits of John Brown, Butler.

Brady, Matthew B., *The Civil War through the Camera* (New York: Trow Printing Company, 1912).
> Hundreds of photographs taken during the Civil War illustrate the text by H. W. Elson.

Carter, Capt. Robert Goldthwaite, *Four Brothers in Blue* (Washington: Press of Gibson Bros., Inc., 1913).
> A true story of the Civil War from Bull Run to Appomattox. (Chapter IX describes Fredericksburg.)

Freeman, Douglas Southall, *Robert E. Lee: A Biography*, 4 vol. (New York: Charles Scribner's Sons, 1934-35).
> Definitive biography.

Garland, Hamlin, *Trail-Makers of the Middle Border* (New York: The Macmillan Company, 1926).
> Second half—Vicksburg, Grant, Sherman, McPherson.

Grant, Ulysses S., *Personal Memoirs*, 2 vol. (New York: D. Appleton-Century Company, 1909).

Hergesheimer, Joseph, *The Limestone Tree* (New York: Alfred A. Knopf, Inc., 1931).
> Interpretation of the Civil War from Kentucky point of view.

Hergesheimer, Joseph, *Swords and Roses* (New York: Alfred A. Knopf, Inc., 1929).
> Vignettes of "the deep South and various phases and leaders of the Civil War."

Johnson, James W., *Book of American Negro Spirituals* (New York: The Viking Press, 1925).

Johnson, Rossiter, *The Fight for the Republic* (New York: G. P. Putnam's Sons, 1917).

Knowles, David, *The American Civil War: A Brief Sketch* (New York: Oxford University Press, 1926).

Lee, Robert E., *Recollections and Letters of General R. E. Lee,* by his son (New York, Doubleday, Doran & Company, 1924).

Lewis, Lloyd, *Sherman: Fighting Prophet* (New York: Harcourt, Brace and Company, 1932).

McMaster, John Bach, *A History of the People of the United States During Lincoln's Administration* (New York: D. Appleton-Century Company, 1927).

Odum, Howard W., and Johnson, Guy B., *Negro Workaday Songs* (Chapel Hill: University of North Carolina Press, 1926).

Pratt, Fletcher, *Ordeal by Fire: An Informal History of the Civil War* (New York: H. Harrison Smith and Robert Haas, 1935).

431

Randall, J. G., *Civil War and Reconstruction* (Boston: D. C. Heath and Company, 1937).

Reese, Lizette Woodworth, *A Victorian Village: Reminiscenses of Other Days* (New York: Farrar & Rinehart, Inc., 1929).

Sandburg, Carl, *The War Years* (New York: Harcourt, Brace and Company, 1939).
> Continued biography and annals of Lincoln and his time.

Scarborough, Dorothy, and Ola Lee Gulledge, *On the Trail of Negro Folk-Songs* (Cambridge: Harvard University Press, 1925).

Sherwood, Robert, *Abe Lincoln in Illinois* (New York: Charles Scribner's Sons, 1939).
> A play.

Smith, Cicely Fox, *A Book of Shanties* (Boston: Houghton Mifflin Company, 1927).
> Sea songs, and ballads.

Tarbell, Ida Minerva, *A Reporter for Lincoln* (New York: The Macmillan Company, 1927).
> Story of a newspaper reporter during the last years of the Civil War.

Villard, Oswald Garrison, *John Brown (1800–1859): A Biography Fifty Years After* (Boston: Houghton Mifflin Company, 1910).

Whitman, Walt, *Specimen Days, Democratic Vistas and Other Poems*, ed. by Louise Pound (New York: Doubleday, Doran & Company, 1935).

——, from *Leaves of Grass:* "The Centenarian's Story," "Cavalry Crossing a Ford," "Bivouac on a Mountain Side," "An Army Corps on the March," "By the Bivouac's Fitful Flame," "The Wounddresser," "Drum Taps," "Come Up from the Fields, Father," "Vigil Strange I Kept on the Field One Night," "Captain, My Captain." Numerous editions.